# Boys and Their Toys?

# HAGLEY PERSPECTIVES ON BUSINESS AND CULTURE

PHILIP SCRANTON AND ROGER HOROWITZ,
SERIES EDITORS

BEAUTY AND BUSINESS
*Commerce, Gender, and Culture in Modern America*
Edited by Philip Scranton

BOYS AND THEIR TOYS?
*Masculinity, Technology, and Class in America*
Edited by Roger Horowitz

FOOD NATIONS
*Selling Taste in Consumer Societies*
Edited by Warren Belasco and Philip Scranton

# Boys and Their Toys?

## MASCULINITY, TECHNOLOGY, AND CLASS IN AMERICA

EDITED BY

# ROGER HOROWITZ

ROUTLEDGE
NEW YORK    LONDON

Published in 2001 by

Routledge
29 West 35th Street
New York, NY 10001

Published in Great Britain by

Routledge
11 New Fetter Lane
London EC4P 4EE

Routledge is an imprint of the Taylor & Francis Group.

10    9    8    7    6    5    4    3    2    1

Library of Congress Cataloging-in-Publication Data

Boys and their toys? : masculinity, technology,
and class in America / edited by Roger Horowitz.
        p.    cm. — (Hagley perspectives on business and culture)
    Includes bibliographical references and index.
    ISBN 0-415-92932-6    —    ISBN 0-415-92933-4 (pbk.)
    1. Masculinity—United States. 2. Men—United States—
    Social conditions. 3. Masculinity in popular culture—
    United States. 4. Men—Employment—United States.
    5. Sexual division of labor—United States. 6. Sex role
    in the work environment—United States. 7. Men—
    Effect of technological innovations on—United States.
    I. Horowitz, Roger.    II. Series.
HQ1090.3 .B68    2001
305.31'0973—dc21                              2001019343

# Contents

Part 3: **Manhood at Play**

# Introduction

**ROGER HOROWITZ**

W hen Ava Baron published her pathbreaking collection *Work Engendered* in 1991, it caused a sensation in social history circles. Arguing for the importance of gender as an analytic category was not new, but Baron's singular contribution was to bring together essays showing how gender was embedded in daily work practices and class relations. In her widely read introduction, the essays in the volume, and the many books later published by her volume's contributors, Baron firmly established among social historians that gender was about men as well as women. The focus of this present volume on masculinity grows out of the germinative impact of *Work Engendered.*[1]

It is worth reflecting on the reception to Baron's collection to see how far we have come in ten years. While reviewers universally praised the essays' qualities, some questioned how much they really added to understanding history. One reviewer asserted that the essays failed to make the case that gender could explain, partially or otherwise, changes over time. Another said flatly that gender as deployed in those essays "did not carry first-order explanatory power." All these reviews, while respectful in tone, doubted that the result would be a reconfigured history of class and work.[2]

The essays in this volume indicate that these assessments were premature. Baron's collection, as part of a larger intellectual movement to make gender central to historical analysis, stimulated a generation of graduate students and practicing historians to see what difference gender made. Among the many productive streams to come out of this scholarship has been new research on masculinity that links class to masculine identities at work and at play. Rather than worry whether or not gender constitutes a "first-order" explanation, these essays place masculinity at the core of class formation along with many other factors. Their methodological strategy reflects a general advance in the use of gender as an analytic category, not to see it as distinct from other factors but instead embedded within the many strands that comprise our social formation.

Work occupies a central place in all the essays. Work, however, is not conceived so simply as productive labor on the job. Work also means playing on the job, and treating play and recreation as forms of work. The poststructuralist theories of Joan Scott are evident in these articles, but so too is the work process analysis that has at its taproot Harry Braverman's *Labor and Monopoly Capital*. The intertwined intellectual strands of Baron, Scott, and Braverman manifest themselves throughout these essays.[3]

The focus on work and experience in this volume—consistent with the themes of *Work Engendered*—as a site of gender formation is at odds, however, with an intellectual trend in the last decade to overly emphasize linguistic approaches to understanding gender and human consciousness. Indeed, Patrick Joyce and some poststructuralist historians have mounted a formidable challenge to the very category of "the social."[4] The sum of these arguments has been to question the value of researching experience and practice though social history methods, and instead to privilege discourse analysis relying on sources more suited to intellectual history. The essays in this volume retain the balance of Baron's collection by linking language to experience in varied and complex ways. Eschewing the old base-superstructure model whereby ideas were derivative of experience, they also avoid imputing to language primacy over structure and practice. Instead, these essays at their best show the messily complex relations between discourse and experience, how each interpenetrates the other so that constructing a causative hierarchy becomes an unproductive enterprise.

## Part 1: Manhood in the Workplace

The volume opens with a section, "Manhood in the Workplace," that comprises a set of essays focusing on the terrain that, as Stephen Meyer puts it, is "central to the forming, nurturing, widening, and deepening of masculine culture." Meyer's essay "Work, Play, and Power: Masculine Culture on the Automotive Shop Floor, 1930–1960" sets the thematic tone for this section (and in some ways the entire volume) by developing two polar forms of masculinity with roots in the nineteenth-century workplace: "rough" versus "respectable" manhood. He defines "respectable manhood" as corresponding to the values of the craft tradition among American workers in which masculine impulses were tempered and channeled to allow for purposeful wielding of mental and physical skills. "Rough manhood" emerged out of traditions among unskilled workers that emphasized risk taking, physical prowess, and disorderly behavior. Situating himself in a wide labor history literature, Meyer employs these notions as ideal types (rather than actually existing discrete forms of masculinity) that "blended" together in varied and peculiar ways as men sought to construct their masculinity in the twentieth-century workplace.

Meyer's essay draws out these tensions through a closely textured study of autoworkers' shop-floor behavior in the mid-twentieth century. Drawing inventively on union grievance files, Meyer shows how the use of play in shop-floor situations merged easily into job actions as male workers used masculine culture to resist the Fordist regime of their mass production industry. Masculine culture cohered work groups in opposition to management and indoctrinated new (especially younger) workers into a manly shop-floor culture that supported unionism. Drinking, cursing, and fighting moved from tavern to workplace and back again as these men combined these older elements of "rough" masculinity with the respectability they could now incur through middle-class wages and benefits. Meyer argues that these practices represented a blend "of the rough and respectable—rough in its relation with managerial authority and respectable in its middle-class standard of living."

In "'To Make Men out of Crude Material': Work Culture, Manhood, and Unionism in the Railroad Running Trades, c. 1870–1900" Paul Taillon postulates a similar rough/respectable dualism to explore the gender ideologies of the railroads' most "manly men"—the engineers, firemen, brakemen, and conductors who comprised the running trades. While Meyer's autoworkers labored on assembly lines under close supervision, Taillon's railroaders operated in largely unsupervised locations where they could selectively apply formal company rules that nominally governed their behavior. In an environment where labor control was deeply problematic, the railroad brotherhoods articulated a masculinity celebrating autonomy, skill, judgment, restraint, and sobriety to win the loyalty of the running trade workers and to convince the railroad companies that they were a useful adjunct to successful train operation. Taillon elaborates on how the railroad brotherhoods consciously developed their version of "respectable" manhood in opposition to both the "rough" informal practices of unorganized railroaders (which interfered with proper railroad operations) and the gentile manhood of the Victorian middle class (which denigrated the physical abilities of the running trades workers).

While placing constructions of manhood at the center of working-class formation, Taillon also shows the limits on respectable manhood as union strategy. The brotherhoods may have shaped the masculine ideals of their growing membership, but rail firms required more than the rhetoric of manhood to accept the brotherhoods. The vagaries of labor supply and challenge of more disruptive workers' actions, he suggests, were necessary conditions for the railroad companies to finally become receptive in the early twentieth century to the respectable manhood—and unionism—promised by the brotherhoods.

Janet Davidson complicates the rough/respectable dichotomy by exploring the fragile masculinity of those liminal railroad employees, male clerks, in her article "'Now That We Have Girls in the Office': Clerical Work, Masculinity, and the Refashioning of Gender for a Bureaucratic Age." The nineteenth-century tradition of office clerking as a management-track occupation persisted into the early twentieth century on the railroads. Consequently, railroad clerks remained almost entirely male on the eve of World War I. Davidson draws on Gail Bederman's notion of a cultural reconfiguration of manhood in the early twentieth century to sketch out how, in an industry that celebrated the manly physical strength of the running trades workers, male clerical workers operated on uncertain masculine terrain—a terrain made even more insecure when over 100,000 women obtained railroad employment during the war. While Bederman stressed the discursive construction of new masculine gender identities, Davidson's emphasis is on workplace conflicts that illuminate clerks' efforts to redefine their masculinity during World War I.[5]

Gender functions as metalanguage in Davidson,[6] explaining not only how clerks struggled to articulate a masculine identity, but more profoundly how these men employed gender "to explain the changes that rationalization and the war had wrought" in their previously stable masculine world. Combining a finely grained analysis of male and female clerks' workplace experiences with discursive efforts by the union to provide a masculine identity for male railroad clerks, Davidson suggests the power and contingency of both discourse and workplace experiences. By incorporating the influence of the federal government (which operated the railroads during the war) and railroad management into her analysis, Davidson makes sense of the remarkable reversion of railroad clerking to a virtually all-male trade by the mid-1920s, in contradistinction to the feminization of clerical work elsewhere in the American economy.

In "Rereading Man's Conquest of Nature: Skill, Myths, and the Historical Construction of Masculinity in Western Extractive Industries" Nancy Quam-Wickham moves this section from eastern rail yards and Midwestern auto plants to western extractive industries. Also drawing on Bederman, Quam-Wickham posits a working-class form of western masculinity that prized skill over brute strength. Considering logging, hard rock mining, and oil drilling, Quam-Wickham argues that the acquisition of skill took place through the tightly knit work groups essential to these trades, and that skill was integral to these worker's sense of masculinity. The "rough" edge to the masculinity in these isolated, all-male settings took extreme form in initiation rites with a degrading sexual edge, through which experienced workers secured new employees' subordination to the work group's values through physical humiliation. Respectability could be earned by applying skill and restraint rather than sheer brawn to the daunting tasks faced by these men. Quam-Wickham creatively explores this lore through the many Paul Bunyan stories told by western working men—not just those few tales that found their way to mass-produced children's books. In these stories Bunyan, as logger, timberman, and oil driller, appears as a buffoon who too often mistakes strength for skill and ability. Quam-Wickham argues that these myths "reveal the folk and class values of western workers, values that downplayed physical prowess in work processes by reinforcing workers' belief in skill as the most important and distinctive attribute of a competent, successful, and manly worker." Skill and ability to use technology properly were what made western workers true men.

Collectively these essays on work trace the highly varied "blending" of rough and respectable manhood among America's working men. They indicate the persistence of "rough" forms of masculinity as a distinctive feature of working-class masculinity. Indeed, the very troubles of the male railroad clerks reflected their unstable manliness in an industry that prized physical prowess along with good judgment. Respectability was as much a strategy as a practice, a means through which working men could demand respect for, and control over, their bodies in the performance of their jobs.

## Part 2: Learning to Be Men

How boys learned the components of manliness is a question only alluded to in the four essays in part 1. The next section in the volume, "Learning to Be Men " addresses this issue explicitly. Through closely textured studies of boys training to become men these essays begin an investigation that deserves far more attention. The three essays in this section illuminate the class-specific character of the training offered to boys, and how what they learned shaped their economic opportunities as men.

Jeffrey Ryan Suzik emphasizes that his article "'Building Better Men': The CCC Boy and the Changing Social Ideal of Manliness" is rooted in a particular context, the Great Depression and widespread fears of the effect of prolonged unemployment on American youth. From its inception, the Civilian Conservation Core (CCC) was a "man-building" project as well as a means to supply work to the unemployed, a program that "would save America's young men both from lives either as transient drifters or as dependent sissies." In the early and mid-1930s the camps emphasized developing physical fitness and imparting basic technological knowledge, principally the operation of machinery common to American construction and manufacturing sites. Drawing on letters from CCC workers and their families, Suzik traces how the grassroots language of masculinity influenced CCC administrators, and validated their policy that it was hard work, and the physical strength it produced, that turned a boy into a man. By the late 1930s, however, growing fears of war encouraged military training to be added to the CCC's existing programs. On the eve of its abolition in 1942, the CCC had bowed to popular sentiment that military service was a necessary component of "building better men."

The role of technological knowledge to turn boys into men, a component of Suzik's essay, is the principal subject of Ruth Oldenziel's article, "Boys and Their Toys: The Fisher Body Craftman's Guild, 1930–1968, and the Making of a Male Technical Domain." Her work emerges out of an overlapping yet distinct body of scholarship on gender emanating from the history of technology field. She is nonetheless in agreement with other authors in this volume that as gender is "intentionally or unintentionally created by people . . . creating and maintaining gender categories often requires an enormous amount of work."[7]

While sharing with the other essays a focus on work and masculinity, Oldenziel's is most interested in how boys learn that becoming comfortable with technology is a distinctively masculine trait. Her essay focuses on General Motors's creation of a national contest that required boys to make an odd technological artifact, a reproduction of a supposed Napoleonic-era horse-drawn coach. Through the GM-sponsored Fisher Body Craftman's Guild teenage boys competed for prizes that could include payment of college tuition. Embedded in this seemingly quaint exercise, however, was a concerted effort by GM to train boys in wood- and metalworking skills and to recruit them to management trainee positions. Unlike the boys prepared by the CCC camps for working-class pursuits, the Fisher Body Craftman's Guild groomed participants for future careers as GM designers and managers by training them in sophisticated technological and conceptual tasks. Creating "technophiles" formed young men whom GM believed could be drawn into the corporate world as loyal and enthusiastic company officials. The complexity of the technological skills learned by these boys, in contrast to the simple operation of machinery inculcated in CCC camps, underscores the class-specific character of masculinity in general, and the relationship between manliness and varieties of technological knowledge in particular.

While considering the same decade as Suzik and Oldenziel, Todd Alexander Postol explores another strategy using work to turn boys into men, in this case into salesmen—in his essay "Masculine Guidance: Boys, Men, and Newspapers, 1930–1939." Focusing on the boys who plied regular subscription routes (not to be confused with "newsies" who sold on street corners), Postol delineates how the strategic "masculine guidance" devised by subscription managers inculcated middle-class values and salesmanship among male teenagers. Catering to the boyhood enthusiasm of their employees, managers devised games with complicated reward structures to motivate boys to recruit and service subscribers. Sales managers devised these methods partly because of the difficulties of supervising the newspaper boys on their regular routes, but also for the purpose of internalizing middle-class values of proper decorum, appropriate dress, and hard work so that the boys would grow up to be respectable men. Similar to GM, newspaper firms used boys' delight in play to inculcate the manly values of work. And unlike the working-class boys trained by the CCC, the skills learned by newspaper boys were those of deportment, presentation, and oral persuasion, situating them by their late teens to move into the white-collar middle class.

The remarkable efforts covered in these three articles to turn boys into men supports the assertion of Oldenziel (and her collaborators Arwen Mohun and Nina Lerman) that making masculinity is a lot of work. The U.S. government, America's largest industrial firm, and the nation's newspaper industry all devoted a great deal of money and effort to separate and distinct "manhood" projects for juvenile boys during the Great Depression. By making work central to becoming men while at the same time training these boys for very different kinds of work, these large institutions steered boys into forms of masculine behavior that reinforced class stratification in America. The respectable manhood depicted by Oldenziel and Postol contrasts sharply with Suzik's discussion of the CCC boys, indicating that even as teenagers "rough masculinity" could serve as a marker of class. Once again these articles show how gender—in this case masculinity— is a constitutive element of class formation.

## Part 3: Manhood at Play

The mixing of play and work within masculine behavior is developed more fully in the volume's final section, "Manhood at Play." Three articles address how playful behavior and recreation contribute powerfully to the formation and perpetuation of masculine forms of identity. The opening essay by Woody Register posits his subjects (men active in the years 1900–1930) as part of the transition in middle-class manhood from a nineteenth-century emphasis on work to a mid-twentieth-century focus on consumptive practices. The next two essays show, in essence, the "blending" of the middle-class "consuming manhood" with working-class masculinity by examining widespread forms of play among America's blue-collar workers. Ben Shackleford (on auto racing) and Lisa Fine (on hunting) extend Register's argument by elaborating how particular forms of recreation become integral parts of working-class manliness.

In "Everyday Peter Pans: Work, Manhood, and Consumption in Urban America, 1900–1930" Woody Register considers the lives and masculine strategies of entertainment-oriented men "who, between 1900 and 1930, helped lay the institutional foundation of twentieth-century consumer capitalism." Men such as Fred Thompson, Steward Culin, and Fred Stone encouraged a new male gender identity celebrating boyish play as an acceptable feature of manly behavior through their efforts to construct amusement parks, play fantasy roles in Broadway plays, and develop museums designed to enrich leisure time. While working as hard as other men, these entertainment industry pioneers refashioned appropriate masculine behavior to include a life devoted to, in essence, play and diversion. Drawing on Michael Kimmel's notion of "consuming manhood," Register traces these men's efforts to fashion a bearing as "manly" as the running trades engineer or auto plant operative.[8] In Register's delightful (and appropriately playful) formulation, their "Peter Pan culture" encouraged middle-class men to look beyond work for manly satisfaction and status and to seek forms of amusement and recreation that would allow them to be men at the same time as they refused to grow up.

Ben Shackleford's article "Masculinity, the Auto Racing Fraternity, and the Technological Sublime: The Pit Stop As a Celebration of Social Roles" takes us to the most popular (measured by attendance and television viewership) form of manly play in the late twentieth century, auto racing, a sport with its root in the rural south but now widely popular among working-class men. Focusing on NASCAR's Winston Cup series, Shackleford employs David Nye's concept of the "technological sublime" to uncover this sport's enormous popularity among spectators and television viewers, as well as product advertisers.[9] Combining the "rough" dangers of cars traveling at high speeds with the "respectable" component of mastery over technology, auto racing constitutes one more blend of these ideal masculine types suggested by Stephen Meyer in this volume's first essay. Auto racing's combination of strength with skill takes its highest form in the pit stop, coordinated high speed racing car maintenance "by experts in control" whose successful performance through "male bravery and productive skill" is essential to a race victory. Like Nancy Quam-Wickham's oil drillers, the pit crews proudly applied technological knowledge and discerning mental judgment under rough and dirty working conditions. Through the (largely rhetorical) assertion by corporate sponsors of a correspondence between race cars and the cars driven by men at home, the NASCAR spectacle establishes bonds of manhood between the men who race and the men who watch. As Shackleford notes astutely, "Racers offer men a chance to publicly associate with the power of masculine aggression in combination with the more socially acceptable potency of mental rigor."

Part of the "technological[ly] sublime" NASCAR experience is the controlled violence of the races, as the cars' sturdy construction allows drivers to "trade paint" by bumping and pushing in a manner that can, but usually does not, result in catastrophic accidents. This controlled yet manly violence is also central to Lisa Fine's remarkable essay,

"Rights of Men, Rites of Passage: Hunting and Masculinity at Reo Motors of Lansing, Michigan, 1945–1975." Fine brings us full circle, back to the Midwestern auto workers who open this volume, considering their masculine activities away from work, in the woods, in recreational pursuit of deer and other game. She rejects simplistic notions of contemporary hunting as atavistic male behavior. Instead Fine historicizes hunting in two separate trajectories: as a *rite* passed from father to son as part of training for manhood, and as a *right* of working men to have similar access to the land and recreation as middle- and upper-class men. Drawing from rich research materials on Reo Motors, Fine shows how hunting's appeal drew on autoworkers' ties to the land as well as a tradition of military service and preparedness. Equally important, though, hunting's popularity grew after World War II such that conflicts over hunters' rights became part of contentious labor-management negotiations and sparked major legislative controversies in Michigan. Rather than seeing hunting as a reaction—to the loss of workplace autonomy, the bureaucratization of American society, or family obligations—Fine contends hunting should be seen in a "proactive" context as a right won, and hence as a constituent element of the masculine lifestyle that these autoworkers expected to enjoy.

Taken together, these essays certainly move us toward the utopian objective of the *Work Engendered*'s subtitle, *Toward a New History of American Labor*. The rough/respectable dualism provides useful generalizations for exploring particular forms of masculinity in relationship to class (and to a lesser degree, race). By contrasting working-class and middle-class forms of masculinity these articles validate recent scholarship by Michael Kimmel and Gail Bederman that stresses the relationship of the male body to conceptions of manhood. The manliness of the deer hunter, CCC boy, and lumberjack all seem to share, to varying degrees, elements of the "rough" masculinity postulated in the Meyer and Taillon essays even as they also seek to be "respectable" men. Their working-class masculinity, despite significant internal variation, still seems quite different from that of the newspaper subscription manager, future GM car designer, or entertainment impresario for whom the "respectable" elements of manhood mattered above all else. It is a fitting testament to the durability of Ava Baron's 1991 collection that it provides a sturdy base upon which new theories of masculinity can be grafted.

This collection began as a fall 1997 conference at the Hagley Museum and Library in Wilmington, Delaware, saw first light as the October 1999 thematic issue of the journal *Men and Masculinities* (coedited by Philip Scranton and myself), and was completed with the inclusion of five new published and unpublished essays. All the articles are part of larger projects that should be emerging as books in the next few years. Ava Baron gave initial intellectual shape to the book by helping to conceptualize and select the papers for the 1997 Hagley conference. Phil Scranton shaped the conference and this book intellectually and with his remarkable energy by participating in the selection process and editing several articles that first appeared in *Men and Masculinities*. Carol Ressler Lockman coordinated the conference and many aspects of this volume's production. Michael Kimmel, *Men and Masculinities* editor and a pioneer in the men's studies field, first suggested the special issue devoted to these papers. Routledge editors Deirdre Mullane, Derek Krissoff, and Brendan O'Malley deserve special thanks for their support of this volume and the series of which it is a part. I also thank Sage Publishers, Johns Hopkins University Press, the *Journal of Social History*, and Oxford University Press for permitting republication of essays from their journals.

## Notes

1. Ava Baron, ed., *Work Engendered: Toward a New History of American Labor* (Ithaca, N.Y.: Cornell University Press, 1991).

2. Reviews of *Work Engendered* by Alan Dawley in *International Labor and Working Class History* 43 (1993), 145–47; David Brody in *Industrial and Labor Relations Review* 46, no. 4 (1993), 744–46; and John Cumbler in *Journal of Social History* 26, no. 3 (1993), 628–30.

3. Joan Wallach Scott, *Gender and the Politics of History* (New York: Columbia University Press, 1988); Harry Braverman, *Labor and Monopoly Capital: The Degradation of Work in the Twentieth Century* (New York: Monthly Review Press, 1974).

4. Patrick Joyce, "The End of Social History?" *Social History* 20, no. 1 (1995), 73–91. For a review and recapitulation of this debate see Geoff Eley and Keith Nield, "Farewell to the Working Class?" and rejoinders by Don Kalb, Judith Stein, Stephen Kotkin, Barbara Weinstein, Frederick Cooper, and Joan W. Scott in *International Labor and Working Class History* 57 (2000), 1–87.

5. Gail Bederman, *Manliness and Civilization: A Cultural History of Gender and Race in the United States, 1880–1917* (Chicago: University of Chicago Press, 1995).

6. For this concept see Evelyn Brooks Higginbotham, "African American Women's History and the Metalanguage of Race," *Signs* 17, no. 2 (1992), 251–74.

7. Nina Lerman, Arwen Palmer Mohun, and Ruth Oldenziel, "Versatile Tools: Gender Analysis and the History of Technology," *Technology and Culture* 38, no. 1 (1997), 2. This entire issue was devoted to gender analysis and the history of technology.

8. Michael Kimmel, "Consuming Manhood: The Feminization of American Culture and the Recreation of the Male Body, 1832–1920," in *The Male Body: Features, Destinies, Exposures*, ed. Laurence Goldstein (Ann Arbor: University of Michigan Press, 1994), 12–41.

9. David Nye, *American Technological Sublime* (Cambridge, Mass.: MIT Press, 1994).

# PART 1

# Manhood in the Workplace

# Work, Play, and Power

*Masculine Culture on the Automotive Shop Floor, 1930–1960*

STEPHEN MEYER

T his is a small article on an enormous topic—the masculine realm of workplace culture. Although it raises some questions about the general nature of working-class masculinity and of leisure-like activities or play at the workplace, some of its major themes concern how workers fabricate a multiplicity of masculinities, how these are fashioned and refashioned, how workers bring male leisure or play activities to a thoroughly controlled shop floor, and how this masculine culture operates within the context of workplace relations of power. Specifically, it distinguishes a rough masculine culture originating in the unskilled laborers' world and a respectable one arising from skilled craftsmen's traditions. Moreover, it heavily relies on a previously neglected labor history resource—the grievances that workers filed about their situations and conditions on the shop floor. These are important windows into the workplace that reveal much about the day-to-day activities and actions of auto workers in their shops and departments and the social relations of power in the American automobile industry.

Though we possess a growing body of recent and suggestive work on the history of masculinity and manhood,[1] Ava Baron pointedly reminds us that "the history of working-class masculinity has yet to be written." In order to write this history, she continues: "we must understand men's and women's efforts to construct and to defend a collective gender identity."[2] Also important, she asserts, is "the significance of gender regardless of women's presence or absence."[3] Although many situations and settings generate, fashion, and nurture masculine culture, this essay focuses on the workplace worlds that men made and remade, and how these functioned for them on the automotive shop floor. From my perspective, two labor scholars, Joshua Freeman and Steven Maynard,[4] point toward a historical analysis based upon the important distinction between *rough* and *respectable* working-class masculine cultures.

Discussing the "vigorous subculture" that existed among "working-class youth," Peter N. Stearns cites an anonymous worker who recalled the broad outlines of his rough manhood: "'When I was eighteen I knew it took four things to be a man: fight, work, screw, and booze.'"[5] Except for the fighting, the young Frank Marquart, an autoworker and later labor radical, seemed preoccupied with these masculine traits. Recalling how he "became increasingly conditioned to the ways of a young factory hand" in the 1910s, Marquart wrote in 1975 about his youthful "peer group" at the Metal Products Company in Detroit. From work, they went home to eat and then later congregated at a bar, Premos on Jefferson Avenue. Though a minor, he was proud to look old enough for the bartender to serve him. "In the saloon," he recalled, "men gathered in groups and usually talked shop. Each tried to impress the others with how important his particular job was, how much skill it required." On Saturday, "the *big* night," the young workers played a few games of pool at Curley's Poolroom, "went downtown to take in the burlesque, either the Gaiety or the Cadillac," and then went to the Champlain Street "red-light" district. For Marquart and his circle, manhood meant work (especially skilled work), daily drinking, and the weekend foray to what they nicknamed "Joy Street."[6]

This regressive manhood possessed many forms and emerged from many settings. The relations of social class, gender, race, and ethnicity influenced and shaped male attitudes, values, and behaviors. Young working-class boys learned to become men from their families at home and in their relations with other people—women, men, girls, and boys—in the larger world. Generationally, fathers taught their sons, craftsmen their apprentices, and senior workers their younger workmates how to become and "be" men. Most important, boys becoming men, young men, and adult men fashioned and refashioned their manliness in a variety of all-male settings—in the schoolyard, on the playing field, or in the locker room; on the hunting field, in the army barracks, in the saloon or tavern, in work camps and, of course, at the workplace.[7]

To be sure, other personal relationships and other social institutions softened the rough edges and mixed up the messages of masculine identity. Also important were the home, the church, the classroom, the fraternal society or lodge, and even the union hall. Also, whenever and wherever men came into contact with women, they had to negotiate and to renegotiate their manhood, sometimes in positive and sometimes in negative ways.

The workplace was central to the forming, nurturing, widening, and deepening of masculine culture. Stan Gray, a Westinghouse worker in the early 1980s and a sympathetic witness to a "female invasion" of the shop floor, describes the workplace as "the last sanctum of male culture." The male world of the shop floor, he continues: "was away from the world of women, away from responsibility and children and civilized cultural restraints. In the plant, they could regale in the rough and tumble world of a masculine world of physical harshness; of constant swearing and rough behavior, of half-serious fighting and competition with each other, and more serious fighting with the boss. . . ." It was "full of filth and dirt and grease and grime and sweat—manual labor, a *manly* atmosphere"; the talk was "vulgar and obscene" and "about football and car repairs."[8]

Generally, working-class masculine culture has surfaced in two distinct forms—a *respectable* culture and a *rough* one. Though analytically quite discrete, these two contradictory forms might result from either personal disposition or social position. Yet they sometimes coexisted with, overlapped with, or blended into each other. Some men certainly carried elements of both the rough and respectable cultures within their individual masculine identities. On the one hand, the respectable masculine culture corresponded with the attitudes, values, and behaviors associated with the craft traditions of skilled workers. David Montgomery, perhaps unwittingly, inaugurated the historical discussion of working-class manhood when he described the aggressive and respectable "craftsmen's ethical" code that demanded a "'manly' bearing toward the boss," connoting "dignity, respectability, defiant egalitarianism, and patriarchal male supremacy."[9] On the other hand, the rough masculine culture correlated to the traditions and values of unskilled laborers and certainly countered the respectable values of the craft tradition. The rough laborers' world formed a lifestyle that, Montgomery observed, "made a mockery of social reformers' efforts to promote habits of 'thrift, sobriety, adaptability, [and] initiative.'"[10] Clearly this rough masculine culture contrasted sharply with both respectable middle-class and working-class virtues.

The rough masculine culture, Joshua Freeman suggests in his examination of construction workers, was one of "aggressive, crude masculinity" or "swaggering masculinity."[11] In his discussion of steel workers and bush workers Steven Maynard adds that: "dangerous conditions . . . reinforced a rugged masculinity."[12] Peter Way's study of antebellum canal workers outlines the basic elements of rough manhood and suggests its deep roots in the North American past—the rough work world of unskilled manual laborers. These unskilled workers, Way observes, were "a swearing, drinking, brawling, hurting, dying mass" shaped by a harsh climate, difficult toil, meager economic resources, and a social life of heavy drinking.[13] These crude male communities were characterized by religious and ethnic identity, vice and violence, alcohol and drinking, brawling and roughhousing, physical prowess and risk-taking, sport and gambling, female dependency and subordination, and a belief in strong egalitarianism coupled with an opposition to employers.[14]

In contrast, the respectable masculine culture emerged from the work skills, social pride, and economic security of the craft tradition.

For late-nineteenth-century construction workers, Freeman asserts: "manliness meant independence, mutuality, and pride in craft." The skilled workers' masculinity also contained a "political construct" that rested on "respect, manhood, and citizenship." Craft workers' monopolization of skilled men's work established their economic security and economic independence, "which was seen as the fruit of skill, hard work, sobriety, and organization."[15] For this reason, craftsmen's social construct of manliness was "firmly attached and even subsumed to ideas of respectability and domesticity." Though "not immune from the temptations of drink, gambling, and extra-marital sex," these respectable workers "sought to temper themselves, to control such impulses, and thereby disassociate themselves from the 'rough working-class culture' dominated by less-skilled, more poorly-paid workers."[16] In his investigation of early-twentieth-century auto workers, Wayne Lewchuk suggests that through their monopolization of skilled work, the respectable craftsmen socially and culturally established and constructed their manhood through "social norms that identified control, independence, and the ability to make decisions as inherent masculine traits."[17] If the laborer's sense of crude manliness emerged from the roughness of physical strength and dangerous work, the respectable craftsman's manhood arose from refined values of control, skill, autonomy, and independence.[18]

Throughout the nineteenth century, working-class men, depending on the individual predisposition or their social location, selected, blended, or fashioned their male identities from disparate values of the rough and respectable masculine cultures. But as the century progressed, the rise of industrial capitalism altered the social boundaries, and ultimately the cultural possibilities, of working-class men. As Maynard indicates, the newly emerging industrial and economic system "not only altered class relations, but also shifted gender relations, precipitating a crisis in masculinity."[19] Moreover, this crisis of masculinity saturated an industrializing American culture, as indicated by the social creation and construction of the late-nineteenth-century immigrant and labor problems. In turn, these social fears fostered assertive and aggressive middle-class identities.[20]

For working-class men, Maynard asserts, "the 'crisis of the craftsman' was . . . both a crisis of work *and* masculinity, of class and gender."[21] Effectively, the internal forces of the American Industrial Revolution emasculated both the physical and the intellectual bases of working-class male identities. They broke the "very explicit connections" that working men made "between their work and their gender identity as men."[22] These forces undermined the rough masculine identity through the elimination of brawn and strength from unskilled work and subverted the respectable identity through the removal of independence and control from skilled work. As Lisa Fine notes about autoworkers, "All the hallmarks of masculinity at the workplace . . . were eradicated by automation, machines, [and] time clocks as well as new management practices, repressive and paternalistic."[23] Furthermore, the continuous and growing movement of women and children into formerly all-male terrain reinforced this deep sense of lost manhood in the laborers' and craftmen's working worlds. Removing the male traits of brawn and brain from workplace skills, Taylorism and Fordism redefined skill as the endurance of repetitious and monotonous tasks and their speedy and dextrous performance. For both craftsmen and laborers, their work became unmanly.

Ultimately, the dual crises of industrialism and of masculinity prompted working-class (and other) men to remasculinize work and identities. To a certain extent, the newly forming masculine culture of semiskilled mass production workers blended and merged elements of rough and respectable manhood. In automobile plants, male workers maintained some of their masculine identity through a boylike playfulness on the shop floor and displayed some of the rougher side of masculine culture—drinking, fighting, gambling, and confrontational opposition to management. At the same time, a relatively high wage permitted some economic stability and independence away from the workplace, feeding the respectable aspect of working-class male culture. Moreover, automotive employers also attempted to fashion and to reshape masculine identities—either through their creation of a male fraternity that glorified hard work and received high wages or their fostering a loyalist male culture emphasizing respectability and cooperation.[24]

In addition to the blending and mixing of the rough and respectable cultures, the working-class idea of manliness in the age of mass production most likely took on more explicit sexual connotations. "Within the craft tradition," Freeman notes, "manhood apparently did not have an explicitly sexual meaning."[25] Yet moving into and through the twentieth century, working-class men remade and reconstructed their manly identities, derogating and demeaning those who appeared to threaten them. For construction workers, manliness took on a "decidedly male idiom" characterized by "physical jousting, sexual boasting, sports talk, and shared sexual activities,"[26] which consciously operated to exclude and debase women. In the second decade of the twentieth century, a factory spy reported on a drafting room worker who made "lewd" blueprints and passed them around to other workers.[27] The oral histories of women who worked in the automobile and auto parts plants in the 1930s testify to the harassment and abuse from their male colleagues at the workplace. One woman, relating the benefits of unionism, is reported by Nancy F. Gabin to have said, "[W]hen you belong to the union, the foreman can't screw you."[28] In the 1970s, John Lippert recounted the full import of such male behavior in an Ohio Fisher Body plant. "Many men are completely unabashed about letting the women know that they are being watched and discussed," he noted, "and some men are quite open about the results of the analysis. Really attractive women have to put up with incredible harassment, from constant propositions to mindless and obscene grunts as they walk by.[29] The remasculinization of the shop floor often resulted in the general degradation and dehumanization of all women.

The gradual creation and evolution of a distinct masculine culture for mass production workers in the early twentieth century forces us to rethink our classic notions of time and work discipline in the transition from precapitalist to capitalist forms of work, discipline, and culture.[30] These notions have emphasized the loose and informal structures and patterns of preindustrial work and the tight and disciplined structures of industrial work. Although in the preindustrial world people worked hard for long hours, typically from sunrise to sunset, their working lives involved a loosely structured mix of work and leisure, of production and play in their daily, weekly, and seasonal activities. With the progressive advance of industrial capitalism, the argument goes, these activities took on a new management-imposed and clock-controlled regularity, which eventually separated the realms of work and leisure. As Edward P. Thompson has noted, the new industrial man required "new disciplines, new incentives, and a new human nature upon which these incentives could bite effectively."[31]

Although the general thrust of this argument captured the essential elements of the transition to an industrial capitalist work culture, it failed to apprehend human abilities and capacities to remake working lives and workplace cultures. Despite efforts to impose new disciplines through the ever-increasing elaboration of factory work rules and managerial work regimes, industrial workers often continued to behave in their pre-industrial and inefficient ways. Pushing Taylorist and Fordist production strategies aside, they continued to act as though their world of work was also a world of play and leisure.

Frequently, autoworkers used the new forms of masculine culture to resist the routinization, degradation, and monotony of disciplined work routines.[32] In his study of the British automobile industry, Paul Thompson discovered that auto workers had three possible responses to disciplined and regimented work—avoiding it, changing it, or accepting it and "putting one's heart elsewhere." In essence, the last strategy meant the redefining and reshaping of male work culture and the transformation of the shop floor and workplace into a site of leisure or play.[33] In his investigation of early-twentieth-century German factory workers, Alf Leudtke distinguishes between the "legal" breaks, the officially sanctioned rest periods for "physical replenishment," and the "illegal" breaks, the workers' expropriation of "bits of time formally designated as working time." Once industrial capitalism separated company time from personal time—that is, work time from

Stephen Meyer

leisure time—managers and workers struggled over the appropriate use of company time. During the illegal breaks, Leudtke observes, factory workers "broke with the demands and constraints of the factory system as well as with the toil of labor and reproduction."[34] Activities such as shop-floor horseplay were "a mixture of claims against supervisors' demands maintaining customary rights and of striving for the humanity of the individual and his comrades."[35] This struggle for independent space connected to working-class masculine culture, and this illicit behavior also connected with male oppositional and confrontational rituals and displays of power to challenge the newly established Taylorist and Fordist industrial order.

Moreover, this behavior suggests that the distinction between work and leisure never fully broke down. Masculine play sometimes meant simply not working dutifully and consistently at one's routinized job. In their individual and collective forms of illegal or illicit behavior, some workers ate, drank alcohol, read books or newspapers, fought, or gambled. Others took overly long breaks, aggressively challenged their supervisors, engaged in incessant play, or conducted work slowdowns or stoppages simply to obtain a break from the factory regimen. Many of these illicit activities and oppositional gestures derived from the rough masculine culture characterized by drinking, violence, and contestation.

For many auto workers, the rest room, the most private of human spaces, often served as a sanctuary from the inhuman rhythms of factory production. Within automobile plants, a most frequent complaint was the contested issue of relief to perform natural bodily functions, an issue that sharply delineated the natural human world from the artificial mechanical world. For recently unionized workers, the position of relief man, along with scheduled breaks, helped to humanize the tightly regimented and controlled workplace.

The shop lavatory remained a private and individual respite and escape from the pressures of mechanized line production. In 1947 the board of review of the United Auto Workers (UAW), a three-man committee that approved grievances sent to the General Motors umpire, denied a worker's appeal of discipline for spending thirty minutes in the rest room. It noted a recent umpire's decision that "a twenty-two minute unobserved absence in the toilet" justified disciplinary action for "loitering." In 1950, the board of review considered a case in which a supervisor charged an autoworker with "reading a newspaper while sitting on the stool with his pants up." Somehow, the worker secured had two witnesses who affirmed his denial of the supervisor's charge. Nonetheless, the UAW board refused to send the case to the umpire since their testimony contained discrepancies.[36]

The shop rest room was also the social space for more collective expressions of relief from work pressures. In 1943, two Bendix Products workers protested William Hornyak's dismissal for his alleged participation in a crap game in the strut division rest room. According to a manager, it was "the worst [toilet] in the plant for crap shooting." Apparently, a plant security guard walked into a circle of eight or nine workers engaged in a crap game with $50–100 lying on the rest room floor. Although another worker admitted to loitering (he "was standing near a post watching the game and smoking"), Hornyak denied violating plant rules. When the guard asked for badge numbers, most of the group, explained a union representative, "walked right by the cop. He asked them for their badges and they said, 'No.'" Hornyak claimed, "I was sitting down and all at once something happened and I got up and was ready to go . . . when the cops came in and stopped me." When the security officer asked for his badge number, Hornyak willingly complied, though he emphasized, "I was not in the game." After a union representative argued that he was not "a habitual hanger arounder of that toilet," management officials eventually rescinded Hornyak's dismissal.[37]

Although the men's lavatory was a frequent site for worker gambling, this male activity occurred throughout automobile plants. In 1965, Thomas Anderson, a millwright in the Baltimore Chevrolet plant, protested his two-day layoff for participating in a crap game during his lunch period. After hearing "the sound of money being thrown on the table and the clicking of dice," two foremen and a plant protection sergeant caught four men—the millwright, two carpenters, and a welder—gambling at a maintenance shop workbench. As the general foreman confiscated a pair of dice, Anderson protested, "This is the first time we shot dice since we were caught the last time [almost three months ago]." Although the union disingenuously claimed that the men were simply "standing or sitting around," that the money was for "coffee, buns, and hot dogs" from the "wagon outside the main gate" and that "no Plant rule" forbade "carrying a pair of dice on your person," Chevrolet management upheld Anderson's suspension.[38]

In 1962, the U.S. Bureau of Internal Revenue, the U. S. Justice Department, and the Ohio State Police discovered a much more extensive gambling operation in the Brook Park Ford plant. Ford officials allowed Curtis Peterson, an FBI undercover agent, to work in the Brook Park foundry to investigate the gambling activities of Ford workers. Over a four-week period the FBI agent found that "a commercial stock and bond 'numbers game' and a Puerto Rican lottery game known as 'Bolita' were operating in the Foundry." In this instance, the FBI agent displayed a racialized conception of illegal masculine play, since he focused on the illicit activities of Puerto Rican and African American workers. During his month in the Ford plant, Peterson worked, socialized, and made bets with eleven Latino and African-American workers. Most of the gambling took place in the plant cafeteria, where Peterson placed his bets and observed others taking bets from Ford workers. Lorenco Cancel was the "Bolita banker" and six others allegedly took one- to two-dollar bets in the Brook Park foundry. Ford officials noted that Cancel had been described as "a kingpin of Bolita gambling." Black Ford workers apparently ran the numbers operation. Louis "Cadillac" Clyde, assisted by three runners, allegedly directed the Ford foundry's "commercial stock and bond 'numbers game.'"

One Latino worker even denied participation in the male culture of drinking and gambling; during the appeal of his dismissal, Carlos Santiago protested, "I don't gamble—I don't drink, and I never gambled in my life." About a slip of paper with numbers in his pocket he said, "I was supposed to buy some T.V. tubes, but I didn't have the money, and I had the slip for about a month."[39]

In many grievances, autoworkers demonstrated how they used their masculine culture to confront and to oppose the relations of authority and power at the regimented workplace. For example, they frequently and publicly postured against their shop foremen, supervisors, and superintendents. In one instance, a Briggs worker insisted on his right to yodel on the job, despite a threatened two-day layoff. With an almost boyish testing of the limits, union officials noted the absence of a specific Briggs rule against yodeling. In this particular shop Briggs workers, they maintained, had a common practice of singing "at the top of their voices" to relieve their monotony at work. "You should be thankful," they counseled Briggs managers, "that you have a department where they are happy." Management thought quite differently, asserting, "this is a place of business and we don't subscribe to yodeling or whistling in our departments at any time," adding that "if the men think they can go out there and yodel, . . . they are badly mistaken."[40]

While male horseplay often redefined the work environment and made it a looser, more friendly space, it sometimes created safety hazards for other workers. In 1937, two Briggs trimmers were "heckling" a third worker and "throwing chalk" at him. According to the union representative at the grievance hearing, the worker "had his head shaved [sic] off and the boys were peppering him with chalk." Angered, the victim "lost control" and "threw a hammer at the man that was throwing chalk at him, missed this man and hit somebody else" who suffered a split lip. Briggs officials fired the two offenders; a few months later they were rehired but lost their seniority.[41]

Yet men were men (perhaps *boys* is the better word), and they persistently insisted on their male right of social interaction on the shop floor. Since horseplay sometimes endangered the personal safety of other union members, union leaders often cooperated with management to contain this illicit behavior. Nonetheless, autoworkers still asserted their right to unsanctioned breaks from the rhythms of mass production. In 1942, twenty-four Briggs workers signed a petition that demanded "a special meeting for setting our chief steward right or electing a new one in his place. . . . " The union steward's offense: he did not "live up to relief regulations" and also reported "horseplay of [union] members to [the] foreman jeopardizing their jobs." In 1944, the executive board members of the Seaman Body UAW local issued a recommendation to discourage horseplay. They complained about the "many cases of horseplay . . . which have caused bodily injury" and the large amount of "lost time for Local Union Officers" on grievances that did not benefit "any great number" of union members. Recognizing management's right to discipline workers, the executive board refused to defend members who "insist[ed] on indulging in the practice of horseplay." [42]

Fighting, another prototypical form of masculine behavior, was a common and frequent means for the aggressive settlement of shop-floor disputes between workers. Numerous grievances concerned workers aggressively displaying their "manly bearing." Sometimes violent behavior involved fists, sometimes boards and two-by-fours, sometimes knives, and sometimes even guns. In 1938, Nelson Saunders, a Briggs worker, protested his layoff and loss of seniority for his involvement in a knife fight. According to the grievance, the other worker was the aggressor who "pulled a knife on Saunders, and Saunders fought back in self defense." Furthermore, it added, "A complete investigation . . . found that the man that attacked Saunders, had on three previous occasions been involved in knife incidents." Saunders had his seniority restored. The rough Briggs plant and numerous other auto plants had many similar incidents. [43]

Another traditional masculine vice was the use and abuse of alcohol at the automotive workplace. For mass production workers in the automobile plants, alcohol numbed the body's senses and reduced the tedium, fatigue, and monotony of their work. Especially when they worked in isolated work areas, men sometimes drank on the job. They also drank in taverns near their plants before and after work. When allowed to leave the workplace for lunch, they drank then, too. Again, another traditional leisure activity persisted in the disciplined modern workplace. Drinking alcohol also complicated workplace personal and social relations. Lubricated by a bit too much drink, an inebriated worker might act overly aggressive toward a coworker, engage in excessively rough horseplay, express more overtly deep ethnic or racial antagonisms, or even verbally deride a shop supervisor.

Consider, for example, the case of Carl "Tex" Leonard, a UAW Local 1250 shop committeeman in the Cleveland Ford engine plant, recently transferred from the night to the day shift. Shortly after his transfer, on a Monday morning, he apparently went on a tear through the assembly room, directly challenging several foremen. After the event, D. W. Starner, the labor relations supervisor, asserted: "A committeeman that goes on a rampage can destroy quite a bit of harmony."

Stephen Meyer

From the moment he arrived on Monday morning at 8 A.M., Leonard began bouncing into and arguing with Ford shop foremen. When foreman Jay O. Reynolds joked with Leonard and another worker inquiring whether they "pulled him off midnights," Leonard replied, "Yeah, I'm on days now and I'd better not catch you working, or I'll pull every f——g man out of your department." He then moved on to another foreman. "I was standing there," Ray F. Hart reported, "instructing [an] employee . . . on a better method of securing the damper onto the crankshaft." Leonard walked up to him with "a strong odor of alcohol on his breath" with an "unshaven face" and "a general haggard appearance," Hart wrote, and said: "I'm the committeeman—goddamn it, lay off these men. You're nothing but a fuckin' production pusher."

After this, Ted Reitz, the shop's general foreman, reported how Leonard threatened to have him fired. "I was talking to a Pipefitter," Reitz explained, "when Leonard waved and said, 'Hey, you, come over here.' I walked a distance of some six or seven feet toward him; and as he approached he said, 'You haven't had any trouble with a committeeman lately, but I'm warning you that if you get out of line the same thing will happen to you that happened to Sprouel.' I asked what was that. He said 'I got his job, and I'll get yours if you get out of line—and if you tell anybody this, I'll deny it.'" Earlier, Sprouel had been dismissed for his overbearing and abusive behavior toward workers. The general foreman too thought that he smelled liquor on the union shop committeeman's breath.

To still another foreman, William Fort, teaching two repairmen how to use a tap extractor, "in a loud and obnoxious manner" Leonard shouted, "You son-of-a bitch, you keep your hands off the f——g tools or I'll have your job."

By this time, the plant superintendent and several foremen reported the incidents to Guy Baker, an industrial relations representative, who initiated a general search for Leonard. Eventually, management found the aggressive committeeman and sent him to the labor relations office. When Leonard arrived there at 12:20 P.M., he had his union representative with him. Starner requested that they go to "the Plant First Aid office to be examined by the doctor." In his report on the incident, the labor relations supervisor noted, "I had reasons to believe that he was suffering from the lingering effects of some type of stimulant . . . ." After conferring with his union committeeman, Leonard told Starner that "the company doctor would be biased and . . . if he could have his own doctor here to be jointly examined, he would comply with the request." After Leonard again refused, the Ford labor official suspended him and escorted him from the plant.

The union committeeman apparently had imbibed a bit too much, but the Leonard incident was much more dense and complicated than the surface facts revealed. First, in the mid-1950s, the Cleveland Ford plant witnessed the genesis of industrial automation and seethed with worker discontent. Automated production technologies wreaked havoc on traditional work processes and skills and resulted in numerous grievances over job classifications. Moreover, in order to protect workers' jobs, UAW contracts often banned foremen from directly engaging in production or actually performing a workman's job. All of Leonard's confrontations involved foremen who either touched a piece of work or instructed workers how to perform their tasks. As a committeeman, Leonard aggressively, perhaps overly so, guarded his coworkers' right to perform their work without supervisory intervention or interference.

Second, within the context of widespread technical change, UAW Local 1250 officials vigorously defended the committeeman against several charges, including "Obscene, Disrespectful and Abusive Language to Supervision; Disobedience to Proper Authority; Out of Assigned Representative Area; Reporting to Work Under the Influence of Alcohol or the Lingering Effects Thereof." Despite this seemingly outrageous behavior, union leaders contended that Leonard never refused to see a doctor and "merely requested" the presence of his family physician. Though shop foremen claimed that Leonard was under the influence of alcohol, the more qualified Baker, they argued, did not "detect the odor of alcohol" in his "small and closed Labor Relations Office." As for being "out [of] his assigned representative area," the union officials maintained that he was new to the daytime shift. They also defended the committeeman's choice of words as the typical masculine talk on the factory floor: "the language of the shop is not the language of the parlor." This premise, they believed, was "universally accepted."

Generally, in Leonard's defense, the Local 1250 leaders asserted that: "in spite of the multiplicity of charges against that aggrieved none of them are warranted nor can be proven." In highly charged and gendered discourse, they charged that the Ford Motor Company was "trying to render our committeemen impotent to do the work of which he and others were elected and are dedicated to. The Union would not be worth the powder to blow it to hell if the company had the right to penalize a committeeman who is willing to fight for the employees he represents."[44]

Often the confrontational games that men played slid into even more direct challenges to managerial power and authority. For sociologist Michael Burawoy, "making out" was "a series of games in which operators attempt to achieve levels of production that earn incentive pay, in other words, anything over 100 percent."[45] Shop managers encouraged such individualistic play or games, because it drew workers into the managerial goal of increased production. "The very activity of playing a game," Burawoy observed, "generates consent with respect to its rules," since "one cannot both play the game and at the same time question the rules." Consent to the industrial order and its power relations, he asserted, "rests upon—is constructed through—playing the game."[46]

Still, the human agency and human will of automobile workers, especially in unionized UAW work settings, often resulted in the creation of different rules for different interests. On the shop floor, soldiering and output restriction—that is, the individual and the collective establishment of shop activities, behavior, and rules—often rested on masculine bonds and understandings developed in the locker room, tavern, union hall, or shop floor. Whether an individual or collective form of "manly bearing," such behavior often took on an oppositional or confrontational posture toward plant management.

In the South Bend, Indiana, Bendix Products plant, department 5B was "infamous for its slowdown tactics in protest of first one thing and then another." The union men in this brake shop turned "making out" into a different game and created their own shop-floor rules. In May 1946, the Bendix workers in 5B engaged in "a concerted slowdown in protest" against new piece rates on the brake shoes that they produced. The workers claimed that the "rates were too tight" and that they could not "make out" on the new piece rates. In fact, during arbitration before Harry E. Shulman, the Bendix workers and their UAW Local 9 union leaders even denied that they were conducting a slowdown strike and "contended that the employees were giving us a full day's work and that they were unable to earn any greater efficiency simply because the rates were too tight." Union officials asserted that "it was impossible for these men to run 100%." In the midst of "confused" testimony, however, several union witnesses said that "they could run from 105% to 112% if they worked at top speed." Shulman declared, "This was not individual action; it was action in concert." Hence, it was impermissible.

The Bendix workers quickly abandoned their work slowdown and over three weeks their "earned efficiency" immediately rose to 157, 161, and then 164 percent. During one month in early 1947, the Bendix brake workers averaged 156 percent. Bendix managers finally recognized that workers had discovered a way "to 'beat' the system." In one instance, brake shoe grinders figured out how to best the counters on the machines that recorded their production. The machine operators, one report noted, "found that they could place two shoes on the fixture and [have] the $1^{st}$ machine run indefinitely with the counter recording two pieces each time that the fixture made a complete revolution. This could be done without removing the shoes from the fixture. Thus, the count increased with each revolution and no parts were produced." In another, the machine operators also discovered "that it was possible to 'fan' the counter manually to increase the count." At the end of the shift, a "weighbill man" took the total off the machine counters and reset it for the next shift. Concerned that worker "cheating" meant that Bendix Products "paid for 34,285 more shoes that were produced," managers installed a scale to "weigh count" the brake shoes produced. This action resulted in another round of slowdowns with the earned efficiency falling from 156 percent to as low as 88 percent. In accordance with state legislation on minimum wages, the Bendix workers then demanded that they be paid the minimum earned rate.[47]

Such male group camaraderie and solidarity also existed in other parts of the same Bendix Products plant. In May 1948, when the department 5B brake shoe grinders conducted an "unauthorized" wildcat strike that resulted in layoffs in other departments, the brake shoe assemblers began their own slowdown. Two days after the grinders struck, the brake assemblers of department 9A were "evidently displeased about something, so that they were running about 80% efficiency." By the afternoon, their efficiency had "fallen to about 25%"; the next day, "they averaged about 10% efficiency for eight hours." Then, the Bendix assemblers demanded the state minimum wage for the day on which they only produced 10 percent.[48]

In both cases, the fraternal bonds of manhood remade and refashioned the rules of the game of "making out." As elsewhere, one can almost hear the smug shop-floor laughter as union leaders and members recounted their disingenuous testimony at the formal grievance hearings. Nurtured in the tavern, the union hall, or the workplace, these bonds of masculine culture facilitated the collective airing of shop-floor grievances and the collective rebalancing of power on the factory floor. To be sure, Shulman certainly did not condone such behavior, but the Bendix workers certainly communicated their oppositional perspective to Bendix management.

Masculine banter and horseplay sometimes verged into homoerotic activities in the all-male space of the automotive shop floor.[49] Reflecting on his Fisher Body experience in the 1970s, John Lippert reported "much time working with men in almost complete isolation from women." Although "none of what happens between men in the plant is considered 'sexuality,'" he discerned in the intensely competitive male environment "a pretty basic need for physical intimacy or reassurance." The Fisher Body workers expressed these needs "very simply, through putting arms around shoulders or squeezing knees, but it can become much more intense and explicit, through stabbing between the ass cheeks or pulling at nipples." Although such behavior "seem[ed] as absurd as possible," Lippert asserted, "many men enjoy[ed] this physical interaction. . . ."[50]

Within this context, arbitrator Edward L. Cushman ruled on a, Reo Motors shop-floor incident of male horseplay that displayed the interconnected themes of work, play, and power. In his ruling, Cushman wrote, "On Wednesday, December 9, 1953, . . . Joe Brzak was walking west, down an aisle, when a lift truck driver, Arthur Trescott, passed him going in the same direction. M. D. Murray, Chief Inspector, . . . claims the he saw Brzak goose Trescott. Foreman Garth Barrett also claims that he saw Brzak move his arm with the apparent intent of goosing Trescott and that . . . he assumed from the startled reaction that Brzak had in fact goosed Trescott." Additionally, two supervisors asserted that Trescott "stopped his truck, stepped off, and chased Brzak a few steps, making an upward motion of his arm as if to goose Brzak." Possibly smiling as he typed his legalistic description of the shop-floor incident, Cushman added: "Both the alleged gooser and the alleged goosee denied the alleged goosing."

For violating three shop rules, "disregard of safety, horseplay, and distraction of attention," the foreman discharged Brzak. On the surface, the goosing grievance appeared a simple case of a reasonable management effort to control possibly dangerous play in the Reo plant. Beneath the surface, however, it represented a more basic conflict over the relative power of labor and management on the shop floor.

In their brief, Reo managers stressed the incident's dangerous nature. The lift truck was "a stand-up type" and the location was "a busy area traversed by a long main aisle" with "many entrances, stairway areas, and intersecting aisles." The location, they maintained, clearly possessed "a high potential of injury, damage or death."

From the Reo management perspective, the factual details were quite simple. Brzak engaged in dangerous horseplay. Brzak, they maintained, "stepped forward toward the driver and 'goosed' him. Brzak's hand touched Trescott's body. There was some reaction on the part of the driver. Trescott then stopped the truck, stepped off, and chased Brzak for two or three steps." Although a foreman witnessed the incident from twelve feet away, he could not confirm that the hand touched Trescott's body. Nonetheless, he was "certain [that] it did because of the position and movement of Brzak's body and arms, and the 'start' by Trescott, followed by a retaliatory chase by Trescott." When the foreman questioned the offender, "Brzak denied that he goosed Trescott, but admitted [that] they were *fooling around*."

In the Reo brief, the most important "real" issue was "Management's right to control dangerous conduct by disciplinary action." Other issues included the right to have "an adequately flexible pattern of penalties," the "credibility of responsible" management officials versus the "self-serving denial" of workers, the "[f]reedom of supervisors to discipline workers," and the union's "responsibility . . . to cooperate with Management in legitimate discipline cases." In management's eyes, "Brzak was guilty of conduct that was most dangerous. Control of unsafe practices is a grave supervisory responsibility." In order to exercise its appropriate managerial authority and power, management required the right to impose severe disciplinary sanctions, "[m]easures . . . sufficiently effective to prevent repetition." Consequently, they held that the arbitrator should deny the union appeal of Brzak's grievance.

Despite management's claim for the power to control illicit behavior, UAW Local 650's brief portrayed an entirely different and more complicated situation. For union officials, the fundamental issue was

Reo management's discriminatory actions toward an aggressive union member. Due to the "discriminatory nature" of Brzak's discharge, the union officials demanded that the referee "reinstate Employee Brzak with full seniority rights and compensate him for lost time."

First, the UAW Local 650 union officials denied that any violation of plant rule occurred. Since chief inspector Murray was sixty feet and not the estimated thirty or forty feet away, he could not have seen the alleged incident. Though only twelve feet away, foreman Barrett "saw no actual goosing, but assumed there had been from the action he observed." Even Trescott, the alleged goosee, presented a notarized statement: "*At no time did Joe Brzak['s] hand come in contact with my body as the company claims.*"

Second, the union officials claimed that management had an established pattern of intimidating aggressive union members who used the grievance process. In 1953, Brzak successfully grieved a three-day disciplinary layoff. In one instance, foreman Barrett attempted "to influence the election of a Union Steward"; in another, someone in the personnel office suggested that the departmental supervisor "was out to get" Brzak's union committeeman. Additionally, the union officials also noted three separate instances in which management disciplined workers who questioned or grieved managerial authority on the shop floor.

Local 650 officials offered the example of a previous goosing grievance to prove management discrimination against Brzak. This involved Herman Lingus, a worker on the truck assembly line, who upon being goosed "turned around and pushed" his assailant "causing him to fall on a sharp edge of a fixture." The other worker even had to go to the hospital. Despite this serious injury, shop officials only gave both workers disciplinary warning slips. Moreover, after six months, management removed the warning from Lingus's personnel record.

In his decision, Edward L. Cushman was "convinced that Brzak was guilty of initiating horseplay with Trescott in disregard for safety." Whether or not an actual goosing took place was "immaterial." Horseplay, the umpire continued, could have "serious adverse results." The two workers had "an obligation to each other and to their families to refrain from horseplay." Although Reo officials had "the right to take steps to prevent" such activities, Cushman believed that discharge was "an excessive penalty" for the Brzak case. In the absence of evidence that Brzak had an "undesirable record" and since a prior goosing penalty was rescinded, Cushman reduced the penalty to a one-week layoff as a "sufficiently powerful inducement for him to refrain from horseplay in the future." Then, Cushman ordered Brzak's reinstatement with full seniority and compensation for lost time since the discharge.[51] In this case, a simple incident of horseplay, an illicit break from the regimented routine of industrial work, was transmuted into a question of power, of management versus union in the Reo factory.

Stephen Meyer

American workers created and maintained a variety of masculine cultures from the mid-nineteenth through the twentieth centuries. They constructed and reconstructed their public postures of manhood in their relations with each other, with their employers, and with women. In broad outline, these masculine cultures paralleled changes in the structures of the industrial economy and the internal social composition of the working class. Both the rough and the respectable patterns of masculine culture originated in the preindustrial laborer and artisan traditions. As the American industrial capitalism matured and developed an American system of mass production, these two masculine traditions persisted and sometimes blended into a complex mixture of the rough and respectable—rough in its relations with managerial authority and respectable in its striving for a middle-class lifestyle.

A social dimension of class contestation always loomed in the shadow of working-class manhood. The fraternal bonds of manhood enabled the creation of collective male identities to resist the Taylorist and Fordist industrial regimes on the automotive shop floor. Whether they simply played on the shop floor or collectively and aggressively restricted output, their "manly bearing" readjusted and redistributed the balance of social power at the workplace. Often, the men who were shop supervisors or union organizers were large men whose physical presence asserted masculine power. These two physical exemplars of male identity frequently reflected an important and combative component of social and class identity in the automotive workplace.

Though not fully explored in this essay, the ethnic and racial elements of working-class manhood beg for additional investigation and consideration. Anglo-American and northeastern European immigrant workers often marginalized southeastern European immigrant and African-American workers as dependent and unmanly, incapable of forging the fraternal bonds of union brotherhood. The Americanization, and indeed the social "whitening," of Polish, Russian, Jewish, Italian, Greek, and other workers certainly meant the adaptation and adoption of the dominant American norms of manhood. So too for African-American workers who were segregated into racialized ghettos of difficult, dangerous, and dirty work; as in the broader social movement, the attainment of social justice at the workplace also meant the assertion of a responsible and respectable African-American masculine identity.

Also not fully explored in this essay is the gendered component of masculine culture of the shop floor. Often, where men and women came together and interacted, rough manhood marginalized, demeaned, and harassed female workers at the workplace. Male autoworkers teased women on the shop floor. Male managers segregated them into low-wage, low-skill jobs and departments. Especially during World War II, as large numbers of women entered the rough male terrain of the automotive workplace, both managers and workers sexually intimidated and harassed them at and away from their work-places.[52] Certainly this and other realms of working-class masculine culture require much more research into additional records and sources.

## Notes

1. Peter N. Stearns, *Be a Man! Males in Modern Society* (New York: Holmes and Meier, 1979, 1990); Michael Kimmel, *Manhood in America* (New York: The Free Press, 1996); Ted Ownby, *Subduing Satan: Religion, Recreation, and Manhood in the Rural South, 1865–1920* (Chapel Hill: University of North Carolina Press, 1990); George Chauncey, *Gay New York: Gender, Urban Culture, and the Making of the Gay Male World, 1890–1940* (New York: Basic Books, 1994); Elliott J. Gorn, *The Manly Art: Bare-Knuckle Fighting in America* (Ithaca, N.Y.: Cornell University Press, 1986); Ava Baron, *Work Engendered: Toward a New History of American Labor* (Ithaca, N.Y.: Cornell University Press, 1991); and Elizabeth Faue, *Labor History* 34, special issue (1993), 167–341.

2. Baron, "Gender and Labor History: Learning from the Past, Looking to the Future" in *Work Engendered*, 30.

3. Baron, "Gender and Labor History," 20.

4. Joshua B. Freeman, "Hard Hats: Construction Workers, Manliness, and the 1970 Pro-war Demonstrations," *Journal of Social History*, 26 (1983), 725–44; and Steven Maynard, "Rough Work and Rugged Men: The Social Construction of Masculinity in Working-Class History, *Labour/Le Travail* 23 (1989), 159–69.

5. Stearns, *Be a Man!* 86.

6. Frank Marquart, *An Auto Worker's Journal: The UAW Crusade to One-Party Union* (University Park: Penn State University Press, 1975), 11–12.

7. Michael S. Kimmel and Michael A. Messner, eds., *Men's Lives* (New York: MacMillan, 1989), passim.

8. Stan Gray, "Sharing the Shop Floor: Women and Men on the Assembly Line," *Radical America* 18 (1984), 77, 79.

9. David Montgomery, "Workers' Control of Machine Production in the Nineteenth Century," in *Workers' Control in America: Studies in the History of Work, Technology, and Labor Struggles* (New York: Cambridge University Press, 1979), 13.

10. David Montgomery, *The Fall of the House of Labor: The Workplace, the State, and American Labor Activism, 1865–1925* (New York: Cambridge University Press, 1987), 58.

11. Freeman, "Hardhats," 725, 732.

12. Maynard, "Rough Work and Rugged Men," 161.

13. Peter Way, *Common Labor: Workers and the Digging of North American Canals* (Baltimore, Md.: Johns Hopkins University Press, 1993), 135, 162.

14. Way, *Common Labor*, 146, 162, 165–76.

15. Freeman, "Hardhats," 727.

16. Ibid., 728.

17. Wayne A. Lewchuk, "Men and Monotony: Fraternalism As a Managerial Strategy at the Ford Motor Company," *Journal of Economic History* 53 (1993), 827.

18. Lewchuk, "Men and Monotony," 833.

19. Maynard, "Rough Work and Rugged Men," 160.

20. Kimmel, *Manhood in America*, 101–12.

21. Maynard, "Rough Work and Rugged Men," 166.

22. Ibid., 160; and Sharon Hartman Strom, "Comments on Review Symposium: *The Fall of the House of Labor*," *Industrial and Labor Relations Review* 42 (1989), 671–72.

23. Lisa Fine, "'Our Big Factory Family': Masculinity and Paternalism at the REO Motor Car Company of Lansing Michigan," *Labor History* 34 (1993), 280.

24. See Lewchuk, "Men and Monotony," passim, and Fine, "'Factory Family,'" passim.

25. Freeman, "Hardhats," 727.

26. Ibid., 731.

27. Report of Operative 15, Box 29, Accession 572, Ford Motor Company Archives, Dearborn, Michigan.

28. Nancy Gabin, *Feminism and the Labor Movement: Women and the United Auto Workers* (Ithaca, N.Y.: Cornell University Press, 1990), 28.

29. John Lippert, "Sexuality As Consumption," in John Snodgrass, ed., *For Men against Sexism: A Book of Readings* (Albion, Calif.: Times Change Press, 1977), 209.

30. Sidney Pollard, "Factory Discipline in the Industrial Revolution," *Economic History Review* 16 (1963), 254–71; Edward P. Thompson, "Time, Work Discipline, and Industrial Capitalism," *Past and Present* 38 (1967), 56–97; and Herbert Gutman, *Work, Culture, and Society in Industrializing America* (New York: Vintage, 1977).

31. Thompson, "Time, Work Discipline, and Industrial Capitalism," 57.

32. Stephen Meyer, *The Five Dollar Day: Labor Management and Social Control in the Ford Motor Company, 1908–1921* (Albany: State University of New York Press, 1981), passim; and Stephen Meyer, "The Persistence of Fordism: Workers and Technology in the American Automobile Industry," in Nelson Lichtenstein and Stephen Meyer, eds., *On the Line: Essays in the History of Auto Work* (Urbana: University of Illinois Press, 1989), 73–99.

33. Paul Thompson, "Playing at Being Skilled," *Social History* 13 (1988), 58.

34. Alf Leudtke, "Cash, Coffee Breaks, Horseplay: Eigensinn and Politics among Factory Workers circa 1900" in Michael Hanagan and Charles Stephenson, eds., *Confrontation, Class Consciousness, and the Labor Process* (Westport, Conn.: Greenwood Press, 1986), 80.

35. Ibid., 82.

36. "Board of Review on Umpire Appeals," Case E-65, December 18, 1947, and Case F-197, September 25, 1950, F. General Motors Board of Review Decisions, V. 1, B. 1, UAW General Motors Department Papers, Archives of Labor History and Urban Affairs, Walter P. Reuther Library, Wayne State University, Detroit. All subsequent cited grievances come from the Archives of Labor History and Urban Affairs.

37. "Discharge Hearing for C. W. Clouse, 21B, and William Hornyak, 165," September 30, 1943, F. Discharge Hearings, 1943, B. 12, UAW Local 9 Papers.

38. "Notice of Appeal, Case L-91," October 27, 1965, F. L Series, B. 169, UAW Region 8 Papers.

39. "Brief for the Ford Motor Company, Umpire Case 23448" and "Meeting in the Offices of Umpire Harry Platt," May 23, 1963, F. UAW Local 1250 Correspondence, B. 5, UAW Region 2 Papers.

40. "Complaint No. I-647," March 14, 1940, F. Grievances, Mack Ave., 1940, Box 10, UAW Local 212 Papers.

41. "Complaint Record, No. 64, August 16, 1937, F. Grievances, Mack Ave., 1937 (2), B. 2, UAW Local 212 Papers.

42. "Petition," October 24, 1941, F. Grievances, Mack Ave., 1941 (2), B. 11, UAW Local 212 Papers, and "Recommendations on Horseplay," August 16, 1944, F. Shop Rules, B. 21, UAW Local 75 Papers.

43. "Complaint Record, No. A-340," October 4, 1938, F. Grievances, Mack Ave., 1938 (12), B. 5, UAW Local 212 Papers.

44. Unsigned, union brief, undated, F. Umpire Cases and "Disciplinary Hearing Held Wednesday, February 20, 1957, Carl Leonard," Reports of J. O. Reynolds, Ted Reitz, William D. Fort, and D. W. Starner, F. Board of Review, Box 5, UAW Region 2 Papers.

45. Michael Burowoy, *Manufacturing Consent: Changes in the Labor Process* (Chicago: University of Chicago Press, 1979), 51. In the auto industry, management structured its piece-rate systems around masculine competitiveness. One hundred percent was allegedly the work pace in number of pieces produced that allowed a normal worker to achieve an expected daily income. "Making out" involved earning as much as possible with the least effort and avoiding a rate cut, which meant more effort for a lesser piece.

46. Ibid., 81–82.

47. M. E. Stone to Harry Shulman, Complaint No. 17758, February 16, 1949, F. Umpire Cases, 1949, B. 58, UAW Local 9 Papers.

48. M. E. Stone to Harry E. Shulman, Complaint No. 15339, February 16, 1949, F. Umpire Cases, 1949, B. 58, UAW Local 9 Papers.

49. Maynard ("Rough Work and Rugged Men," 166–68) and Chauncey (*Gay New York*, passim) have interesting and suggestive points to make about all-male work spaces and homoerotic and even homosexual activities in work camps and boarding houses.

50. Lippert, "Sexuality As Consumption," 208.

51. Edward L. Cushman, "Decision of the Impartial Chairman, Grievance No. 54," March 31, 1954; "Management Brief," Grievance 54, Joe Brzak, Disciplinary Discharge," n.d.; "Union Brief," March 9, 1954; and "Union Exhibit G," F. Umpire Decisions, n.d., B. 20, UAW Local 650 Papers.

52. Stephen Meyer, "'The Woman in Red Slacks': Men and Women on the Automotive Shop Floor during World War II," unpublished paper presented at the North American Labor History Conference at Wayne State University, October 1999.

Stephen Meyer

# "To Make Men out of Crude Material"

## *Work Culture, Manhood, and Unionism in the Railroad Running Trades, c. 1870–1900*

PAUL MICHEL TAILLON

S peaking at the annual convention of the Brotherhood of Locomotive Firemen in Chattanooga, Tennessee, in September 1902, Theodore Roosevelt warned the assembled delegates that "there is in modern life with the growth of civilization, with the growth of luxury a special tendency to the softening of the national fiber." "I feel that professions like yours," he continued, "have a tonic effect upon the whole body politic. It is a good thing that there should be a large body of our fellow citizens in whom the exercise of the old, old qualities of courage and daring resolution and unflinching willingness to meet danger. . . . A man is not going to be a fireman or an engineer or serve in any other capacity well on a railroad long unless he is a man. . . ."[1] While the presence of a standing United States president at the convention of a labor union like the Locomotive Firemen's might have been unusual, Roosevelt's choice of rhetoric was not. With his comments, Roosevelt acknowledged the power and respectability of the Brotherhood of Locomotive Firemen and at the same time took the opportunity to promote one of the key themes of his presidency. Along with such figures as the frontiersman, Theodore Roosevelt knew that the railwayman embodied the "rugged virtues" he held so dear. For good reason, then, Roosevelt glorified railroad workers as manly and held them up as examples of manhood in his call for a return to the "strenuous life."[2]

Roosevelt's address, however, also acknowledged railroaders as not simply abstractions but as living, thinking subjects who were aware of their place in American culture and who, it seems, were receptive to his message.[3] Railwaymen produced for the commercial market autobiographies, narratives, and reminiscences recounting and extolling their experiences. Railway unions published magazines that treated readers to hagiographic stories, prescriptive essays, and letters expounding upon the finer points of railroad work and the character of railroad workers. In addition to the self-consciousness it reveals, what stands out about this writing is the prominence of a highly "gender-ized" language, especially with regard to the idea of manhood. While this language may appear evidence simply of the florid, sentimental style of Victorian-era prose, railwaymen took such language quite seriously. Historically, but especially in the late nineteenth and early twentieth centuries, workers like railroaders made very explicit connections among their work, their organizations, and their gender identity as men.[4]

The workers in the railroad running trades—the engineers, conductors, firemen, and brakemen—understood the experience of work, their claim to that work, and the honor they derived from it in terms of gender.[5] Elaborated in running trades work culture, the skills required for the job and the hazards they faced in the course of their work contributed to railroaders' sense of themselves as men and as unique workers in a unique industry.[6] The "rough" quality this style of masculinity often took and its celebration of physical strength, toughness, and courage had much in common with Roosevelt's celebration of railwaymen's manhood.

At the same time, the unions that organized these workers, the "Big Four" railroad brotherhoods, employed a gendered language to constitute themselves and to articulate their grievances and goals.[7] However, the style of manhood articulated in the railroad brotherhoods was not entirely the same as that which Theodore Roosevelt attributed to railwaymen, and differed markedly from that of the workplace.[8] For railroaders organized in the brotherhoods, manhood was if anything more firmly connected to ideas about respectability than Roosevelt's "rugged virtues." As a number of historians have argued, late-nineteenth-century skilled workers sought to dissociate themselves from the rough culture of the less skilled and more poorly paid by taking on the bearing of "respectable" men.[9] To distinguish their work culture from "coarse" workplace behavior, the conservative railroad brotherhoods articulated a "respectable" version of manhood that had much in common with middle-class norms. Still, the conservatism of the railroad brotherhoods and the respectable style of manhood they embraced represented more than simply class collaboration or an urge to achieve bourgeois respectability. For one thing, the idea stood as an expression of organized railwaymen's sense of dignity, serving as an ideal and code of behavior. For another, the ideal of respectable manhood and the language of which it was part represented a self-conscious strategy for brotherhood leaders to mobilize skilled railroaders and convince railroad managers that they could be trusted as dependable partners in labor relations.

While the brotherhoods' strategy fit with prevailing Victorian understandings of gender identity and propriety as well as their own fraternal culture, it had an important basis in the nature of train operation and the railroads' methods of labor control. Direct labor-control strate-

Paul Michel Taillon

gies have characterized management thinking in the mass production industries, but in sectors less conducive to the separation of conception from execution, like railroading, management has relied on methods that Andy Friedman has termed "responsible autonomy."[10] By incorporating workers' autonomy into the organization of production, this strategy sought to redirect workers' initiatives in concordance with a firm's priorities. Railroads in the United States attempted to ensure responsibility through an elaborate set of rules, a quasi-military style of discipline, and by supplying such positive inducements as high wages and encouraging the privileged status of running trades workers. But the railroads' bureaucratic structures proved weak instruments of labor control. At bottom, running trades workers' adherence to the rules remained under their own discretion. In fact, contesting managerial authority, train crews developed a rich work culture, elaborated a rough style of masculinity, and applied the rules as they saw fit or refused to comply with them altogether. Management found that it had to accept some limitation on its workplace authority and bargain for voluntary cooperation.[11] The railroad brotherhoods inserted themselves into this gap in managerial authority beginning in the late 1860s. In return for recognition as not only the representatives but the sole suppliers of skilled railway labor, they promised responsible, reliable *men*.

Railwaymen in the United States worked in an industry that was national in scope and bureaucratically complex. The creation of a national railroad system occurred in three distinct phases: the decade before the Civil War, when the first major trunk lines linking the east and the Midwest were completed; the years following the Civil War, when the first transcontinental railroad became a reality; and, above all, the years from the late 1870s through the early 1890s, this last phase marked by a rate of construction that outpaced earlier periods of growth, intense competition, and the consolidation of existing railroads into giant regional systems. By 1900, the outlines of the national rail network and major systems were complete, with close to 200,000 miles of track in operation.[12]

The huge scale and investment in railroad construction and operation distinguished this sector from other nineteenth-century enterprises and prompted early railroad managers to craft pioneering private-sector management techniques. One of the first truly modern technological systems, railroads depended on the synchronized operation of sophisticated equipment and the activities of thousands of men. To coordinate these operations, railroads developed the first administrative hierarchies staffed by full-time, salaried managers with specialized skills. Following the Civil War, railroads divided operations into two departments, each with its own managerial hierarchy. The road department concerned itself with the construction and maintenance of rails and road beds, while the mechanical department maintained rolling stock and coordinated the movement of traffic.[13] By the 1880s, the railroads had made important steps toward the integration of national rail operations with agreements upon standard time (1883), a uniform gauge (1886), and a standard code of operating rules (1887), and had formed the American Railway Association (1886) to coordinate industry interests.[14]

The contours of railwaymen's work took shape within this geographically dispersed and bureaucratically structured environment. From the beginning, the railroads organized their labor force into a complex job hierarchy segmented by multiple gradations of skill, prestige, arduousness, and race. Young men drawn from the lower echelons of the labor market predominated in the industry's unskilled construction and maintenance sectors. Depending on the region of the country these men could be African American, Latino, Asian, or the "new" immigrants from southern and eastern Europe. By contrast, the skilled running trades were composed almost exclusively of white men who were native-born in the United States of old immigrant stock. Both popular and managerial assumptions about the relative worth and ability of "white" and "dark" races informed the construction of this racially segmented labor force. Whereas the racial hierarchy of railroad work required some justification, however, its gender composition occasioned little, for it seemed self-evident. Customary notions of what constituted men's work dictated that men only would be hired for railroad construction, maintenance, and operation. Like many industrial and craft workplaces during these years, the locomotive footboard and the caboose were homosocial environments inhabited exclusively by men. Railroading in the late nineteenth and early twentieth centuries was a man's world, and in the running trades it was a white man's world.[15]

Train operation in the late nineteenth century was demanding, requiring a combination of skill, physical strength, and stamina. Engineers ran that distinctive piece of railroad technology, the steam locomotive, monitoring its mechanical workings while watching the rails for signals and hazards, all the while trying to "make time."[16] For this work, engineers were recognized as the most highly skilled and remunerated workers in the industry. Firemen, who shoveled coal into the locomotive's firebox and worked under the engineer's supervision, had less prestige and skill. While the position of firemen may have demanded greater physical endurance than mental ability, providing sufficient steam at just the right moment required a certain amount of skill.[17] The railwayman officially in charge of the train, the conductor, supervised the crew and saw that his train arrived at its destination on time without interfering with other trains.[18] The bulk of the conductor's duties, however, made him something of a traveling clerk. On passenger trains he collected fares and assisted passengers while on freight runs he was responsible for the cargo manifest. Conductors needed to be literate as well as have practical judgment, record-keeping ability, and for passenger runs, courteous manners.[19] Brakemen's principal duties included operating the brakes, coupling and uncoupling cars, and opening and closing switches. In the days before air brakes and automatic couplers these operations required brakemen to scramble atop moving cars to set brake wheels or to step between cars during coupling to insert a link between the drawheads.[20] Obviously dangerous, this kind of labor demanded physical coordination of the individual brakeman and teamwork of the entire crew.

Railroading, indeed, came with more than its share of burdens and risks. Work in the running trades involved long hours of labor and unpredictable work rhythms. The nature of train operation demanded that train crews put in long hours—twelve to twenty-four hours (and sometimes more) at a stretch—and absent themselves from home for days or weeks at a time.[21] The hours of work were unpredictable as well as long.[22] Even steadily employed railroaders rarely knew how many days out of the month they would be on duty, and even when it was steady, railroad work involved its own uniquely unpredictable brand of industrial time. The majority of train workers operated freight trains, which ran twenty-four hours a day, on irregular schedules that varied by season and weather, for the greatest portion of their careers.[23] Train crews could be called at any hour of the day or night for a run, particularly if they were on the "extra board."[24] Once en route on a freight run, there was no quitting time—work was finished when the train arrived.[25] Surveying these conditions in his 1900 report on railroad labor to the U.S. Industrial Commission, Samuel McCune Lindsay characterized railroad service as "a life in itself, somewhat apart from that of the ordinary man . . . in an occupation that follows the conventional hours of work."[26]

While the hours and rhythms of work represented a "burden" of railroad labor, it paled in comparison to the awful hazards of the job. Railroaders, especially those in the running trades, toiled under the constant threat of crippling injury or death. Boiler explosions, derailments, and, above all, the primitive hand braking and "link and pin" coupling systems made railroading one of the riskiest occupations in nineteenth-century North America.[27] Figures from the Interstate Commerce Commission (ICC) show that railroaders outpaced almost every other occupation in terms of injury. In the year ending June 30, 1889, the ICC found that one out of every 117 train workers were killed and one of twelve were injured in some way;[28] brakemen were the principal victims of these accidents.[29] State-level figures confirm the ICC's reports: in 1908, well after U.S. railroads began introducing safer technologies like air brakes and automatic couplers, the Illinois Bureau of Labor Statistics found that in that state railroaders accounted for 56 percent of broken ribs, 50 percent of broken arms, 41 percent of broken legs, 54 percent of all hand injuries, 30 percent of lost fingers, 71 percent of severed arms, and all legs amputated. In 1907 and 1908, 47 percent of the workers killed in Illinois were railroaders and 38 percent of the workers injured labored on railroads.[30]

More so than the risks, work rhythms, and unique equipment, however, another element defined running trades work: the rules.[31] Company rule books, upwards of one hundred pages long (referred to as the "Company Bible" by employees), governed the movement of traffic as well as how railroaders performed their work and conducted themselves on the job. The "Book of Rules," for example, formally placed conductors in charge of train runs; they had to follow strict guidelines governing the loading of freight and boarding of passengers, collecting of fares and waybills, and reporting of delays and accidents. Along with train orders, which were written, numbered, dated, and signed directives modeled on military orders, rule books specified which trains had priority over others, the speeds at which they could travel, the use of signals and switches, and the procedures at stations, bridges, and crossings. Rule books also established codes of behavior for railway employees. The Chicago, Burlington and Quincy Railroad, for instance, called the attention of employees "to the importance of neatness in their personal appearance, of orderly and manly deportment whether on or off duty. . . ."[32] "Rule G" prohibited the consumption of alcohol while on duty as well as on or around railroad property and called for the dismissal of intoxicated employees.[33]

Since bosses could not be present in the cab, caboose, or depot, adherence to operating rules was the principal manifestation of effective supervision and discipline. Before promotion, every engineer and conductor, fireman and brakeman had to pass an examination given by a rules examiner and pledge to carry the rule book with him at all times on duty. Company officers attempted to monitor the performance of train crews through the use of "spotters" (spies who boarded passenger trains and reported on workers' conduct) and "mechanical spotters" (devices installed in cabooses that recorded train speed). The penalty for violating the rules typically involved a military-like hearing before the division manager in which the guilty worker might be suspended without pay or dismissed. Even with such penalties, however, managers were acutely aware that they were dependent upon the cooperation and trust of their employees.[34]

Train crews enjoyed a high degree of control over the execution of their work through their application of railroad rules. Railroaders had to judge, select, and apply the appropriate rules in particular operating situations. Since it was impossible to mandate absolute guidelines for every possible exigency that might arise on the road, train crews had to be flexible. A unique combination of cognitive and perceptual-motor skills—when, where, and how an action must be performed—defined railroad work; it was as much a mental use of "the rules" as a manual

Paul Michel Taillon

endeavor. The tension between the rules and the physical actions and accompanying "sensory" skills they governed set railroading apart from all other occupations.[35] Workers in the running trades occupied a singular niche in that they were "all-around" craftsmen within a highly bureaucratic environment defined by elaborate rules.

The work culture of the running trades, then, was rooted in the application of official rules dictated by management, and informal practices developed by workers.[36] It was the accumulated experience and collectively held knowledge embodied in work culture that provided the individual railroader with the information to interpret and apply the rules. As applied, these rules often bore little resemblance to their written form. Indeed, most train workers found that if they followed the rules to the letter they would never get their trains in on time, if at all. The mark of good railroading was the ability not to follow the rules exactly but to interpret and apply them with common railroad sense as situations arose. In fact, some rules had to be consistently broken to complete the task expeditiously. As conductor Harry French recalled, "in the early [eighteen] nineties the train crews made their own rules to fit various occasions. The general idea was to keep trains moving. Any man's ability to do just that determined, to a large extent, how highly he was rated as a railroadman."[37]

French's comments indicate not only the autonomy and skill of railroaders but also reveal how ideas of masculinity informed those concepts. For running trades workers, the complexity of train operation, not to mention the physical aspects of the job, were, in the words of theorist Paul Willis, "essentially masculine problems, requiring masculine capacities to deal with them."[38] Like other nineteenth-century craftsmen, the notion that a workingman's masculinity was connected to his skill enjoyed currency among railroaders. Because skilled workers saw reasoning, skill, and muscle as specifically masculine attributes, this "embodied capital" could be the property only of men.[39] Railroaders' relationship with the technology and the rules, as well as the strength, endurance, and knowledge required for railroading, mediated their sense of themselves as men. Canadian brakemen and conductors who worked in the 1920s and 1930s remembered the skill and strength required to throw switches and to couple or uncouple cars, as well as the dangers involved in such operations. Engineers and firemen enjoyed a sense of mastery operating their locomotives: one engineer recalled, "I loved the engines. I loved the power."[40] In the way railwaymen described their relationships, the technology and its operation were often invested with sexual or gender-specific metaphors: "[W]hat fireman doesn't call his machine his girl or his beauty?" asked the *Locomotive Firemen's Magazine* in 1890.[41] On a variety of levels, the skill and physical abilities required to handle switches, cars, and locomotives made railroading a masculine calling. At the same time, the act of railroading—the acquisition of skill, interpretation of rules, enduring the elements, and facing injury and death with bravery—made railroaders masculine.

The running trades work culture incorporated definitions of manhood and male bonding that fit with the demands of railroading. If the contemporary research of anthropologist Frederick Gamst is any guide, a "'rail' is a self-assured and reliable *man*, who does not resort to an 'alibi' for not performing properly on the job or for unsociable job behavior. A 'good rail' is operationally skilled, knowledgeable, and efficient—saving time and effort for all on the crew. And the 'rail' is reasonably careful with personal safety, but much more with the protection of fellow employees." A "rail" was a team player; he did not turn stool pigeon on another "rail" bending the rules.[42] Indeed, improvisation, teamwork, and cooperation were essential to getting a train over the road and to minimizing the effects of long, irregular hours and workplace hazards.[43] Rails looked out for each other on the job, executing their work according to the rules and warning fellow workers of danger. When speaking of fellow train workers, men used terms such as *brother* and *fraternity* and observers have compared the bonding of train crews to that of soldiers under battlefield conditions.[44]

Running trades work culture had its "rougher" aspects. Laboring in a workplace that was homosocial and apart from "civilized" heterosocial society, train crews had a sense of themselves and their workplaces as men and spaces apart from the mainstream of "polite society."[45] The rhythms and content of their work set them apart, as did the fact that for all their skill and popular romanticization of their work railwaymen still labored with their hands. Even engineers and conductors, "aristocrats" of labor, were not free of the disdain with which middle-class society held manual labor. Brakemen and firemen, who performed labor-intensive, semiskilled, entry-level work, stood out as objects of suspicion.[46] Awareness of this attitude led many skilled workers to distance themselves from the "roughness" of the unskilled working class by embracing the trappings of bourgeois respectability and demanding respect for their skills as a signifier of manhood.[47] But at the same time, perhaps making a virtue of necessity, or perhaps emerging from "manly" confrontation with their working conditions, railroaders celebrated toughness and physical strength as badges of masculinity.[48] Writing in 1860, engineer Henry Dawson characterized a good railwayman as "dependable" and "unromantic"—"the stuff a man was made of." By contrast, he insisted, in emergencies, "Your lily-handed, romantic gentry would have failed. . . ."[49] This style of masculinity celebrated the qualities of toughness and the ability "to take it," enabling men to cope with harsh working conditions through "sheer mental and physical bravery."[50] In the workplace, this sensibility often revealed itself in coarse behavior, bawdy humor, "hard swearing," "hard drinking," and manly defiance toward management.[51]

Paul Michel Taillon

This kind of "rough" behavior, and the work culture of which it was part, conflicted with management's goals in running a railroad. At its best, management and workers had different ideas as to what constituted "good railroading." Indeed, railwaymen could be openly and deliberately defiant when it came to the manner in which work should be performed. A classic example of workplace autonomy and rules violation was that of "running on smoke orders." The great majority of railroads in the nineteenth century were of the single-track variety. Trains were dispatched and coordinated in head-on and overtaking movements in such a way that certain trains were given priority over others. Local freights and work trains usually had inferior rights to through freights and passenger runs. If the crew of a work train fell behind in its schedule, it might elect to run on the main line without the necessary train order authority to do so. To avoid a collision the errant crew watched for smoke from the engine of the train having the right to run on that section of track.[52] Such practices gave rise to the *American Railroad Journal*'s 1858 complaint that "railroad employees lack the right kind of sentiment. They establish their own rules for the regulation of their own conduct."[53]

Train crews routinely bent the rules to get their work done as well as to secure informal perquisites, such as allowing friends or fellow "rails" to ride free of charge. Conductors found themselves uniquely situated to take advantage of their workplace autonomy. By performing transport-related odd jobs, conductors could supplement their income. During his career as a conductor in Oregon, Harry French carried messages and packages for a fee and even shopped for people who did not have access to the city. Such activities, however, could easily spill over onto "criminal" terrain, like the embezzlement of fares. A conductor on the Chicago, Burlington and Quincy Railroad, for example, kept from $65 to $200 per trip and over a five-year period accumulated $17,000. The Pinkerton Detective Agency, hired by the Philadelphia and Reading Railroad in 1862, discovered that the company's conductors embezzled 32 percent of their collections. Companies attempted to deal with embezzlement, in addition to free rides, through spotters disguised as passengers and well-publicized discharges. Incidents like the Concord Railroad of New Hampshire's wholesale dismissal of its entire corps of conductors did not solve the problem, but they gave conductors an unseemly reputation for dishonesty.[54]

Tarnishing railwaymen's reputations more thoroughly was their renowned propensity to imbibe alcoholic beverages. In 1898, for instance, the U.S. Commissioner of Labor included conductors, engineers, switchmen, and, above all, brakemen among the leading occupations in which employees were addicted to alcohol.[55] Railroaders drank not only off the job but frequently during work hours, too, contributing to their reputation, in the words of historian James H. Ducker, as "a boastful, rough-speaking, hard-living, immoral lot."[56] Part of railroad work culture, occupational drinking fostered a common, if not oppositional identity, among train crews. Indeed, occupational drinking may be understood as a ritual of resistance that set railway-men apart from management, white-collar labor, and women. Railway-men's beliefs about drinking informed their understanding of themselves as men and as a distinctive category of workers.[57] Of course, railroaders' inclination to consume intoxicating beverages also, more dramatically than in any other industry, ran up against industrial discipline—the dangers of mixing train running and alcohol were obvious.[58]

The negative image of railroaders created by the rougher aspects of running trades work culture both presented a problem and created opportunities for the organizing efforts of the railroad brotherhoods. In an era when labor unions' public standing was dubious at best, organizing disreputable workers invited public hostility. However, claiming to reform those workers, to make them upstanding citizens and dependable employees, could provide an avenue for acceptance by the public and railroad management. If railroad firms were unable to ensure that their employees conducted themselves responsibly on the job, perhaps the unions representing those workers could. With this in mind, and implicitly acknowledging conductors' blemished image, Grand Chief Conductor C. S. Wheaton emphatically stated, "The Order [of Railway Conductors] are doing all they can and using their whole influence . . . to place the conductor where we believe he rightly belongs, not as an object of ridicule and jest, but in an honorable position . . . so that his position is a desirable position, and he is placed above the imputations which are so many times cast at conductors."[59]

Brotherhood leaders saw their mission in the late 1860s through the early twentieth century as ensuring that organized railroaders had the necessary skills and appropriate habits for railroad work. Belonging to a tradition of fraternalism that infused much of the North American labor movement, the brotherhoods were well suited to such a task. From their beginnings, the brotherhoods committed themselves to programs of fraternal uplift aimed at making members good railroaders. This, brotherhood leaders believed, would convince railroad managers of the validity of their unions and the efficacy of their leadership. At the same time, they had no doubt that occupational uplift in its own right was a desirable goal for railwaymen. By associating on a fraternal basis, railroaders could benefit themselves individually as they improved their material situations collectively. With a little help from one's peers, a man could attain competency within the craft, hone his skills through technical instruction, and learn good work habits such as punctuality and tidiness. Brotherhood men assumed their employers would then recognize and reward employees accordingly and acknowledge the brotherhoods' role in this effort, accepting them as partners in labor relations and as suppliers of dependable labor. Eugene V. Debs, then secretary for the Brotherhood of Locomotive

Firemen and editor of the *Locomotive Firemen's Magazine*, stated these ideas simply in 1881: "The object of our institution is to make men out of crude material, and when we have succeeded in that . . . when we are fully qualified to receive our rights, they will be accorded us."[60]

At a basic level, this effort involved provision of educational programs running the gamut of railroading. Individual lodges, for instance, often set aside a portion of the monthly meeting for technical and industrial education, and brotherhood journals provided special sections devoted to these topics. The *Locomotive Engineers Monthly Journal*'s "Technical Department" featured articles addressing issues such as "Freight Train Handling" and "Brake Application."[61] And the *Locomotive Firemen's Magazine* included a "Mechanical Department" containing titles like "Primary Lessons in Steam Engineering," "Scientific Firing," "Saving Coal and Avoiding Smoke," and "What Should a Young Fireman Know?"[62] Technical drawings of locomotive and train-car mechanical systems abounded as well as articles and illustrations on new railroad technologies. These essays, and similar offerings in the *Railway Conductor* and *Railroad Brakemen's Journal*, expounded upon the technical aspects of railroading.[63]

At the same time, brotherhood educational work attempted to ensure that the men conducted themselves in a manner becoming of their stations by indoctrinating them in the appropriate attitudes, habits, and mental skills necessary for railroad labor—to "be faithful and conscientious in the discharge of [one's] calling. . . ."[64] This effort included "prescriptive" essays in brotherhood journals on proper work habits and exhortations at union meetings promoting responsible conduct such as punctuality, neatness, not sleeping on the job, and avoiding alcohol.[65] A series of articles in 1893 entitled "Practical Talks to Young Engineers" stressed adherence to company rules while acknowledging the necessity for on-the-job decision making: "When you receive your train order, read it thoroughly and give it to the fireman . . . *never read an order the second time* . . . have it thoroughly impressed on your mind at the first reading. . . . Imagine any contingency that is liable to occur to prevent the successful completion of your trip; disaster overtakes the person who is not looking for it." In similar fashion, hoping to persuade its members to comply with company rules, the Order of Railway Conductors launched a campaign for "perfect service" in the late 1880s.[66] As these essays suggested, railroading demanded not just technical skills but also "good character."

Brotherhood leaders knew, however, that exhortations to follow good habits and technical instruction were not enough. They were competing against an entrenched workplace culture with its customary practices and norms. Thus, brotherhood leaders worked to construct an alternative identity for railroaders. In contrast to the "rough" style of masculinity that emerged from the workplace, they articulated a vision of "respectable" manhood for railroaders. As developed by brotherhood leaders from the 1870s through 1900, "respectable" manhood involved living up to responsibilities in multiple arenas of men's lives: workplace, union lodge, and household, but they emphasized the workplace above all. Brotherhood leaders assumed that their members would earn a family wage as a result of productive labor and support their households as breadwinners, and they expected brotherhood men to dedicate themselves to their crafts and conduct themselves as dependable employees at work.[67] All of this came together, in the words of Brotherhood of Locomotive Firemen member H. J. Facke, in "fidelity to obligations, honorable ambitions [and the] building of a good, pure manly character." For one brotherhood official, this process amounted to nothing less than "successful man-building."[68]

To realize this vision of manhood, and to supplant the "rough" masculinity of railwaymen, brotherhood leaders attempted to translate the virtues they preached—cultivating manners, practicing self-control, and striving for self-improvement—into "heroic," "manly" qualities. An 1882 editorial by Eugene V. Debs entitled "The Square Man" presented self-restraint, responsibility, and courage as "manly" and "heroic." As Debs saw it, "If the square man grasps the throttle of an engine there will be no sleeping at that post. Lives are entrusted to him; all his faculties are on the alert for danger. . . . Clear-brained, keen-eyed, strong-armed he stands at his post, and if the hour of danger overtakes him while there, he will never desert it. Duty does not call to him in vain. All the time while his engine is skimming along the rail . . . he stands there silent, watchful, fearless."[69] In this vision Debs emphasized responsibility, control over the body, coolness in the face of danger, and willingness to sacrifice oneself to save others. But if in Debs's opinion railroading commanded bodily control in the best middle-class fashion, he nevertheless acknowledged the physically taxing aspects of the job. In an 1884 essay, Debs painted a portrait of manhood based in corporeal ability and practical mental aptitude: "[Railroaders] are remarkable for common sense. They are bronze-browed, hard-fisted, noble-natured men. They are forever dealing with problems which demand and command serious thought. A locomotive fireman cannot, in the nature of things be a dude."[70]

A glorified vision no doubt, but as this passage from the *Locomotive Firemen's Magazine* indicated, Debs's understanding of gender identity was bound up in the skilled work demanded by railroading. For Debs and others, control and restraint of the body, firmly grounded in the railroad work process, had distinctly working-class, not middle-class, meanings. In contrasting railwaymen to "dudes," Debs ridiculed the "unmanly" conduct of leisure-class men who did not work with their hands. By contrast, respectable working-class manhood celebrated the risks and rewards of physical labor, emphasizing its ennobling effects and stressing the superiority of manhood based in "authentic experience." "The cultured and refined with their silks and laces and arrogant pride, sweep by in majestic disdain when meeting this class of workers, little dreaming that beneath that blouse beats a heart as brave and chivalrous as ever distinguished knights of old," wrote A. J. Schmidt, a fireman from Cleburne, Texas, in 1891. "What matters the rough exterior, the soiled over clothes and the grease and coal dust? 'A man's a man for that.'"[71] Brotherhood railroaders insisted that regardless of their appearance, their character and the content of their work made them respectable, heroic men. In this manner, brotherhood spokesmen redefined as "respectable" the "rough" aspects of manhood in running trades work culture.

While union leaders sought to reconcile the workplace and brotherhood notions of manhood to win railwaymen's allegiance, they also presented workplace responsibility and employer loyalty as manly virtues. "The most sacred and binding seal known by civilized men is the pledge of honor," lectured Eugene Debs in an 1882 editorial. "No man, with any moral scruple, would be able to contemplate, without a keen feeling of shame, the record of a broken pledge." He continued, "It is our aim to impress this fact upon the minds of our members . . . the obligation they take to support the rules and principles of our Order is as binding upon a man as a bond backed by millions, and anyone who violates that obligation strikes down his very manhood with his own hand."[72] It did not matter whether a pledge was made to a fellow man, to one's union, or to one's employer; a pledge was a contract to be honored. Debs intended this passage as a reminder of brotherhood members' duty to their employers. By doing so, Debs was addressing not only union membership but also railroad executives.

Thus, while brotherhood efforts sought to raise the status and respect of skilled railwaymen, they also worked to position themselves with railroad management. In return for material benefits and recognition, the brotherhoods promised "to give to railway corporations a class of sober and industrious men."[73] The brotherhoods' project of "man building" would provide the railroad corporations with skilled, dependable labor. Indeed, they argued that it was in the interests of the railroads to encourage the brotherhoods in this effort. By 1889, as Grand Chief Engineer Peter M. Arthur believed, "The [Brotherhood of Locomotive Engineers] had been instrumental in giving the railway companies a better class of men than they would otherwise have had."[74] Brotherhood leaders aimed at nothing less than ensuring what management had been unable to accomplish—proper conduct at work.

Such bold promises required expression at a more practical level than pronouncements in public or in the pages of brotherhood journals. Ultimately, the test came in the brotherhoods' policies and actions in specific work situations.[75] Central to the brotherhoods' moral stewardship, and, by extension, their claim to respectability and legitimacy was their ability to guarantee that their members indeed were skilled, trustworthy, sober, respectable, and manly.[76] The brotherhoods' police power extended beyond matters internal to the lodge or between members to include the conduct of brotherhood men at work. The brotherhoods followed strict procedures to discipline members who failed to conduct themselves as respectable men on the job or who violated the employer's trust. The Brotherhood of Locomotive Engineers, for instance, made it an offense to conduct oneself as anything other than an exemplary employee: should any brother "neglect his duty or injure the property of his employer, or endanger the lives of persons" he would be brought up on charges. Such was the case when in 1893 the secretary of Brotherhood of Railroad Trainmen Lodge No. 93, in Moosic, Massachusetts, "preferred charges against Frank A. Green for stealing goods from the F. R. R. Co. and recommended that he be expelled for same."[77] Indeed, brotherhood officers willingly made unfavorable reports on members to management. As master of his local lodge, in 1885 Eugene Debs voluntarily informed the Vandalia Railroad about the poor medical condition of a member who had applied for a job as engineer. Upon learning that the individual in question had a poor heart, the road declined to hire him and thanked Debs for his action.[78]

Actions like Debs's revealed a conception of class relations in which workers and their representatives played the role of junior partner to capital. As Nick Salvatore has argued, before his conversion to socialism Debs placed responsibility for social discord on the shoulders of working people. He looked to employers as both personal and social models to maintain the qualities of manhood and citizenship necessary for harmonious labor relations and advancement for railwaymen. In Debs's view, since railway managers had already demonstrated their virtue and ability by rising to their eminent stations, and because workers themselves were responsible for social disorder, the union should emulate corporations' success and focus on making their members responsible citizens and workers.[79]

This kind of rhetoric, together with moral uplift, technical education, and disciplinary procedures, yielded results in the judgment of brotherhood leaders and members. "Our employers are not slow in discovering this marked advance in morality, as is evidenced on every hand by the frequent advancements and promotions, and the seeking in our ranks, as is often done, for good, trustworthy, sober men," maintained Grand Master Frank W. Arnold at the Brotherhood of Locomotive Firemen's 1882 convention.[80] "The Brotherhood of Railroad Brakemen are doing a great deal of good here," agreed a brakeman in 1886. "They have been the means of reforming a great many men. A man who belongs to this order must be upright, sober and industrious. Railroad officials are beginning to see the good of the order and are giving brotherhood men the preference."[81] Likewise, a writer to the *Locomotive Firemen's Magazine* argued in 1891 that the Brotherhood of Locomotive Firemen had educated "the membership up to a high standard." Railroad officials, he conceded, used to oppose organized labor, but the "wise" ones no longer did, for "the train service has attained to such a degree of perfection a high order of skill and training is essential on the part of the men in charge. . . . Railroad managers have discovered this, and have accepted the inevitable. . . ."[82]

It seemed that many railroad managers did accept the inevitable in the 1880s and 1890s. William Riley McKeen, president of the Vandalia Railroad and Eugene Debs's original employer, not only maintained a friendly relationship with Debs after he joined the Brotherhood of Locomotive Firemen but signed the bond that Debs posted when he became the union's secretary. Some managers wrote to brotherhood leaders and spoke of their organizations, as Debs described it, "in the kindliest terms." William H. Vanderbilt of the New York Central Railroad, recorded Debs in 1880, was "greatly pleased to notice the rapid development of the organization."[83] New York Central president Chauncey Depew, known for his tolerant view of organized labor, spoke of the engineers in 1886 as "a model for trades unions. You are not only the most successful of labor organizations, but you have the respect of and confidence of those whom you so admirably serve—the people and the corporations." Five years later, Depew's outlook had not changed: "Every reasonable, helpful labor organization, controlled by its own members, in their own interest, is to be encouraged. We welcome such a trade union as the locomotive engineers. We would rather have it than not have it."[84] The words of these officials appear to be borne out by the brotherhoods' record during the 1880s. Experiencing something of a golden age, they negotiated agreements providing favorable wages and working conditions for train crews.[85]

Brotherhood success during these years, however, may be attributed as much to a tight railroad labor market and threats from more radical labor organizations as to the brotherhoods' educational and uplift programs and their language of respectability and manhood. The men directing the nation's railroads looked upon the brotherhoods in a decidedly more favorable light in the aftermath of the 1877 railroad strikes and 1894 Pullman boycott, conflicts the brotherhoods studiously avoided. And these officials seemed interested in dealing with the brotherhoods only as long as they had to. As new railroad construction tapered off in the late 1880s and early 1890s and the labor market turned to the employers' advantage, the brotherhoods found themselves confronting railroad executives determined to gain control over the supply and direction of railroad labor. The engineers' and firemen's strike on the Chicago, Burlington and Quincy Railroad in 1888 grew out of these dynamics and highlighted the inability of brotherhood-style unionism to protect skilled railwaymen's interests, much less win acceptance by railroad managers. And the defection of thousands of members to the brotherhoods' archrival, the American Railway Union (ARU), in 1893–94, suggests that for many, the messages of manhood, mobility, and respectability no longer resonated.[86] In light of these events, brotherhood leaders' claims to success take on something of a strident quality.

Yet in 1900, before the U.S. Industrial Commission, Peter M. Arthur was still testifying along these lines: "I think that we have convinced [railroad managers] by our work that we are sincere and honest in our efforts to give to the railway companies a reliable, trustworthy class of men." Similarly, reasoned Brotherhood of Locomotive Firemen Grand Master Frank P. Sargent, "If they did not have respect for us and the work in which we are engaged they would not ask for our men to take service on their lines."[87] Arthur and Sargent had good reason to feel as though railroad executives valued their organizations. Following the Pullman boycott of 1894 and the destruction of the American Railway Union, the railroad brotherhoods found themselves favored by a state-sanctioned regime of collective bargaining mandated by the 1898 Erdman Act and a real degree of acceptance by the nation's railroad corporations.[88] The testimony of Illinois Central Railroad president Stuyvesant Fish in an 1899 statement before the U.S. Industrial Commission appears to confirm this. He referred to the Brotherhood of Locomotive Engineers and the Order of Railway Conductors as "useful and honorable organizations of intelligent railroad men."[89]

In this context, William S. Carter, who took over editorship of the *Locomotive Firemen's Magazine* after Debs left in 1893, probably was more on the mark than his colleagues when in 1901 he wrote that the ARU "taught railway corporations a useful lesson. It taught them that if corporations during times of distress could succeed in enforcing defeat upon the organized old brotherhoods they would also create a mob of unorganized workers who ignored law and order and entered into what came near being an insurrection."[90] Carter's remarks reveal a good deal. The Pullman boycott, like the 1877 railroad strikes before it, stood as a dramatic example of what angry, undisciplined workers could do—just the sort of thing the brotherhoods had promised to prevent. So, while the brotherhoods' success after 1900 arguably had less to do with their own strategy than more radical alternatives, neither was it irrelevant. To become the beneficiaries of the ARU's actions and the state's largesse, the brotherhoods had to present something of substance. That substance came forward in the brotherhoods' avoidance of the boycott and earlier labor conflagrations as well as in their efforts to provide the corporations with dependable disciplined men.

The railroad brotherhoods efforts to establish a disciplined and reliable membership while winning the confidence of railroad employers through the construction of respectable manhood was only partially successful. Many brotherhood members no doubt wholeheartedly adopted the ideals promulgated by their unions. Other members, however, probably joined, or felt compelled to join, *in spite of* such rhetoric.

Either way, to varying degrees, skilled railwaymen in the workplace resisted, limited, and altered the brotherhood message just as they resisted, altered, and challenged the directives of railroad managers in the conduct of their work.[91] At the same time, railroad management recognized the brotherhoods only when they had to or when the alternative was too unpleasant.

The brotherhoods' efforts to act as brokers of dependable, skilled labor indicates the salience of gender for the relationships among technology, the workplace, workers, unions, and employers.[92] The ability of nineteenth-century craft unions to control the market for their members' labor and to engage in collective bargaining depended on their members' conduct in the workplace.[93] Railroading technology and the nature of train operation, however, created a unique environment in which running trades workers had a tremendous degree of control over their labor. In this environment they developed an intense sense of masculine pride that challenged not only managerial authority but also the strict moral codes and conservative gender ideals of the railroad brotherhoods. In turn, the brotherhoods articulated a style of respectable manhood through which they sought to influence their members' behavior in line with the goals of railroad firms.

The brotherhoods' practices and the difficulties they experienced securing acceptance by management reflected how masculinity on the railroads was contested at the same time as it was ubiquitous. Masculinity provided a terrain for the interplay of managerial efforts at labor control, workers' practices for asserting workplace autonomy, and union efforts to attain growth and stability. It was fitting, then, that President Theodore Roosevelt upheld railroaders as exemplars of manhood in his 1902 address for the very ground upon which workers, managers, and union officials interacted was imbued with gender. However, that ground was riven with debates about appropriate forms of manhood, revealing that the masculine practices of the "manly" railroader were a great deal more diverse and complicated than Roosevelt may have thought.

## Notes

1. "The President a Grand Honorary Member," *Locomotive Firemen's Magazine* 33 (1902), 547–56; magazine hereafter cited as *LFM*.

2. On Theodore Roosevelt and the "strenuous life," see Gail Bederman, *Manliness and Civilization: A Cultural History of Gender and Race in the United States, 1880–1917* (Chicago: University of Chicago Press, 1995), 170–215; Michael Kimmel, *Manhood in America: A Cultural History* (New York: The Free Press, 1996), 181–88.

3. The Firemen returned the favor by making Roosevelt an honorary member.

4. Steven Maynard, "Rough Work and Rugged Men: The Social Construction of Masculinity in Working-Class History," *Labour/Le Travail* 23 (1989): 159–60.

5. See Joy Parr, *The Gender of Breadwinners: Women, Men, and Change in Two Industrial Towns, 1880–1950* (Toronto: University of Toronto Press, 1990), 166–68.

6. Work culture is the ideology and practice by which workers stake out a relatively autonomous sphere of action on the job. See Barbara Melosh, *The Physician's Hand: Work Culture and Conflict in American Nursing* (Philadelphia: Temple University Press, 1982), 5–6; Susan Porter Benson, "'The Customers Ain't God': The Work Culture of Department-Store Saleswomen, 1890–1940," in Michael H. Frisch and Daniel J. Walkowitz, eds., *Working-Class America: Essays on Labor, Community, and American Society* (Urbana: University of Illinois Press, 1983), 185–86.

Reed C. Richardson and Walter Licht identify the factors making railroaders unique. See Reed C. Richardson, *The Locomotive Engineer, 1863–1963: A Century of Railway Labor Relations and Work Rules* (Ann Arbor: University of Michigan Press, 1963), 15–16; Walter Licht, *Working for the Railroad: The Organization of Work in the Nineteenth Century* (Princeton, N.J.: Princeton University Press, 1983), 5, 80–81.

7. The "Big Four" included the Brotherhood of Locomotive Engineers, the Order of Railway Conductors, the Brotherhood of Locomotive Firemen, and the Brotherhood of Railroad Trainmen. Sometimes the Switchmen's Mutual Aid Association is included in this group. Together, these groups organized the workers of the running trades: engineers, conductors, firemen, brakemen, and switchmen.

8. For most industrial workers, knowing firsthand the unromantic realities of "abundant experience" in the workplace, Roosevelt's call for a return to the "strenuous life" probably sounded absurd. In fact, Roosevelt's glorification of working-class masculinity reveals more about the anxieties and longings of middle-class men and elites at century's end than the realities of working-class experience. See Thomas Winter, "The YMCA, Workingmen, and Imagining the Male 'Other,' 1877–1920," paper presented at the Eighty-ninth Annual Meeting of the Organization of American Historians, Chicago, March 1996, 1–3; E. Anthony Rotundo, "Body and Soul: Changing Ideals of American Middle-Class Manhood, 1770–1920," *Journal of Social History* 16 (1985): 32.

9. See Nick Salvatore, *Eugene V. Debs: Citizen and Socialist* (Urbana: University of Illinois Press, 1982), 46; Ken Fones-Wolf, *Trade Union Gospel: Christianity and Labor in Industrial Philadelphia, 1865–1915* (Philadelphia, Penn.: Temple University Press, 1989), 20–29; Elliott J. Gorn, *The Manly Art: Bare-Knuckle Prize Fighting in America* (Ithaca, N.Y.: Cornell University Press, 1986), 129–47; John Tosh, "What Should Historians Do with Masculinity? Reflections on Nineteenth-Century Britain," *History Workshop Journal* 38 (1994): 185–86.

10. See Andy Friedman, "Responsible Autonomy versus Direct Control over the Labour Process," *Capital and Class* 1 (1977): 47–48, 51–53.

11. See Jonathan Zeitlin, "Shop Floor Bargaining and the State: A Contradictory Relationship," in Steven Tolliday and Jonathan Zeitlin, eds., *Shop Floor Bargaining and the State: Historical and Comparative Perspectives* (Cambridge: Cambridge University Press, 1985), 13–15; Licht, *Working*, 93.

12. Alfred Chandler Jr., *The Visible Hand: The Managerial Revolution in American Business* (Cambridge, Mass.: Harvard University Press, 1977), 81–86, 88, 145–87; Lance E. Davis, Richard A. Easterlin, and William N. Parker, eds., *American Economic Growth: An Economist's History of the United States* (New York: Harper and Row, 1972), 493–94, 500–505, 512–13; U.S. Department of Commerce, Bureau of the Census, *Historical Statistics of the United States, Colonial Times to 1970* (Washington, D.C.: Government Printing Office, 1975), 728–31.

13. Chandler, *The Visible Hand*, 81, 87, 94–109.

14. Ibid., 122–43; George Rogers Taylor and Irene Neu, *The American Railroad Network, 1861–1890* (Cambridge, Mass.: Harvard University Press, 1956), 49–83.

15. On the racial division of railroad labor, see Licht, *Working*, 67–69, 224–25; Sterling D. Spero and Abram L. Harris, *The Black Worker: The Negro and the Labor Movement* (Port Washington, N.Y.: Kennikat Press, 1931), 284–86; Herbert Hill, *Black Labor and The American Legal System: Race, Work, and the Law* (Madison: University of Wisconsin Press,

1985), 335. On the exclusion of women from railroad work in the nineteenth century, see Licht, *Working*, 214–16; James H. Ducker, *Men of the Steel Rails: Workers on the Atchison, Topeka, and Santa Fe, 1869–1900* (Lincoln: University of Nebraska Press, 1983), 72.

16. John Farrington, *Life on the Lines* (Derbyshire, England: Mooreland Publishing, 1984), 94–95; B. B. Adams, "The Every-Day Life of Railroad Men," in *The American Railway: Its Construction, Development, and Appliances* (New York: Scribner's Sons, 1889), 402–403.

17. Farrington, *Life on the Lines*, 52–55; Brotherhood of Locomotive Firemen and Enginemen, *Feeding the Iron Hog: The Life and Work of a Locomotive Fireman* (Cleveland: Brotherhood of Locomotive Firemen and Enginemen, 1927), 19–20.

18. Fred L. Feick, *The Life of Railway Men* (Chicago: H. O. Shepard, 1905), 38–40; Adams, "The Everyday Life of Railroad Men," 398–99; U.S. House of Representatives, *Report of the Eight-Hour Commission*, appendix VII, "Employment Conditions in Train and Yard Service Under the Eight-Hour Law," by Victor S. Clark, H. doc. 690, 65th Cong., 2d sess., 1918, 384.

19. Feick, *Railway Men*, 40–41; U.S. House of Representatives, "Employment Conditions in Train and Yard Service," 384–85.

20. Although first used in 1869 and 1873, respectively, it was not until 1910 or so that these technologies enjoyed anything approaching widespread use. See Charles Clark, "The Railroad Safety Movement in the United States: Origins and Development, 1869–1893" (Ph.D. dissertation, University of Illinois-Urbana, 1966), 319–52; Steven W. Usselman, "Air Brakes for Freight Trains: Technological Innovation in the American Railroad Industry, 1869–1900," *Business History Review* 58 (1984): 31–32.

21. U.S. Commissioner of Labor, *Fifth Annual Report of the Commissioner of Labor, 1889: Railroad Labor* (Washington, D.C.: Government Printing Office, 1890), 163–65; U.S. Department of Labor, Bureau of Labor Statistics, *Railway Employees in the United States, Bulletin No. 37*, by Samuel McCune Lindsay (Washington, D.C.: Government Printing Office, 1901), 1036, 1046; U.S. House of Representatives, "Employment Conditions in Train and Yard Service," 402–403.

22. Licht, *Working*, 164–74; U.S. Commissioner of Labor, *Fifth Annual Report*, 82, 108, 122, 126, 136, 139.

23. U.S. House of Representatives, "Employment Conditions in Train and Yard Service," 382–83.

24. The "extra board" was a list of those running trades workers, usually low in seniority, who did not have regular runs but who were available on call.

25. U.S. House of Representatives, "Employment Conditions in Train and Yard Service," 393–94.

26. U.S. Industrial Commission, *Report of the Industrial Commission on Labor Organizations, Labor Disputes and Arbitration, and on Railway Labor*, vol. 17 (Washington, D.C.: Government Printing Office, 1901), 848. See also Mark Rosenfeld, "'It Was a Hard Life': Class and Gender in the Work Rhythms of a Railway Town, 1920–1950," *Historical Papers* (1988), 245–48.

27. Licht, *Working*, 190–94. Observers at the time noted the dangers of railroad work. See, for example, "Railway Accidents," *The Nation*, February 26, 1880, 159–60; Henry C. Adams, "The Slaughter of Railway Employees," *The Forum*, June 1892, 550–56; "Harvest of Death," *The World's Work*, March 1907, 85–98.

28. U.S. Interstate Commerce Commission, *Second Annual Report on the Statistics of Railways in the United States to the Interstate Commerce Commission for the Year Ending June 30, 1889* (Washington, D.C.: Government Printing Office, 1890), 36–38.

29. Although brakemen represented no more than 10 percent of the total workforce before 1880, they accounted for 35 to 50 percent of all fatalities and injuries resulting from railroad accidents. See U.S. Commissioner of Labor, *Fifth Annual Report*, 42.

30. Illinois Bureau of Labor Statistics, *Biennial Report of the Bureau of Labor Statistics of Illinois* (Springfield, Ill.: Illinois State Journal Co., State Printers, 1908), 13, 17, 74, 156. The closest Illinois industry in fatalities was coal mining, which claimed 35 percent of those killed and 36 percent of those injured. Together, mining and railroads accounted for 78 percent of industrial deaths in Illinois; see Illinois Bureau of Labor Statistics, *Biennial Report*, 13, 153, 156.

31. Frederick C. Gamst, "The Railroad Apprentice and the 'Rules': Historic Roots and Contemporary Practices," in Michael W. Coy, ed., *Apprenticeship: From Theory to Method and Back Again* (Albany: State University of New York Press, 1989), 65–66.

32. Operating rules were standardized in the United States and Canada in 1887. Richardson, *Engineer*, 96–98, 168–69; Licht, *Working*, 80–86. Chicago, Burlington and Quincy rule quoted in Licht, *Working*, 85.

33. Paul V. Black, "Experiment in Bureaucratic Centralization: Employee Blacklisting on the Burlington Railroad, 1877–1892," *Business History Review* 51 (1977): 444–59.

34. Licht, *Working*, 122–23, 93.

35. Gamst, "The Railroad Apprentice," 70–71.

36. Ibid., 66. In the words of Barbara Melosh (*The Physician's Hand*, 5–6), work culture provides "the critical link between a job's official protocol and its actual performance."

37. Gamst, "The Railroad Apprentice," 73; Chauncey Del French, *Railroadman* (New York: MacMillan, 1938), 153–55. See also "Breaking the Rules in the Old Days," in B. A. Botkin and Alvin F. Harlow, eds., *A Treasury of Railroad Folklore: The Stories, Tall Tales, Traditions, Ballads and Songs of the American Railroad Man* (New York: Bonanza Books, 1953), 312–13.

38. Paul Willis, "Shop-Floor Culture, Masculinity and the Wage Form," in John Clarke, Charles Crichter, and Richard Johnson, eds., *Working Class Cultures: Studies in History and Theory* (New York: St. Martin's Press, 1979), 196. Ava Baron argues that nineteenth-century printers considered the nature of their work essentially masculine; see Ava Baron, "The Masculinization of Production: The Gendering of Work and Skill in U.S. Newspaper Printing, 1850–1920," in Dorothy O. Helly and Susan M. Reverby, eds., *Gendered Domains: Rethinking Public and Private in Women's History* (Ithaca, N.Y.: Cornell University Press, 1992), 279.

39. Focusing on printers, Ava Baron argues that nineteenth-century male workers considered wage work and skill measures of manliness. See Ava Baron, "The Masculinization of Production," 279; Ava Baron, "Questions of Gender: Deskilling and Demasculinization in the U.S. Printing Industry, 1830–1915," *Gender and History* 1 (1989): 181, 184. Keith McClelland notes the moral worth skill carried in the British working class; see Keith McClelland, "Some Thoughts on Masculinity and the 'Representative Artisan' in Britain, 1850–1880," *Gender and History* 1 (1989): 164–77.

40. The material on Canadian railroaders, their relationships with technology, and the engineer's quote are drawn from Rosenfeld, "'Hard Life,'" 270.

41. "Dead Men's Brains," *LFM* 14 (1890), 495. See Rosenfeld ("'Hard Life,'" 271) on Canadian railroaders' use of sexual metaphors.

42. Gamst, "The Railroad Apprentice," 72; Rosenfeld, "'Hard Life,'" 265.

43. U.S. House of Representatives, "Employment Conditions in Train and Yard Service," 383–84.

44. See Rosenfeld, "'Hard Life,'" 262, 264.

45. Speaking of the contemporary all-male workplace, Stan Gray argues that masculine work culture is a form of rebellion "against civilized society's cultural restraints"; see Stan Gray, "Sharing the Shop Floor," *Canadian Dimension*, June 1984, 24.

46. Ducker, *Steel Rails*, 59. On middle-class attitudes toward manual labor, see Jonathan Glickstein, *Concepts of Free Labor in Antebellum America* (New Haven, Conn.: Yale University Press, 1991), 9–10, 14–16.

47. See Salvatore, *Eugene V. Debs*, 46; David Montgomery, "Workers' Control of Machine Production in the Nineteenth Century" in David Montgomery, ed., *Workers' Control in the United States* (Cambridge: Cambridge University Press, 1979), 13.

48. Meeting and mastering the difficult conditions under which they labored informed railwaymen's sense of masculinity. Given the difficult, dangerous, or oppressive work situations railroaders faced, they reinterpreted their experiences as heroic, manly confrontations with "the task." See Willis, "Shop-Floor Culture," 188–89; Rosenfeld, "'Hard Life,'" 270.

49. Henry Dawson, *Reminiscences in the Life of a Locomotive Engineer* (Columbus, Ohio: Follett, Foster, 1860), 215. See also "The Engineer," *Locomotive Engineers Monthly Journal* 1 (1867): 6; journal hereafter cited as *LEMJ*.

50. Willis, "Shop-Floor Culture," 189; Rosenfeld, "'Hard Life,'" 270, 272–73. Michael Yarrow identifies the ability to "do hard work, to endure discomfort, and to brave danger" as essential to miners' sense of masculinity. See Michael Yarrow, "The Gender-Specific Class Consciousness of Appalachian Coal Miners: Structure and Change," in Scott G. McNall, Rhonda F. Levine, and Rick Fantasia, eds., *Bringing Class Back In: Contemporary and Historical Perspectives* (Boulder, Colo.: Westview Press, 1991), 294, 302–303.

51. Rosenfeld ("'Hard Life,'" 275–76) notes Canadian railwaymen's proclivity to "hard swearing" and "hard drinking." See also Paul Willis, *Learning to Labor: How Working-Class Kids Get Working-Class Jobs*, (Farnborough, England: Saxon House, 1977), 52, 148.

52. Licht, *Working*, 98–100; Gamst, "The Railroad Apprentice," 75.

53. Quoted in Licht, *Working*, 97.

54. French, *Railroadman*, 138; Licht, *Working*, 95–97, 140–41. See also Paul V. Black, "Development of Management Personnel Policies on the Burlington Railroad, 1860–1900" (Ph.D. dissertation, University of Wisconsin-Madison, 1972), 455–56.

55. U.S. Commissioner of Labor, *Thirteenth Annual Report of the Commissioner of Labor, 1897: Economic Aspects of the Liquor Problem* (Washington, D.C.: Government Printing Office, 1898), 72–76.

56. Ducker, *Steel Rails*, 59.

57. See William J. Sonnenstuhl, *Working Sober: The Transformation of an Occupational Drinking Culture* (Ithaca, N.Y.: Cornell University Press, 1996), 26–27.

58. The U.S. Commissioner of Labor found in 1897 that of the industries surveyed, transportation (of which the railroads was the largest) was most concerned about the drinking habits of their employees. U.S. Commissioner of Labor, *Thirteenth Annual Report*, 71–72.

59. C. S. Wheaton to Chief Conductors, Secretaries and Brothers, n. d., Order of Railway Conductors Records, box 2, folder 5, Kheel Center for Labor-Management Documentation and Archives, M. P. Catherwood Library, Cornell University.

60. *LFM* 5 (1881), 169.

61. See, for example, "Freight Train Handling," *LEMJ* 35 (1901), 49–50; "Running Problems to Answer," *LEMJ* 35 (1901), 187; "Explanation of Side Rod Problems," *LEMJ* 35 (1901), 500; "Fuel Economy, Etc.," *LEMJ* 35 (1901), 568–69.

62. "How to Fire a Locomotive," *LFM* 17 (1893), 55–56; "Primary Lessons in Steam Engineering," *LFM* 20 (1896), 465–66; "Scientific Firing," *LFM* 26 (1899), 107; "Saving Coal and Avoiding Smoke," *LFM* 27 (1899), 61; "What Should a Young Fireman Know?" *LFM* 45 (1908), 192.

63. See, for example, "Drummond's Water-Tube Fire Box," *LFM* 27 (1899), 179; "The Kincaid Locomotive Stoker," *LFM* 32 (1902), 156–62.

64. George W. Heidenthal to the Locomotive Firemen's convention, 1876. See Brotherhood of Locomotive Firemen, *Journal of Proceedings of the Tenth Annual Convention of the Brotherhood of Locomotive Firemen* [1876], in *Journal of Proceedings of the First Twelve Annual Conventions of the Brotherhood of Locomotive Firemen. From 1874 to 1885, Inclusive* (Terre Haute, Ind.: Moore and Langen, 1885), 7.

65. See, for example, "To The Members of the B. of R. R. B. in General," *Railroad Brakemen's Journal* 3 (1886), 28. In many ways, these essays resembled Gilded Age success manuals; see Judy Hilkey, *Character Is Capital: Success Manuals and Manhood in Gilded Age America* (Chapel Hill: University of North Carolina Press, 1997).

66. "Practical Talks to Young Engineers," *LFM* 17 (1893), 53–55; C. S. Wheaton to Chief Conductors, Secretaries and Brothers, n. d., Order of Railway Conductors Records, box 2, folder 5. See also, "Dead Men's Brains," *LFM* 14 (1890), 495.

67. Nick Salvatore, *Eugene V. Debs* (23) discusses this style of manhood with regard to Debs. See also Baron, "Questions of Gender," 181; Baron, "Masculinization of Production," 279–80; Tosh, "What Should Historians Do?" 185–86.

68. "A Fireman's Duties," *LFM* 13 (1889), 17–18; "Successful Man-Building," *LFM* 14 (1890), 997.

69. "The Square Man," *LFM* 6 (1882), 16.

70. "The Mission of Our Brotherhood," *LFM* 8 (1884), 277.

71. "The Square Man," *LFM* 6 (1882), 16; "He's Only a Fireman," *LFM* 15 (1891), 634–35.

72. "Personal Honor," *LFM* 6 (1882), 128. Nick Salvatore (*Eugene V. Debs*, 46) argues that Debs intended this passage as a reminder of a fireman's work-related duties.

73. *LFM* (1879), 17–18.

74. U.S. Commissioner of Labor, *Fifth Annual Report*, 38.

75. Salvatore, *Eugene V. Debs*, 30–31.

76. See, for example, "To the Officers and Members of All Division of the B. L. E. on Southern System," April 1, 1901, Brotherhood of Locomotive Engineers, Simpson Division No. 210 Records, box 311, folder 2, Southern Labor Archives, William Russell Pullen Library, Georgia State University.

77. Brotherhood of Locomotive Engineers, *Constitution and By-Laws of the Grand International Brotherhood of Locomotive Engineers* (Cleveland: J. B. Savage, 1885), 21; Brotherhood of Locomotive Engineers, *Constitution and Statutes of the Grand International Brotherhood of Locomotive Engineers* (n. p.: 1918), 80; Brotherhood of Railroad Trainmen, Moosic Tunnel Lodge No. 93 Minute Book, December 24, 1893, Kheel Center for Labor-Management Documentation and Archives, M. P. Catherwood Library, Cornell University.

78. Salvatore, *Eugene V. Debs*, 31.

79. Ibid., 37.

80. Brotherhood of Locomotive Firemen, *Proceedings* [1882], 14–15.

81. *Railroad Brakemen's Journal* 3 (1886), 27.

82. "Organization," *LFM* 15 (1891), 725–26.

83. David A. Shannon, "Eugene V. Debs: Conservative Labor Editor," *Indiana Magazine of History* 47 (1951): 361; *LFM* 5 (1881), 169; *LFM* 4 (1880), 347–48; *LFM* 7 (1883), 492–93.

84. Quoted in Stevenson, 172–73; *The Monthly Balance* 1 (1891), 40.

85. Shelton Stromquist, *A Generation of Boomers: The Pattern of Railroad Labor Conflict in Nineteenth-Century America* (Urbana: University of Illinois Press, 1984), 56.

86. Ibid., 54–60, 79–99.

87. U.S. Industrial Commission, *Report*, vol. 4, 87, 117.

88. Stromquist, *Generation*, 262–65. In the wake of the 1894 Pullman boycott, key figures among railroad management and in the federal government agreed upon the necessity for promoting "responsible" labor organization and establishing a framework for the voluntary settlement of industrial disputes. The 1898 Erdman Act not only reflected the growing perception among lawmakers of the brotherhoods as conservative, socially responsible unions but also recognized that unions could be legitimate parties to the relationship between employer and employee. With this in mind, the Act mandated federal arbitration of railway labor disputes. See Stromquist, *Generation*, 259–61; Gerald Eggert, *Railroad Labor Disputes: The Beginnings of Federal Strike Policy* (Ann Arbor: University of Michigan Press, 1967), 213–25; Christopher Tomlins, *The State and the Unions: Labor Relations, Law, and the Organized Labor Movement in America, 1880–1960* (Cambridge: Cambridge University Press, 1985), 84–86.

89. "Statement to the United States Industrial Commission by Stuyvesant Fish, President of the Illinois Central Railroad Company, and of the Yazoo & Mississippi Valley Railroad Company," October, 1899, 11. Pamphlet in Newberry Library general collection, Chicago, Illinois.

90. "Is History to Repeat Itself?" *LFM* 30 (1901), 987.

91. On hegemony and resistance, see Raymond Williams, *Marxism and Literature* (Oxford: Oxford University Press, 1977), 132.

92. On these connections see Philip Scranton, "None-Too-Porous Boundaries: Labor History and the History of Technology," *Technology and Culture* 29 (1988): 731.

93. On nineteenth-century unions' effort to control members in the workplace, see David Montgomery, "Industrial Democracy or Democracy in Industry?: The Theory and Practice of the Labor Movement, 1870–1925," in Nelson Lichtenstein and Howell John Harris, eds., *Industrial Democracy in America: The Ambiguous Promise* (Cambridge: Cambridge University Press, 1993), 31.

# "Now That We Have Girls in the Office"

## Clerical Work, Masculinity, and the Refashioning of Gender for a Bureaucratic Age

JANET F. DAVIDSON

I n August 1918, the *Railway Age Gazette* published an editorial entitled "Give A Man a Man's Work," which called for women to replace
men in railway offices.[1] This marked a change in the industry's attitude toward women employees. Railroad companies came of age
within the nineteenth century's increasingly segregated gender system and masculinity was deeply embedded in railroad work culture,[2]
but during World War I, the gendering of railway work, previously
taken for granted, came under fire. The long held association of railway clerical work with men was questioned and threatened.

Even before the war, gender was a powerful influence on the railroads. A distinctly gendered hierarchy structured the railroad world in
which, as sociologist Fred Cottrell succinctly explained, "not all
employees of a railroad are 'railroaders.'"[3] Cottrell's 1940 study illumi-
nates how railroad workers differentiated among the many different
jobs on modern railroads. At the top of the hierarchy were "real" railroad jobs, characterized by dangerous working conditions and a
unique association with railroading.[4] Brakemen, locomotive engineers,
and firemen, for example, were clearly "real" railroad men. Lower
down the scale were the workers laboring in the maintenance and
repair shops (20 percent of all railroad employees), those caring for
the tracks (25 percent), clerks and station employees (16 percent), and
the telegraph operators, crossing guards, and other miscellaneous jobs
(16 percent).[5] Clerks ranked far below the prestigious trainmen in this
hierarchy and, as Cottrell noted, were "seldom identified as railroaders
at all."[6]

Before women entered the workplace, then, railroad clerks had an
attenuated relationship to the manly railroader ideal. Male clerical
workers sat at an uneasy crossroads, stationed between manual
worker and manager, between skilled and unskilled, between gentleman and proletarian. Railways, as the nation's first big businesses, had
to develop bureaucratic systems to cope with the scale of their enter-

prise, and thus they needed more clerical workers than the typical nineteenth-century office,[7] limiting individual employees' advancement opportunities. Still, during the nineteenth century working in a railroad office could open significant career options: "by 1885, the largest percentage of railway managers actually had begun their careers as station clerks."[8] Even after railway clerks' promotional prospects began to decline in the early twentieth century, as the Brotherhood of Railway Clerks (BRC) put it, albeit nastily, railroad clerks were "dominated by the railroad officials, [and] stultified by the notion that they were confidential employees."[9]

Because of the strong cultural identification of men with railroad work and the continued practice of promotion from within, the overwhelmingly male railroad offices in the early twentieth century were an anomaly. By the time the United States entered World War I, clerical work had, for the most part, become the province of women.[10] Indeed, as Lisa Fine has noted, by 1912 the "typical" clerk depicted in *System* magazine was a woman.[11] In contrast, in both the *Railway Clerk*, the BRC's union magazine, and the *Mutual Magazine,* the company union magazine for the Pennsylvania Railroad (PRR), continued to assume the vast majority of railway clerks were men throughout the war and into the 1920s.[12] Thus, while male railway clerks had an uneasy relationship to the dominant ideal of railroad masculinity, the railroading world continued to imagine clerking as an appropriately male domain.

Still, male clerks' masculinity was threatened and questioned during World War I as women entered the workplace in increasing numbers. Labor shortages encouraged PRR officials to examine their hiring policies, and even before America's formal declaration of war on Germany companies started to hire more women workers. Most critically, however, the federal government took over the railroads, setting up the United States Railroad Administration (USRA), which ran the nation's rails from January 1, 1918, to March 1920. The USRA, in turn, created a Women's Service Section (WSS) to monitor and control women's access to railroad work.[13] The net effect of the all-female WSS's recommendations limited the types of jobs women could do, and helped increase the numbers of railroad women as a whole.[14] Within the strictures placed upon them by railroad and federal officials, women actively sought railroad work and, at the peak of the women's hiring, over 100,000 women worked on the nations railroads. The majority of those women, over 70 percent nationwide, worked in railroad offices.

The introduction of thousands of women into railway offices ushered in a visible, dramatic, noticeable, and contested change in the railroads' gender organization. The United States's entrance into World War I presented a profound challenge to the railroads' assumptions about who was an appropriate employee. As women went to work on the railroads, as male employees grappled with the idea that their

Janet F. Davidson

work could be done by women, and as PRR and government officials argued about what, precisely, women could do on the railroads, ideas about work were all examined closely, revealing deeply held assumptions about gender.

The World War I railroads let us literally see gender in operation. The ways in which members of the railroading world coped with women's introduction into their workplace culture and identity illustrate the dynamic and relational features of historically contingent constructions of gender.[15] The arguments, negotiations, debates, and conflicts over gender, as well as the experiences of women workers, reveal that workers' day-to-day lives were saturated with presumptions about the meanings of masculinity and femininity. Furthermore, the railroads suggest that ideas about work could be refashioned to stretch the railroads' organizational identity so as to accommodate a temporary reordering of gender relations for the war's duration.

Railroading women disrupted the ways in which men understood railroad work. Even before they entered railroad offices, women were a presence in the railway world. Both male railroad clerks and male company officials deployed ideas about womanhood and manhood in order to understand workplace relations. Just the idea that women could adequately perform some railroad work presented a challenge to the assumption that the railroads were a male preserve. And, clearly, during the war women railroaders became much more than threat; they became a reality. Working women tried to make a place for themselves on the railroads. They actively applied for work, joined unions to safeguard their rights once hired, and tried to make sure they were paid what they were owed under federally mandated pay scales. Yet, in spite of their actions on their own behalf, women could not overcome the powerful connections between the railroad and masculinity.

Those connections were perpetuated by railroad men, regardless of class. Male trade unionists deployed ideas of femininity and masculinity to affirm the railroad's masculine character and limit the number of women workers. At the same time, male railroad officials used gendered ideology to prop up their own power and to assert corporate control over the labor force. Even though their motivations were different, both railroad officials and trade unionists tried to mitigate women's challenge to the railroads' gendered status quo. And, in part because workers and managers had complementary and overlapping interests, despite the introduction of women clerks into the railroad, the railroads remained at heart a masculine enterprise.

## The Contours of Women Clerks' Work Experiences

PRR women railroad clerks' work was varied even though they all worked for one company. Given the size and complexity of railroad corporations, a wide range of jobs fit under the rubric of clerical work,[16] and women did a fair number of them. The ranks of female railroad clerks included women such as Eleanor Cahill, an assistant bookkeeper in Bridgeport, Connecticut, who was described in May 1917 as performing the following "indispensable" tasks: she "sorts freight bills, in ledger from A to H, charges ledger bills same, forwards weekly statements to patron and does many other duties in and around the cashier's department."[17] Cahill's colleague Evelyn Post also did a range of work including typing, indexing, filing, answering the phone, and "other duties whenever there is time."[18]

Although clerks like Post and Cahill performed a variety of tasks during the day, other women had more specific duties. Their specialized job titles included storehouse clerk, file clerk, freight clerk, office clerk, relief clerk, shop clerk, and billing clerk. A woman might work in a station office, in the shops' office, in a storehouse, or in a number of other settings; in each case, her job would be shaped by her environment. Yet even when two women technically had the same job title, even when they were simply described as clerks, they did not necessarily have exactly the same job responsibilities. As historian Lisa Fine noted in her discussion of the varieties of corporate clerical work, "The work experiences of the female stenographer-typist varied greatly depending upon the type of office in which she worked."[19]

On the PRR, geographic location shaped women's employment in significant ways. A person who worked in a small rural Pennsylvania office, for example, would have had a very different environment and work experience than a clerk in the Broad Street Station main office would have. Agents in small stations needed to understand how freight and passengers moved about in the PRR system, and needed to accomplish a range of tasks including selling tickets, keeping the books, setting the signals, and using the telegraph.[20] In contrast, a typing-pool stenographer had a much more regimented work life and a narrower skill base.

Although female clerks had both sorts of experience on the PRR, the vast majority labored in large urban offices, such as the Philadelphia-based general office, with other female workers. Few women clerked out in the field. In the course of the war, women clerical workers became even more concentrated in large offices: in November 1919, one-fourth of all female railroad clerks were employed in the general office, an increase of 11 percent in a year. As more women workers were hired, they were increasingly likely to be hired as a part of a pool.

Despite being part of a large office staff with a narrowly defined set of jobs, women had comparatively good railroad work experiences. As Maurine Weiner Greenwald has commented, "Had women been asked during the First World War which industry offered them the most favorable wages and working conditions, they surely would have chosen rail-

Janet F. Davidson

TABLE 3.1    *Percentage of the total number of PRR women clerks in selected locations, by date, November 1918 to November 1919, from PRR Monthly reports.*[21]

| date | 11/18 | 2/19 | 5/19 | 8/19 | 11/19 |
|---|---|---|---|---|---|
| General Office | 14% | 15.7% | 17.3% | 16.4% | 25.9% |
| Elmira Division | 1.1% | 1.1% | 1.2% | 1.1% | 1.1% |
| Philadelphia Terminal | 7.3% | 8.0% | 8.8% | 7.2% | 7.3% |
| Juniata Division | 0.2% | 0.29% | 0.3% | 0.3% | 0.3% |
| Altoona Shops | 5.4% | 6.0% | 7.6% | 4.7% | 4.4% |
| Total PRR | 8,073 | 7,884 | 5,874 | 5,680 | 5,615 |

road work."[22] Railroad work's appeal for women can be best glimpsed through the employment records of 112 PRR treasury department employees. These Philadelphia-based women were hired between 1910 and March 1920, but 96 of them started work during the war emergency.[23] A small segment of the women hired on the railroads did not like or were not suited for the work and quickly resigned their newly acquired positions. Usually, such a woman would not last six months.[24] Yet in the treasury department, at least, these women were in the minority; in 1920, over 60 of the 112 women were still employed. Given that rapid job turnover was a common characteristic of the labor market in the Progressive and war eras, such loyalty to a single firm was fairly rare.[25] This pattern suggests that there were good reasons for women to remain with the railroads.

Money was clearly a big draw. Most of the treasury department women started out earning between $50 and $60 a month. Those wages increased when the federal government, in the form of the USRA, took over. In May 1918, the USRA raised the wages of all but the best-paid railroad workers. In September of the same year, they instituted a minimum wage of $87.50 a month for clerical workers. The PRR's Treasury Department tried to avoid complying with the provisions of the order, and continued to pay women less than men and less than the mandated minimums. Nonetheless, women's wages did go up during 1918. On other parts of the PRR, officials complied with the USRA's wage orders without hesitation. When Helen Ross inspected the Altoona yards' scale office in January 1919, she found that the nineteen women and fifty men who were employed there worked eight hours a day, six days a week. Because they lacked seniority, most women were clustered at the low end of the new pay scale, earning $87.50 a month, but that entry-level salary was significantly higher than the kinds of wages that they were used to. As the WSS noted, "women [clerks] are receiving exceptionally high wages as compared with the usual remuneration given them for similar work outside the railroad service."[26]

While general clerical wage statistics are sparse, in 1911, a survey of 143 clerical workers in Boston showed the women earned, on average, $9.61 per week.[27] In the same city, over a year ending in July 1914, 148 of the 167 women surveyed who worked in department stores' offices earned less than $9 a week.[28] Because of wartime inflation, wages and the cost of living rose between 1915 and 1920.[29] Still, in Kansas in 1919 to 1920, a survey showed that approximately 15 percent of women earned under $9 a week, nearly 26 percent earned between $9 and $12, and another 16.6 percent earned between $12 and $15 a week. Only just over one-fourth of the women earned over $18 a week.[30] Entry-level female railway clerks who took home over $21 a week were clearly paid vast sums in comparison to other female office workers.

Money was not, and is not, the only measure of a decent workplace. Clerical work rated highly in other ways. In the Altoona yard's scale office, women worked in three rotating shifts so they all did night work, despite government directives that night work for women should be avoided if at all possible. Still, the WSS field agent inspecting Altoona gave the scale office a good rating, in part because women had access to a "very nice, comfortable rest room, with toilet adjoining."[31] Other PRR women worked under equally nice conditions. Nine women worked in the division superintendent's office in Oil City, Pennsylvania. This office was "one of several nice bright Division offices in the station building, with a pleasant atmosphere for work."[32] In it, the women worked alongside sixteen men. All workers started at 8 A.M., had an hour for lunch, and finished at 5 P.M. They worked a forty-eight hour week, did no overtime or night work, and got Sundays off. Working conditions were not perfect—the office staff had to go to the toilet in the public waiting room in the station because there were no other facilities available—but they were good.

Railroad jobs qualified as good work because they paid well and were performed steadily under decent conditions, usually for a set number of hours. All of these attributes were the exception, rather than the norm, for Progressive-era workers of either sex. Domestic servants, for example, the largest female occupation, worked long hours, under their employers' watchful eyes.[33] One contemporary survey showed that most women in personal service got Saturday afternoons off, but that they often worked at night, on Sundays, and on holidays.[34] They were also badly paid: on average, domestic servants of both sexes received the paltry sum of $432 a year in 1918.[35] This translates into $36 a month, less than half the pay that entry-level female railroad clerks received. Most other types of traditionally female employment were not much better than servitude. Cannery work, for example, was physically demanding and seasonal. As Virginia Yans-McLaughlin has noted, it "required many hands working long hours during the busy season."[36] Women canners, along with other family members, worked ten-hour days, seven days a week during the busy season. Women candy makers, box makers, boot and shoe workers, laundry workers, and other factory operatives also worked long hours for little pay.[37] Much of the industrial employment that women obtained was physically grueling, performed over long hours, and yet also, paradoxically, seasonal and intermittent.

The kinds of women who sought and obtained railroad employment had education and office skills.[38] Thus, they were unlikely to apply for work as canners or domestic servants. Wartime female railroad clerks would have, in other eras, found employment as teachers, clerks in other businesses, or in department stores. Teaching required similar skills to those utilized by an office worker, and in the cities, at least, it paid well if not better than clerical work. But all jobs were not in the cities. Clerical work may have been more appealing to women in urban centers than the option of leaving home to teach in a rural community, where teaching salaries were lower. Teaching also left women without an income for part of the year, and while it was a respectable job, it often came with high social costs for the individual. Many teachers were subjected to surveillance and restrictive rules designed to limit their behavior. Even if a woman did not mind the regulation of her life and was willing to work in small-town America, Lisa Fine points out that "teaching could not absorb the large number of women entering the labor force during the first decades of the twentieth century."[39] White, native-born women had to look for other employment opportunities if they needed or wanted to work. The "palaces of consumption," department stores, provided one opportunity.[40] Department store work was respectable employment, and became the province of native-born white women. Nevertheless, store clerks needed less education and training than a teacher or an office worker. According to Susan Porter Benson, "Within the realm of white-collar work, clerical workers consistently earned more than saleswomen, and the gap apparently widened over time."[41] Thus, becoming an office worker may have often seemed more appealing to literate women with access to job-training.

Railroad clerking, with comparatively high salaries and good conditions, was a top-notch job for an educated, native-born, respectable white woman. Ironically, however, the very attributes that made railroad office work appealing to women also produced gender-based tensions on the job. The wages women railroad clerks made were particularly challenging and threatening to male workers. Railway women made good money in a society that did not expect them to, and did not quite know what to do with the idea that women could make enough money to potentially support themselves outside of their families.

## Women's Wages and the American Standard of Living

Women's wages were often understood within the context of the assumption that good men were breadwinners who earned a living wage sufficient to support a family without monetary contributions from wives or children.[42] According to Lawrence Glickman, as the ideal of the independent yeoman farmer became even more of a pipedream for most Americans, "[i]n the period between the Civil War and World War I, workers learned to accept wages and to identify themselves as wage earners because they had no alternative."[43] During that time, white male workers remade themselves as "wage-earning citizens" and tried to "link economics to morality and politics . . . to create a new discourse of virtue, replacing a producerist republicanism with a consumerist one."[44] In the process, they ardently advocated the idea of a "living wage" for workers.

That wage was fluid and changed over time, but it was predicated on the idea that male workers deserved good wages for their labors, that workers in the United States should have access to more than a minimal, subsistence wage level, and that the living wage would increase over time. The definition of the wage promulgated by Rev. B. W. Williams in 1887 in *Knights of Labor* was fairly typical: "The American laborer should not be expected to live like the Irish tenant farmer or the Russian serf. His earning ought to be sufficient to enable him to live as a respectable American citizen. His living therefore must include not only food and raiment for himself and family, but also such other items as taxes, school books, furniture, newspapers, doctors bills, contributions to the cause of religion, etc."[45] The "American standard of living" presumed that workers should have access to a broad range of goods and services. While Williams's definition only implied that the living wage was a white man's prerogative, other proponents made their racial assumptions more explicit. The title of the American Federation of Labor's 1906 pamphlet "Meat vs. Rice: American Manhood against Asiatic Coolieism. Which Shall Survive?" suggests the virulent racism that infused the living-wage debate. When unionists and other living wage advocates spoke of an American laborer, their definition of *American* did not include immigrants, women, blacks, and the unskilled, who numerically constituted the bulk of the members of the U.S. working classes.[46]

As well as being heavily influenced by claims of American exceptionalism, the living-wage discourse was profoundly affected by the participants' gendered assumptions about the role of men in families. Some commentators tried to extend the idea of a living or minimum wage to women, often because of connections between low wages and vice.[47] But, for the most part, women were excluded from discourse about, and the direct benefits that accrued from, a living wage, and as a result female wage earners as a category were a threat to white male workers. As Glickman succinctly points out, "The problem was not that women had low standards but that they possessed no standard of living whatsoever. It was, after all, defined as a male quality."[48] Sociologist Henry Seager, then president of the American Association of

Labor Legislation, remarked in 1913 that women "have no definite, independent, standard of living and consequently are contented to accept wages that lighten more of the burdens of their support for their fathers, brothers or husbands, but are pitifully inadequate for that increasing number who do not live at home."[49] Since women's work was not highly valued, the ideal female wage was low. According to Joanne Meyerowitz, "Before the period of rapid inflation beginning in 1915, numerous social investigators found that a woman needed a minimum of eight to twelve dollars per week to cover her cost of living."[50] The calculations Progressive investigators made rarely included much of a safety net for female workers. As Alice Kessler-Harris has noted, "in practice, survival was the best, not the worst that the [female] wage embodied."[51] And most women, including many clerks, did not even earn this survival wage.

The "American standard" and the "woman's wage" were two sides of the same coin. Historians of the family wage and the living wage have quite rightly pointed out that "the family wage became a convenient means for male workers to retain their control of jobs and conditions."[52] In order for men to claim that they needed to make enough to support their families, women had to rhetorically be confined to supporting family roles.[53] The *Railway Clerk*, for example, described an appropriate standard of living for men that included "comforts, necessities, and extravagances of life" such as education and vacations.[54] At the same time, the magazine also published a column suggesting that a single woman needed only the ridiculously low amount of $6.70 per week to live on in 1916.[55] Yet despite the proclamations of the Brotherhood of Railway Clerks, women on the railroads earned a lot more than $28 a month. The treasury department women's salaries of $50 to $60 a month were a substantial contribution to their own and their family's livelihood. And women who were actually paid the entry level USRA rate made at least an additional thirty dollars a month on top of that.

## Male Clerks and the Meanings of Masculinity

Women's presence in well-paid railroad jobs posed a challenge to the male railroading clerical community. Those tensions were, partially, a product of the absolute and proportionally deteriorating position of male railroad clerical workers during the early twentieth century. As railroad companies consolidated their holdings and their lines and added more employees to their payrolls it became less and less likely that an individual railroad worker would rise through the ranks into management. Between 1900 and 1912, the number of railroad workers increased from 1 million to 1.7 million, and there were twice as many clerks to managers in 1912 as there had been in 1900.[56] This trend continued during the war era. In 1915, the railroads employed 141,095 clerks and 5,923 general officers.[57] By 1920 the railroads employed over 233,000 clerks and 8,606 managers;[58] the ratio of clerks to managers increased from 24:1 to 28:1 in the five years between 1915 and 1920. Railroad clerks had a lot more colleagues, and a lot less likelihood of being promoted than in the past. Unlike other male railroad workers, clerks experienced declining opportunity. For example, the ratio of firemen to engineers remained fairly constant from 1900 to 1920. That meant, all things being equal, that a fireman had about the same chance of being promoted to engineer in 1900 as in 1920. Thus, despite the traditional assumption that clerking on the railroads led to promotion and opportunities within the corporations, the opportunities for railroad clerks diminished absolutely and relatively during the first two decades of the twentieth century.

At the same time, however, federal control improved salaries for the great majority of clerical workers. In 1915 the majority of railroad clerks earned less than $900 per annum; by 1918 almost two-thirds of all clerks earned more than that, and in 1919, over 90 percent of clerks exceeded this level. Yet, clerical salaries still lagged behind those of other railroad workers. Before the war, most railroad clerks earned about half the average hourly wage of a machinist or a fireman, and about one-third of a locomotive engineer's hourly pay. In 1919, despite the increases in clerical salaries, clerks still, on average, earned less than all three of these groups of employees.[59] If one was a railroad clerk, as the war progressed, one's salary improved, but one's position relative to other railroaders did not.

Women did not cause the railroad clerks' circumscribed opportunities, but the threat that women presented, and the entrance of a larger number of women into the workplace, created a discursive site for the railroad world to come to terms with the rationalization of railroad office work. Although male clerks experienced declining opportunity before the wartime introduction of thousands of women employees, and although they would have likely continued to experience such diminishing opportunities even if the workforce had remained overwhelmingly male, the introduction of women sharply focused attention on that decline and sparked much debate about railroad clerical work.

Some of this discussion did not bode well for the men. Despite the fact that clerical work had remained a masculine preserve on the railroads, employers began to question the necessity of keeping men in the offices. For example, the August 1918 *Railway Age Gazette* editorialized, "The most striking fact noted by a recent visitor to numerous railroad offices, both general and divisional, was that after more than a year of war, there are still a great many men employed in purely clerical positions. Why should men, particularly young men, cling to jobs that can be held as well, if not better, by girls when there is so much real man's work to be had, a large part of which pays equal or higher wages?"[60] Although this editorial provoked debate, leading one clerk to state, "This article brings home forcibly the fact that the rail-road clerk is not understood or appreciated in a general way,"[61] the perceived need for soldiers and workers put male clerical workers backs, ideologically speaking, against the wall.

## Union Ideology and Masculine Identity

The Brotherhood of Railway Clerks (BRC), the American Federation of Labor union with jurisdiction over railway offices, responded to the threat that women workers presented in a number of ways. Although they were the most "woman friendly" of the railway unions, the BRC deployed ambiguous yet complementary visions of masculinity and femininity in order to explore their working situations, explain their lack of organizing success, and promote the idea that clerical work was working-class employment. As they did so, they used ideas of mas-culinity to promote unionization, affirm clerical workers' manhood, and construct their class and racial identity in opposition to women, blacks, and railroad managers. While the union did not necessarily persuade male railroad officials or female workers that their ideas about railroad work were right, these ideas were an important part of the process of making and remaking gender at work.

The BRC was concerned with gender identity before the introduction of women workers. Before the war, the BRC examined the relationships between clerical work and manliness, and used ideas of masculinity in order to exhort men to join unions, yet the BRC's visions of their own relationship to masculinity and to other railroad men were not simple. During the first decades of the twentieth century, the *Railway Clerk* pub-lished paeans to railroad men's masculinity interspersed with denuncia-tions of clerks' potential for cowardliness and class betrayal.

The union's history, as well as the nascent threat of workplace fem-inization, helped cause this contradictory representation of railroad clerks' masculinity. The BRC was a weak latecomer to the railroad union scene;[62] founded in 1899, it limped along in its early years. Before the war, the union only had about 5,000 members out of a potential pool of more than 100,000 workers.[63] The BRC attributed its weakness to several factors: First, the union argued that the white-col-lar nature of clerical work impeded class consciousness. Second, they quite rightly believed that the vehement anti-unionism of the railroad companies hindered organization. Third, the BRC recognized that company unionism hindered their attempts to organize real unions; through organizations such as the PRR's Mutual Benefit Association, the PRR used corporate welfare provisions in order to try to persuade workers that they did not need to join a union to have a good working environment.[64] And, finally, the union blamed the individual failings of male railroad clerks for the BRC's weakness.

Although the union underwent the first stirrings of a transformation in 1915, when its members replaced the old guard leadership with a new slate of officials, the real turning point came with the outbreak of war. Guaranteed the right to organize by the federal government, the union saw, in stark contrast to other office workers, a rapid rise in the number of organized clerical workers from about 5,000 in October 1915 to over 150,000 in June 1919.[65] Weak railroad unions like the clerks' benefited immensely from the federal takeover and they knew it. In a very real sense, the clerks were war profiteers: their strength did not come from their unity or from their manly demeanors. It came from federal support.

With women entering railroad offices in increasing numbers and the BRC's membership growth due to federal protection the union expressed considerable ambivalence concerning male clerks' claims to manhood. Within the pages of the *Railway Clerk*, unionists—both national officials and the rank and file—demonstrated an ambivalence about their status as men and as members of the working class, and as they did so they used gendered imagery in order to explain their relationships to other members of the railroad community.

The *Railway Clerk*, like many union journals of the time, combined editorials, cartoons, joke pages, advertisements, and exhortations to unionize. Often the "jokes" were fairly cutting. In March 1916, for example, the journal quipped, "Physicians in Philadelphia recently discovered what they thought to be a great human freak—a man without the semblance even of a back-bone, but were disgusted to learn that he was a railroad clerk, and that there were thousands more like him."[66] This theme of clerical workers' spinelessness recurred in the journal. At various times, the brotherhood characterized railroad clerks as yellow-bellied, cowardly, stupid, and as parasites on the body politic.[67] Since women had come to be identified as parasites on society, this last characterization was especially vitriolic.[68] For the most part, union men often accused the unorganized as being the font of these negative traits.

Figure 3.1 succinctly expressed the BRC's disdain for unorganized clerks; in this illustration men who are organized are literally bigger men than the unorganized. This portrayal buttresses the observation of Gail Bederman that in the 1890s "an ideal male body required physical bulk and well-defined muscles."[69] The unionist's large size provided a quick visual identification with strength, health, and positive masculine traits. While it is unclear if his manliness derived from some inherent trait or if he acquired a more manly bearing from membership in the BRC, the illustration endowed the unionist with a large quotient of masculinity. The unionist, by virtue of his size and strength, had access to the railroad official; the two men came to agreements over wages and conditions. In contrast, the unorganized worker literally and figuratively came to the door with his hat in his hand. According to this representation, the unorganized clerk was a supplicant, hoping for a

Janet F. Davidson

Official: No time to bother with individuals: we are doing business with a committee now.

**FIGURE 3.1** *"The Difference." Reprinted from* Railway Clerk *XV (June 1916), p. 189.*

handout. Not surprisingly, given his lack of stature, the nonunionist was humiliatingly rebuffed by the general manager.

The themes expressed in figure 3.1 were typical for the BRC's journal, and provided a way to show clerical workers' conditions and their aspirations. In figure 3.2 the benefits of union membership were juxtaposed with working conditions in the absence of unions.

In this representation, the nonunion clerical worker was still at work even though it was past 9 P.M. The man himself was depicted as older, looking drawn and tired. He longed to be with his wife and child but he was chained to his desk. In contrast, at the same time of night, the union man sat at home, surrounded by his family and creature comforts. The family members were well dressed and portrayed as if they are content in each other's company. The union wife was happily reading the *Railway Clerk*, suggesting that the whole family both supported and benefited from the union. In this illustration, organized clerks were better able to support their families, had more access to leisure, and were better family men. Sometimes the pages of the journal made the connection between manliness and unionized clerkdom even more explicit. In January 1918, for example, B. H. Baxter exhorted his fellow clerks to "[g]et in; make it [the union] strong and *keep* it strong, for if you don't you will be right back where you were before our organization sought you out and taught you to be a man."[70]

Despite making numerous claims that unionized men had access to a valorous form of manliness, however, the BRC continued to portray

NO HOME LIFE HERE        THE JOY OF LIVING

**FIGURE 3.2**   *"Join the Brotherhood."*

*Reprinted from* Railway Clerk *XV (June 1916), pp. 92–93.*

male clerical workers as cowardly and weak, and sometimes, they did not distinguish the unorganized from the organized. In the aforementioned "joke" that described railroad clerks as spineless, the author did not differentiate between union and nonunion; according to him, all clerks were weak. The following poem, "Looking for an Easy Job," made fun of clerks' bourgeois pretensions. Finding it laughable that clerks believed that they had access to a privileged, white-collar life, the poem satirized conditions on the railroad:

> I want to be a railroad clerk
> And draw his princely pay
> When all I have to do is work
> Some eighteen hours a day
> I'd like to join those happy guys
> With hearts so full of cheer
> Who overstrain their weary eyes
> Six hundred days a year.[71]

This poem was written in 1916, before the federal government took over the railroads, and introduced mandatory pay scales and the eight-hour day. In contrast to figures 3.1 and 3.2, the poem depicts railroad work (for union and nonunion alike) as ill-paid, physically debilitating, and emotionally enervating. While the poem clearly exaggerated, the message remained that railroad work was misery-inducing, unremitting toil. Unless they managed to organize an entire company or line, union members worked as many hours as nonunion members. The

    Janet F. Davidson

BRC's cartoons might make distinctions between union and nonunion, but they did not accurately represent the ways in which most union members experienced work on the PRR in 1916.

Other segments of the union's journal reflected this grimmer reality. Before the war, most clerks did not have enough power to obtain union recognition. Before federal control, because of their weak absolute and relative bargaining position, members of the clerks' union were exhorted to follow the example of other railway men who had stronger unions. In April 1917, for example, Wade Shurtleff, president of the BRC's Cleveland Lodge No. 47, put a prediction about post-war conditions in his local report, writing, "Many of the little gentlemen who make a living as clerks have looked down with scorn upon the union man. The little man with the respectable black coat and nice necktie, clean collar, and large family of children will see his income cut down. And the Mechanic, with the oil-stained jumper and the dinner pail on his arm, who makes often twice as much, and nearly always more than the average Clerk, will see his income go on as big as it was before."[72] Men such as Wade Shurtleff believed that clerical "gentlemen" were fools; men who worked as clerks but knew that they were workers, Shurtleff and the union believed, were much more likely to join a union and get better wages and working conditions. As the *Railway Clerk* stated in 1919, "If we would quit wasting our breath emphasizing the fact that we are the 'brains' of the railroad and stick up for our rights, we might convince the managers that we have more brains than they credit us with having"[73] One of the BRC's techniques for getting clerks to consider themselves part of a broader union movement involved juxtaposing their conditions to those of other railroad unionists. The contrasts, which were often explored through a trope of masculinity, rarely made male clerks look good.

Illustrations such as figure 3.3 characterized less-educated but more class-conscious and better-organized members of the railroad community as having a number of advantages over educated clerical workers. Under the rallying cry of "take heed," the illustration visually and textually showed the plight of the railroad clerk; it uses the higher pay of bricklayers and sweepers to promote unionization, but at the same time the male clerks were characterized as middle class and highly skilled.

Figure 3.3 used gendered racial imagery to promote white male unionization, but it did not do so in a straightforward manner. Semiotically, this illustration gives off very mixed messages. In *Stylin'*, Shane White and Graham White note that "the masks that whites imposed on blacks 'veil the humanity of Negroes,' in the process reducing them 'to a sign,' which, like most signs, can be readily manipulated to an ideologically serviceable end."[74] Clearly, this BRC illustration is an overblown lampoon. It visually denigrates the black laborer, who is drawn in an unrealistic "Samboesque" style and "speaks" in a kind of fake black dialect that railroad union journals delighted in using, pre-

It's A Fact.

**FIGURE 3.3**  *"Take Heed!" Reprinted from* Railway Clerk *XV (June 1916), p. 125.*

sumably because it made white workers feel superior. Yet despite the style of drawing, and the syntactically challenged mode of speech, the African American laborer did not have a simple ideological function. While he remained a sign, his textual meaning was made more complicated by the words he was given to speak. Since the sweeper's message was that he received more pay than the clerks in the window, the cartoonist put words in the sweeper's mouth that undercut the clerks' claim to superiority.

Throughout the war era, the BRC made explicit and implicit connections between race and masculinity. For example, in 1916, the *Railway Clerk* described the social gulf separating managers and clerical workers by observing, "Why the agents wife would no more make a social call on your wife than she would on some old 'nigger' washerwoman."[75] By appealing to white men's pride in their social status, this comment was designed to reveal to clerks the true working-class nature of their employment and interests. The BRC also made repeated connections between railroad clerical work and slavery. In January 1917, the BRC claimed that being a member of the union and fighting for union rights meant one was engaged in a struggle for "the right to uphold that principle of the fundamental law of our nation which says that 'involuntary servitude shall not exist within these United States. . . . '"[76] In this instance, the BRC used the language of the Thirteenth Amendment, which originally dealt with the issue of actual chattel slavery, in order to assert their rights to organize.

In other places the *Railway Clerk* referred to clerical workers' "emancipation." This kind of rhetoric had been appropriated by white Americans during the Revolutionary War era and throughout the ante-bellum period,[77] and it continued to be used by trade unionists during the late nineteenth and early twentieth centuries—notably by Samuel Gompers, the president of the American Federation of Labor.[78] Despite its long heritage, the rhetoric was particularly provocative in an era filled with overt racism and discrimination.[79] For a whites-only organization to use this imagery in a country in which blackness and enslavement were inextricably connected in the public imagination, and at a time when segregation, Jim Crow laws, African American disenfranchisement, and lynchings were facts of life suggests the depths to which the BRC feared its membership had fallen.

The BRC was not the only union to use African American men as a symbol of the degradation white workers experienced at the hands of railroad officials. Both Eric Arnesen and Paul Taillon have persuasively argued that skilled white male railroad workers defined their manhood and their respectability in opposition to black men.[80] Thus, when they made comparisons to themselves and African Americans and when they used a trope of slavery to explain their condition, railroad brothers did so within a climate in which their assumed superiority over people of color was a given. The rhetorical use of slavery was predicated on the writers' assumptions that white men deserved better treatment than blacks.

Yet when the BRC used the metaphors of slavery to claim that their treatment at the hands of railroad officials was demeaning and potentially emasculating, they conflated their work situations with those of the most exploited workers in the land, African Americans. Figure 3.3 associates whites' situations with those of African Americans, and, because it showed that some African Americans earned higher wages than some whites, it tangentially questioned the innateness of white superiority since it showed that it did not always exist as a matter of course. In these small ways, the *Railway Clerk* undercut the bases of white men's claims to superiority. Yet the sweeper in figure 3.3 ultimately reinforces white superiority, since the image only "worked" as a joke if the audience knew that it was palpably ridiculous that a black man should earn as much as a white.

The African American man is not the only "other" in the cartoon. Figure 3.3 also included a white bricklayer, whom the clerks represented as both less educated and less skilled than themselves. And yet, like the sweeper, the bricklayer was a union man, and he earned more money than the clerks. Furthermore, the seemingly older blue-collar worker refered to one of the clerks as "son," creating a faux familial connection between the bricklayer and clerk, implying that he was the dominant half of an inequitable power relationship. Again, having the blue-collar bricklayer call the clerk "son" worked as a joke if both the author and the viewer assumed that in the "natural" order of things clerical workers should be paid more than bricklayers.

Despite its underlying assumption that clerical workers are better than other workers, the illustration foregrounded the "outside" workers, who were organized and better paid. In doing so it suggested that, for all their skills, the clerks were less manly because they accepted poor wages, long hours, and their status as unorganized workers. While the whites-only Brotherhood of Railway Clerks appealed to, and ultimately reinforced, the racism and elitism of its membership, it did so in ways that showed the attenuated claims of male clerks' to racialized masculine superiority over their blue-collar and African American brethren.

Not all of the BRC's attitudes about its own masculinity were so negative. In addition to admonishing its membership to be class-conscious and demand their rights as workers, the BRC adhered to a more positive vision of manhood, one to which the organized clerk could aspire. While railroad clerks were not the brawn behind the railroad enterprise, the BRC made a case that they were the critical employees on the roads. As they did so, the union implied that male clerical workers could flex their collective muscle and, potentially, influence corporate policy. In July 1916, for example, a poem entitled "The Manly Man" exhorted the virtues of "the spirit of manly cheer" whereby men fought, toiled, worked, and served the "country's need" with great stoicism.[81]

In other places, the *Railway Clerk* more directly constructed a manly railroad man. In the following poem "The Railroad Clerk," written by BRC Seattle Local 392 member Leonard Plush, one can see an alternate, nonphysical vision of manliness:

There's a man in railroad circles
That you don't hear much about,
But if he wasn't at his duty
He would put the rest to rout.
For the man who does the work
And who hasn't time to shirk
Is the clerk

Now you hear old-timers talking
Of the good old days of yore;
And they talk about the firemen
And the brakies, maybe, more.
But the man behind the train
And the one who bears the strain
Is the clerk.[82]

In this (admittedly dreadful) poem, a clerk reconfigured the meaning of his work, placing it at the center of the railroad community.

Rather than being a passive, spineless lackey, this railroad clerk bore the strain of the organization and claimed to be better than a brakeman or a fireman, the two most physically dangerous operating-crafts jobs. Plush's definition of manhood validated loyalty, steadiness, and withstanding the mental pressures of work; it was a definition of manhood for a newly bureaucratic age, one that sought to narrate the story of the railroad industry in a way that revamped the world of work so that bureaucrats took center stage.

## Male Clerks and the Meanings of Femininity

While male clerks continued to debate the effects of clerical work on their status as men, the BRC's discussions about gender took a new turn during World War I, when the introduction of women made the *Railway Clerk* focus more directly on women's roles in the workplace. During the war, the prospect of railway women presented a profound challenge to the gendered status quo. As the following examples show, male workers often envisioned women as threatening. Railway women, even women in railroad offices, were seen as a catalytic and disruptive influence at work. As the poem "Girls in the Office" put it,

> The office is really a different place,
> For every man works with a smile on his face,
> It's certainly evident such is the case,
> Because we've got girls in the office.[83]

Although this poem started out suggesting that women workers make men smile, as the poem's verses progress, women distract men from their jobs, and cost men money as male workers treat their female colleagues to car fare. Women's presence transforms the workplace's manners and morals. As one of the later verses put it,

> From using strong language the older men shrink,
> The effort it costs them you really can't think,
> And the Manager never goes out for a drink,
> Now that we have girls in the office.[84]

In this poem, women's presence made men smile, stop swearing, and start addressing each other formally. As well as civilizing men, however, "woman" also profoundly disrupted imputed existing office relations, creating tension between male workers and managers who competed, in the poem at least, for women's attentions.

The introduction of women into a previously male sphere shone a light on to the increasing distance between male workers and managers in offices. While a myth of upward mobility and gentlemanly bonds between clerks and officials was perpetuated by PRR officials,[85] introducing "woman" into the mix—in representation as well as in fact—threatened to rupture those mythical male bonds. "Woman" in this instance created a significant, and at least partially recognized, breach in the seemingly seamless promotional possibilities of the railroad office.

The BRC's public pronouncements illustrate that gender relations became a more visible and contested part of the railroad world during the war. Despite their public commitment to organizing women, unionists employed gender as an explanatory tool as they sought to explain the changes that rationalization and war had wrought on the work of the (presumed to be male) membership.[86] Initially, the union was fairly ambivalent about the introduction of women into the working world. Women rarely rated a mention in the prewar union journal; when they did, they were characterized as wives of workers, not workers themselves.[87] Immediately prior to and following the United States's entrance into the war, however, women became a larger presence on the railroad and in the BRC.

The pages of the *Railway Clerk* track the increasing importance of women in the workplace in a number of ways. There were more frequent references to women as workers during the war years, and some of those comments were even positive. In April 1916, for example, a contributor noted, "The progress of working people's battle for existence is greatly simplified by the advent of the ladies into the councils of Brotherhood."[88] And in April 1917, an observer of the Boston and Maine System noted that "Worcester, once upon a time a heart-breaking proposition, is now one of the brightest spots on the system and up-to-date in every respect, even to sending that ornament to her sex, Sister Rose A. Yates, to represent them on their Board of Adjustment. We lift our hats and congratulate them on their prescience."[89] To these writers the introduction of women and their integration into the union were markers of modernity, something to be valued and encouraged because they contributed to a solidly unionized workplace.[90]

At the same time that the BRC began to represent women more positively and more realistically, however, the *Railway Clerk* also published a spate of "beauty pages," with photographs of female members. As the accompanying texts noted, a number of women clerks were unwilling to have their pictures published, but a fair number agreed;[91] when they did so, their images were presented along lines that "not only are all these girls good, true and loyal members of the Brotherhood, but good and efficient railway clerks as well. At some stations there is objection to lady clerks by the male clerks, but not at Bridgeport, and after you take a good look at 'Beauty page No. 4' we know you will say we are right."[92] In this report, women's commitment to unionism and their claims to efficiency were juxtaposed with comments on their good looks. At the same time as they noted their presence, writers

FIGURE 3.4    *"Impressions of National Agreement."*

*Reprinted from* Railway Clerk *XV (June 1916), p. 121.*

often belittled women by objectifying them. By valuing women for their ornamental or social contributions as much as for their work or organizing abilities, union members created a distinction between the idea of *woman* and the idea of *worker* in ways that weakened women's claims to skill, jobs, and union credentials. In the quote above, the male worker/writer positioned himself and other men so that they seem to "allow" women access to employment and the union. In doing so, the male clerk implicitly claimed the right to object to women in the workplace even as he admonished his fellow employees to accept "lady clerks" in stations.

Other sources, such as figure 3.4, show the same kinds of mixed reaction to women workers. This cartoon, in a rare exception to the norm, depicts a woman as a worker, rather than a wife or a mother.[93]

Furthermore, the centrality of the female figure and the fact she holds the union's new national labor agreement seems to legitimize women's place in the workplace and the union. But the woman's words, "The contract protects me as a wage earner, too!" undercut women's claims to the right to earn wages as a matter of course. Discursively appearing as an addendum, figure 4 places women workers on the periphery of the union, the company, and the industry.

These reactions were the most positive brotherhood responses to women's introduction into railroad offices.[94] The pages of the *Railway Clerk* were much fuller of cautionary tales about the potential for women to undermine male workers. When cast in the most favorable light, one BRC member remarked in April 1916 that "it is most distasteful to picture our wives, sisters and sweethearts as competitors in the field of labor . . . but it follows that it is a vital necessity to absorb them and make of them our allies."[95] This statement recognized the existence of women workers, even as it positioned women's wage-earning as a necessary evil. Yet its rhetoric was not rooted in actual hiring practices; by claiming that wives had to work, the writer illustrated male workers' lack of access to decent wages and symbolized the depths to which employers would sink to make a profit. Since married women were virtually nonexistent on the railroad company's employment rolls, the writer invoked a specter that rarely haunted real railroad offices. Clearly, for this author, the working wife was a value-laden symbol, not a verifiable phenomenon. In the end, however, while this particular male railroader did not want to work alongside women, he believed that if he had to, the introduction of female workers should be controlled so that they did not undermine his salary and his status. While this unionist desired a woman-free workplace, he was pragmatic enough to recognize that the BRC did not have the power to control the PRR's hiring practices.

Often union members were more straightforwardly hostile to the idea of women replacing men. In November 1917, for example, the *Railway Clerk* expressed the union's fears about the introduction of women workers: "'Suffer the women to come unto us, for out of their cheap labor we shall amass fortunes for unknown railroad stockholders. This we will do while the war lasts, and after it is over use them to beat down wages,' say the railroad corporation managers."[96] In this instance, the journal abused the pattern of a religious verse ("Suffer the Little Children . . .") in order to rhetorically link women's employment to war profiteering, stock-watering, and the evils of business monopoly. The journal characterized women's introduction into the work world as unpatriotic, nefarious, and as a threat to men's wages.

At other points, the union employed the idea of industrial democracy to caution against hiring women indiscriminately.[97] In a column entitled "Home-Grown Autocrats," culled from the *Oregon Labor Press*, the *Railway Clerk* passed on to its members the idea that "[a]nyone who employs a woman under the cloak of a patriotic claim to replace a man in industry and pays her less than a man's wage is a hypocrite, and no worse appellation can be applied to a two-legged man. He is not only using his country's necessity to further his own selfish ends, but is laying the foundation for a low standard of wages for the soldiers when they return to industry from the task of making the world safe for democracy."[98] In this case, the juxtaposition of democracy, war, and employers' hypocrisy was designed to perpetuate men's claims for power in the workplace in the postwar world. By invoking and appropriating President Woodrow Wilson's pledge to make the world safe for democracy, and by linking the independence of workers to patriotism, the clerks' union positioned itself as a defender of American values against tyrannical bosses who sought to undermine the supposedly democratic fabric of American society.[99]

Seemingly, the BRC's fears about women's introduction into the workplace had much more to do with concerns about men's job rights and family rights than they did about a job's effect on women. The pages of the *Railway Clerk* tell us more about the ways in which men thought about family life and their roles as wage earners than they do about the lives of women railroad workers. With the rare exceptions of articles on women's jobs, journal writers used women as a floating signifier, a concept through which to express male workers' fears. Yet these ideas about gender were an important part of the context of women's work. The BRC fostered ideas that made women workplace anomalies. Subtly and not so subtly, the clerks' union undermined women's status as legitimate wage earners.

## Male Officials and the Practice of Gendering

Male workers were not the only men engaged in the process of fashioning gender on the railroads. Railroad officials, although they did not use manliness to exhort workers to unionize, also affirmed that railroads were a male domain. In these instances (although it was not always the case) male workers and officials' ideas about gender resonated with each other; their consensus over the roles that women should play often served to create barriers to women's opportunity.[100] Since railroad officials made the hiring decisions, however, their understandings of gender were an especially powerful influence on women's work experiences.

Officials' assumptions shaped women's job prospects and their day-to-day work lives. The following case study shows the ways that employers applied gender at work. In this instance, despite the USRA's insistence that women should receive the same pay as men, women's rights to those wages were undermined by their superiors. This attempt to abrogate federal labor policy shows the lengths to which male officials were willing to go to palliate the destabilizing effects of having to pay women the same wage as their male counterparts.

The USRA's wage orders, with which the PRR was supposed to comply, tried to make railroad wages and working conditions uniform.[101] Since they were complicated and voluminous, however, it was not always clear how to follow the orders and what the regulations meant on a practical level.[102] Consequently, railroad managers routinely sought the "common sense" advice of the men under them to create working interpretations of the orders. Local railroad officials, the people in charge of implementing USRA wage policies, were powerful figures in the railroad companies' corporate structure. They had developed their own practices for hiring, retaining, and paying workers in their regions. And they did not throw out their understandings of what people should be paid simply because their titular bosses had changed. Often local supervisors' interpretations differentiated between men and women.

For example, Allegheny region General Superintendent A. J. Whitney abrogated part of the intent of the USRA's wage policies by creating a "student" category of worker. According to Whitney, while women were paid the requisite minimum in most cases, exceptions were permitted in "the case of Student-Clerks, who serve a probationary period of preparation and to whom we do not understand the minimum of $87.50 applies until they fully qualify for clerical positions at which time they are allowed the minimum of $87.50."[103]

While the local superintendent was responsible for initiating this "student" policy, senior PRR officials were aware that Whitney might not have followed the USRA's guidelines. Although they wrote to Whitney asking him to explain "just what duties are performed by these 'student clerks'; what rate of pay is allowed during probationary period, and how long they have to serve in this capacity before being qualified for a clerical position,"[104] and informed local officials that the minimum pay scale should be adhered to,[105] they did not follow up on the use of student clerks in Oil City until they were forced to do so by the USRA's Women's Service Section (WSS).[106]

When WSS agent Edith Hall paid a routine visit to the PRR's Allegheny division at the end of March 1919, she went to the road offices in Oil City, in western Pennsylvania. Following the standard inspection practice, Hall noted the available toilet facilities, the standard hours of work, the status of the women's union membership, and their pay. In general, field agent Hall's Oil City report was positive. In fact, she remarked that the women were not union members because "they felt pretty well contented with their conditions of work and looked upon the union chiefly as a help in time of trouble."[107] Yet at the same time, Hall documented a pattern of widespread evasion of the USRA's minimum pay scale. She found evidence of approximately twenty employees who were designated as "students" in contravention of USRA regulations.

Janet F. Davidson

Edith Hall's inspection of the Allegheny region of the PRR uncovered a drama unfolding over the status of women workers in Oil City that was replicated elsewhere in U.S. railway systems during World War I.[108] In an effort to avoid paying some women (especially young women) $87.50, railroads, including the Pennsylvania Railroad, tried to create an unregulated category of employee: "students." Despite the descriptions of the Oil City workplace as "pleasant" and filled with "contented" workers, women in the offices surrounding Oil City were subjected to systemic wage discrimination on the basis of their sex as their supervisors tried to subvert the USRA wage orders and avoid paying women the mandated minimums.

There was a cluster of railroad offices in Oil City that routinely hired young women at rates far below the federally mandated minimum wage. The dispatch office, for example, hired Mabel Pfaff, Marie Moore, and Martha Monkhern as student messengers between September 1918 and January 1919, paying them $23 per month rather than the regular messenger rate of $64. Other young women—and it seems only young women—were similarly exploited by the PRR in the Oil City offices. They were, however, more commonly employed as clerks. The assistant trainmaster's office, the trainmaster's office, the division superintendent's office, the engineer's office, the supervising agent's office, and the road foreman's office all hired young women as "student" clerks and paid them from $35 to $55 a month for their work.[109] These women, as Edith Hall pointed out with increasing vehemence as she went from place to place uncovering this practice, did the work of regular clerks.

For example, Cecilia Henry, a high school graduate, started work in June 1918 for $32.05 per month. Henry was the road foreman's personal stenographer. She did "all his official correspondence, had charge of the filing, and [made] out engine reports, &c." According to the WSS, this was "a plain case of ignoring the minimum established by Suppl. 7."[110] Peppered all through the region, these cases were clearly sanctioned by superintendent Whitney. The chief clerk in the trainmaster's office reported to Hall that "the matter of student clerks had been taken up with the Genl. Supt. about two months ago, and the ruling was that for the present they should be continued."[111] This practice was systemic on the Allegheny division and as well as decrying the practice because it abrogated USRA wage policy, Hall condemned the student wage as "doubly unwarranted because many of the girls can no longer be looked upon as learners."[112]

In Oil City offices, despite claims that the girls were being trained for promotion, one could go back to being a student clerk. And invoking gender may have seemed to officials a good way to justify their inconsistent behavior. As one of Hall's reports noted, a woman in the trainmaster's office "was recently promoted from a student position to a desk paying $91.65, was later bumped to $89.14 and again to

$52.05."[113] This woman was a student clerk one day, a regular clerk the next, and a student clerk again on the third day. And she was not the only one: Mildred Terwillinger and Hazel Wade were both hired, promoted, and demoted to student clerks again. This practice, for Hall, showed that the idea of a student clerical worker was a fiction perpetuated by the company to undermine women's access to equal pay.

The USRA forced the railroads to pay women the right amount when it caught them subverting government pay scales. The clarity of the wage orders and the established clerical minimum made it much harder for officials to claim ignorance of the regulations, or that the rules were ambiguous. Yet, while the Oil City cases were an extreme example of the abrogation of the wage orders, they illustrate a fairly commonplace railroad company tactic. Paying women less than men and misapplying wage orders was a strategy that, to varying degrees, male PRR officials used throughout the system.[114]

Although it was not the only cause of the PRR officials' attempts to underpay women, gender was a compelling way to explain and justify pay differentials.[115] Officials routinely paid women less than the guaranteed federal minimums because they found it hard to imagine that women's work, especially work done by young women, was worth the money. Thus, when PRR officials looked around and tried to work out how to keep the company's payroll down, one of the ways in which they did so was through the employment of contemporary understandings of gender difference. Since the PRR consistently subverted wage orders by discriminating on the basis of sex, it seems that PRR officials believed that gender could, possibly, trump federal regulations. By calling them students, Oil City railroad officials distinguished between women's work, and the valuable work of "real" clerks: men who had worked in the railroad offices for years. As young interlopers into a masculine world of work, girls who were hired as clerks clearly presented a problem for management.

Just as PRR officials found it almost impossible to imagine that women were worth the salaries mandated by the USRA, so too did they find it hard to accept that women could climb the promotional ladder. Since most railroad promotions were governed by seniority, and most women were hired during the war years, it was rare for a female clerk to gain enough seniority in a railroad office to bid on a chief clerk's position. Yet while the question of promoting women remained for the most part academic, as the war continued a few women did work their way up in the railroads' hierarchy. Because they did so, they, and their coworkers, had to face questions of what to do when women were in line for top jobs.

On the New York Central Railroad, for example, Ella Barnett took advantage of the WSS's presence and new work rules to get her job reclassified. Barnett, an employee with thirty-one years' seniority and standing, ran the return tickets department, an all-female subdepartment with a staff of over ninety. Having started work in the department at age fourteen, Ella Barnett climbed up a promotional ladder that was artificially cut off when she became an assistant chief clerk: "although performing the entire duties of a chief clerk, she had carried the title of Asst. Chief clerk, and her pay had been less than that of the men throughout the offices in the same positions."[116] Taking advantage of the government's grievance procedures, Barnett asked to be rerated as a chief clerk. Her complaint bore fruit and when her supervisors agreed to rerate her, her salary rose from $165 to $225 a month.

Even though "her services had been absolutely satisfactory and of a high quality judged even by the standard of the best men holding these positions," and Barnett's career trajectory made her into a good railroad "man," male workers opposed her promotion. Using a technicality, the men on her division insisted that when the job was renamed, it changed, and that this change opened up the position to the whole department. Four men applied for the job, and officials still hired Barnett. When one of the men protested with the backing of the clerks' union, the company started to back down. While the final disposition of this case was unclear, Barnett's comment that "the trouble is primarily jealousy on the part of the men at having a woman raised to a position of rank and pay equal to their own" was insightful.[117] Barnett's case was exceptional in two respects. First, other women were similarly passed over, but usually at earlier career stages. Second, Barnett's promotion was blocked by the union whereas more often women were passed over by male PRR officials of those officials' own accord.

Elizabeth Campbell of Pittsburgh, for example, wrote to the WSS and complained that despite her thirteen-and-a-half years service with the railroad she had been ignored at least three times when the possibility of promotion had arisen.[118] WSS inspections all over the PRR system uncovered wage differentials and discrimination. In the Altoona yards' freight master's office "in adjacent offices where the work is almost identical, the men work in one at $114.80; women in the other at $87.50."[119] After a routine WSS inspection in Harrisburg, four women were, after some pressure brought to bear by WSS, allowed to be "holding down the jobs as held by men" according to Mr. Baldwin, the office's chief clerk. Yet they remained underpaid.[120] WSS field agent Florence Clark went so far as to state that "there has been universal discrimination in regard to women" throughout the PRR system.[121]

Just like their trade union counterparts, PRR officials believed that male workers had family and other obligations that entitled those workers to better pay than female workers. As the Oil City example shows so starkly, and the thwarted promotion prospects of women such as Elizabeth Campbell confirm more subtly, when women went to work, gender exerted a powerful influence over the ways that their work was understood by railroad officials. Despite the increasing numbers of women who performed railroad clerical work during the war, women remained an anomaly on the railroads. Male railroad workers' and officials' ideas about the connections between masculinity and railroading worked together to create an environment in which women remained on the periphery of the work culture. All classes of railroad men assumed that the typical railroad clerk was, and would remain, a man. And because they did so, despite their differing attitudes toward pay, hours, and unionization, unionists and corporate officials helped to buttress the association between railroads and masculinity.

## Conclusion

For clerical workers of both sexes, day-to-day work life on the railroads was saturated with gendered assumptions. Workers and officials, at the same time as they did the work that made the trains run engaged in the ambiguous and complex processes of gendering and re-gendering work. During the beginning of the twentieth century, as male railroad clerks experienced a decline in their promotion prospects, male trade unionists actively created and deployed ideas about masculinity. As the BRC struggled to get itself off the ground as an organization, it tried to recruit members by appealing to workers as men.

Despite union leaders' efforts before the war, the advent of federal control caused the union to take off. At the same time, federal control posed a threat to men because the USRA encouraged the introduction of larger numbers of women into the workforce. Women, like men, benefited from the regulations of the federal government. Male and female clerks had access to trade union membership, they worked eight-hour days, and were paid according to federally mandated scales. The gender-blind application of these principles threatened male railway clerks' masculinity and helped foment male workers' evaluations of their own masculinity and its relationship to their work. And unionists' ambiguous representations of clerical manhood reveal their anxieties about their status as men in a changing world of work.

To make matters worse for male clerks, when railroad officials began hiring women in larger numbers, they put them to work in the larger office settings, in rationalized workplaces. Women's entrance into railroad work thus functioned as a visible marker of a more generalized set of changes in male clerks' work opportunities. Still, while individual male clerks were increasingly unlikely to get promoted into management as the century progressed, during the war era clerical workers' salaries increased, more clerks were hired, and joining the union became easier. In the short term, at least, railroad clerking improved for many men.

Moreover, despite male clerks' anxiety about their relationship to the rest of the railroad world, the wartime regendering of clerical work had a more profound and deleterious effect on women's employment prospects. Despite their class antagonisms, male railroad clerks and male railroad officials subscribed to a similarly gendered vision of work. Consequently, railroad clerical work remained male dominated. Male railroad officials' assumptions limited the locations and the types of jobs in which women were hired. Officials also tried to create special job categories such as "student clerk" that undermined women's access to equal pay. Furthermore, with the occasional assistance of male workers, they curtailed women's promotional possibilities. Thus, despite the increasingly widespread cultural connection between women and clerical work in nonrailroad settings, even during the war, the idea of female railroading clerical workers remained an anomaly.

The hegemonic power of the idea of railroads as a masculine domain is illustrated by the rapid removal of women from the railroad world after the end of World War I and the termination of federal control. PRR corporate officials quickly and actively sought to remove women from many of the jobs they had held during the war.[122] The numbers of railway women working fell by almost one-third during the six months after war's end.[123] Although in the first three months after the war the numbers of women clerical workers actually rose, by July 1919 there were fewer PRR women working in any job category than there had been female clerical workers just three months previously.[124] Ironically, women experienced a diminishment in opportunity at a time when the railroads were still employing huge numbers of people. In 1918, the railroads employed over 1.8 million people. That number rose to over 1.9 in 1919 and to over 2 million in 1920. As the railroads increased their workforce, the number of railroad clerks rose both numerically and proportionately. In 1918, clerks constituted 11.1 percent of all railroad employees; by 1928, they were 17.2 percent of railroad workers.[125] The PRR began firing women clerical workers at a time when their need for clerical help was increasing.

Despite women's forays into the working world, despite their pride in their accomplishments and their skills, and despite the on-paper policies of the federal government, many women were summarily ejected from the railroad world. When PRR officials decided that they no longer needed women's services, it was only a matter of time before most of the women who had been hired during the war were gone. Women who worked in nontraditional jobs or in nontraditional locations were the most quickly fired from their posts; clerks were the last to go. Regardless of the tasks women were hired to do, however, existing seniority systems, the reversion to old hiring policies, the changing postwar economic and political climate, and the PRR's commitment to keeping railroad work gendered male combined to provide the PRR with the impetus to revert to their old practice of hiring men to do the overwhelming majority of the tasks on the railroads. The ties between railroad work and manliness remained securely fastened.

# Notes

1. "Give a Man a Man's Work," *Railway Age Gazette* 65 (1918): 285.

2. Paul E. Johnson, *Shopkeepers' Millennium: Society and Revivals in Rochester, New York, 1815–1837* (New York: Hill and Wang, 1978); Jean Boydston, *Home and Work: Housework, Wages, and the Ideology of Labor in the Early Republic* (New York: Oxford University Press, 1990).

3. W. Fred Cottrell, *The Railroader* (Stanford, Calif.: Stanford University Press, 1940), 4.

4. Cottrell, *The Railroader*, chapter 3.

5. Bureau of Railway Economics, *Statistics of Railways, 1903–1913*, Consecutive No. 75, Miscellaneous Series, No. 19 (Washington, D.C.: Government Printing Office, 1915).

6. Cottrell, *The Railroader*, 33.

7. For a concise description of the nineteenth-century office, see Sharon Hartman Strom, "'We're No Kitty Foils': Organizing Office Workers for the Congress of Industrial Organizations, 1937-50," in *Women, Work and Protest: A Century of U. S. Women's Labor History*, Ruth Milkman, ed. (Boston: Routledge and Kegan Paul, 1985), 208.

8. Walter Licht, *Working for the Railroad: Organization of Work in the Nineteenth Century* (Princeton, N.J.: Princeton University Press, 1983), 26.

9. Phil E. Ziegler, "History of the Brotherhood of Railway Clerks, Freight Handlers, and Station Employees," *Railway Clerk* 18 (June 1919): 420.

10. Angel Kwolek-Folland, *Engendering Business: Men and Women in the Corporate Office, 1870-1930* (Baltimore, Md.: Johns Hopkins University Press, 1994); Lisa M. Fine, *The Souls of the Skyscraper: Female Clerical Workers in Chicago, 1870-1930* (Philadelphia: Temple University Press, 1990); Cindy Sondik Aron, *Ladies and Gentleman of the Civil Service: Middle Class Workers in Victorian America* (New York: Oxford University Press, 1987); Sharon Hartman Strom, *Beyond the Typewriter: Gender, Class, and the Origins of Modern Office Work, 1900-1930* (Urbana and Chicago: University of Illinois Press, 1992); Margery W. Davies, *Woman's Place Is at the Typewriter: Office Work and Office Workers, 1870-1930* (Philadelphia: Temple University Press, 1982).

11. "How to Select a Stenographer," *System Magazine*, 1912, cited in Fine, *The Souls of the Skyscraper*, 60.

12. *Railway Clerk*, 1915–1930.

13. Margaret A. Hobbes, "War Time Employment of Women," *American Labor Legislation Review* 8 (1918): 335.

14. USRA, Division of Labor, *Annual Report* (Washington, D.C.: Government Printing Office, 1919), 59. Janet F. Davidson, "Women and the Railroad: The Gendering of Work during the First World War Era, 1917–1920" (Ph.D. diss., University of Delaware, 1999), 94–95.

15. For a theoretical starting point for understanding gender see Ava Baron, ed., *Work Engendered: Toward a New History of American Labor* (Ithaca, N.Y.: Cornell University Press, 1991); Gail Bederman, *Manliness and Civilization: A Cultural History of Gender and Race in the United States, 1880-1917* (Chicago: University of Chicago Press, 1995); Judith Butler, *Gender Trouble: Feminism and the Subversion of Identity* (New York: Routledge, 1990); Judith Butler and Joan W. Scott, eds., *Feminists Theorize the Political* (New York: Routledge, 1992); Joan W. Scott, *Gender and the Politics of History* (New York: Columbia University Press, 1988).

16. I compiled a database of over 1,100 women who worked on the PRR. Sources included lists of union members, WSS inspection and complaint reports, Pennsylvania Railroad generated seniority lists, union magazines, and the PRR files at the Hagley Museum and Library as a whole. I also collected information from the 1920 manuscript census on approximately 500 women railroad employees. In my census data set, there were 9 accountants, 7 bookkeepers, 87 stenographers, and 250 clerks, as well as a series of women were specific sorts of clerks—billing, relief, record, shipping, shop, etc. In my PRR sample, there were 481 clerks, and 49 storehouse clerks. The PRR did not separate stenographers out.

17. *Railway Clerk* 16 (May 1917): 124.

18. Ibid., 125.

19. Fine, *The Souls of the Skyscraper,* 85.

20. Thomas C. Jepsen, *Ma Kiley: The Life of a Railroad Telegrapher* (El Paso: Texas Western Press, University of Texas at El Paso, 1997), 14–15.

21. National Archives and Records Administration, United States Railroad Administration, Record Group 14, Entry 97 Box 11, Pennsylvania Railroad, Eastern Lines, Statement showing by Grand Divisions and by Occupations Number of Women Employees (subsequently cited in the following format: NARA, USRA, RG-14-97-11).

22. Maurine Weiner Greenwald, *Women, War and Work: The Impact of World War I on Women Workers in the United States* (Westport, Conn.: Greenwood Press, 1980), 87.

23. Pennsylvania Railroad Records, Hagley Museum and Library, Wilmington, Delaware, Accession 1810, box 191 (subsequently cited in the following format: PRR-Hagley, 1810–191). Ninety-six of the women were hired between January 1917 and June 1918.

24. PRR-Hagley, 1810–191. Eight women had worked less than three months, and another four worked three to six months. Of the other four women, one woman had worked for ten years, another for over two years and two others fell between six and fifteen months.

25. Daniel Nelson, *Managers and Workers: Origins of the Twentieth-Century Factory System in the United States, 1880–1920,* 2d ed. (Madison: University of Wisconsin Press, 1995).

26. "Annual Report of Women's Service Section," *Railway Age* 68 (1920): 354.

27. Louise Marion Bosworth, *The Living Wage of Women Workers: A Study of Incomes and Expenditures of 450 Women in the City of Boston* (New York: Londmans, Green, 1911), 9, 37.

28. U. S. Department of Labor, Bulletin of the United States Bureau of Labor Statistics, Women in Industry Series No. 8, *Unemployment among Women in Department and Other Retail Stores of Boston* (Washington, D.C.: Government Printing Office, 1916), 29.

29. Alexander M. Bing, *Wartime Strikes and Their Adjustment* (New York: E. P. Dutton, 1921), 212–21.

30. U.S. Department of Labor, Bulletin of the Women's Bureau no. 17, *Women's Wages in Kansas* (Washington, D.C., 1921), 15. In Women's Bureau studies of industries in Kentucky, Arkansas, Rhode Island, South Carolina, Alabama, Georgia, and Maryland, no mention of office workers was made. For the Kansas survey, office workers were recorded only when they worked for the industries surveyed, but were not studied in their own right. See U.S. Department of Labor Bulletin of the Women's Bureau No. 10 (Virginia), no. 21 (Rhode Island), no. 22 (Georgia), no. 24 (Maryland), no. 26 (Arkansas), no. 29 (Kentucky), no. 32 (South Carolina), no. 34 (Alabama).

31. NARA, USRA, RG 14-97-Altoona Series no. 13, Helen Ross, Scale Office, Altoona Yards, Middle Division, PRR, January 29, 1919.

32. NARA, USRA, RG 14-97-16-174a, Edith R. Hall, Allegheny Region Inspection no. 41, Oil City, Pennsylvania, Division Superintendent's Office, March 29, 1919, 2.

33. For work on domestic service see Phyllis Palmer, *Domesticity and Dirt: Housewives and Domestic Servants in the United States, 1920–1945* (Philadelphia: Temple University Press, 1985); David M. Katzman, *Seven Days a Week: Women and Domestic Service in Industrializing America* (New York: Oxford University Press, 1978).

34. Illinois Industrial Survey, *Hours and Health of Women Workers: Report of Illinois Industrial Survey, December 1918* (Springfield, Ill.: Schnepp and Barnes State Printers, 1919), 57.

35. Scott Derks, ed., *The Value of a Dollar: Prices and Incomes in the United States, 1860–1989* (Detroit: Manly, 1994), 150, does not differentiate between male and female domestics.

36. Virginia Yans-McLaughlin, *Family and Community: Italian Immigrants in Buffalo, 1880–1930* (Urbana: University of Illinois Press, 1982), 184.

37. In Arkansas in 1922, for example, women candy makers earned, on average, $8.50 a week; U.S. Department of Labor, Bulletin of the Women's Bureau no. 26, *Women in Arkansas Industries: A Study of Hours, Wages, and Working Conditions* (Washington, D.C.: Government Printing Office, 1923), 30; In a 1920 Manchester, New Hampshire,

survey in which the majority of the women worked in the shoe industry, over 32.6 percent of women earned less than $800 a year, another 56.3 percent earned between $800 and $1,200 per year. In contrast, more than 40 percent of men earned over $1,200 a year, U.S. Department of Labor, Bulletin of the Women's Bureau no. 31, *The Share of Wage-Earning Women in Family Support* (Washington, D.C.: Government Printing Office, 1923), 45–46.

38. Davidson, "Women and the Railroad," chapter 3.

39. Fine, *Souls of the Skyscraper*, 44.

40. William Leach, *Land of Desire: Merchants, Power and the Rise of a New American Culture* (New York: Vintage Books, 1993) uses this phrase.

41. Susan Porter Benson, *Counter Cultures: Saleswomen, Managers, and Customers in American Department Stores, 1890–1940* (Urbana: University of Illinois Press), 183.

42. For more information on the history of the family/living wage, start with Lawrence B. Glickman, *A Living Wage: American Workers and the Making of Consumer Society* (Ithaca, N.Y.: Cornell University Press, 1997). Other work on the subject, much of it looking more closely at women, includes Martha May, "The Historical Problem of the Family Wage: Ford Motor Company and the Five Dollar Day," *Feminist Studies* 8 (1982): 399–424; Martha May, "Bread Before Roses: American Workingmen, Labor Unions and the Family Wage," in Milkman, ed., *Women, Work and Protest*; Joanne Meyerowitz, *Women Adrift: Independent Wage Earners in Chicago, 1880–1930* (Chicago: University of Chicago Press, 1988); Alice Kessler-Harris, *A Woman's Wage: Historical Meanings and Social Consequences* (Lexington: University Press of Kentucky, 1990); Nancy Fraser and Linda Gordon, "A Genealogy of Dependency: Tracing a Keyword in the U.S. Welfare State," *Signs: A Journal of Women in Culture and Society* 19 (1994): 309–36.

43. Glickman, *A Living Wage*, 2.

44. Lawrence B. Glickman, "Inventing the 'American Standard of Living:' Gender, Race and Working-Class Identity, 1880–1925," *Labor History* 34 (1993) 231, 235.

45. Cited in Glickman, *A Living Wage*, 82.

46. Glickman, *A Living Wage*, 86–87.

47. Thomas H. Russell, *The Girl's Fight for a Living: How to Protect Working Women from Dangers Due to Low Wages* (Chicago: M. A. Donohue, 1913).

48. Glickman, *A Living Wage*, 91.

49. Henry A. Seager, "The Minimum Wage As Part of a Program for Social Reform," *Annals of the American Academy of Political Science* special issue, The Cost of Living, July 1913: 4; cited in Glickman, "Inventing the 'American Standard of Living,'" 234.

50. Meyerowitz, *Women Adrift*, 34.

51. Kessler-Harris, *A Woman's Wage*, 14; Meyerowitz, *Women Adrift*, 34–36.

52. May, "Bread Before Roses," 13.

53. Fraser and Gordon, "A Genealogy of Dependency," 309–36.

54. "Prosperity?—No," *Railway Clerk* 16 (March 1917): 49.

55. *Railway Clerk* 15 (August 1916): 264.

56. Bureau of Railway Economics, "Table 24, Number of Employees," *Statistics of Railways, 1902–1912, United States* (Washington, D.C.: Government Printing Office, 1914), 28.

57. Interstate Commerce Commission, *Twenty-eighth Annual Report of the Statistics of the Railways in the United States for the Year Ended June 30, 1915* (Washington, D.C.: Government Printing Office, 1916), 25.

58. Interstate Commerce Commission, *Thirty-third Annual Report of the Statistics of the Railways in the United States for the Year Ended Dec. 31, 1920* (Washington, D.C.: Government Printing Office, 1921), p. XX.

59. Compiled from Interstate Commerce Commission, *Twenty-eighth Annual Report of the Statistics of the Railways of the United States* (1915) through *Thirty-third Annual Reports of the Statistics of the Railways of the United States* (1920).

60. "Give a Man a Man's Work," 285.

61. N. H. Greenberg, "Women As Railroad Clerks," *Railway Age Gazette* 65 (1918): 422.

Janet F. Davidson

62. There is no good scholarly work on the Brotherhood of Railway Clerks (or the Brotherhood of Railway and Steamship Clerks, Freight Handlers, Express, and Station Employees, as it came to be known in 1919). BRC grand-secretary-treasurer Phil E. Ziegler wrote an article for *Railway Clerk* in 1919. Two other books provide some information: Harry Henig, *The Brotherhood of Railway Clerks* (New York: Columbia University Press, 1937) and Nixon Denton, *History of the Brotherhood of Railway and Steamship Clerks, Freight Handlers, Express and Station Employees, with Emphasis on the Years in which George M. Harrison was Grand President* (Cincinnati, Ohio: The George M. Harrison Biographical Committee, 1956). Henig's book is much more valuable to the scholar, but he seems to have glossed over the early conflicts within the organization that manifested themselves in the pages of *Railway Clerk* in 1915 when the old guard were thrown out of office.

63. ICC statistics, 1915, show that there were over 140,000 clerks. According to *Railway Clerk*, membership hovered around 5,000 at that time; Interstate Commerce Commission, *Twenty-eighth Annual Report of the Statistics of the Railways in the United States*, 26; *Railway Clerk* 14 (1915).

64. PRR-Hagley, 1810-950-1, Mutual Beneficial Association, 1913–1923.

65. Unions of other office workers were few and far between. While some workers were organized, the AFL consistently refused to let office workers organize an international union, partly on the basis that they were too few in number to warrant such a step; American Federation of Labor Records, The Samuel Gompers Era, 1877–1937, Executive Council Minutes, January 20–27, 1917, Reel 5, frame 1298 and October 18–20, 22–27, 1917, frame 1445. For statistics on the BRC's growth see Phil E. Ziegler, "History of the Brotherhood of Railway Clerks, Freight Handlers, and Station Employes," *Railway Clerk* 18 (June 1919): 391.

66. *Railway Clerk* 14 (March 1915): 75.

67. "If we would quit wasting our breath emphasizing the fact that we are the 'brains' of the railroad and stick up for our rights, we might convince the managers that we have more brains that they credit us with having"; *Railway Clerk*, 18 (July 1919): 432. For an illustration about nonmembers as parasites: *Railway Clerk* 19 (July 1920): 475. For reference to "dry-land jelly-fish" *Railway Clerk* 17 (July 1918): 206. For reference to men being "too yellow and too pro-German to join" union, *Railway Clerk* 19 (July 1920): 241.

68. According to one woman who, in 1914, defended her decision to pass as a man, "the well-cared for woman is a parasite"; San Francisco Lesbian and Gay History Project, "'She Even Chewed Tobacco': A Pictorial Narrative of Passing Women in America," in Martin Duberman, Martha Vicinus, George Chauncey Jr., eds. *Hidden from History: Reclaiming the Gay and Lesbian Past* (New York: Meridian Book, 1989), 186.

69. Bederman, *Manliness and Civilization*, 15.

70. B. H. Baxter, "Along the Rail," *Railway Clerk* 17 (January 1918): 8.

71. *Railway Clerk* 15 (September 1916): 284.

72. Excerpt from *New York Journal* in Wade Shurtleff, "Editorial: After the War, What?" *Railway Clerk* 16 (April 1917): 73.

73. *Railway Clerk* 18 (July 1919): 432.

74. Shane White and Graham White, *Stylin': African American Expressive Culture from Its Beginnings to the Zoot Suit* (Ithaca, N.Y.: Cornell University Press, 1998), 133.

75. *Railway Clerk* 15 (January 1916): 17–18.

76. "Retrospect of the Past Year," *Railway Clerk* 16 (January 1917): 8.

77. See, for example, the Declaration of Independence, and Sean Wilentz, *Chants Democratic: New York City and the Rise of the American Working Class, 1788-1850* (New York: Oxford University Press, 1984).

78. Samuel Gompers, *Labor and the Employer* (New York: E. P. Dutton and Company, 1920), 8.

79. Evelyn Brooks Higginbotham uses the word "nadir" to describe American race relations at the turn of the century; Evelyn Brooks Higginbotham, *Righteous Discontent:*

*The Women's Movement in the Black Baptist Church, 1880-1920* (Cambridge, Mass.: Harvard University Press, 1993), 1.

80. Eric Arnesen, "'Like Banquo's Ghost, It Will Not Down': The Race Question and the American Railroad Brotherhoods, 1880–1920," *American Historical Review* 99 (1994): 1601–1633; Paul Taillon, "Culture, Politics, and the Making of the Railroad Brotherhoods, 1863–1916" (Ph.D. diss., University of Wisconsin-Madison, 1997), 210–26.

81. *Railway Clerk* 16 (July 1916): 230.

82. *Railway Clerk* 17 (October 1918): 380.

83. PRR-Hagley, 1810-987-14, "Girls in the Office," circa 1918.

84. Ibid.

85. The Mutual Benefit Association, a company union set up to counteract unionization in the PRR, had members from the supervisory classes as well as clerical and other members. They tended to stress connections across class divisions, playing on white-collar workers' associations with "respectable" and loyal corporate employees. The *Mutual Magazine*, the MBA's official organ, was full of antistrike and procooperation messages.

86. Like the United Electrical Workers in World War II, the BRC was fairly amenable to women members, in part, it seems, because of the relatively high numbers of women clerks. For UE and World War II, see Ruth Milkman, *Gender at Work: The Dynamics of Job Segregation By Sex During World War II* (Urbana: University of Illinois Press, 1987).

87. *Railway Clerk* assumed the reader-clerk was a white man. See, for examples, *Railway Clerk* 15 (January 1916): 17–18; *Railway Clerk* 15 (March 1916): 92–93.

88. *Railway Clerk* 15 (April 1916): 139.

89. *Railway Clerk* 16 (April 1917): 94.

90. According to Angel Kwolek-Folland, "Often, women's presence seemed the most salient fact separating the new corporate workplace from the traditional male office." Angel Kwolek-Folland, *Engendering Business*, 11.

91. *Railway Clerk* 16 (April 1917): 91, 94.

92. *Railway Clerk* 16 (May 1917): 126.

93. For an insightful analysis of union journals' depictions of masculinity and femininity see Elizabeth Faue, *Community of Suffering and Struggle: Women, Men and the Labor Movement in Minneapolis, 1915–1945* (Chapel Hill: University of North Carolina Press, 1991), chapter 3. Faue points out that even when unions had large numbers of women members, the journals often depicted workers as male, marginalizing and misrepresenting women's role in union building and strike activity.

94. "Lets raise a special fund to send some lady solicitor to take subscriptions for the Journal. Think of the fun we will have hammering these nons every month and making them pay for it"; *Railway Clerk* 16 (January 1917): 23.

95. R. E. Nutting, Witch City Lodge, Salem MA, *Railway Clerk* 15 (April 1916): 139.

96. *Railway Clerk* 16 (November 1917): 262.

97. Joseph McCartin employs the idea of industrial democracy with great aplomb in his study of unions in World War I (*Labor's Great War: The Struggle for Industrial Democracy and the Origins of Modern American Labor Relations, 1912-1921* [Chapel Hill and London: University of North Carolina Press, 1997], 1–12 and passim).

98. *Railway Clerk* 17 (December 1918): 518.

99. For an example of linking the bosses and Germans, see "Pennsylvania Clerks," *Railway Clerk* 17 (January 1918): 23.

100. For an example of male officials and workers who did not have overlapping interests, see Davidson, "Women and the Railroad," chapter 5.

101. United States Railroad Administration, *General Order 27, Wages of Railroad Employees, Washington, May 25, 1918* (Washington, D.C.: Government Printing Office, 1918), 3.

102. For example, the primary wage order affecting the bulk of the railroad workforce, which was enacted at the end of May 1918, was twenty-five pages long and designed to cover as many eventualities as possible. According to it, "no problem so vast and intricate as doing justice to the 2,000,000 railroad employees of the country can be

Janet F. Davidson

regarded as completely settled and disposed of by any one decision or order" (United States Railroad Administration, *General Order 27*, 3).

103. PRR-Hagley, 1810-976-2, A. J. Whitney, General Superintendent to R. L. O'Donnel, General Manager, January 18, 1919.

104. PRR-Hagley, 1810-976-2, R. L. O'Donnel to A. J. Whitney, February 8, 1919.

105. PRR-Hagley, 1810-976-2, R. L. O'Donnel to R. V. Massey, N. W. Smith, Joseph Gumbes, F. Latrobe, H. M. Carson, A. J. Whitney, A. M. Parker, December 19, 1918.

106. PRR-Hagley, 1810-976-2, A. J. Whitney, General Superintendent to R. L. O'Donnel, General Manager, January 18, 1919. HAE to WAB, annotation on letter.

107. NARA, RG 14-97-16-174a, E. R. Hall, Memorandum, Organization of Clerks, P.R.R., Oil City, Pennsylvania, Allegheny Division, P.R.R., Oil City, Pennsylvania, No. 41.

108. Docket C-173, Railway Board of Adjustment No. 3, Mobile and Ohio Railroad versus Clerks. Docket C-304, C-305. *Railway Clerk* 18 (August 1919): 488.

109. According to General Order 27, even the lowest paid monthly worker got a $20 pay raise. Women who had been hired before May 1918, then, even if they were hired at $35 a month, should have been making $55 a month after General Order 27, Supplement 7 (September 1918), made the lowest possible clerical salary $87.50 a month.

110. NARA, RG 14-97-16-174a, No 49, Adjustment Re Student Clerk, Inspection by Edith Hall, March 31, 1919, 2.

111. NARA, RG 14-97-16-174a, No. 46, Adjustment Re Student Clerks, Allegheny Division, Edith Hall, March, 31, 1919, 2.

112. NARA, RG 14-97-16-174a, No. 46, Adjustment Re Student Clerks, Allegheny Division, Edith Hall, March, 31, 1919, 2. For a similar case see NARA, RG 14-97-16-174a, Adjustment Re Student Messengers, Allegheny Division, Inspection by Agent Edith R. Hall, March 31, 1919.

113. NARA. RG 14-97-16-174a, No. 46, Adjustment Re Student Clerks, Allegheny Division, Edith Hall, March 31, 1919, 2.

114. PRR-Hagley, 1810-191. In the treasury department, for example, Elsie Albright, who was hired in 1917 and paid $56.50 a month, was given a raise to $68.65 under the department's misinterpretation of the 1918 wage order. Anna Robinson, who earned $55 in January 1918, got a raise of $10 under the order; Marsha Shoenberg, who started work in 1915, earned $66.50 in October 1917 and got an $11.05 raise in June of the next year.

115. The PRR also wanted to keep its wage bill down. In all these cases it seems clear that the PRR used whatever means it had at its disposal to save money and deflate its wage bill. During the war, the government shouldered the costs of running the railroads and paid companies for the privilege. Railroad officials were nonetheless concerned about the ways in which the governmental decisions inflated their wage bills. Even though they were not yet paying themselves, the PRR was concerned about the precedents such raises set for the postwar period. They feared, quite rightly, that unions and workers would try to hold onto, and consolidate, the gains that they had made during the war if and when the companies were returned to private control. Employers were surely motivated both by their commitment to retaining their power and reaping big profits when they sought to pay women less than men.

116. NARA, USRA, RG 14-97-22, Complaint 58, n.d. (c. May 1919), 1.

117. NARA, USRA, RG 14-97-22, Complaint 58, 3.

118. NARA, USRA, RG 14-97-19-193D, Elizabeth Campbell to Helen Ross, March 2, 1919, Pittsburgh, Pennsylvania.

119. NARA, USRA, RG 14-97-17-181, Altoona Series No. 22, February 4, 1919.

120. NARA, USRA, RG 14-97-18-197a, Harrisburg, Pennsylvania, Stores-Shopkeeper, Inspection, January 22, 1919.

121. NARA, USRA, RG 14-97-18-187a, Memoranda-Clerks, Store House Office, Pennsylvania Railroad, Harrisburg, Pennsylvania, Harrisburg Shops, Florence Clark, 4.

122. The WSS report noted that "a tendency has been not to take on more women when vacancies occur, even in positions formerly held by them"; "Annual Report of Women's Service Section," *Railway Age* 68, January 30th (1920): 352.

123. From 14,992 in October 1918 to 9,977 in March 1919. Compiled from U.S. Railroad Administration, *Number of Women Employed and the Character of Their Employment for Dates Jan. 1, April 1, July 1, Oct. 1, 1918 (class 1 roads) Eastern, Southern, and Western Territories* (Washington, D.C.: Government Printing Office, 1919); USRA, *Number of Women Employed and the Character of Their Employment for Dates Jan. 1, April 1, July 1, Oct. 1, 1919 (class 1 roads) Eastern, Southern, and Western Territories* (Washington, D.C.: Government Printing Office, 1920).

124. In July 1919, there were 9,357 PRR women; USRA *Number of Women Employed and the Character of Their Employment for Dates Jan. 1, April 1, July 1, Oct. 1, 1919 (class 1 roads) Eastern, Southern, and Western Territories* (Washington, D.C.: Government Printing Office, 1920).

125. Interstate Commerce Commission, "Number, Service, and Compensation of Employees, 1916–1929," *Statistics of Railways in the United States, Year Ending 1930,* (Washington, D.C.: Government Printing Office, 1931): 21.

Janet F. Davidson

# Rereading Man's Conquest of Nature

*Skill, Myths, and the Historical Construction of Masculinity in Western Extractive Industries*

## NANCY QUAM-WICKHAM

In our popular national imagination, the American West of our past was a land of rugged terrain, untamed wilderness, unruly rivers, and unpredictably harsh climes—an unforgiving landscape populated by savage beasts and uncivilized men. Both contemporary writing and subsequent scholarship on the West have tended to amplify the region's inherently *wild* nature. From the Turnerians' stress on the creation of a national character by our expansion onto the "primitive" frontier to the dramatic opening scenes of Ken Burns's *The West* television series (a decidedly "new western" interpretation of our past), in such western exceptionalist eyes the West was clearly a place like no other in this country.[1] The West was also a profoundly gendered region: a place where *men* conquered Mother Nature. As historian Richard White has so aptly stated, early scholars erroneously formulated "an essentialist West, a West that produced . . . men to match its mountains—that is, men able to overcome and dominate a feminine nature. From their domination they derived their distinctiveness." More simply stated, in the literature of regional myths, the West was indeed "the He-Man Land."[2]

As economic historians have reminded us, the West was also a land of natural resources—a land with towering forests, rich mineral deposits, seemingly limitless pools of oil—all there for the taking. Significantly for this discussion, it was men who exploited these resources, men who labored in the forests and mines, men who built a distinctive regional economy. The stories of western extractive industries (mining, lumber, oil) are peopled with such masculine heroes, images of men "conquering" the resources of nature—images that, states historian Katherine Morrissey, "epitomize imagined masculine virtues" thus creating and maintaining an "ideology of the West [that] celebrates a particular, and gendered, form of American identity."[3] To comprehend just how close this association of conqueror of nature with the ideal of manliness was, consider one man's rather breathless description of late-nineteenth-century loggers. In 1929 John Emmett Nelligan wrote, "The lumberjacks of the Northwest, those hardy fore-runners of our present-day civilization, walked the streets in all their pristine glory. I shall never forget how splendid those young giants of the North first appeared to my impressionable eyes. They were strong and wild in both body and spirit, with the careless masculine beauty of men who live free lives in the open air. They seemed the finest speci-mens of manhood I had ever seen."[4]

While recent scholars have written extensively and perceptively about Western women, with few exceptions historians have ignored the particular experiences of men as gendered individuals whose ideas about manhood and masculinity were consciously created.[5] This article examines how workers in western extractive industries culturally con-structed a "masculine ideal," the defining qualities of which were brotherhood, solidarity, and a pride in the acquisition of skill.[6] This ideal was then translated into a "cultural process," in the words of his-torian Gail Bederman, "whereby concrete individuals are constituted as members of a preexisting social category—as men. The ideological process of gender . . . works through a complex political technology, composed of a variety of institutions, ideas, and daily practices. Com-bined, these processes produce a set of truths about who an individual is and what he . . . can do, based upon his . . . body."[7] Skill was the crit-ical element in this process through which workers asserted their mas-culinity. This is a study of how workers constructed and expressed the slippery concept of skill: defined here as the ways in which workers and managers conveyed in thought and words a man's experience, manual ability, occupational knowledge, and the inventiveness needed to accomplish any particular task.[8] As a social concept, *skill* served as the most important component of workers' culture in the West's dark mining shafts, damp forests of redwood and Douglas fir, and dusty oil fields, and it contributed to workers' ideas about man-hood and class pride. Workers expressed their sense of skill—and thus their manliness—through initiation rites, story- and myth-telling, and occupational language.

In each of the three settings that I examine, solidarity between workers grew out of distinctive social and working conditions. It is well known that skilled immigrant (particularly Welsh and Cornish) miners were instrumental in developing western hard rock mines, and that loggers from Maine and the upper Midwest were among the first workers to fell the tall trees of the West.[9] Less well known, but of equal importance, is the fact that many of the first western oil-field workers were trans-plants from the oil and coal fields of Pennsylvania and West Virginia.[10]

An often tenuous social cohesion brought about by a common occu-pational heritage was reinforced by the dictates of work. The work process in lumbering, oil production, and hard rock mining demanded teamwork among the members of any individual work unit. Producing ore, oil, or lumber was a collective process: after the mid-nineteenth century, no man could do so by laboring alone. Even into the twentieth century, managers recognized this fact in their pay schemes, awarding bonuses to men based not on their individual performance but on the performance of the entire work unit. Cooperation between workers was essential. Consider these examples. In lumbering operations, the particularly dangerous task of driving of logs downriver required two crews of men working in harmony, one of which handled the fore part of the drive, breaking up jams, sluicing, and so forth, and the other the rear end, picking up logs that were stranded when the high water receded. Such work required men to gauge carefully the speed of the river current, taking into account the distance and course of the river, the size of the "drive," and any number of other factors that could cause a logjam. A log drive was "an epic drama," claimed Nelligan, who conveyed how clearly workers coordinated their efforts when he wrote, "Down the river it wended its way, around bends, over falls, through rapids. Upon the constantly shifting carpet of logs the agile rivermen labored in a Herculean manner. Whenever there became discernible the slightest cessation in the steady, downstream movements of the logs, a jack was on the job to remedy the matter. Every effort was made to avoid jams, which were apt to exact a heavy toll in both men and money."[11] In the Pacific Northwest, loggers understood that learning the skills of various "logging systems," in the words of one historian of the region, were "important means of enhancing earning power and asserting independence."[12]

Similarly, in the dangerous work of underground mining operations, safe operations required not only cooperation, but also a keen understanding of local conditions to prevent workplace disasters. These were the kind of dangerous working conditions out of which arose the Wobblies' (Industrial Workers of the World) watchword, "an injury to one is an injury to all." Before the widespread adoption of automatic drilling machines hard rock miners were reportedly men of great skill, noted folklorist Wayland Hand in his study of Butte miners, whose knowledge of underground conditions, "individual initiative and 'savvy' were appreciated and . . . commonly possessed by the crew as well as by shifters and foremen."[13] Early attempts to exploit the West's great silver deposits had, in fact, been hampered by the lack of experienced underground miners.[14] Moreover, geological conditions varied widely throughout the region, requiring different excavation techniques to ensure the stability of the mine. "Traditional miners" reportedly were "experts" in choosing the tunnel or shaft methods, determining where to sink mineshafts and dig crosscuts, deciding how to set timbers in mine drifts, and judging where to set stulls, galleries, and floors.[15]

In some instances, workers themselves contributed greatly to the evolution of the industry. In western oil-field operations, the technology of oil production was largely rudimentary in the early twentieth century. In an industrial environment where technological practices were in great flux, workers not only had great control over their labor processes but also participated actively in improving the techniques of producing oil. Drilling is a case in point: Skilled drillers learned their trade through direct experience in the region's oil fields; a "good driller is only developed by practice," asserted the author of one popular oil field engineering manual.[16] A man's experience was immediately apparent to observers, workers, and managers alike. "The skilled driller will know as soon as his hand touches the drilling cable whether the drill is working properly or not," advised one University of California professor of petroleum engineering in a textbook he authored to prepare university students for specialized training in the technology of petroleum production.[17] The "sensitive hand of the driller" was an experienced hand, one that could judge the effectiveness of the tools by the vibrations in the drilling cable, taking into account the different elasticities of steel and hemp cables of varying diameters.[18] Moreover, only an experienced worker could determine the geological strata by the action of the tools in the drill hole and then adjust the temper screw accordingly, "as conditions require . . . observing the cutting and the depth being obtained in order to determine the necessity for . . . a newly-sharpened drill."[19] Skill and experience made it possible for the driller to distinguish the "depth and thickness of each set of formations penetrated" by the tools.[20] The "value of an able and experienced drilling crew," observed one government publication, "is evident to anyone who will take the trouble to review the hundreds of cases where wells have been spoiled through bad judgment or preventable accidents, or in which the oil sand has been injured or ineffectually tapped."[21] An inexperienced man, or "Sears-Roebuck driller" as novices were often called in the fields, commonly impeded the production process because he lacked the experience, "presence of mind and ingenuity" that made a skilled worker "preeminent in his field."[22]

Out of the social recognition of skill emerged a group identity defined by shared experiences, common values, and the solidarity brought about as men labored in distinctive industries. A rich language and occupational subculture developed from these bonds of worker solidarity. There are several dimensions to this thick and dynamic subculture: workers' cultural construction of masculinity, their elaboration of stories and myths that highlighted skill, and their development of occupational languages that, according to one lexicographer, "cannot be understood without some acquaintance" with the work itself.[23]

Work in the mines, forests, and oil fields was a profoundly gendered activity. Material conditions reinforced prevailing gender ideologies that prescribed a particular economic role for men—that of the family breadwinner. Certainly, in all three industries neither were all men married nor could all those who were married fulfill this role, a point

Nancy Quam-Wickham

that I will not expand upon here. The significance of large numbers of single men may have been important in the construction of a sense of manhood in these industries, but it was by no means the only factor in men's elaboration of their sense of manliness. For married men in the fields and mine camps of the West, contemporary ideas about proper gender roles reflected the social organization of work and the distribution of power under capitalism. Women's labor was not unvalued. Quite the opposite: for most married workers, women's labor, consisting mostly of unpaid work, was an absolutely necessary yet subsidiary activity contributing to the reproduction of labor, making it possible for men to work under conditions dictated by capital.[24] Moreover, in some instances, women participated in the cultural construction of men's manliness: during organizing drives in the late 1910s, Mary Harris ("Mother Jones") frequently admonished oil-field women to refuse to sleep with their husbands until they joined the new union. Other times, Jones asserted that men who failed to join the union "have not the right to be called men."[25]

This discussion proposes a different definition of manhood that was based neither on male occupational exclusivity nor a man's status as family breadwinner. Here masculinity—or "manliness"—was not just some social construction of collective gender identity serving to uphold male hegemony, born of contention and divisiveness, as men struggled to exclude women from occupations in Western extractive industries. Manliness was not simply a personal quality distinguished by certain characteristics, such as strength or ability. To assert one's manliness was part of the process through which male workers quite self-consciously expressed their identity and authority as men in both body and spirit. At least for the moment, I will consider the case of oil-field workers in the early decades of this century. An oil worker might have to be "a special breed of man," big, rough, strong, and have experience, but he also had to engage his own class oppression by the forces of capital.[26] Working conditions were brutal; in California during the early 1920s, one in four workers was hurt or killed on the job. Thus one encounters courageous manhood in the corporeal sense, as a worker risks his life and limb for work. Many men, one oil worker remembered, "[w]ouldn't work in the oil fields because it was . . . so treacherous and dangerous. . . . You're working with big, heavy equipment, and stuff breaking and a lot of people getting hurt, getting killed . . . arms getting cut off, dropping pipe on their feet, cutting their fingers off on the catheads drumming them. Just various things."[27]

Local newspapers in oil regions regularly reported oil-field accidents, recounting injuries and deaths in strikingly graphic detail: a worker was caught in the rotary machinery and whirled to his death, his arms torn off in the process; another was crushed to death in a fall from the top of a slippery derrick as his coworkers watched in horror.[28] Themes of exploitation ran thick in such descriptions of industrial accidents. One Signal Hill, California, newspaper lamented the death of a roughneck: "Only a worker gone, just another cost in the game of oil. A loop, a twirl, a cathead turn, then a knock at the door and no more sun. Somebody else puts on his gloves. The swish of the rotary still goes on. Only a worker gone."[29]

In the oil fields, everyday work routines also elicited narratives illustrating the inextricable relationship between a man's labor and his exploitation. The masculine virtues of tough, rough gangs of men who worked together were often subjects of special acclaim; men who laid the pipelines and built the tanks to receive the oil, whose jobs "required not only enormous strength and skill, but split-second interaction," were one such group of workers.[30] Pipeline crews working quickly in unison were described by one oil worker as "lads with guts," "cocky roosters" and "manhood boosters," but were also slaves who would never get rich—men who sweat and swore, who had to hustle, jump, heave, and up and run to "put money in the bank for their bosses."[31]

While themes of exploitation highlighted the commonality of workingmen's experiences, western workers also sought to define masculine virtues in other ways. An assertion of manhood and celebration of masculinity came only with accomplishment on the job. Accordingly, workers routinely subjected new employees to humiliating and often vicious initiation rites. Some pranks were relatively innocuous, save for the new worker's embarrassment: in the oil industry drillers, derrick men, and other experienced crew members would send a new worker off on a long hunt for a "left-handed wrench," a "maiden head," a "Thompson's bar," a "set of pipe-stretchers," or some other "imaginary tool." Some time later, the chagrined new worker would return to the laughter of his fellow workers on the rig, knowing that he had been had.[32] Other initiation rites were more risky. Workers in Santa Fe Springs in the early 1920s would play jokes on one another, and especially on new workers. One such stunt was setting on fire the greasy wipe rags workers carried around in their backpockets; Pete Davis remembered having "the whole ass of my coveralls burnt off that way" when he began work in the fields.[33] Still other rituals confronted directly workers' beliefs in the interconnections between gender and skill, and served to define a worker's masculinity in relation to his occupational proficiency. In his short book on oil-field language, Gerald Haslam describes an initiation rite widely practiced in the California fields in the early 1960s, when he began work as a roughneck; there is ample evidence that this ritual was not new to the oil regions.[34] In a sadistic ritual that at least symbolically resembled a form of rape, a novice worker on a drilling rig was tricked into lying on the ground, where two of his fellow workers pinned him down. A third worker stripped the pants off the newcomer, then applied a "liberal coating" of a "semi-caustic sealing compound" to the new man's genitals. The initiate was then left to fight his way from the grasps of the other workers. Says Haslam about the social functions and perpetuation of this "lifting" rite, "While it is considered good form for an initiate to fight while being lifted, it is further necessary for him to accept his misfortune with good humor. The older workers continue the rite, in a sense, by openly discussing the lifting, and the trick or tricks used to "seduce" their victim, in front of him. Good form calls for an acknowledgment of inferiority at this point. . . . One important function is to show that the group cannot be easily entered; it says that the profession is special. . . ."[35]

Timber workers, too, had their versions of brutal initiation rites. Like the oil-field workers' lifting ceremony, loggers engaged in highly sexually charged, violent group attacks on men new to work in the woods in a ritual that one observer called the "sheep game." As part of the initiation ceremony, staged in a crowded bunkhouse for the "amusement" of other more experienced loggers, two skilled loggers (called "jacks") would take on the roles of a farmer and a sheep buyer. A "greenhorn new to camp" was then "rolled up tightly in a heavy blanket and became the "sheep." He was carried by two other jacks. The farmer and the sheep buyer would stage an argument over the weight of the sheep. To determine its real weight they would let it down repeatedly on the "scales." The "scales" was a sharply pointed stick and the "sheep" was always thrown onto the "scales" in such a way that the point of the stick came into violent contact with the tender, rear central portion of his anatomy. This was very uncomfortable for the greenhorn and very laughable for the rest of the crew."[36]

Hard rock miners in Butte engaged in somewhat less violent initiation rites. In the 1920s, newcomers to the area's many copper mines were "made to mount a Burley drilling machine which had been provided with stirrups. When the air was cut in and the machine began to jiggle they were fervently admonished: 'Stay with 'er kid! If she gets loose she'll kill every man in the drift!'" At other times, experienced miners placed "tender notes from pseudonymous lovers" in the lunch pails of new men.[37]

Such initiation rituals affirmed the special character of work in the oil fields, mines, and woods of the West, highlighting the manliness of older workers' experience and skill by emphasizing a novice's sexual, social, and occupational inferiority. Such "rough" practices also brought workers together, by bringing them into conflict with management. Pete Davis recalled that "the bosses put a stop' to workers' tricks of 'setting one another on fire'—'it was either stop or lose your job if you were caught.'"[38] At least some workers were fired for organizing initiations of new men into drilling gangs; in one incident, an oil company production manager, who "opposed . . . such initiations," discharged two employees for treating two initiates "a little roughly." The manager refused to rescind these discharges, despite the pleas of his foreman to do so, and even though the foreman and others reminded the manager, Mr. Smith, that they had "observed the initiations of new men in rotary crews in the presence of Mr. Smith which Mr. Smith greatly enjoyed and at which Mr. Smith had hearty laughs."[39] The issue here thus became one of workers' rights to determine and define the elements of their own identities as oil workers, free from managerial supervision, in ways that accentuated both their skill and, sometimes implicitly and sometimes quite explicitly, their gender and class. To assert one's manhood was to claim one's authority and independence from the boss.

More than this, the assumptions behind initiation rites reveal the duality of individualism and collectivity so critical in the processes through which workers socially constructed *skill*: oil-field work, mining, and lumbering jobs all required a combination of ability, perseverance, and strength that could be mastered by relatively few men. The process of acquiring skill was an individual endeavor, but the evaluation of skill—the process through which any individual worker was deemed to *possess* skill—was a collective enterprise, one in which other *workers* determined the attainment of skill. The process of acquiring and then demonstrating one's skill was an important part of workers' occupational subculture. In the settings of Western extractive industries, inexperienced workers stood out in the work gang, sometimes presenting danger to others as well as increasing the daily burden of work for most experienced men. Furthermore, in many settings, such as the oil industry and some logging and mining operations through the 1920s, the authority to hire and fire new workers normally rested with supervising workers (drillers, shift foremen) even within companies having "modern" centralized employment bureaus. A prospective worker would have to prove his ability to the man who would become his immediate supervisor before the latter would offer him the job.[40]

Occupational language, a "folk language of labor" in the words of folklorist Archie Green, further reinforced a highly gendered and sexually charged work world in which male workers defined and asserted their manliness. Words specific to each industry served two purposes: to describe and signify real objects of a specialized and technical nature, and to impart and amplify attitudes that formed the basis of collective identity for this group of industrial workers. It is this latter purpose with which I am concerned in this essay. Most terms used commonly in work settings derived from common English words, and consequently, at least in oil, seemed "incomprehensible and sometimes shocking to the uninitiated."[41]

Workers used words in abstract ways, to signify difference—between workers, between social classes, and between their industry and others. Words thus used become symbols of power relations, used to convey meanings that suggest a collective sense of exploitation and class injustice, indicating a distinctive (if not entirely inclusive) group identity from which an occupational subculture arose. Nowhere is this use of language more apparent than in the creation and employment of derogatory terms. Working-class chauvinism underlied terms of derision and disparagement. As Lalia Phipps Boone notes in her extensive work *The Petroleum Dictionary*, "Field workers generally deride college-trained men who come to the oil fields by the use of various uncomplimentary names. Engineers are called *brainstorms, educated gassers, the guessing department, slip stick artists,* and *the stress and strain department*. Geologists are called *pebble pups, rock hounds, roxies, wrinkle chasers, [mud] smellers,* or *witchers*, depending on their experience and dependability. . . . Representatives from the main offices are *czars* or *wheels*. . . . Employees who secure their positions because they are friends or relatives of the boss are known as *connections* or *parasites* regardless of their skill. Those who maintain very friendly relations with their superiors are known as *meat augers, drapers,* or *grapers*."[42]

In all three industries, "farmers" were men new to the industry, inexperienced and unskilled in the work processes. In the logging camps, experienced men effeminized inexperienced workers by calling them "fuzz faces," (as in pubescent boys), "chics," or "chicadees." Slow workers were called "grandmas." Still more revealing was the use of the phrase "seducing the dog," "dogging it," or "catching the dog" (or "seducing the canine," as it appears in Boone's work) to indicate a loafing employee—at once conflating a despised worker's laziness, inability, and questionable sexuality.[43] Such words of disparagement were imbued with visions of a sexualized class struggle, the meanings of which were readily apparent to a group of men who based their gender identity as workers on the shared values of skill and experience, and the capacity to perform honest manual labor: in short, the ability to produce.

Ritual and language are integral components of cultural dynamism; in this case, myth, too, played a part in the construction of an occupational subculture that celebrated a supposed manliness. Heroic tales of giant men conquering nature in the West are legendary and have assumed often demigod status.[44] More to the point, however, was the appearance and retelling of mythical tales, such as Paul Bunyan stories. The legends of Paul Bunyan, hero of the woods, appeared in workers' oral culture sometime before 1900, then first appeared in print in 1910. Bunyan tales soon spread to other industrial settings: they were apparently first appropriated by oil workers about the turn of the century, perhaps in West Virginia or in Texas.[45] California is the setting for several Bunyan stories, and it is clear that some workers in this state repeated such tall tales by 1920. Although scholars dispute the origin of some Paul Bunyan tales, it is clear that workers created or elaborated upon at least some of these stories.[46] To understand the relationship's among skill, myths, and masculinity, it is essential that one understand the nature and character of mythmaking and myth-telling in the distinctive work cultures of the West's extractive industries. Paul Bunyan myths, as they were told by workers and recorded by ethnologists, folklorists, and lexicographers, are an oral expression of the Midwestern and Western working class. Too often, the Bunyan myths of American mass culture have been excised from the multilayered occupational subculture—ideas about skill and workers' solidarity, the assertion of manhood, the language of work—in which these myths were embedded. Some understanding of the work processes of any given set of workers is needed before one can appreciate the subleties and nuances, the humor, the double meanings, and the subtext of workers' myths.

Let us turn again to the case of oil. Like his woodsman persona, Paul Bunyan the oil worker was a man of gigantic proportion, a worker so strong that he could build a derrick by himself in one day, a man so full of "childish pride" that he seldom admitted defeat. Yet for all his fantastical physical powers, Paul Bunyan made grave mistakes—the clumsy errors of a beginner—that betrayed any causal correlation between strength and skill. Paul was such an eager worker that he consented to labor high up in a tall derrick in Bakersfield during one of that region's legendary wind storms, nothing a straight-thinking worker would have agreed to do. Consequently, he found himself blown five hundred miles out into the Pacific Ocean. On another occasion, when shooting a well with nitroglycerin, his charge exploded before it reached the bottom of the hole, unleashing a "terrific flow of oil" that Paul stopped by sitting on the geyser. This action, however, was ill advised, as the "incredible pressure of gas and oil thus restrained forced the casing out of the ground," carrying Paul with it. In various other tales, Paul Bunyan unknowingly drilled such a crooked hole that the drill pipe exited through the far side of a nearby mountain before his error was detected—hardly the actions of a competent driller. On another rig, Paul encountered a rock formation so hard that it could not be drilled through, so enraging him that he "grabbed the drill pipe, raised it, and threw it down so hard that it broke the rock," causing the entire derrick to collapse—a sure sign that he, as driller, had pushed the tools too forcefully. On yet another occassion, Paul "carelessly allowed himself to be caught in the steel drilling cable while the bit was being lowered into the hole"—a normally horrendous accident feared by all cable drilling crews. In the manner of all tall tales, however, Paul redeemed himself for his careless (and normally fatal) blunder: he found himself carried to hell, where he had a disagreement with the devil, who "chased him back up the well."[47]

In the woods, Paul Bunyan the logger took on two identities. Sometimes he was nothing more than a common worker; more often, he took on the character of the boss. In one story the worker Paul arrives in the Pacific Northwest (from Michigan) in the midst of winter, but is befuddled by the lack of snow and is unable to log successfully the vast stands of Douglas fir, even as "lesser" men continue to harvest the forest all around him. Ever resourceful, Paul and his great blue ox Babe travel to Alaska to harness a glacier and gather loads of snow to bring back to Washington and Oregon, where he uses the slippery snow and ice to skid the logs to their landings along the riverbank, as he had done in Michigan. Unlike other migrant loggers, Paul was unable to adapt to Western conditions, where most logging was carried on in the spring and early fall months; the steepness of Western mountains made snow-assisted logging redundant and dangerous. On another occasion, Paul falls victim to jealousy as another logger matches Paul's Herculean production; as a result, while on a drive down the Columbia River, Paul carelessly permits his logs to jam up the mouth of the great riverway, creating the bar that forever after threatened mariners and fishermen in the region. Recall that all loggers dreaded a logjam and worked fervently to prevent them, sometimes at the risk of their lives.[48] In yet a third story, Paul worked like a madman to log—in clear-cut method—the Dakotas; at the end of his labors, he had removed any semblance of a tree from those upper plains states.

Bunyan also appears as boss—as "man-grabber" in the logger's vernacular—in numerous stories told by western loggers. Here again, Paul's efforts often are for naught. In one story, he takes his gang to the Southwest, where he puts them to work logging the petrified forest of northern Arizona. But, of course, the average logger cannot cut stone; as Paul pushes them to work on New Year's Day, a traditional holiday in the woods, the workers defiantly confront Bunyan the boss, laying down their tools and quitting work in a sit-down strike. Angered by their actions, Paul—in a dual role as boss and scab—chops at the stone trees for "five days and nights," suffering "intensely" before admitting defeat.[49] Elsewhere, Paul builds a huge "uplift camp" full of modern conveniences and luxuries, modeled after Henry Ford's early lumber camps in the upper peninsula of Michigan; but, of course, because such luxuries mask awful exploitative working conditions, the workers refuse to live there. In another story, Paul becomes an "efficiency engineer" and attempts to rid his camp of all those men he perceives as slackers, "moral cowards," and poor workers. But the men strike in response, foiling Bunyan's efforts to increase his profits by speeding up the work process.[50]

The degree to which workers repeated such tall tales is unknown; at least some folklorists collected Paul Bunyan myths, reporting as a mythical figure he was well known throughout the West's timber and oil regions.[51] Furthermore, scholars disagree on the function of myths in establishing a group's identity: is the mythical hero some "projection of the folk" or is the "literature of exaggeration" merely part of an oral culture that is specific to, and arises out of, a particular communal context?[52] Such questions are important, but also remain tangential for the purposes of this discussion. Rather, I would argue, such myths as these Bunyan stories satisfy both categories above, but even more, they are valid expressions of both the person as performer and the community of workers in which these myths first arose before being retold to scholarly audiences.[53] In this case, Paul Bunyan myths reveal the folk and class values of Western workers, values that downplayed physical prowess in work processes by reinforcing workers' belief in *skill* as the most important and distinctive attribute of a competent, successful, manly worker. Paul Bunyan, for all his superhuman strength, often fails in his efforts to harvest the wealth of the forests or to bring in a successful, producing oil well. In both settings, Paul's actions often become blunders, and his persona borders on buffoon-ery—facts readily apparent to skilled workers but imperceptible to most academic observers.

More than this, such myths appeared at a particular historical moment, as new machinery and technologies were introduced to rationalize production processes in both lumbering and oil production in the late nineteenth and early twentieth centuries. In western log-ging operations, mechanization arrived early, turning the skilled log-ger into "merely a timber worker" whose work pace and routine was determined more by the dictate of the donkey engine, Caterpillar trac-tor, and railroad than by the traditions and skill of the hand logger.[54] Even into the mid-twentieth century, gyppo loggers—subcontractors who worked with little machinery—bemoaned the loss of skill inher-ent in the highly mechanized, clear-cut logging operations of western Oregon and Washington. Some gyppos who preferred to log selectively the best trees even considered clear-cutting a waste of western resources brought on by indiscriminate use of heavy machines. Indeed, old-timers referred to mechanized logging as the process of harvesting small trees, known derisively as "dog hairs" and "pecker poles."[55] Similarly, in the oil industry changes in the technology of oil production (brought about by the rapid adoption of the rotary drill in the 1910s and 1920s) led to changes in the labor process that tended to dilute a traditional worker's skill and autonomy even as they allowed a worker to acquire a new set of competencies, thus facilitating changes in the definition of skill. Essentially a large steel augur that ground its way thousands of feet into the ground, the rotary drill was less precise in its operations than cable drilling. Thus, rotary crews had a more difficult time discerning the advance of the drill in oil-bearing geological strata, necessitating the involvement of geologists in determining when to "finish" a well. Rotary drills were both more likely to be abandoned (due to mechanical breakdown) and, con-versely, more likely to cause a disastrous blow-out of a well as the bit pierced the layer of natural gas blanketing oil pools. Nothwithstand-ing these troubles, however, the rotary drill had one definite advan-tage for employers: its production process was easier to learn; it took

Nancy Quam-Wickham

considerably less time to become an experience rotary driller than it did to become a skilled cable-tool driller.[56]

So what should we make of the manly western worker? At a fundamental level, this is a question of agency. Just as they invented their rituals, language, and myths, men who labored in these distinctive industries of the American West helped to develop—and, in the case of oil, create—their industries. Unfamiliar geological, geographical, and natural conditions posed formidable challenges to men as they sought to exploit the region's resources. As they evolved here, these Western industries—mining, oil, and lumbering—were massive, collective enterprises that required ability, inventiveness, and resourcefulness at each step in the production process. Only a few men could do such jobs well. The social acknowledgment of such qualities—ability, inventiveness, and resourcefulness—invested workers with a strong sense of ability. In their language and behavior, workers could possess skill; in turn, *skill* was a defining element in that process by which workers identified themselves as manly men: it separated the men from the boys. The cultural construction of masculinity, of manliness, cannot be disentangled from the very real occupational and historical contexts in which it emerged. Thus, we need to acknowledge the centrality of work in the construction of the legendary manliness of western extractive workers—the men who conquered nature. In the wild and savage West of our imagination, the legends of the manly man—the he-man— might express some idealized masculine virtues. But in the industrialized West, these same legends of manly men signify those qualities that male workers needed to succeed in some of the nation's most dangerous and challenging industries.

## Notes

1. The literature on the West as wild place is so extensive that I will cite only representative works here. See Frederick Jackson Turner, *The Frontier in American History* (New York: Henry Holt, 1921); Henry Nash Smith, *Virgin Land: The American West As Symbol and Myth* (Cambridge, Mass.: Harvard University Press, 1960); Richard Slotkin, *Regeneration through Violence* (Middletown, Conn.: Wesleyan University Press, 1973); and *The Fatal Environment* (New York: Atheneum, 1985); Patricia Nelson Limerick, Clyde A. Milner II, and Charles E. Rankin, eds., *Trails: Toward a New Western History* (Lawrence: University Press of Kansas, 1991).

2. Richard White, "Trashing the Trails," in Limerick, et.al., eds. *Trails: Toward a New Western History*, 35; Charles J. Finger, *A Paul Bunyan Geography* (York, Penn. [privately published], 1931).

3. Katherine G. Morrissey, "Engendering the West," in William Cronon, George Miles, and Jay Gitlin, eds., *Under an Open Sky: Rethinking America's Western Past* (New York: W. W. Norton, 1992), 133.

4. John Emmett Nelligan, *The Life of a Lumberman* (n.p., 1929), 37.

5. Among those few scholars who have examined manhood as a cultural and social construction in the West are John Mack Faragher, *Women and Men on the Overland Trail* (New Haven, Conn.: Yale University Press, 1979); Susan Lee Johnson, "Bulls, Bears, and Dancing Boys: Race, Gender, and Leisure in the California Gold Rush," *Radical History Review* (Fall 1994): 4–37; *Roaring Camp: The Social World of the California Gold Rush* (New York: W.W. Norton, 2000); and Mary Murphy, "Making Men in the West," in Valerie J. Matsumoto and Blake Allmendinger, eds., *Over the Edge: Remapping the American West* (Berkeley and Los Angeles: University of California Press, 1999), 133–47.

6. My discussion of workers' subjective experience of gender, and especially manhood, is informed by Ava Baron's essay "Gender and Labor History: Learning from the Past, Looking to the Future," in Ava Baron, ed., *Work Engendered: Toward a New History of American Labor* (Ithaca, N.Y.: Cornell University Press, 1991), 1–46, especially 14, 27–32; Joan Wallach Scott, *Gender and the Politics of History* (New York: Columbia University Press, 1988), chapters 2 and 5; Joshua B. Freeman, "Hardhats: Construction Workers, Manliness, and the 1970 Pro-War Demonstrations," *Journal of Social History* 26, no. 4 (1993): 725–44; Gail Bederman, *Manliness and Civilization: A Cultural History of Gender and Race in the United States, 1880–1917* (Chicago: University of Chicago Press, 1995), esp. 1–42; Steven Maynard, "Rough Work and Rugged Men: The Social Construction of Masculinity in Working-Class History," *Labour/Le Travail* 23 (1989), 159–69; Margaret S. Creighton, "Davy Jones' Locker Room: Gender and the American Whalemen, 1830–1870," in Margaret Creighton and Lisa Norling, eds., *Iron Ships, Wooden Women: Gender and Seafaring in the Atlantic World, 1700–1920* (Baltimore, Md.: Johns Hopkins University Press, 1996), 118–37, and W. Jeffrey Bolster, "'Every Inch a Man': Gender in the Lives of African-American Seamen, 1800–1860," in Creighton and Norling, eds., *Iron Ships*, 138–68; Peter Stearns, *Be a Man! Males in Modern Society* (New York: Holmes and Meier, 1979), esp. 13–78; Alice Kessler-Harris, "A New Agenda for American Labor History: A Gendered Analysis and the Question of Class," in J. Carroll Moody and Alice Kessler-Harris, eds., *Perspectives on American Labor History: The Problems of Synthesis* (DeKalb: Northern Illinois University Press, 1990), 217–34.

7. Bederman, *Manliness and Civilization*, 7.

8. This theoretical concept of skill is largely drawn from Harry Braverman, *Labor and Monopoly Capital: The Degradation of Work in the Twentieth Century* (New York: Monthly Review Press, 1974), 50–51; Charles More, *Skill and the English Working Class, 1870–1914* (London: Croon Helm, 1980), 15–17, 22–23.

9. Mark Wyman, *Hard Rock Epic: Western Miners and the Industrial Revolution, 1860–1910* (Berkeley and Los Angeles: University of California Press, 1979); Richard Lingenfelter, *The Hardrock Miners: A History of the Mining Labor Movement in the American West, 1863–1893* (Berkeley and Los Angeles: University of California Press, 1974); Caroline Bancroft, "Folklore of the Central City District, Colorado," *California Folklore Quarterly* 4 (1945): 315–42, esp. 316–22; Vernon Jensen, *Lumber and Labor* (New York: Farrar and Rhinehart, 1945); Thomas Cox, *Mills and Markets: A History of the Pacific Coast Lumber Industry to 1900* (Seattle: University of Washington Press, 1974); William G. Robbins, *Lumberjacks and Legislators: Political Economy of the U.S. Lumber Industry, 1890–1941* (College Station: Texas A&M University Press, 1982).

10. Paul F. Lambert and Kenny A. Franks, *Voices from the Oil Fields* (Norman: University of Oklahoma Press, 1984); Nancy Quam-Wickham, "Petroleocrats and Proletarians: Work, Culture, and Politics in the California Oil Industry, 1917–1925" (Ph.D. diss., University of California-Berkeley 1994).

11. Nelligan, *Lumberman*, 141, 135–36.

12. Richard Rajala, "Bill and the Boss: Labor Protest, Technological Change, and the Transformation of the West Coast Logging Camp, 1890–1930," *Journal of Forest History* 33 (1989): 168–79, quote from 170.

13. Wayland D. Hand, "The Folklore, Customs, and Traditions of the Butte Miner," *California Folklore Quarterly* 5 (1946): 155.

14. Walter R. Crane, *Gold and Silver* (New York: John Wiley, 1908), 11–12.

15. For comprehensive discussions of the technological differences in western mining regions, see Crane, *Gold and Silver*; Rossiter W. Raymond, *Silver and Gold: An Account of the Mining and Metallurgical Industry of the United States* (New York: J. B. Ford, 1873).

16. Victor Ziegler, *Oil Well Drilling Methods* (New York: John Wiley, 1923), 11–12, 35.

17. Lester Charles Uren, *A Textbook of Petroleum Production Engineering* (New York: McGraw-Hill, 1924), 127, v, vi.

18. Ibid., 127–128.

19. U.S. Bureau of Labor Statistics, Bulletin No. 297, "Wages and Hours of Labor in the Petroleum Industry, 1920" (Washington, D.C.: Government Printing Office, 1920), 9.

20. F. J. S. Sur, *Oil Prospecting, Drilling and Extraction* (Calgary, Alb., n.p. [the author?], 1914), 26.

21. California State Council of Defense, *Report of the Committee on Petroleum* (Sacramento: State Printing Office, 1917), 125.

22. Frederick R. Pond, "Language of the California Oil Fields," *American Speech* 7 (1932): 270; Ziegler, *Methods*, 111.

23. Ibid., 265.

24. Women workers were rare in all industries under discussion here. They constituted less than 1 percent of all wage earners in the oil industry in California in 1920, a percentage that remained constant until the early 1970s, except for a very brief time during World War II, and then only temporarily and mostly in the refining branch. See U. S. Department of Commerce, Bureau of the Census, *Fourteenth Census: Population,* vol. 4 (Washington, D.C.: Government Printing Office, 1923), 882–85; and Beth Randolph, "Women in the California Oil Industry during World War II," 1986, seminar paper; manuscript in possession of author. Similarly, in logging and mining operations, women were equally unrepresented in the labor force, where they seldom appeared before the 1930s, and then generally only as camp cooks. Among western miners, so rare were women that some men refused to go into the mine if there was a woman nearby, as a woman in the mine was considered a "bad omen." The origin of this belief seems to lie in the fact that women appeared at the mine face only after fires or other disasters, as they waited for their menfolk—or, more commonly, the bodies of their deceased menfolk—to be retrieved from the mine. On miners, see Wayland D. Hand, "Folklore from Utah's Silver Mining Camps," *Journal of American Folklore* 54 (1941): 132–61. On logging, see Julie Anderson, *I Married a Logger* (New York: Exposition Press, 1951); Margaret Elley Felt, *Gyppo Logger* (Caldwell, Idaho: Caxton, 1963).

25. *Kern County Union Labor Journal*, February 8, 1919; *Taft Daily Midway Driller*, December 23, 1918.

26. Dyer Bennett provides these attributes in an interview with Jean Howlett, November 17, 1981, Brea, California, for the Brea Community History Project, Oral History Program, California State University-Fullerton, 27.

27. Ivan "Red" Carey, interview with Kaye Briegel, Long Beach, California, 1978, in Petroleum Collection, Special Collections, California State University-Long Beach.

28. See, for instance, *Kern County Union Labor Journal*, January 18, 1919, and March 18, 1919.

29. *Signal Hill Leader*, December 23, 1927.

30. Jimmie Cook, "The Oil Patch: A Part of the Passing Parade," *Journal of American Culture* 14, no.2 (1991): 121–24, quote on 123.

31. *Signal Hill Leader*, January 6, 1928.

32. Oil-field memoirs, fiction, and other works abound with such stories of hazing new workers. See, for instance, Gerald Lynch, *Roughnecks, Drillers, and Tool Pushers: Thirty-three Years in the Oil Fields* (Austin: University of Texas Press, 1987), 4–6; Roger M. Olien and Diana Davids Olien, *Oil Booms: Social Change in Five Texas Towns* (Lincoln: University of Nebraska Press, 1982), 146–47; Lorecia East, *The Boomers: The Autobiography of a Roughneck's Wife* (Baton Rouge, La.: Legacy, 1976), 17–18.

33. Pete Davis to [Richard] Hathaway, n.d., [c. 1978?], in Richard Hathaway Collection, Hathaway Ranch Museum, Santa Fe Springs, California.

34. See below; also see, for instance, the accounts of "Robert the Roustabout," who wrote euphemistically about how older workers viewed new workers, especially "college boys" like himself, with disdain in the 1920s: "It is no place for a weakling, nor for a sensitive individual . . . those who are left are pretty well case-hardened to all kinds of profanity, shocks, and various other evils." ["Robert the Roustabout"], "A Freshman in the Oil Country," (2d installment), *Petroleum World: A Western Journal of the Oil and Allied Industries* 9, no.9 (1924): 30.

35. Gerald Haslam, *The Language of the Oil Fields: Examination of an Industrial Argot* (Penngrove, Calif.: Old Adobe Press, 1972), 48–54, quote from 51.

36. Nelligan, *Lumberman*, 125–26. The name loggers gave to this ritual—the "sheep game"—deserves some comment here. Westerners commonly scorned the sheep as a range animal, destructive to the land and its workers alike: cowboys of the day referred to sheep as "maggots" and shepherds as "scab-herders." In the nineteenth-century West, a "sheep" was sometimes an opprobrious term for a "second-class" man; in the maritime trades, a "sheep's-pen" was where midshipmen were housed aboard ship. And an association of the animal with the generic human qualities of stupidity and timidity goes back to Shakespearean times. More particular to logging, a "sheepherder" was the "logger's idea of a useless man." See Ramon Adams, *Western Words* (Norman: University of Oklahoma, 1968); Dean Walter F. McCulloch, *Woods Words: A Comprehensive Dictionary of Loggers Terms* ([Portland]: Oregon Historical Society, 1958), 161.

37. Wayland D. Hand, "The Folklore, Customs, and Traditions of the Butte Miner (Conclusion)," *California Folklore Quarterly* 5 (1946): 153–78, quotes from 164–65.

38. Davis to Hathaway, n.d. c. 1978?, Hathaway Collection, Hathaway Ranch Museum, Santa Fe Springs, California.

39. Charles V. Hatter to Mr. F. C. Ripley, Chanslor-Canfield Midway Oil Company (CCMO), Los Angeles, November 22, 1932, in file folder: "Confidential Reports on Field Activity (1932–1936, Partial)," F. C. Ripley Papers, California Petroleum Industry Collection, Long Beach Public Library, Long Beach, California. This file, one of two such folders, consists of extensive labor spy reports, covering a span of seven years and amounting to more than three hundred pages of text, submitted by various operatives to the management of CCMO.

40. Paul F. Brissenden, "Labor Policies and Labor Turnover in the California Oil-Refining Industry," *Monthly Labor Review* 9 (1919): 970–71; Richard Rajala, "Bill and the Boss: Labor Protest, Technological Change, and the Transformation of the West Coast Logging Camp, 1890–1930," *Journal of Forest History* 33 (1989), 168–79, esp. 169–71.

41. Lalia Phipps Boone, *The Petroleum Dictionary* (Norman: University of Oklahoma Press, 1952), 4; Pond, "Language of the California Oil Fields," 261–72; Clark S. Northrup, "The Language of the Oil Wells," *Dialect Notes* 2 (1903/1904): 338–46, 393–93; Leon Hines, "Pipe Line Terms," *American Speech* 17 (1942), 280–82; A. R. McTee, "Oil Field Diction," *Publications of the Texas Folk-Lore Society* 4 (1925): 64–67; Arthur T. King, "Oil Refinery Terms," *Publication of the American Dialect Society* 9 (1947); Haslam, *The Language of the Oil Fields*, 14–15.

42. Boone, *Dictionary*, 32. Emphasis in the original.

43. See Boone, *Dictionary*, 34, 265, on this phrase, and, more generally, Haslam, *The Language of the Oil Field*, 54–60, more generally on derogatory language and sexual symbolism.

44. On this point, see Richard W. Etulain, *Re-imagining the Modern American West: A Century of Fiction, History, and Art* (Tuscon: University of Arizona Press, 1996), xviii–xx.

45. John Lee Brooks, "Paul Bunyan: Oil Man," *Publications of the Texas Folk-Lore Society* 7 (1928), 46–47, asserts that Bunyan stories were familiar to the West Virginia cable-tool drillers that he worked for in Texas about 1920; Mody C. Boatright, on the other hand, could not locate any workers from the Appalachia fields who remembered

Paul Bunyan tales, suggesting that Texas was the place of their first appearance; see Boatright, *Folklore of the Oil Industry* (Dallas: Southern Methodist University Press, 1963), 168–69.

46. Gladys J. Haney, "Paul Bunyan Twenty-five Years Ago," *Journal of American Folklore* 55 (1942), 155–68; Nelligan, *Lumberman*, 126; McCulloch, *Woods Words*, 132; Charles P. Loomis, "Lineman's English," *American Speech* 1 (1926), 659–60; Archie Green, *Wobblies, Pile Butts, and Other Heroes: Laborlore Explorations* (Urbana: University of Illinois Press, 1993), 19. In the latter work, laborlore specialist Green cautions that "we ought not to be deflected by questions of where particular heroes originated. Rather, we need to understand the complex relationship of folklore to popular culture. Who expanded the Paul Bunyan narratives—and why?"

47. Boatright, *Folklore of the Oil Industry*, 165–69 ; Acel Garland, "Pipeline Days and Paul Bunyan," *Publications of the Texas Folk-Lore Society* 7 (1928): 59.

48. Ida Virginia Turney, *Paul Bunyan Comes West* (New York: Houghton Mifflin, 1928), 24; James Cloyd Bowman, *The Adventures of Paul Bunyan* (New York: The Century Company, 1927), 243–67; Charles J. Finger, *A Paul Bunyan Geography*.

49. Finger, *A Paul Bunyan Geography*, 32–33.

50. Stan Newton, *Paul Bunyan of the Great Lakes* (Chicago: Packard and Company, 1946), 120–28; on Ford's lumber camps, which remakably resembled Bunyan's "uplift camp" down to the weekly bath requirement, see Nelligan, *Lumberman*, 127–28; Bowman, Paul Bunyan, 143–50; Rajala, 168–79.

51. Brooks, *Oil Man*, 50–51; Garland, "Pipeline Days," 59; Boatright, *Folklore of the Oil Industry*, 165; Pond, "Language of the California Oil Fields"; Haney, "Paul Bunyan Twenty-Five Years Ago," 155–68. Lexicographers also note the universal nature of oilfield language and storytelling; see Thomas L. Crowell, "Universality of Petroleum Terminology," *American Speech* 24 (1949): 201–06.

52. Boatright, *Folklore of the Oil Industry*, 192.

53. Folklorists classify such myths and "belief stories" as "culturally liminal," expressing themes that mediate between personal experience and the shared culture of a particular community. See Gillian Bennett, "'Belief Stories': The Forgotten Genre," *Western Folklore* 48 (1989): 289–322, esp. 301; Donald War, "On the Genre Morphology of Legendry: Belief Stories versus Belief Legend," *Western Folklore* 50 (1991): 296–303; Dan Ben Amos, "Toward a Definition of Folklore in Context," *Journal of American Folklore* 84 (1971), 3–15. I argue that Bunyan myths constitute part of workers' laborlore, defined by Archie Green as covering all forms of "expressivity by workers themselves and their allies: utterance, representation, symbol, code, artifact, belief, ritual." See Green, *Wobblies, Pile Butts, and Other Heroes*, 7. I have emphasized here those stories that individual authors have identified as having come directly from workers themselves. See, for example, the foreword to Newton, *Paul Bunyan of the Great Lakes*, 13–15.

54. Jensen, *Lumber and Labor*, 23, 102–103; Rajala, "Bill and the Boss," 169–71; Rajala, "The Forest As Factory: Technological Change and Worker Control in the West Coast Logging Industry, 1880–1930," *Labour/Le Travail* 32 (1993): 73–104.

55. On this point, see Felt, *Gyppo Logger;* William G. Robbins, *Hard Times in Paradise: Coos Bay, Oregon, 1850–1986* (Seattle: University of Washington, 1988), 121–22; Richard White, "'Are You an Environmentalist or Do You Work for a Living?': Work and Nature," in William Cronon, ed., *Uncommon Ground: Toward Reinventing Nature* (New York: W. W. Norton, 1994), 171–85.

56. Various authorities disagree on the length of time it took a man to become a rotary driller. One government report estimated that it took "more than one year" for "drillers, tool-dressers, pumpmen, machinists, engineers, gagers [*sic*], foremen, geologists, superintendents and others" to "acquire the necessary skill and experience in their work." California State Council of Defense, *Report of the Committee on Petroleum*, 125. Uren, *A Textbook*, 184, implies that it took only "several" years, rather than the twelve or

more needed for a cable tool driller, for a man to become a skilled rotary driller. Some men worked as roustabouts (general laborers) or roughnecks for several years before working on rotary rigs or as rotary drillers. See Perry Chansler, interview with Gail Norman-Bilby, May 18, 1982, Brea, California, for the Brea Community History Project, Oral History Program, California State University-Fullerton; Ivan Carey interview; Paul F. Lambert and Kenny A. Franks, eds., *Voices from the Oil Fields,* 38, 41 (quote), 56.

# PART 2

# Learning to Be Men

# "Building Better Men"

## The CCC Boy and the Changing Social Ideal of Manliness

JEFFREY RYAN SUZIK

Less than one month after his inauguration as president of the United States in March 1933, Franklin D. Roosevelt signed a bill creating the Civilian Conservation Corps (CCC). The CCC was the first work relief program instituted by Roosevelt's New Deal.[1] Young unmarried and unemployed men between the ages of eighteen and twenty-five were chosen from relief rolls and sent to live and work in wooded camps where they planted trees, built bridges, and fought forest fires. The program undoubtedly developed out of Roosevelt's personal interest in the conservation of natural resources, but even more so, it grew out of a societal concern about the uncertain occupational prospects of America's jobless male youth.

The CCC quickly became a rallying point around which society discussed and debated the precarious future of young American manhood. Supporters of the CCC—as well as the organization itself—argued that it could literally "build better men" by offering out-of-work youth the jobs society had denied them. Furthermore, the CCC, its proponents contended, would help prepare these inexperienced working-class male youths for future lives as independent breadwinners by teaching them to use and manipulate heavy machinery such as mechanized backhoes, tractors, and electric lathes. According to official program statements and publicity reports, this technological skill, built in the CCC, would make its alumni more attractive candidates to industrial employers hiring in the private sphere. In addition, by gaining relatively small amounts of technological and vocational training in the CCC, jobless boys could attain a most powerful social validation of their manhood—self-sufficient breadwinning—and in turn become bona fide men themselves. In much of the publicity they generated concerning the "man-building" aspects of the program, CCC administrators made strong connections between masculinity, work, and the development of technologically based skills.[2]

From its inception in 1933 to its termination in 1942, the CCC fostered a great deal of social discourse over what masculinity meant to American society, what it did and did not consist of, and how the CCC could best ensure its development in boys coming of age in a time of economic crisis. This essay traces the representation of the "rebuilt" CCC boy as a symbol of ideal American manliness. It examines statements concerning the program's goals of building "better" men that appeared in official publicity materials and press releases as well as in stories and articles from popular sources. At the same time, the essay shows how voices from the grassroots, heard mainly through the exchange of letters with the CCC director's office, helped to shape and define the manly ideal that the program promised its enrollees. Finally, this essay suggests that societal conceptions of ideal gender types—in this case, of men—cannot be divorced from an ever-changing social context.[3] How a society understands and defines "appropriate" roles and behaviors for men and women, I argue, is not transhistorical; rather, it is connected to changes that may occur in the political, economic, or social spheres.

## Setting the Sociocultural Context: Masculinity in the Depression Era

The CCC and the image of the ideal CCC boy did indeed emerge out of a specific social and cultural context. By the early 1930s, American society had become increasingly aware of a growing number of youth problems born out of the ravages of the Great Depression. As the following poem, published in a June 1933 issue of the social work journal *Survey Graphic* so well reveals, during the Great Depression, work—or the lack thereof—seems to have been on virtually every man's mind.

Idle Men

Slowly great buildings rise while men
Look on who may not aid,
Those who had thought no task too great
Now idle, and afraid.

Deftly the stones are placed while they,
With hunger in their eyes,
Dream in a mute, half-hopeless way
Of work as paradise.[4]

This, I would argue, held doubly true for young men on the verge of adult manhood in the early 1930s. Coming of age at a time of economic crisis in a society that placed so much cultural emphasis on the connections between adult masculinity and independence, breadwin-

Jeffrey Ryan Suzik

ning, and work had made more than a few young American men nervous and insecure about their futures, quite simply, as men.[5]

Social commentators had grown increasingly worried about the large number of young men who were unable to find work. In their now-classic 1937 study, *Middletown in Transition*, Robert and Helen Lynd found that people in that particular American community saw hard work as the key to a man's success and that his societal worth was measured almost entirely upon his economic solvency.[6] Similarly, psychologist Winifred V. Richmond warned that the lack of self-sustaining job opportunities for boys coming of age in the early 1930s presented them with tremendous difficulties in "attaining manhood in a world [that had become] practically as unstable as adolescence itself."[7] Without work, and a concomitant ability to provide for himself and his family, a "boy" could not really become a "man" at all. This cultural understanding of adult masculinity left unemployed boys, ones on the cusp of adult manhood, in a particularly precarious position.[8]

By 1932 a full 25 percent of boys between the ages of fifteen and twenty-four were totally unemployed; and an additional 29 percent could find nothing but low-paying part-time work.[9] If work itself was "paradise," a well-recognized cultural symbol of manly independence and strength, then for most young men hoping to strike out on their own in the 1930s it was a paradise postponed, and an adult manliness as of yet unrealized.

Working-class boys, especially, had reason to be concerned about their abilities to rise to a "man's estate" through regular, full-time employment. A study completed in Menden, Connecticut, in 1935 found that working-class youth on average were waiting from between one and five years to find "permanent" jobs after finishing school.[10] Overall, working-class boys tended to have had very little technological or vocational training or experience and were subsequently turned away time and again from prospective industrial employers who favored better skilled, more experienced workers.[11] Even those boys who had been "trained" for future careers as machinists and machine operators were more often than not coming up empty-handed in the job market. A 1934 report prepared by the Division of Instruction and Research of the Milwaukee Vocational School found that one year after graduation, a whopping 74 percent of the school's male graduates were still without jobs.[12] In 1937, looking back at the "nascent" youth problem of 1932 and 1933, Aubrey Williams of the National Youth Administration described the occupational dilemma facing young men (not just working-class ones) well. "Youth had the door of opportunity closed to him," Williams noted. "A boy reaches that stage of life where he should begin to be self-supporting; to take his place as a functioning unit in society; to make the final transition from youth's to man's estate. The traditional means of such a step is through a job, but there is no job for him. He trudges the streets day after day. He becomes discouraged and the fear dawns that his society which his elders have built does not need him."[13]

Due, then, to the convergence of widespread economic depression, an overly saturated industrial job market, and most working-class boys' lack of vocational and technological training or job experience, the "normal life sequences" of working-class male youth were being either interrupted or totally blocked in the early 1930s.[14] Instead of entering adult male jobs in industry, earning adult male wages, and subsequently assuming adult male roles as self-sufficient breadwinners, many a young working-class man was wasting away, it was argued, in an emasculated state of perpetual dependency. Without gainful employment, a boy coming of age could never truly be self-sufficient and economically independent. And without that self-sufficiency and independence, very possibly, he would remain a mere boy in the eyes of society. Even worse yet, he would be in danger of being labeled a "sissy."

The term *sissy* took on new meaning when in 1948 British cultural anthropologist Geoffrey Gorer published a provocative account of early-twentieth-century American society. Gorer based his arguments in *The American People: A Study in National Character* on research trips he made to the United States between 1935 and 1939. Americans, Gorer argued, were overwhelmingly concerned—obsessed, even—with proving their independence and their self-reliance. American society perceived dependence of any kind as weak, and labeled those who were unduly dependent on others as "sissies." "Being a sissy," Gorer wrote, "is a key concept for the understanding of American character; it has no exact parallel in any other society. Although it is analogous to some English terms of opprobrium (e.g. milksop, cry-baby, nancy, mother's darling) it is more than any of them. Schematically, it means showing more dependence or fear or lack of initiative or passivity than is suitable for the occasion."[15] Americans, Gorer argued, were deathly afraid of being called sissies. He described American parents as preoccupied by an "overwhelming fear . . . that their child would turn into a sissy." He even suggested that a good deal of American speech and public activity was "designed solely to avert this damning judgement."[16]

But according to Gorer, one was not born a sissy; one *became* a sissy. What is most important here is the connection Gorer made between what Americans defined as sissified behavior and what they considered unnaturally prolonged dependency. To prevent the possibility of permanent emasculation, or, to coin a phrase, "sissification," many Americans believed boys coming of age needed to be given every opportunity to strike out on their own, thereby proving their manly independence and self-reliance—even if social or economic forces did not fully cooperate.

By 1933, most social commentators agreed that the young male unemployment problem lay well beyond the capabilities of local charitable organizations and job placement agencies. In response to what was now deemed to be a calamitous situation for the nation, calls went out for a new system of youth relief, one able to quell societal fears over young men's uncertain prospects as future independent bread-winners and, consequently, as men. Not surprisingly, with the coming of Roosevelt's New Deal policies and the subsequent burgeoning of the American state, that call was answered (in part) by the U.S. federal government. Within three weeks of his inauguration as president, Roosevelt had successfully pushed legislation through Congress that would (he and many others hoped) solve the occupational and psychological crises facing male youth. That legislation created the CCC; and with it, the federal government's involvement in the "man-building" process began in earnest.

## Social Discourse and the Construction of an Ideal CCC Boy

From the outset, public interest in the CCC was tremendous. The program promised to give discouraged, unemployed young men the chance to support themselves financially and in so doing to attain manly independence. At the same time, it would seek to build up their bodies and their self-esteem through the virtues of hard work. Furthermore, the CCC camp experience would teach boys to master technological skills that would (ostensibly) make them more attractive job candidates to industrial employers. Without a doubt, supporters suggested, the CCC would save America's young men both from lives either as transient drifters or as dependent "sissies." While the CCC built bridges, fought forest fires, planted trees, and repaired diesel engines, the program also set out to transform the country's at-risk boys into self-supporting men.

Grassroots voices, including special interest groups, reformers, and concerned individuals—as well as legislators and policymakers—contributed to and shaped the social discourse of ideal manliness that developed around the CCC and the CCC boy. Policymakers and CCC administrators, I contend, did not (nor could they) define the program's goals within a social vacuum. Publicity reports and press releases reveal the CCC administration's awareness of, and interplay with, grassroots opinions.[17]

Gaining and later maintaining the popularity of the CCC was a major goal of the director's office.[18] To do this successfully, administrators like CCC directors Robert Fechner and James McEntee had to tap into grassroots sentiments of all kinds.[19] Without at least acknowledging such sentiments, they could not hope to "sell" the program to the American public. Without a doubt, the CCC's goal of transforming wayward youth into upstanding young men rested squarely upon society's general understanding of who an upstanding young man was. For instance, in the program's early years pacifism and anti-war sentiments bubbling up from the grassroots strongly shaped the masculine ideal offered by the CCC. Calls for a peaceful, nonmilitaristic CCC boy dominated the discourse. When publicity reports portrayed the socially reformed CCC boy in both texts and photos, his manly identity revolved almost entirely around his financial independence, his physically enhanced body, and his role as a productive, technologically adept worker. In the program's early years, a military model for manliness was never offered, at least officially.

By the late 1930s, however, the tides of public opinion had begun to change as American society prepared itself for yet another war. As early as 1938, the need for wartime preparedness began to replace pacifist isolationism as the dominant voice in the social discourse;[20] along with this marked change in public opinion came a strikingly different societal understanding of masculinity, and this, in turn, led to a reconceived ideal for the CCC boy. Military service was no longer perceived by many in American society as anathema. In fact, it resurfaced as an integral stepping stone to adult manhood. In light of the new national emergency—war—society's conception of true manliness almost necessarily included young men in roles not only as workers and providers but as soldiers as well.[21]

## A Day in the Life of the CCC Boy

After a boy enrolled in the CCC, he went through a two-week period of physical hardening and body conditioning at army outposts. Enrollees then filled positions in camps located in all forty-eight states, as well as the territories of Alaska, Hawaii, Puerto Rico, and the U.S. Virgin Islands. Boys entered these camps, generally numbering two hundred enrollees in all, for six-month periods, and many reenlisted for up to twelve additional months. In addition to receiving room, board, medical attention, and educational opportunities, enrollees earned one dollar per day in wages. Every month, CCC boys were required by law to remit a substantial twenty five of their thirty dollars in wages to parents or guardians. Enrollees retained five dollars in pocket money for their personal expenses.

Like many other New Deal relief programs, the CCC made use of existing governmental infrastructure to coordinate its efforts. A total of four Federal departments administered the CCC, with a director's office coordinating the necessary interactions between the cooperating departments. The U.S. Department of Labor was responsible for enlisting state and local relief agencies to select enrollees from relief rolls; the Departments of Agriculture and Interior organized the actual conservation work projects and provided experienced foresters and woodsmen to supervise the labor. Finally, the Department of War—

specifically, the army—controlled the camps themselves. Reserve army officers received peacetime commissions as commanding officers of the camps, and as a result, a modified system of military rules and regulations shaped the CCC boys' camp experiences.

During their eight-hour workdays, enrollees were under the supervision of local foresters who assigned them to various projects. Perhaps the most lasting—and visible—contribution of the CCC to the American conservation movement, however, was the program's reforestation effort. More than half of the trees ever planted in the United States can be credited to the CCC.[22] In fact, one of the first nicknames given to the CCC by the enthusiastic press was "Roosevelt's Tree Army," indicative of the major role it played in the reforesting of America.[23] After a full day's work, enrollees left the supervision of the forestry services and were turned over to the army officers, who supervised the camps themselves. Following a formal "company" dinner for which they were required to change into clean dress uniforms, enrollees were generally free to spend the evening hours as they wished. Most camps were equipped with canteens where boys could congregate, play pool, smoke cigarettes, and listen to music.

Camps also offered a wide range of athletic opportunities. Boys participated in frequent baseball tournaments and boxing matches, and teams from other nearby camps were invited to weekend competitions. Weekends also provided free time for boys to explore the local surroundings, and many chose to frequent taverns, dance halls, and even houses of prostitution in the nearest towns. Although these were among the influences from which the CCC ostensibly was attempting to "save" the boys, few restrictions were placed upon enrollees' behavior when they were away from camp, as long as they returned by the start of the workday on Monday morning.[24]

Needy boys enrolled in the CCC in three-month intervals. Typically, some 100,000 new enrollees entered the camps at any one enrollment period, joining the 250,000 or so experienced CCC boys who "re-upped" their tours of duty for an additional six months. By the time of the CCC's termination in June 1942, over 2.9 million young men had gone through the program.[25] In the minds of administrators and much of American society in general, boys who had entered camp listless, broken down, and discouraged emerged six months or a year later as responsible breadwinners, self-reliant workers, and all-around better men.

## Defining the Ideal—Correspondence with the Grassroots, 1933–1936

From virtually the moment of its inception, the CCC and its administrators had to contend with questions and criticisms about the role of the army in what, by all accounts, was intended to be a purely civilian relief enterprise. Robert Fechner, director of the CCC from 1933 to

1939, and others in the organization who had control over publicity and press releases were extremely concerned with dispelling rumors about militaristic training occurring in the camps. Press releases were worded with care so as not to suggest that the army played any more of a role than was deemed "appropriate" in the shaping of the boys' new manly countenances. When visuals like photographs and drawings began to be used in publicity as well, anything that might appear even remotely militaristic was censored. Again and again, from the program's creation in March 1933 right up until Congress approved noncombatant military training for CCC enrollees in 1941, the director's office would downplay and/or deny any aspect of camp life that may have smacked of militarism or warmongering.[26]

Throughout its existence, the CCC was publicized as a training ground in which boys could develop into self-sufficient adult men. But CCC training would not, at least initially, include military drills. Rather, the CCC's instructional schemes would revolve around the development of technological skills befitting CCC boys' eventual absorption into the working-class world of industrial production. In the program's early years, from its inception in 1933 to about 1937, any training CCC boys received, and any skills they were taught, were linked explicitly to job attainment and the concomitant manly self-sufficiency those skills would bring. As Fechner took great pains to point out, the CCC's daily regimen would remain free of "militaristic routine of any character."[27] The army, he explained, had been incorporated as an organizational necessity and nothing more.[28] The CCC boy was not going to be molded into a soldier, but rather into a competent worker and economic provider.

In a society that had grown weary of war and skeptical of too many European entanglements, many did not believe military training camps to be appropriate places for men to assert their manly characters.[29] And as Michael Kimmel has argued, even though heroic victories in World War I temporarily provided positive affirmation of doughboys' masculinities, real "military glory had proven elusive" to most American servicemen. Throughout the 1920s and 1930s cases of "paralysis, convulsions, paraplegias, tics and tremors of the battle-weary soldiers . . . flooded the psychiatric literature."[30] In the long term, the lasting effects of the Great War proved more debilitating than uplifting to veterans' masculine identities.

At the same time, grassroots pacifist organizations were achieving substantial successes in their postwar campaigns to "agitate against and to [publicly] argue the folly" of war. Groups like the Women's Peace Society were determined to protect the next generation of Americans from the horrors of rampant militarism, going so far as to hand out leaflets in front of department stores "protest[ing] against the display and sale of war-like toys."[31] Pacifists responded forcefully to anything they saw as an attempt to indoctrinate children or youth—

particularly males—with militaristic rhetoric. The CCC, with its army-controlled camps, therefore became an immediate object of pacifist scrutiny. Concerned citizens maintained that manliness need not be affirmed through military training, and they sought to forcefully impose that vision on the CCC's training programs as well.

Official statements by the CCC administration tried to reassure wary pacifists and other groups that the CCC was not in any way a military training camp masquerading as a relief program. Fechner's first informational bulletin to prospective enrollees assured them that joining the CCC was not the same thing as signing up for boot camp. The bulletin, released to the press on April 17, 1933—several weeks before large-scale selection had even begun—was the most comprehensive explanation to date of just what the CCC was intending to do for out-of-work American youth.[32] At the same time, the bulletin made definite statements about what the program would not be doing to them. Even at this early date Fechner seems to have anticipated the questions that would hound him for several years to come.

The report was literally a list of questions, followed by Fechner's answers. Would army regulations in the camps turn CCC boys into gun-toting soldiers ready for frontline duty? Of course not, Fechner said. The men "will be civilians and will be treated as civilians." Would desperate boys looking for no more than a chance to work and to be self-supporting arrive at camp only to find themselves marching in formation to a military beat? Fechner assured that there would be "neither military drill nor military discipline" in the camps. And furthermore, Fechner promised, CCC boys would not even look like soldiers: "The clothing which they receive from the Army will be work clothes, not military uniforms."[33] Military training and battlefield heroics were not to be the focus of the ideal, hardworking, financially independent CCC boy's life.

As much as Fechner might have hoped that tackling the issue head-on would calm societal fears over the program's "militarism," he would have no such luck. During the program's first three years, from 1933 until about 1936, the director's office was forced to respond to nearly constant written inquiries on the subject.[34]

Letters voiced concerns over the role the army was playing, had played, and should or should not continue to play in the administration of the camps. Pacifists from around the country wrote to Fechner asking him either to confirm or deny press reports of militaristic activities in the conditioning camps.[35] Labor unions mounted letter writing campaigns, in some cases inundating the director's office with multiple copies of the same motion. In February and March of 1935 Fechner received individual letters from thirteen local units of the Illinois Workers' Alliance. Each one demanded, in almost identical fashion, that the army's role in the camps be abolished. This, they said, was the only way to ensure working-class youth's "right to live as human beings" and not as conscripted soldiers.[36]

CCC boys themselves often wrote to Fechner or Roosevelt complaining that officers in their camps were attempting to enforce military discipline upon them and asked that it be stopped.[37] Mothers of enrollees made emotional pleas against military training in the CCC as well. One mother visited her son at camp and found it to be a "paradise for the boys." Yet, even though she herself had not witnessed anything at all militaristic about the camp, people she trusted ensured her that the boys there were being transformed into war-hungry soldiers. If her boy was indeed being trained for war, she said, "I would like to have [him] back."[38]

When Ellen Starr Brinton of the Women's International League for Peace and Freedom wrote to Fechner in June 1933, she voiced the mixed feelings a good deal of Americans were starting to have about the army's role in the program. Brinton acknowledged the debt the American public owed to the CCC for its attempts to save young men from the degradations of poverty; she hoped that the program could still prove to be a "marvelous opportunity" for the "handling of human beings and re-dignifying labor." The program's present format, however, worried her. As she warned Fechner, the "military institution builds a military mind." Army officers, she said, were incapable of doing much more than teaching "men to shoot straight." With army men parading about the camps, boys would be transformed not into better workers and independent economic providers, but rather into war-hungry militants. To train boys appropriately for lives as adult male workers in a peaceful world, Fechner needed to "place civilians with authority in every one of those camps."[39]

Letter writers such as these contributed a great deal to the ongoing social discourse about what the identity of a truly masculine, reinvigorated CCC boy should be. In their letters, writers like Brinton intimated that American masculinity need not (and should not) be affirmed through military training. Additionally, they offered suggestions as to how the CCC might go about making weak, undernourished boys into strong, stalwart men free from the presence of guns, uniforms, marching, or warfare.

Yet it was more than just idle talk. Grassroots opinions such as these undoubtedly influenced the administration's development of camp policies and procedures, and in turn, the evolving image of the remasculinized CCC boy. A relevant example of this came in mid-May 1933, a month after the first camp was mobilized. The CCC Advisory Council (CCCAC), which included Fechner and one member from each of the four coordinating departments, was still only beginning to outline various aspects of camp organization. One policy not yet determined was how the camps would deal with discipline problems. In a letter dated May 15, 1933, W. Frank Persons, U.S. Labor Department representative to the CCCAC, counseled Fechner on the evolving camp disciplinary system.[40] He reminded Fechner of how "exceedingly important" it would be to word the order carefully "as to avoid the public impression that military discipline in disguised form is being imposed."[41] As Fechner was already well aware, much of the public was not willing to accept too strong a role for the military in the lives of the enrollees, nor in its still nascent man-building agenda.

To allay the possible societal fears, Persons suggested a system of penalties based on those customarily used by industrial employers. Penalties for infractions would include admonition, suspension of certain privileges, or a substantial fine of up to three dollars—more than half the CCC boy's allotted pocket money for a month. There would be no military-styled detention cells, nor would military techniques of discipline be used. Indeed, it was befitting that an organization so ostensibly wedded to the notion that its enrollees were being trained in the skills necessary in the workaday world of industrial production would choose to model its in-camp penal system after an industrial model. Fechner obviously agreed with the recommendation, and on June 12, Roosevelt approved the order exactly as Persons had worded it.[42]

Of course, not everything that special interest groups suggested was implemented as policy by the CCC; nor did all grassroots correspondence in this period come strictly from pacifists or liberals. The National Rifleman's Association of America (NRA) petitioned the CCC in early 1934 to make recreational target shooting available to any interested CCC boy. The NRA even offered to pay all possible expenses incurred while setting up rifle ranges in the camps.[43] Fechner, after brief consultation with the CCCAC, declined the offer, holding with his and the program's opinion that anything that appeared even remotely militaristic be banned from the CCC's agenda, skeet shooting included.[44]

While groups like the Committee on Militarism in Education quickly congratulated Fechner on his determination to keep the CCC the way they wanted it—free from guns—the right-wing *New York Daily News*, along with other concerned citizens, was outraged.[45] All boys loved guns, the *Daily News* roared. Young men all over the country could take advantage of local shooting clubs, so why not the CCC boys? Fechner, the article concluded, simply insisted on treating the boys of the CCC "as if they were somehow abnormal." Stripped of their right to bear arms, CCC boys, for some, were clearly less than "real" men in the making.[46]

As the CCCAC's decision shows, however, antimilitaristic sentiments carried the day in the program's early years. In fact, guns, one of the ultimate symbols of militarism to pacifists, would never play a role in the CCC's training program, even during its later years when it was absorbed into national defense preparation for World War II. CCC boys were not training to be soldiers and therefore would not be permitted to handle weapons in the camps—even if it were only for the sake of skeet shooting. Manliness in this overwhelmingly pacifistic social context—despite strong dissenting voices—did not, for many, include training for war.

The public image of the CCC boy cannot be divorced from the anti-war social context in which it developed in the early 1930s. While right-wing political groups and other conservatives would continue to challenge the CCC's nonmilitary status, periodically calling for outright military drill in the camps as early as 1935, pacifism and noninterventionist ideologies proved the more powerful influence on the program for several years.

In response to the pacifist protests, the organization would promote a CCC boy who, while in the process of becoming a better man, was also free from too much overt militaristic influence. But if he could not be portrayed as a valiant soldier fighting his way to manhood, then what could he be? What was the program doing for him to help ensure his transition into an adult male role? It was fine for Fechner to declare that there were "no drills, no guns, no bugle calls, or anything of a military nature" in the CCC.[47] But if the CCC boy's masculinity was not being defined through any these things, then through what?

## The Ideal CCC Boy Emerges

"The CCC—A Builder of Men"; W. Frank Persons of the Labor Department coined this phrase in 1934, and the program soon adopted it as one of its official slogans.[48] But what precisely made a fresh CCC enrollee into an ostensibly "better" man by the time his tenure at camp was over? How had he supposedly benefited from his experience?

The CCC boy could not just be defined in the negative. His identity could not revolve solely around his *not* being a soldier. Once again, grassroots sentiments were integral to the evolving definition of who the reformed and remasculinized CCC boy was. Fechner, McEntee, and especially Persons reached out to assess public opinion at regular intervals. They encouraged those who had firsthand experience with the camps to speak openly about the changes they had witnessed in the enrollees and to comment on the extent to which the program was succeeding in its goal of making the boys into better men. In fact, Fechner addressed the need to look to the grassroots for information on the benefits of the program in his second director's report, distributed to the president and members of Congress in early 1935. Fechner said that because it had been impossible for either him or his assistants "to spend very much time in the field" visiting the camps, they relied upon those who had more firsthand knowledge.[49]

Publicity reports regularly included eyewitness accounts of how the CCC had transformed the weakened boys in some way. Persons requested information from local relief agents, foresters, and the boys themselves, asking them to give personal testimonies about the program. Official publicity brochures and pamphlets often included snippets from these narratives, but of course including only those that extolled the CCC's positive, nonmilitaristic role in training boys for adult manhood.

In May 1934, Persons sent a circular letter to all state directors of enrollee selection. News correspondents had been making constant requests for information on what the social benefits of the program were. Persons asked the state directors to then consult with local relief agents who had had the most contact with individual boys and their families. Those at the local level, Persons said, would be the most "qualified observers of the work being done."[50] As it turned out, Persons received thousands of replies. Letters came in not only from relief workers, but also from local and state politicians, business people, parents, and enrollees.

Becoming a man, many correspondents seem to have agreed, consisted foremost of learning how to labor. A relief director from Vermont wrote to Persons saying that after only a few days on the job "the boys seem more manly, more self-reliant and better able to cope with their individual problems."[51] An enrollee from Arkansas thought there was nothing better in life than having a "real job with cash pay," and now that he was in the CCC, he said, "I have a man's size [sic] job."[52] A sense of manliness developed when a boy had the opportunity, as he did in the CCC, to depend on himself to earn his own living.

Manliness, within this social context of deep economic depression and widespread unemployment, undoubtedly was linked all the more powerfully to a boy's attainment of financial independence. Yet to be truly independent and self-supporting, boys—even working-class ones—simply needed to master a certain level of technological expertise in order to make themselves marketable to prospective industrial employers. During the Depression, many societal observers claimed, large numbers of boys were attempting to enter the world of adult work without training in the vocational skills they so desperately needed to be able to compete in an already overly saturated industrial job market.

By the 1930s, as education reform advocate Dorothy Canfield Fisher pointed out, young men could no longer look to industrial firms themselves to provide them with the types of on-the-job training that had once been common for boys fresh out of school.[53] And while in the first two decades of the twentieth century public school districts across the country had toyed with the idea of providing more comprehensive industrial and vocational training for those young men predisposed to lives of manual labor and blue-collar work, the development of separate public high schools focusing on industrial training had been a short-lived and rather unpopular phenomenon.[54] For as Reed Ueda's study of secondary schooling in Somerville, Massachusetts, has shown, "for secondary education . . . parents and youths preferred the comprehensive high school over the vocational school." And by the mid-1920s, enrollment in such institutions had dropped off precipitously.[55]

The CCC, then, was in part designed to provide the occupational coming-of-age experience that was no longer available to the bulk of young men aspiring to working-class careers. Due to a combination of factors—the overwhelming economic instability of the 1930s, the persistent inability of secondary schools to provide meaningful vocational training for high-school-aged boys, and the end of industry-sponsored apprenticeship programs—the CCC emerged as a place where, at least occupationally, American boys could learn to be adult male workers and self-sufficient breadwinners. And they would do so, in large part, through their harnessing of modern workplace technologies.

"The young man of today has been literally brought up with machines," CCC director Fechner trumpeted in his 1938 report to Congress. The CCC, he continued, would therefore strive to provide the types of vocational and technological training young men needed to secure coveted private-industry jobs. Looking back on the first five years of the program, Fechner said that there had been a "constant attempt" on the part of the CCC's job-training schemes to "balance the efforts of men and machines," since "that [would be] the condition which the enrollee [would] encounter when he left the Corps for private industry."[56] Teaching inexperienced boys to master fairly low-level technological skills—among them tractor and steam-shovel operation, welding, concrete construction, blasting, and drainage construction—would increase their chances of private employment away from the CCC and subsequently would bring about their economic self-sufficiency.

The CCC's publicity regularly made explicit cultural links between an adult manliness based on financial independence and employment with the development of a boy's technological skills. In the CCC's annual report for 1937, Fechner argued that the vocational and technological instruction that CCC enrollees received while on the job had been "focused with increasing sharpness on the problem of training the individual enrollee to obtain and hold a job in private industry."[57]

The CCC would argue time and again in its publicity reports that the types of technological skills its work projects focused upon would make jobs all the more attainable for young unemployed men; work would bring boys independence, which would lead to their economic self-sufficiency, which would in turn bring with it the societal validation of adult male status. [58] Therefore, while these working-class boys definitely were not being encouraged to "make" technology themselves (they merely were learning how to use it), technology definitely was "making" them.[59] Learning to harness technology was—at least in part—what made working-class boys into men.

Yet technological and vocational skills were not the only man-building aspects of the program that were lauded by its publicity and its proponents. The hearty character of the outdoor work itself was often cited as having had a profound effect on the boys, transforming them into hardened men.[60] This was particularly true about tree planting, perhaps the most tedious of all tasks a CCC boy ever did. In his 1940 book about the CCC, *Now They Are Men*, McEntee remarked that once a CCC boy planted 25,000 trees, he "felt like a man."[61] One enrollee, Harold Lubrit, discussed the "art" of tree felling in similar terms, a skill he said all "rookies" needed to master on the road to self-improved manhood. The boy's vivid depiction of his skillful wielding of an axe is an intently physical affirmation of his developing manliness. As Lubrit wrote, "I begin to make an uppercut. I swing the axe with vigorous movements. After a short time has elapsed, my skin prickles with wee drops of perspiration. I remove my shirt and upper underwear. The sun is now in full view and shines down on a beautiful tan I have acquired through many days similar to this. I feel wonderful! Again I swing my axe into the tree. Soon my undercut is finished. Now I am commencing the uppercut. I "slough" into the tree with a vicious precision that time alone has taught me. The former wee drops of perspiration have now enmassed into streams of running sweat. . . . My entire body is wet and gleaming in the sun. The underwear beneath my overalls is drenched, but oh boy, I feel glorious!"[62]

Official publicity statements lauded physical conditioning, muscle hardening, and weight gains as particularly crucial "man-building" aspects of the program. Fechner said the CCC "assured decent manhood" for scores of boys who developed "new skills [and] new bodies." Those new bodies, the surgeon general reported in 1936, were stronger, healthier, and on average eight to fourteen pounds heavier after six months in the CCC.[63] Family members of CCC boys said much the same thing. A young woman named Orville Thogmartin described the unbelievable physical metamorphosis she witnessed in her brother after he returned home from the CCC, writing, "God's great outdoors had sent us home a husky—he had gained fifteen pounds—tanned young man. My brother had gone to camp a boy and had come home a man."[64]

To attain full social validation as a man, it seems, one needed to be brawny and bronzed along with being financially self-sufficient and technologically adept. Reportedly, narratives objectified the CCC boys' bodies, intimating that an even more exemplary manliness came with outstanding physical conditioning. In an era when Charles Atlas was having tremendous success selling his muscle-building techniques in the back pages of boys' magazines, the CCC publicized its own man-building method by advertising the success stories of its enrollees.[65]

In their narratives CCC boys often described a marked change in their physical statures after they entered camp. One boy spoke of being "gaunt and undernourished" going in, but within four months the CCC had built up his broken body through "invigorating physical exertion" and he "glowed with health again."[66] Other tales were more fantastic and worthy of a spot in Atlas's advertisements themselves. A former CCC boy from Cleveland reported that he went from being a veritable "Ninety-Eight-Pound Weakling" to a hefty 186 pounds in only eighteen months in the corps.[67]

Boys rarely mentioned hearty camp meals or abundant food as the causal factors in this process, however. Rather, physical growth usually was credited to the rigors of the work alone. Learning to work, therefore, remained the determining factor in a boy's transition into manhood. Bigger bodies might make men feel more manly, but work, quite simply, made one a man. The overwhelming emphasis on the value of work—and, in this case, on low-skill-level manual labor—reveals just how narrowly the socially acceptable roles for working-class men were defined. If a man were not a worker or a man were not a provider, then that man could not really be a man at all.

Official photographs and illustrations of enrollees provide outstanding examples of how the program visualized the physically masculine CCC boy. Photos from the early to mid-1930s heavily emphasized the rebuilt physical stature of the boys and explicitly focused on the value of their labor and the skill-building work they were performing. Boys appear most often in the process of working—swinging an axe, driving a tractor, repairing a broken-down diesel engine, or pounding a nail. In all of these instances, boys wear dungarees and work shirts, and rarely, if ever, were they photographed wearing the military-style uniforms that were prevalent in most of the camps. The consistent focus on the CCC boy's labor further reinforces the cultural connection between masculinity and work, while deemphasizing the possible connections between military service and manliness at the same time.

Most often, however, official photographs of CCC enrollees focused on boys who were shirtless (see figs. 5.1 and 5.2). Boys performing all types of work appear bare chested, their bronzed bodies exuding physical manliness. All of the chests are hairless, perhaps to highlight the enrollees' youthful vigor. For the most part their muscles are well-defined, although not all of the boys in photos had yet developed a true "man's" body. Some very well-developed men's torsos are juxtaposed with less mature ones, drawing attention to the fact that the CCC billed itself as a "builder of men." Therefore, at any given time, some of the boys would have already attained full-blown manhood while others were still in the developmental stages. With a little more work, the photos suggested, they could one day attain the ideal body— and an ideal manliness—as well.

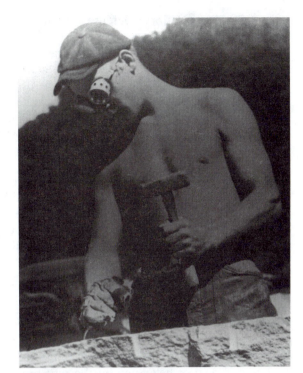

**FIGURE 5.1**

*"Shirtless Boy with Hammer."*

*Reprinted from* The CCC at Work: A Story of 2,500,000 Young Men *(Washington, D.C.: Government Printing Office, 1941), p. 41.*

**FIGURE 5.2**

*"Shirtless Boy with Shovel."*

*Reprinted from* The CCC at Work: A Story of 2,500,000 Young Men *(Washington, D.C.: Government Printing Office, 1941), p. 41.*

## The CCC Meets National Defense—The Revival of Military Manhood

By 1938, worries over Europe's deteriorating peace made many Americans increasingly nervous about the state of the United States's defenses. As much of the world openly prepared for war, pacifist groups that had agitated so vocally against the army's role in the CCC now "abandoned their position to support Roosevelt's policy of preparedness and collective security."[68] If there were to be another war, men would once again be expected to perform roles not only as workers and as providers but also as soldiers.

A Gallup poll taken in late 1938 indicates that a vast proportion of American voters believed that current conditions favored military training as part of the CCC boy's daily routine.[69] Seventy-five percent of those polled sided with advocates of preparedness who were calling for anywhere between two and six hours of military drill per week in the camps. With increasing regularity, voices began to speak out in support of the benefits CCC boys would receive from military training.

Thus, as the social climate changed, so too did the public's perception of who the ideal CCC boy should be.[70] A masculine identity revolving almost exclusively around self-sufficiency and an honest day's labor would be challenged, eventually giving way to a markedly different ideal of young American manhood. After much public debate—and a good deal of hesitancy on the part of CCC administrators—the CCC boy became a soldier.

Some Americans now saw the seeming imminence of another world war as a perfect opportunity for boys to develop their manliness. Speaking at a CCC camp dedication in 1939, Colonel C. L. McGee took an extreme position when he told the boys that it was "great to get into war. It broadens you." He went on to say that it was "a glorious thing for an American youth to lay down his life for defense of his country."[71] Yet, as extreme as McGee's speech was, views like his gained increasing credibility as the war approached. By 1940, letters calling for military training in the CCC appeared regularly in the *New York Times*, quite unlike the earlier period in the program's development; one writer even praised military service as "the greatest character-building opportunity" a boy could possibly receive.[72] The CCC administration, however, moved cautiously and did not publicly endorse military training as part of the CCC boy's routine despite the obvious changes in the social discourse. In fact, CCC publicity continued to downplay the army's role long past the time when it had needed to do so.

The CCC continued to hold onto its traditional man-building goals even when another poll showed that an astounding nine out of ten Americans now backed proposals for the program's militarization.[73] A scripted radio interview used for recruitment in October 1939 reveals the program's stubborn inability to see that the social context had begun to change markedly. "The CCC is a strictly civilian organiza-

Jeffrey Ryan Suzik

tion," the interviewee announced. "We are on a strictly civilian basis. We are seeking to build men, not soldiers. Or, if you want to put it another way, soldiers of peace and not of war."[74]

However, in June 1940 Congress mandated noncombatant military training for all CCC enrollees. The CCC boy underwent an immediate metamorphosis in the official discourse. Director McEntee, having assumed the position after Fechner's death in December 1939, was now obliged to extol the virtues of noncombatant military training for the boys, even though he himself was still adamantly opposed to it.[75] CCC boys now received training in various defense-related fields, including an increased emphasis on industrial mechanics, first aid, motor vehicle operation, map reading, and signal communications. In meeting the new emergency head-on, McEntee suggested, the vocational and technological training CCC boys had been offered for the last seven and a half years had in fact always been fitting them for military service. The corps, he said, had been "converting unemployed young men without work experience into strong, vigorous young men who could drive trucks, tractors, which are the first cousins to tanks, build roads, bridges, telephone lines . . . which would aid in the advancement of industrial defense and in . . . the strengthening of the military forces."[76] In a November 1940 radio interview McEntee went even further, proclaiming that CCC boys lacked nothing in their training as future members of the military but drill with a gun.[77] With that one exception noted, McEntee claimed, they were soldiers through and through.

Photos of the "new" CCC boy appearing in recruitment brochures and publicity reports from the national defense period are striking. Whereas earlier shots of the CCC boy in action had carefully camouflaged his uniformed body or had presented him shirtless, the new enrollee-turned-soldier often appeared in full military glory. Photos showing rows of CCC enrollees standing at attention became a regular feature in recruitment brochures by 1941 (see fig. 5.3).

Sharply pressed uniforms cover the CCC boys' once-bare upper bodies, and army-styled hats sit atop their well-groomed heads. In one shot, dutiful, patriotic boy soldiers stand in military formation, saluting two of their fellow enrollees as they gravely lower the American flag (see fig. 5.4). The caption appearing under this recruitment brochure photo is particularly telling: "CCC boys become better qualified for self-support and for their proper place in American life." Their proper place, it seems, was in the military. And their proper role, at least for the time-being, was to be a soldier.

Yet, for many, the CCC boy was still not "soldier" enough. It was becoming less and less tenable for the CCC to define a man-building experience for boys that was not more explicitly linked to military training. In June 1940, a mother of two teenage boys expressed outrage at the CCC's lack of a "real" military emphasis. In a letter to the

**FIGURE 5.3** *"Rows of Civilian Conservation Core Boys Standing at Attention."*

*Reprinted from* The CCC at Work: A Story of 2,500,000 Young Men *(Washington, D.C.: Government Printing Office, 1941), p. 5.*

**FIGURE 5.4** *"Two Civilian Conservation Core Boys Lowering the Flag."*

*Reprinted from* The CCC at Work: A Story of 2,500,000 Young Men *(Washington, D.C.: Government Printing Office, 1941), p. 103.*

Jeffrey Ryan Suzik

*New York Times*, she attacked Congress's decision to institute noncombatant training in the CCC instead of outright military drill. Did Congress really believe it was "catering to our desires in not insisting on military training?" she asked. "As a mother I want my sons trained and I feel sure other women share my desire. Millions are being raised for guns and planes, but who is to use them? Enough of this namby-pamby talk of noncombatant training."[78] From her perspective, without more military training, the CCC was not building the kind of men America now needed. Society's definition of a "real man" no longer was limited almost entirely to economic self-sufficiency and physical hardiness. Boys needed military training and military drill, many now argued, to enable them to assume manly roles as soldiers. Refusing to train CCC boys in this way had become "namby-pamby" nonsense. With war looming, "age-old masculine attributes of courage, endurance, toughness, and guts" were once again unfurled.[79] Military service had resurfaced as an earmark for American masculinity. And the CCC boy would need to be reconceptualized accordingly or fade away forever.

Yet as John Salmond puts it, "with [war production] employment rising, and the armed forces expanding, the CCC had lost its main function."[80] The vast numbers of unemployed boys were, quite simply, no longer unemployed. Few needed—or even wanted—the CCC to provide manly independence for them any longer; boys could rise to a self-sufficient "man's estate" elsewhere, on their own, and for far more money. In fact, the CCC boy was about to be unseated as a dominant model for ideal American masculinity: G.I. Joe stood tall, waiting right around the corner. Just a few months after the Japanese attack on Pearl Harbor, the Senate Committee on Education and Labor held hearings concerning a proposal to terminate the CCC.

At the hearings, Tennessee senator Kenneth McKellar, longtime supporter of the program and author of the proposed bill, now voiced numerous objections to the CCC's continued existence. First, the CCC was, to McKellar, quite simply a waste of money. The war effort demanded economy, and the CCC was far from economical. In fact, one boy's CCC training cost the American people approximately two hundred dollars more per year than one year spent in the military did. Second, with its less rigorous military training, the CCC was merely "duplicating what the army [was] so well doing" anyway. Finally, McKellar said he thought the CCC actually hurt rather than helped boys' self-reliance. The program handed enrollees everything they needed "the easy way." In fact, instead of building up the better men it so regularly professed to do, McKellar believed it was doing exactly the opposite. The CCC, he argued, was making "mollycoddles out of our young people."[81] Young men were not being trained for lives of self-sufficiency and independence; instead, they were learning to depend on the state for their livelihood. By 1942, boys could become men—real men, better men—in a much more patriotic and far more exotic location: an international war. Stripped of its role in leading working-class boys to manhood, the CCC had no chance for survival. Two months later, the program was dead.

## Conclusions

For nine years, from 1933 to 1942, the Civilian Conservation Corps put young men to work. The program's supporters said it was "building better men"; at the same time, however, its early detractors claimed it was "making a military mindset." Champions of the program celebrated it as a pathway to self-sufficient adulthood for jobless boys. Others eventually criticized it as no more than a redirection of boys' dependency away from their families and onto the state. When World War II loomed in the future, defenders believed the program could help train stronger soldiers, whereas its enemies were convinced it could do no such thing. Yet amid all the debate, conflicting voices and dissenting opinions, most held at least one in common: the CCC had the ability—the power, if you will—to transform the boys it enrolled in some way. Whether it be for good or bad, better or worse, positive or negative, supporters and antagonists alike generally agreed that the boy who went in to the CCC would not be the same when he came out.

A constant discourse of masculinity swirled around the CCC: how did Americans define masculinity, what did they think it meant, and what role did they believe it played in their society? The economic insecurity and financial destitution that accompanied the Great Depression had made many people nervous about men's futures, quite simply, as men. Without a way to support himself, or to support a family, could a man really be a man at all?

Undeniably, the CCC developed as a way of providing economic relief for out-of-work male youth. But we can also read it as a federally instituted antidote to societal worries over young men's uncertain futures. Without a doubt, the program provided a state-sanctioned (and in part controlled) space in which boys could make the transition into manhood when jobs were not forthcoming.

Nevertheless, CCC boys had plenty of room away from the gaze of the state to construct their own personal identities as men and as workers. While the CCC may have encouraged conformity to certain rules of order, efficiency, and hygiene (to name a few), it certainly did not have the all-encompassing power to eliminate all of the boys' options for self-expression and/or self-definition as they matured into men. The state may indeed have become a more visible presence in the lives of American citizens through their participation in New Deal relief programs like the CCC; but it never could have become the only one.[82]

The state—and in this case, the CCC—did not, I argue, have hegemonic control over the future lives of the boys it employed. Rather than being hegemonic, I maintain that the state was (and is) reflexive. It is by necessity open to voices from below, adapting itself and its policies according to public opinion. Grassroots sentiments had incredible influence over how the CCC promoted itself, how it developed policies and procedures for the handling of enrollees, and how it conceptualized the ideally reformed CCC boy.

As it sought to transform wayward youth into honorable young men, the program necessarily took into account what the public wanted and thought it needed from its young men. CCC administrators produced a program that could "build better men" according to society's changing conceptions of what "real" manhood should be. When that conception changed from men merely being good providers and dependable, technologically adept workers, the CCC's man-building goals had to change as well. When society worried over boys' lack of economic self-sufficiency, the CCC gave them jobs and made them workers; later, when it worried over boy's lack of military training, the CCC gave them drill and made them soldiers. In each case, one thing remained the same; both times, the CCC promised to make them into men—the men that America needed.

## Notes

1. For classic liberal approaches to the New Deal, see William E. Leuchtenberg, *Franklin D. Roosevelt and the New Deal* (New York: Harper and Row, 1963); and Arthur Schlesinger Jr., *The Coming of the New Deal, 1932–1940* (Boston: Houghton-Mifflin, 1959). A more recent work refuting the liberal analysis is Stanley Vittoz, *New Deal Labor Policy and the American Industrial Economy* (Chapel Hill: University of North Carolina Press, 1987). For a good historiographical essay tracing changing interpretations of the New Deal state in recent historical works see Stuart Kidd, "Redefining the New Deal: Some Thoughts on the Political and Cultural Perspectives of Revisionism," *Journal of American Studies* 22, no.3 (1988): 389–415.

2. In a recent article, Ruth Oldenziel deftly illustrates how by the early twentieth century in the United States the relationship of men and women to technological processes had solidified into a "world where men design systems and women use them; men engineer bridges and women cross them; men build cars and women ride in them; in short, a world in which men are considered the active producers and women the passive consumers of technology." As provocative and persuasive as Oldenziel's argument may be about the cultural implications of technological change and development, I think that her argument pertaining to the social gendering of men as merely "producers" of technology might have limited application. The boys that her study of the Fisher Body Craftsman's Guild traces, who were encouraged to become engineers and technological producers via their participation in the Guild's Napoleonic coach design contests, were, I would argue, by and large from the middle class. Prospective CCC enrollees, on the other hand, being selected at first exclusively from local relief rolls, were solidly working class in origin. In all of the vocational and technological training programs the CCC ever offered in its nine-year existence, never did the program attempt to offer boys

training in technological production. Instead, it offered them vocational training that would allow them to become skilled users of mechanical technology. See Ruth Oldenziel, "Boys and Their Toys: The Fisher Body Craftsman's Guild, 1930–1968, and the Making of a Male Technical Domain," *Technology and Culture* 38, no.1 (1997): 60–96; reprinted as chapter 6 of this volume.

3. I am using here Joan Kelly Gadol's now classic definition of gender as a category of historical analysis, one that she argues is "socially rather than naturally constituted, varying with changes in social organization"; see Gadol's "The Social Relation of the Sexes: Methodological Implications of Women's History," *Signs* 1 (1976), 814. For a more recent take, see Judith Lorber and Susan A. Farrell, eds., *The Social Construction of Gender* (London: Sage, 1991). On the cultural construction of gender identities in the New Deal, see Barbara Melosh, *Engendering Culture: Manhood and Womanhood in New Deal Public Art and Theater* (Washington, D.C.: Smithsonian Institution Press, 1991). And for another approach to the CCC and its "man-building" agenda, see Eric Gorham, "The Ambiguous Practices of the Civilian Conservation Corps," *Social History* 17, no. 2 (1992): 224–49.

4. Catherine Cate Coblentz, "Idle Men," *Survey Graphic,* 1933, 323.

5. Joe L. Dubbert, *A Man's Place: Masculinity in Transition* (Englewood Cliffs, N.J.: Prentice-Hall, 1979), 219.

6. Robert S. Lynd and Helen Merrell Lynd, *Middletown in Transition* (New York: Harcourt Brace Jovanovich, 1937), 410–12.

7. Winifred V. Richmond, *The Adolescent Boy* (New York: Farrar and Rinehart, 1934), 18.

8. Historians of American masculinity have generally agreed that by the early twentieth century, societal understandings of masculinity (at least the working-class varieties) revolved almost entirely around a man's earning potential and his capability to support his family. Therefore, the Depression proved to be a sharp blow to many working-class men's very identities. For examples, see Peter N. Stearns, *Be a Man! Males in Modern Society* (New York: Holmes and Meier, 1979), 127; and James A. Doyle, *The Male Experience* (Dubuque, Iowa: William C. Brown, 1983), 42.

9. George P. Rawick, "The New Deal and Youth: The Civilian Conservation Corps, the National Youth Administration, and the American Youth Congress," Ph.D diss., University of Wisconsin, 1957, 18–29.

10. Mark A. May, "The Dilemma of Youth," *Progressive Education,* January 1935, 5–6.

11. Paula S. Fass, *Outside In: Minorities and the Transformation of American Education* (New York: Oxford University Press, 1989), 66.

12. Milwaukee Vocational School Division of Instruction and Research, "Survey of Employment and School Status of Milwaukee High School Graduates—Class of June, 1933," February 5–6, 1934. Unpublished.

13. Aubrey Williams, "Youth and the Economic Problem," in Alfred C. Oliver Jr. and Harold M. Dudley, eds., *This New America: The Spirit of the Civilian Conservation Corps* (New York: Longmans, Green, 1937), 30.

14. May, "Dilemma," 5.

15. Geoffrey Gorer, *The American People: A Study in National Character* (New York: W. W. Norton, 1948), 85.

16. Ibid., 85–86.

17. I am indebted here to Barbara Melosh's definition of social discourse, which she calls "the social negotiation of meaning, [an] on-going process of making sense of (or even constituting) social life." See Melosh, *Engendering Cultures,* 5.

18. In early 1934, CCC director Robert Fechner demanded—and subsequently gained—full control over the dissemination of all official documentation concerning the CCC and its agenda. From that point on, all pamphlets, press releases, and publicity had to be cleared by the director's office before being circulated. Fechner was responding to instances that had occurred recently in which unauthorized reports had been leaked to the press without his knowledge. Robert Fechner to the Departments of Agriculture, Interior, Labor, and War, January 1, 1934, Documents Relating to the Organization of the CCC, RG 35, National Archives.

19. Robert Fechner was the first director of the CCC. Roosevelt appointed Fechner, a vice president of the International Association of Machinists (IAM), to the position in 1933 in part to calm protests coming from organized labor. The AFL had been particularly vocal in its cry that the CCC boys' one dollar per day would drive wages down in general. Born in 1876, Fechner had been an active unionist his entire life, and he had developed great skill as a strike negotiator. He administered the CCC until his death on December 31, 1939. Fechner's successor, James J. McEntee, had been the CCC's assistant director from the beginning and saw the organization through to its termination in 1942. A few years younger than Fechner, McEntee was also an officer in the IAM. McEntee had worked as a negotiator for the New York Arbitration Board during World War I, settling several munitions plant disputes. Both men held a great deal of affinity for their work with the CCC, and neither ever wanted to see the program militarized. See Fechner's biographical entry in *The National Cyclopaedia of American Biography* vol. 29 (Ann Arbor, Mich.: University Microfilms, 1967), 70–71. On McEntee, see his *New York Times* obituary, October 16, 1957, 35.

20. John A. Salmond, *The Civilian Conservation Corps, 1933–1942: A New Deal Case Study* (Durham, N.C.: Duke University Press, 1967), 193.

21. Dubbert, *A Man's Place*, 231–32.

22. Leuchtenberg, *Franklin D. Roosevelt*, 174.

23. "Roosevelt's Tree Army," *New Republic*, June 12, 1935, 127–29.

24. Personal narratives by former CCC boys and others involved with the camps often reveal wide tolerance for, and even outright glorification of, boys' sexual escapades outside of camp. In his memoir, a CCC camp commander approvingly described his "young Paul Bunyans" off on weekend leaves looking for a wild time that "wasn't hard to find. This or that girl was supposed to be a hot mamma . . . and there followed sagas of traveling men who always 'made' the town—there was such good hunting!" See Albert W. Jernberg, *My Brush Monkeys: A Narrative of the CCC* (New York: Richard R. Smith, 1941), 143–44.

25. James J. McEntee, *Final Report of the Director of the Civilian Conservation Corps* (Washington, D.C.: Government Printing Office, 1943), 39.

26. Much of Fechner and his associates' concern with downplaying the military side of the program can be traced to American apprehensions about the mobilization of youth occurring in several European countries at the same time. Many were especially worried about the Nazi Party's transformation of preexisting voluntary work camps in Germany into obligatory military training centers for all German youth. The CCC made every attempt to disassociate itself from comparisons that could be made between it and the Nazi program. For a good contemporary discussion of the European examples, see Kenneth Holland, *Youth in European Labor Camps* (Washington, D.C.: American Council on Education, 1939).

27. Fechner to Jessica Henderson, chair, New England Committee for U.S. Congress against War, September 18, 1933, Personal Correspondence of the Director (hereinafter PCD), RG 35, National Archives.

28. Charles William Johnson, "The Civilian Conservation Corps: The Role of the Army," Ph.D diss., University of Michigan, 1968, 12–16. Johnson argues further that the army was never particularly comfortable with its obligatory participation in the CCC anyway, seeing it as a huge drain on its resources as well as a restriction on its ability to provide adequate national defense.

29. For a World War I counterexample to this trend, see Nancy K. Bristow, *Making Men Moral: Social Engineering during the Great War* (New York: New York University Press, 1996). Bristow's study concerns the Commission on Military Training Camp Activities, a federal agency set up during World War I to reform army training camps notorious for their immorality. In the process, Bristow suggests soldiers were indoctrinated with middle-class values and a sense of virtuous manhood that centered on the glories of military service, quite unlike the early CCC.

30. Elizabeth Lumbeck, quoted in Michael Kimmel, *Manhood in America: A Cultural History* (New York: The Free Press, 1996), 192.

31. Robert Cooney and Helen Michalowski, eds., *The Power of the People: Active Non-violence in the United States* (Philadelphia: New Society Publishers, 1987), 74. On American pacifist movements in the interwar period more specifically, see also Charles Chatfield, *For Peace and Justice: Pacifism in America, 1914–1941* (Knoxville: University of Tennessee Press, 1971).

32. U.S. Department of Labor, "A Chance to Work in the Forests." Emergency Conservation Work Bulletin no. 1, April 17, 1933, 3.

33. This was an outright fallacy on Fechner's part. CCC boys would consistently wear uniforms throughout the program's existence. They only did so, however, after returning to camp after their day's work. Until 1939, when the advisory council approved a new, distinctive, forest-green CCC uniform, enrollees wore secondhand army uniforms, many of which dated back to World War I. Early publicity concerning the idealized CCC boys, however, almost always focused on them working, and hence, on their work attire—dungarees and work shirts. U.S. Department of Agriculture, "CCC Chronological Reference Material by Subjects," No. 1 Special Enrollee Uniforms, Documents Relating to the Organization and Operation of the CCC, RG 35, National Archives.

34. The Civilian Conservation Corps records in the National Archives include voluminous files of written correspondence between the cooperating departments as well as the director's office's correspondence with the population at large. The records contain a large number of letters from pacifists up until 1936, when they seem simply to stop writing. Even groups like the Women's International League for Peace and Freedom, which wrote to Fechner eight times between 1933 and 1936, did not write to him at all in the later period.

35. Mary Winsor, Haverford, Pennsylvania, to Fechner, May 22, 1933, PCD, RG 35, National Archives.

36. Illinois Workers' Alliance, thirteen letters total, to Fechner, various dates ranging from February 28, 1935, to March 20, 1935, PCD, RG 35, National Archives.

37. Lawrence Bye, Soapstone, Utah, to Franklin D. Roosevelt, September 19, 1934, PCD, RG 35, National Archives.

38. Bessie Lowy, Brooklyn, New York, to Franklin D. Roosevelt, April 17, 1933, PCD, RG 35, National Archives.

39. Ellen Starr Brinton, Women's International League for Peace and Freedom, to Fechner, June 14, 1933, PCD, RG 35, National Archives.

40. W. Frank Persons was a longtime social welfare and reform advocate. Born in 1876, Persons attended Cornell College in Iowa and graduated from Harvard Law School in 1900. In 1906 he became the director of New York City's Charity Organization Society. During World War I, Persons served in Europe with the International Red Cross, and on his return to the United States was named vice chairman of the American Red Cross. He was deeply interested in the problems of youth and was a long-term member of the National Council of the Boy Scouts of America. Roosevelt personally selected Persons in 1933 to direct CCC enrollment and to sit on the CCCAC as Labor Department representative. Persons retained these positions until the program was terminated in 1942. See Persons's obituary in the *New York Times*, May 29, 1955, 45.

41. W. Frank Persons to Fechner, May 15, 1933, PCD, RG 35, National Archives.

42. Emergency Conservation Work, Office of the Director, press release, June 12, 1933, Public Relations File, RG 35, National Archives.

43. M. A. Reckord, Executive vice president of the National Rifleman's Association, to Fechner, February 20, 1934, PCD, RG 35, National Archives.

44. Emergency Conservation Work, Minutes of the Advisory Council to the Director, February 28, 1934, RG 35, National Archives.

45. Edwin C. Johnson, Committee on Militarism in Education, to Fechner, December 18, 1934, PCD, RG 35, National Archives.

46. "Fechner Says No Guns for CCC," *New York Daily News*, December 12, 1934, clipping in PCD, RG 35, National Archives.

47. Fechner to Bessie Lowy, May 23, 1933, PCD, RG 35, National Archives.

48. W. Frank Persons, CCC Circular Letter Number 35, Series 4, 1934, Documents Relating to the Organization and Operation of the CCC, RG 35, National Archives.

49. Fechner addressed the need to look to the grassroots for information on the benefits of the program in the second of six annual reports he submitted to Congress each year he presided as director of the program (McEntee would continue the tradition after him). In his second report, Fechner said that because it had been impossible for either him or his assistants "to spend very much time in the field" visiting the camps, they relied upon those who had more first-hand knowledge to assess the finer points of the program for them. See Robert Fechner, *Report of the Director of Emergency Conservation Work* (Washington, D.C.: Government Printing Office, 1935), 1.

50. U.S. Department of Labor, "A Summary of the Social Values of the Civilian Conservation Corps (1933–1934)," Documents Relating to the Organization and Operation of the CCC, RG 35, National Archives.

51. Mary Jean Simpson, Director, Women's Division, Vera Vermont, to Persons, January 10, 1935, Documents Relating to the Organization and Operation of the CCC, RG 35, National Archives.

52. W. R. Dyess, to Persons, July 14, 1934, State Procedural Records, RG 35, National Archives.

53. Dorothy Canfield Fisher, *Our Young Folks* (New York: Harcourt Brace, 1943), 40–41.

54. For an exhaustive overview of the development of vocational schooling in the United States in the early twentieth century, see Edward A. Krug, *The Shaping of the American High School, 1880–1920* (Madison: University of Wisconsin Press, 1969), 217–48; also see Herbert M. Kleibard's more recent *Schooled to Work: Vocationalism and the American Curriculum, 1876–1946* (New York: Teachers College Press, 1999).

55. Reed Ueda, *Avenues to Adulthood: The Origins of the High School and Social Mobility in an American Suburb* (Cambridge: Cambridge University Press, 1987), 198–200.

56. Robert Fechner, *Annual Report of the Director of the Civilian Conservation Corps, Fiscal Year Ended June 30, 1938* (Washington, D.C.: Government Printing Office, 1938), 13.

57. Robert Fechner, *Annual Report of the Director, Fiscal Year 1937* (Washington, D.C.: Government Printing Office, 1937), 4.

58. Historian Wayne A. Lewchuk has argued that changes in the industrial production process in the early twentieth century progressively alienated men from their work, as assembly-line jobs became increasingly "unskilled, repetitive, and monotonous." In response, workers commonly voiced complaints about the mundane, unappealing nature of their industrial tasks. According to Lewchuk, in order to placate workers, managers at the Ford Motor Company reconstructed nineteenth-century conceptions of masculinity that had formerly linked manliness to artisanal skill and shop-floor decision making. Industrial employers like Ford reconceptualized the masculine role in industrial production as one in which men were encouraged to gain personal sustenance from little more than "working hard in the company of other men." See Wayne A. Lewchuk, "Men and Monotony: Fraternalism As a Managerial Strategy at the Ford Motor Company," *Journal of Economic History* 53, no. 4 (1993): 824–56. In the same time period, the CCC's vocational training schemes were also encouraging young men to in part define themselves in relation to the "group," as the small-group-oriented work setting of the camps attests. But quite unlike Ford, however, the CCC also encouraged boys to see the technological tasks they performed as personally valuable, life-enriching, and, without a doubt, "manly."

59. See Oldenziel's argument about the Fisher Body Craftsman's Guild and the gendering of engineering and design—in other words, technological production—as an inherently masculine domain. Oldenziel, "Boys and Their Toys," (see chapter 6 in this volume, 139–68). My argument about working-class CCC boys and the masculinization of technology, on the other hand, suggests that in that program boys were not being encouraged to develop manly countenances based upon their production of technological knowledge, but rather on their skillful manipulation and usage of it. Regardless of the low-level skills this vocational training often entailed, the cultural connection, I think, between manly independence and technological knowledge was no less profound.

60. The cultural connection between the "great outdoors" and American conceptions of masculinity was strongly reinforced in the Progressive era through the life and activities of Theodore Roosevelt, and that connection continued well into the twentieth century. On Roosevelt and the concept of the "strenuous life," see John Higham, "The Reorientation of American Culture in the 1890s," in John Higham, ed., *Writing American History* (Bloomington: University of Indiana Press, 1970), 79; E. Anthony Rotundo, *American Manhood: Transformations in Masculinity from the Revolution to the Modern Era* (New York: Basic Books, 1993), 268–69.

61. James J. McEntee, *Now They Are Men: The Story of the CCC* (Washington, D.C.: National Home Library Foundation, 1940), 18.

62. Harold Lubrit, "Adventure with an Axe," in Oliver and Dudley, eds., *This New America*, 69–70.

63. Robert Fechner, *Annual Report of the Director of Emergency Conservation Work* (Washington, D.C.: Government Printing Office, 1936), 3–5.

64. Orville Thogmartin, "My Brother Went to the CCC," in Oliver and Dudley, eds., *This New America*, 96–97.

65. Michael Kimmel has argued that body-building aficionados like Atlas proved so successful during the Depression because they marketed aggrandized physical strength to men as a replacement for their lost economic solvency. On the 1930s body-building craze, see Kimmel, *Manhood*, 210–12.

66. Paul J. Stone, "The Rehabilitation of Paul J. Stone," in Oliver and Dudley, eds., *This New America*, 85.

67. Helen M. Walker, *The CCC through the Eyes of 272 Boys* (Cleveland, Ohio: Case Western Reserve University Press, 1938), 29.

68. Cooney and Michalowski, *The Power and the People*, 84.

69. "Military Training in CCC Is Favored," *New York Times*, December 16, 1938, 26.

70. Beginning in May of 1939, letters urging some form of military training for CCC boys appeared regularly in the *New York Times*. From that point on, not a single writer argued for the program's continuation on a strictly civilian basis.

71. Colonel C. L. McGee, quoted in Salmond, *Civilian Conservation Corps*, 195.

72. "Overlooking Our Assets," *New York Times*, February 11, 1940, sec. IV, 9.

73. "Public Backs Voluntary Military Training for CCC by Wide Majority, Survey Shows," *New York Times*, October 1, 1939, 41.

74. *OGR State Broadcast: Civilian Conservation Corps*, Number One-A, Division of Planning and Public Relations, RG 35, National Archives.

75. McEntee had just six months earlier passionately debated Raymond J. Kelly, National Commander of the American Legion, on the Radio Forum of the Air. The issue was the probable militarization of the CCC, and McEntee voiced vehement opposition to the plan.

76. James J. McEntee, *Annual Report of the Director of the Civilian Conservation Corps* (Washington, D.C.: Government Printing Office, 1940), 2.

77. Office of Government Reports, "United States Government Reports," Program Number 13, "National Defense Series." State Procedural Records, RG 35, National Archives.

78. "Training: Mother Wants It," *New York Times*, June 2, 1940, sec. IV, 9.

79. Doyle, *The Male Experience*, 42.

80. Salmond, *Civilian Conservation Corps*, 208–9.

81. Congress, Senate, Committee on Education and Labor, *Termination of the Civilian Conservation Corps and the National Youth Administration*, 77th Cong., 2nd Sess., March 28, 1942, 242.

82. On the increased role of the state in people's lives during the New Deal, see Leuchtenberg, *Franklin D. Roosevelt*, 331–33. For a more recent discussion of the same phenomenon, see Lizabeth Cohen, *The Making of a New Deal: Industrial Workers in Chicago, 1919–1939* (New York: Cambridge University Press, 1990), 281.

# Boys and Their Toys

*The Fisher Body Craftsman's Guild, 1930–1968, and the Making of a Male Technical Domain*

RUTH OLDENZIEL

n 1931, an advertisement for the Fisher Body Craftsman's Guild in *National Geographic* invited teenage boys to participate in a model-making contest. It showed a boy offering a girl a miniature version of a "Napoleonic coach"—an image that had been chosen as the emblem of the Fisher Body Company in 1922 to convey luxury, comfort, and style. The emblem had been modeled on the coaches Napoleon I of France used for his wedding and for his coronation as emperor. Fisher Body, the organizer of the guild, was the world's largest manufacturer of automobile bodies, which supplied principally to General Motors. The Fisher Body Craftsman's Guild aimed to train "the coming generation" and to secure "fine craftsmanship" (see fig. 6.1). Intended to appeal to boys of high school and young men of college ages (between 12 and 20), the ad portrays the "Fisher boy" as fatherly, mature, and responsible, ready to take a bride—a far cry from the boisterous bachelor or daredevil hot-rodder. Opposite the Fisher boy stands a girl, positioned as the passive and grateful but critical recipient of his Napoleonic coach and suggesting the kind of future that such a gift seems to promise. The illustration implies that the Fisher boy is not only a builder of coaches, but also a builder of families and security as a future husband and breadwinner.

The Fisher Body Craftsman's Guild (1930–68), the organization that sponsored the ad, marks one of the most playful by-products of the very successful partnership between Fisher and cosponsor General Motors (GM). At first glance, the guild invites us to view the world of boys' toys hidden in attics, basements, barns, and backyards as whimsical, playful, and innocent, but a second reading reveals an intricate web of institutions that defined and maintained a male technical domain. The fascinating but now forgotten history of the guild suggests that the definition and production of male technical knowledge involved an extraordinary mobilization of organizational, economic, and cultural resources.[1] The guild, "an educational foundation devoted to the development of handi-

THOUSANDS of boys all over America are completing miniature model Napoleonic coaches in the first year's activity of the Fisher Body Craftsman's Guild. These models they will shortly submit in a nationwide competition for four university scholarships of four years each, 98 trips to Detroit, and 882 other valuable awards.

The Fisher Body Corporation sponsored this inspiring movement, believing that this exercise of creative talent, this quickening of the hand of youth, are essential steps toward the development of high ideals—that only by training the coming generation can fine craftsmanship be perpetuated and superior coachcraft be assured.

CADILLAC · LA SALLE · BUICK · OAKLAND · OLDSMOBILE · PONTIAC · CHEVROLET

FIGURE 6.1  *"Fisher Boy Offers Girl His Napoleonic Coach" Advertisement for the Fisher Body Craftsman's Guild.*

*From the collections of the Henry Ford Museum and Greenwood Village, neg. 91.303.2027*

FISHER BODIES

GENERAL MOTORS

Throughout the years, the success of "Body by Fisher" has
been completely identified
with the success of the cars
which are recognized leaders
in their respective price groups

FISHER

**FIGURE 6.2**    *"Fisher Bodies,"* Life *(June 1927).*

*From the collections of the Henry Ford Museum and Greenwood Village, neg. 64.167.657.531*

work and craftsmanship," directly appealed to boys and relied on the
Boy Scouts, the YMCA, and the public school systems for recruits.[2]
Girls found themselves excluded as a matter of course.

This explicitly male technical domain came into existence at precisely the same time that "the consumer" became more and more
explicitly gendered female, as scholars of consumer culture have
argued.[3] Through various means such as the "Body by Fisher" ad campaign, GM and the Fisher Body Company aligned their companies with
women as their potential consumers.[4] To consider a single example
among many, the same Fisher Body Company that created the Craftsman's Guild ran an advertisement in *Life* magazine in 1927 in which
we find a different Fisher girl, a flapper whose body sensuously repli-
cates the curves of an automobile (see fig. 6.2).[5] Seen side by side,
these two Fisher promotional campaigns exemplify the complemen-

tary ways in which we have come to portray men and women in their stereotypical relationships with the technological world—a world where men design systems and women use them; men engineer bridges and women cross them—men build cars and women ride in them; in short, a world in which men are considered the active producers and women the passive consumers of technology. Both ads point to a specific historical moment in which these roles were being articulated and shaped by GM and the Fisher Body Company. Considered in this light, the exclusion of girls from the Craftsman's Guild was not so much a culturally determined oversight as it was an expression of the need to shore up male identity boundaries in the new world of expanding consumerism precariously coded as female.

The case study of the Fisher Body Craftsman's Guild also suggests that an exclusive focus on women's supposed failure to enter the field of engineering is insufficient for understanding how our stereotypical notions have come into being; it tends to put the burden of proof entirely on women and to blame them for their supposedly inadequate socialization, their lack of aspiration, and their want of masculine values. It also runs the risk of limiting gender, as an analytical tool for historical research, as merely an issue affecting women.[6] An equally challenging question is why and how boys have come to love things technical, how boys have historically been socialized into technophiles, and how we have come to understand technical things as exclusively belonging to the field of engineering. The focus on the formation of boy culture is not to deny that girls and women often face formidable barriers in entering the male domain of science and engineering; they do. The story of the Fisher Body Craftsman's Guild introduces one episode into the institutionalized ways in which boys, male teenagers, and adult men have been channeled into the domain designated as technical.[7]

This article considers one side of the gendering processes. The most substantial part focuses in detail on the male gendered codes in the Fisher Body Craftsman's Guild and its miniature world of model cars to show how from the 1930s to the 1960s the guild helped socialize Fisher boys as technophiles and sought to groom them as technical men ready to take their places as managers or engineers in GM's corporate world. If the first guild advertisement points to the making of a corporate male identity, the second ad suggests, as the Fisher Body Company explained, that the making of the "technical," "hard," and "male" coded worlds of production also has been produced by and produced its opposite: a world of consumption coded as nontechnical, soft, and female.

## Building Model Cars and Male Character

Between the 1920s and 1940s, boys' toys developed into a booming consumer market.[8] Wagons, sleds, scooters, bicycles, airplanes started

Ruth Oldenziel

to clutter boys' rooms, while chemistry and Erector sets were sold because "every boy should be trained for leadership."[9] Girls also acquired toys from their parents, of course, but theirs were less varied and not aimed to help smooth a career path. Toys were not only intended to amuse and entertain, but also "as socializing mechanisms, as educational devices, and as scaled-down versions of the realities of the larger adult-dominated social world."[10] Many toy makers such as the Gilbert Company, the Wolverine Company, and Toy Tinkers exploited the new passion, but none of these companies turned play with toys into the totalizing experience that the Fisher Body Craftsman's Guild managed to create. Under the auspices of GM, the guild combined the appeal of toys and the model-making tradition with corporate needs for training new personnel while crafting consumers' tastes.

The annual Fisher Body Craftsman's Guild contest awarded a $5,000 scholarship at an engineering school to the American or Canadian teenage boy who managed to build the best miniature Napoleonic coach (1931–47) or car (1937–68) (see figs. 6.3 and 6.4). One recruiting sign in 1930 read, "BOYS! Enroll here in the FISHER BODY CRAFTS-MAN'S GUILD. No dues . . . no fees. An opportunity to earn your college education or one of the 980 other wonderful awards" (see fig. 6.5). When the guild was founded in 1930, $5,000 was an average worker's income for three years and would buy eight Chevrolets or Fords; in 1940 Americans could buy a house for that price.[11] With a college education perceived as an avenue for upward mobility, young men and their families could gain a great deal from participating in the guild. GM's investment in the organization was not trivial either: beyond the $20,000 to $100,000 spent on actual awards, the company budgeted at least twenty times more for organizational expenses and publicity each year.[12] Promotional literature boasted that the guild had the largest membership of any young men's organization in the United States except for the Boy Scouts of America, and claimed that by 1960 over eight million male teenagers between the ages of twelve and twenty had participated in the guild through national, state, and local contests and clubs. Whether these figures are trustworthy or not, it is clear that through its recruitment efforts alone the guild influenced numbers of male adolescents much greater than that of the high school students who actually managed to finish and submit the complicated models each year.[13]

If the stakes were high, so were the requirements. The teenage boy who built a miniature coach or car had to be willing to invest an extraordinary amount of time, possess a large measure of patience, and acquire a high level of skill. The guild's officials apparently realized that the completion of a coach would be extremely challenging without substantial corporate encouragement. Hence, they ensured that replicas would be prominently displayed in department store windows and that color prints and scale drawings were printed in local newspa-

FIGURE 6.3    *Example of Napoleonic Coach model built for the Fisher Body Craftsman's Guild contest during the period 1930–47. Built from scratch, each coach demanded on average 960 hours to complete.*

*From the General Motors Media Archives; neg. 20134-L-1. Copyright © General Motors Corporation, used with permission.*

FIGURE 6.4    *A 1962 example of free design model for the Fisher Body Craftsman's Guild contest. It took on average 275 hours to complete a model after one's own design.*

*From the General Motors Media Archives; neg. X42371-101-L4. Copyright © General Motors Corporation, used with permission.*

**FIGURE 6.5** *Applicant to the Fisher Body Craftsman's Guild in 1930 in Detroit's Fisher Building. Note that the sign on the wall reads: "An opportunity to earn your college education or one of the 980 other awards."*

From the General Motors Media Archives; neg. 19206-2. Copyright © General Motors Corporation, used with permission.

pers and in the guild's newsletters. To be sure, displays of the Fisher coach served promotional purposes as well. Contest rules demanded that all parts be handmade, which necessitated the ability to build a miniature Napoleonic coach (measuring 11 x 6 x 8 inches) from scratch, to read complicated patterns, to draft accurately, carve wood painstakingly, work metal, paint, and make upholstery with utmost care (see fig. 6.6). Boys of high school and college ages had to construct functioning mechanical parts: windows that could slide, steps that could be folded away, spoked wheels and cambered axles that could turn, and a working leaf-spring suspension. The interior also needed painstaking attention to evoke the proper royal texture of lush upholstery, silk covers, rabbit fur carpets, and brocade curtains. Harking back to the time-consuming labor of craft traditions, the completion of a miniature Napoleonic coach to specification demanded an extraordinary amount of dedication and time—about three hours a day for over ten months—not to mention the investment in materials.

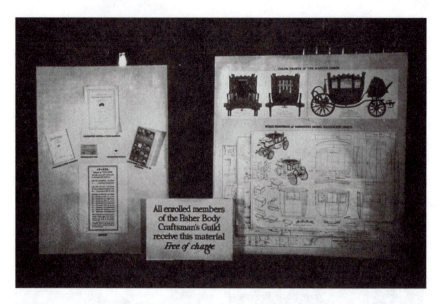

**FIGURE 6.6** *Application materials for Fisher Body Craftsman's Guild, c. 1932.*

*From the General Motors Media Archives; neg. 19206-1. Copyright © General Motors Corporation, used with permission.*

The craft theme presented the organization with a full range of medieval symbols tailored to contemporary corporate needs. These were smoothly mixed with the most up-to-date technologies of the time: during the 1930s live radio broadcasts announced the winners to parents, family, friends, and neighbors; after World War II, airplanes carried the boys to GM's headquarters in Detroit for the festive four-day Fisher Body Convention. Here, GM officials staged events ranging from essay writing contests to matches in swimming, golfing, and other athletic events in order to foster the boys' competitive spirit (see fig. 6.7). Finally, the teenage boys toured carefully selected industrial sites and GM laboratories that served as windows through which they could view their possible future in the corporation (see fig. 6.8).

The evocation of the medieval theme found its culminating moment during the last day of the convention, when the organization offered the contestants a banquet and an initiation rite at a candlelit table against a Gothic backdrop. Clad in medieval costumes, the state finalists entered into the corporate world as apprentices under the blare of trumpets. In 1939 Embury A. Hitchcock, a guild judge and engineering educator, vividly described the spirit of the ritual and showed how the ceremonies marked the transition from apprentice to master craftsman and from boyhood to manhood. He fondly recalled how "the light of flickering candles shows the ornate walls, the heavy-beamed ceil-

FIGURE 6.7 *Fisher Body Craftsman's Guild contestants who had won in their home states were treated to a four-day Fisher Body Convention where they competed in sports and games.*

*From the General Motors Media Archives; neg. 37633-2. Copyright © General Motors Corporation, used with permission.*

ings, and shields and draperies much as they were in the guild halls of Brussels. . . . The trumpeteers [*sic*], dressed in doublets, breeches, and buckled shoes . . . lead the procession of contestants, each man carrying his own coach. After the seating, a casement window on the second floor swings open and a representative of the master workmen of the guild days addresses the group on what is required in the way of long years of service to qualify as a craftsman." Most of all, the guild succeeded in updating the old "corporate" world of medieval guilds to modern times. Hitchcock described how—after the evocation of European guild traditions—the medieval ornaments served as a backdrop for GM's American corporate modernity: "a picture of the modern boy, using power-driven tools in building his coach, shows the contrast between work in the Middle Ages and today."[14] By deftly wedding medieval motifs to symbols of the modern age, then, the ritual trumpeted the past and broadcast the future, reaching millions through radio shows, news bulletins, department store displays, photographs, short films, and advertisements.

FIGURE 6.8 *Fisher Body Craftsman's Guild contestants, wearing their Guild berets, with corporate officials inside a Fisher Body Plant. Four contestants lift a body top. One worker looks on.*

*From the General Motors Media Archives; neg. 37633-4. Copyright © General Motors Corporation, used with permission.*

The Fisher guild did more, however, than just update the medieval values of apprenticeship for the modern corporate world. As the guild's ads suggested, the company sought to create a future generation of corporate workers while also expanding consumer markets. During the guild festivities organizers allotted time for shopping trips in downtown Detroit, suggesting that in the expanding consumer society men were no longer just breadwinners and producers but were also expected to take on new roles as consumers. At the same time, the guild's advocates and GM officials explicitly encouraged guild winners to seek GM jobs after graduation. During a 1931 radio broadcast announcing that year's winners, GM President Alfred Sloan Jr. extended "to all you boys the opportunity to become employees of the corporation as soon as your schooling is completed."[15] In the depths of the Depression, this was a powerful message indeed.

Sloan's 1931 invitation turned out to be more than a public relations ploy, for it was sustained by the corporation's active recruitment policy. As many participants later testified, the sumptuous banquet offered the teenagers easy access to key GM officials, and indeed the event was designed to encourage the boys to converse with men held up as successful role models and potential mentors. Local business leaders, GM chief designers and upper management, and the presidents and deans of major engineering colleges all fraternized with the contestants. GM's attention to the teenage boys went beyond fleeting moments of attention at banquets. By sponsoring an alumni organization, the guild held winners of past contests up as examples to others. Each year all members of this exclusive club were invited back to the banquet as guests of honor, giving GM ample opportunity to monitor their advances as they grew up. The guild newsletter, *The Guildsman*, printed biographical narratives next to instructions on how to design the miniature coaches and cars. Working together, these narratives and technical instructions advised simultaneously on building perfect models and proper male character.

The corporation's recruiting efforts paid off handsomely: many of the winners later became chief designers and high-level managers at General Motors and elsewhere in the corporate world. By 1968, for example, 55 percent of the creative design staff at GM had been involved in the Fisher Body Craftsman's Guild, while many other former contestants occupied key positions in other large corporations.[16] "These cars," a design director for Walter Dorwin Teague Associates, Ken Dowd, recalled in 1985, "were truly the beginning of my design career."[17] The guild, another alumnus remarked, "was very much part of my teenage years. I was a scholarship winner in 1963. . . . The Guild and the Soap Box Derby got me started on the road to being an industrial designer."[18] Over the years, the winners constituted a true fraternity of designers, still voicing deep emotions when recalling the pleasures of joining the guild.[19] Although the story of these winners fails to account for the many who never managed to complete a model or lost the contest, the guild's carefully planned effort reached many more teenage boys than those who actually submitted models for the contest.[20] Even those who merely learned about the guild's existence through friends or at school praised its impact. Carroll Gantz, for example, recently recalled its lasting influence when he wrote, "I was not a participant, but I certainly recollect the program's introduction in 1948 as inspirational to my career choice."[21]

The public narratives in the media stressed individual merit and preached "rugged competition," faithful as they were to the middle-class American ideal of the self-made man, but personal recollections suggest that the efforts were often collaborative. Many of the entrants came from the lower middle classes and from small towns, and building the coaches and models fitted into the family economy and ambitions for upward mobility. After all, college education was the prize, a potential reward difficult to ignore for a teenage boy and his family. In 1930, Raymond Doerr's father, for instance, allowed his son to postpone entry into the job market after high school graduation. Young Doerr lived off the family's income for about a year to devote all of his time to the competition. This family decision indeed paid off, because Doerr won the 1931 competition. Other fathers assisted their sons with advice, tools, capital, or skills. Mothers helped with the complicated and elaborate work on the majestic upholstery that adorned the Napoleonic coach. Myron Webb recalled that his mother "had at one time worked in a millinery shop designing and making hats and did beautiful handiwork. She did the sewing on the inside trim [of the coach]." Brothers assisted by exchanging skills and sharing earlier experiences in the competition. The Pietruska brothers, Richard, Ronald, and Michael, were all national winners: "[N]eedless to say we were very proud of our accomplishments, individually and as a family."[22] Thus while the contest pushed a masculine identity of autonomy, individuality, and honor in building the cars, actual practices suggest that model making was embedded in the family economy, in which family members shared their talent, capital, and time. Such pooling of family resources is perhaps not surprising given the promise of a scholarship, but it contrasted sharply with the guild's representations of building proper male character as a lone, individual effort.

These family strategies developed in tandem with GM's search for personnel. The company sought to socialize male teenagers not only as future corporate employees, but also as breadwinners and consumers. As one contemporary observer close to the automobile industry remarked, the goal of General Motors's sponsorship of the guild "was to build good will, rather than to sell automobiles," but also considered "the boy's influence in automobile selling . . . a very powerful factor."[23] In another appreciative assessment an advertising trade journal stated that the guild served to whet the boys' appetite as prospective consumers."[24] If this trade-literature assessment is correct, it is particularly significant that the guild presented the boys in their new consumer roles as knowledgeable producers and builders—a portrayal that stood in marked contrast to the passive roles mapped out for girls in GM's advertisement campaign "Body by Fisher," initiated a few years earlier, and the craft's recruiting literature during this period.

## Building Male Institutional Networks

The guild owed its remarkable success to more than the luster of banquets and the promise of substantial scholarships, however important they might have been in motivating the Fisher hopefuls. In an age of increasing marketing sophistication, the guild's promoters succeeded particularly well because GM's organizational apparatus enabled the company to reach and recruit young men from across the United States and Canada, in a manner so convincing that the contest appeared to be an integral part of the life of the teenage boy and his family. This was due both to GM's deft mobilization of leading economic, social, and cultural institutions to support the competition and to the intimate organizational parallels between the guild and its corporate parent.

The organizational shape of the Fisher Body Craftsman's Guild's contest closely resembled General Motors's business organization and followed the company's strategy of multidivisional management structure in various ways. In Sloan's formulation of GM's corporate strategy, the company sought "decentralized operations through coordinated control." While centralized control played an important role, the guild, like its parent company, invested in local economies and communities around the United States and Canada. By 1933, the guild's organization had covered over six hundred major cities and many other communities.[25] As is well known, GM's management approach contrasted with the Ford Motor Company's hierarchical and centrally organized structure, which sought to integrate production vertically.[26] Ford and GM differed not only in their internal management structure but also in their views on the world outside the confines of their companies. For one thing, Sloan sought to manage the reproduction of skills and the succession of people through calculated and predictable bureaucratic means. Promoting the virtues of the "Organization Man" as the model of the new corporate worker, Sloan detested idiosyncratic personalities such as Ford's.[27] If the Ford company emphasized vertical and backward integration of production, Sloan's strategy stood out because it also crafted a consumer framework for GM's products by seeking to integrate both personnel and consumers forwardly into the organization in a more planned and organic fashion. GM's sophisticated advertising campaigns, such as "Body by Fisher," represented one means of accomplishing that integration. The guild represented another.

The guild also marked an important alliance between the corporation and educational institutions. Its judging system, for example, cemented GM's collaboration with educators by integrating the school system into its ranks. Teams of judges enlisted from local and national educational elites evaluated the models for faithfulness to the original and level of craftsmanship (see fig. 6.9). On the national level, GM recruited a group of judges that reads like a roll call of engineering's educational elite. In 1937, for example, five presidents of engineering schools and seven deans of engineering colleges participated. An advisory committee included heads of secondary public school systems and leaders in manual arts teaching. These leading educators had ample opportunity to fraternize with GM's high-level managers and to exchange views with Harley H. Earl, head of the GM Art and Color Section, or Daniel C. Beard, president of the Boy Scouts, while they were in Detroit to judge the many models and participate in the festivities.[28]

**FIGURE 6.9**  *Fisher Body Craftsman's Guild judge examining 1960 entrants in the free model design contest.*

*From the General Motors Media Archives; neg. X-36690-11. Copyright © General Motors Corporation, used with permission.*

How did a boy get involved in such an institutional mobilization in 1930? How did the guild succeed in becoming such an integral part of the life of the teenager and his family that he would be willing to spend at least three hours a day after school on his work for the guild?[29] Based on information supplied by nearly two hundred contestants, a composite biography emerges of how a boy got drafted smoothly into the guild and learned to nurture his passion for cars as if it were his second nature.[30] There were at least three all-male institutional settings in which the teenage boy might be introduced to the guild: the YMCA, which organized local guild chapters, provided the first avenue; the Boy Scouts, which also participated in recruitment and integrated the contest into their merit badge program, was the second; and finally, the high school, where the vocational counselor's advice to participate often received further endorsement from the high school principal's active support, offered a third.[31] GM secured the sponsorship of high school principals, rewarding that collaboration by presenting a trophy not only to the boy who had won the contest but also to the school he attended.[32] To further wed these networks with the appropriate educational message, GM arranged for some thirty-two renowned athletes to narrate stories about enduring difficulties and overcoming initial failures on the path to ultimate success. Finally, GM organized promotional teams that visited 1,200 high schools each year. Some even visited the contestants at home.[33]

Once introduced to the guild and encouraged to participate in it, the teenager enrolled by submitting his name to the local Chevrolet, Buick, Oakland, Cadillac, or Oldsmobile dealer in his area well in advance of the deadline; officials calculated that on average seven boys enrolled at each GM dealership throughout the country. After enrolling, they received a membership card, a bronze guild button, a guide for their parents, a detailed manual with plans and instructions, and a quarterly newsletter called *The Guildsman*, which counseled them on how to proceed and paraded previous winners who showed off their successful careers as additional trophies.[34] To cap it off with a show of personal attention, members of the guild received greeting cards wishing them a Merry Christmas with the compliments of GM.[35] In some cases the support was much more substantial than that: GM divisions such as Delco Remy, the Packard Electric Company, the Mansfield Tool and Die Company, and the Fisher Body plant in Hamilton, Ohio, organized local guild clubs in their own communities under management supervision to help guide and encourage the boys making their models.[36] James Barnett recalled that community and industrial support for the guild program in his hometown of Anderson, Indiana, was substantial: "it is only in retrospect that I can fully appreciate that guidance we guildsman received."[37] The judging system, as has been mentioned already, brought GM's corporate management together with the Boy Scouts, high school teachers, and engineering educators. All of these institutional networks and rituals helped reproduce distinctly male patterns of paternal mentoring.

The emerging social and economic network extended beyond the coalition between the corporation and the engineering education elite to include the active support of the media. More than twenty national and local newspapers participated in weaving these intricate social and economic networks together into a seamless web. Among several newspapers, the *Detroit News* directly sponsored the guild by providing weekly instructions on how to plan, design, and build a model; other newspapers faithfully helped to build suspense by carrying accounts of deadlines, events, displays, or announcements of winners throughout the year.[38] The guild's advocates structured the annual cycle of each contest in such a way that reports on the Fisher Body Craftsman's Guild appeared in the press monthly and sometimes even weekly.

In other words, the contest was as much about building media events and suspense as about building models and male character to which girls had no access. A photograph taken at the annual banquet in 1931 just moments before the winners were announced symbolizes these close parallels most graphically. The photograph shows rows of

FIGURE 6.10    *Top: Winners of the 1932 state contests with their Napoleonic coaches awaiting the announcement of the four national winners. Bottom: The senior and junior winners.*

*From the Smithsonian Institution, National Museum of American History, Division of Transportation, neg. 9988.*

straight-backed boys identically clad in guild attire: jacket, beret, tie, and pin. Facing the camera with similar expressions of suspense on their faces, each boy clings to his exact miniature replica of the Napoleonic coach (see fig. 6.10). We can read this 1931 photograph as a perfect rendition of the emerging male corporate ideal. The contest's demand for exact imitation of the original coach model is neatly replicated in the demand for identical male character, something that would come to symbolize the ideal of the "organization man." As propagated so eloquently by Sloan, GM's corporate male ideal demanded patience, hard work, and a willingness to conform to the rules and regulations of a large organization, the very antithesis of the behavior associated with unpredictable and colorful personalities.[39]

Although many of the contest's features remained the same throughout the years, over time organizers gradually introduced one important change. Until the outbreak of World War II, the contest required that entrants build a miniature replica of the coach featured in the Fisher Body logo, but after the war, the guild's organizers decided to change this requirement, and began to ask for an original design instead of the faithful imitation. This change occurred neither suddenly nor in straightforward fashion, but reflected the contradictions and challenges General Motors faced. If the "free model" design seemed a radical departure from the straitjacket of careful imitation of the craft as represented by the 1931 photograph, a closer look at the change also shows continuities between the values at work in the coach and in the free model contests and between the idealized nineteenth-century culture of production and the twentieth-century culture of consumption.[40]

## The Napoleonic Coach versus the Free Model: (Dis)continuities and Contradictions

Why would an automotive giant such as GM and a body company such as Fisher sponsor an organization that harked back to the European Middle Ages and their craft traditions? Why would Fisher Body go to such extraordinary lengths to instill "craftsmanship" in a younger generation when auto manufacturers changed their production methods so thoroughly? How did the guild fit into the company's overall strategy? The premium put on skilled craftsmanship and endurance entailed a historic irony. At first glance, the guild's emphasis on craft seemed at odds with the growing economic trend toward a Fordist mode of mass production that sought to eliminate workers and replace them with machinery.

The Fisher Body Craftsman's Guild celebrated the craft ideal and demanded undivided labor (from the purchase of raw materials through toolmaking, design, execution, and finishing) at the same moment that production in the Fisher Body plants moved toward the assembly of parts by semiskilled workers. Because of the extraordinary degree of difficulty, many teenagers who started the process never finished; others negotiated the craft challenge by competing year after year; some competed for as long as eight consecutive years—from age 12, when they were first allowed to join the contest until age 20, when they lost eligibility. The guild's initial emphasis on craft as a path of male socialization disguised the emasculating nature of corporate America that produced it. The borrowing of guild past attempted to recapture and remake a masculine culture in the context of a twentieth-century society looking for new resources. In time, the guild evolved to fulfill the dual purpose—one concerned with the crafty imitation of existing models, the other based on the inspiration of new designs.[41] This tension of near opposites reflected an often uncomfortable transition within the company and the automotive industry as a whole. The guild expressed the contradictions, tensions, and solutions of GM's conflictual world of corporate culture that the Fisher family confronted as it moved into the corporation. As historian Roland Marchand has shown, many of GM's corporate strategies during the 1920s not only reflected an "outward quest for prestigious familiarity" but also sought to promote internal loyalty and corporate centralization.[42] The guild and Fisher's promotional campaigns were no exception.

From a thriving German-American family firm in Detroit during the second half of the nineteenth century, Fred Fisher and his six brothers swiftly built their company into the world's largest manufacturer of automobile bodies when they began to mass-produce closed bodies for various automobile companies during the first two decades of this century. Before World War I, combustion-engine cars had been mainly associated with utilitarian farmers or upper-class male adventure and racing.[43] Soon thereafter automotive design changed dramatically as manufacturers sought to broaden its appeal and market to include women.[44] Closing the automobile's body on all sides did just that; it moved motoring away from an exclusively sporting, summer, and leisure-time activity to a practical mode of transportation all year round, in all weather conditions. The Fisher brothers simultaneously stepped into and created this new market.[45] "The Fishers kept their eyes on closed car possibilities from the start," one chronicler of the firm explained in 1928 in detailing the Fishers' particular need for women as the company's market niche. "They saw that motoring would remain a summer sport until drivers and owners could be comfortable in the winter months. Women would never be really pleased with the automobile so long as their gowns and hats were at the mercy of wind and weather. After pressing these points on car manufacturers they were at last rewarded . . . for the first 'big order' for closed car bodies."[46] Thanks to the closing of the car's body, the mass of middle-class and urban women could venture out on the road in any weather. More important, perhaps, is that the car's body became the selling point of the automobile as a whole, over its technical specifications. The body of the car "is emphasized by thousands of successful automobile salesmen as an introduction to their selling effort and as an easy and sure way of having the buyer accept the entire car."[47] In this technical and marketing transformation of the automobile, the Fisher

Body Company played a critically important role as the world's largest producer of closed bodies and became the key company in GM's marketing strategy to beat Ford and other competitors.

Not only was the Fisher firm phenomenally successful in carving out a powerful new niche in the market, it also succeeded in making a smooth transition from a traditional, craft-oriented nineteenth-century family firm to a twentieth-century division of GM, despite the rapid changes in product and modes of production this new market strategy entailed. The seven Fisher brothers were brought into GM's managerial structure and without exception became leading corporate managers. At first they successfully negotiated for their continuing control within General Motors; holding onto their craft-inspired past and playing a crucial role in helping to bring about General Motors's success at styling, the Fisher clan moved into GM's managerial command during the 1930s. Fisher Body remained a family firm tightly embedded into the corporate structure; eventually, however, the brothers became the victims of their own success precisely because their very effective incorporation into the corporate structure rendered them obsolete.[48]

The Fisher Body Company's choice of the handmade Napoleonic coach as its logo illustrates the emblematic ways in which Fisher reworked the discontinuities and contradictions with the corporate world. Fisher Body's Napoleonic coach did not draw on an old family trademark, but represented an invented tradition. "This symbol" read an announcement in 1922, "will appear, from this time forward, on all finished products of the Fisher Body Corporation [and] records the care which the motor car manufacturer has exercised in providing your car with a body of the very best quality obtainable."[49] The imperial coach harked back to an old craft tradition and symbolized comfort and luxury—values believed to appeal to women in particular. Registered in 1922 and officially introduced as a trademark in 1923, the Napoleonic Coach logo began to circulate in the commercial and visual domain in 1926. That year also marked Fisher's incorporation into GM and the surrender of its autonomy as a coach-making firm.[50] Ironically, the Napoleonic coach—symbol and model for the guild-represented the craft tradition that the Fisher family was about to lose to GM. The coach perhaps breathed nostalgia for a Fisher that was long gone, but in the hands of GM it became less a symbol of the past than a malleable and invented tradition suitable for present and future use.[51] The trademark proved so successful that the coach became a stand-in for GM's own logo well into the 1980s. Inside GM, Fisher and its Napoleonic logo mitigated the contradictions between the worlds of craft and of mass production; outside, they carved out a new market. The Fisher slogan "Body by Fisher" in advertisements, featuring the suggestive curves of the female body, sought to convey an image of beauty, elegance, luxury, and craftsmanship associated with European royalty, and held it as a promise to the newly emerging middle classes.

Strictly speaking, of course, the European hand-crafted Napoleonic coach was out of reach for American middle classes, but the emperor's mass-produced coach by Fisher beckoned consumers to enter its fantasy world through the illusion of a custom-made body—something a Ford could not and would not provide. Most important was that the emphasis on comfort, luxury, and safety aimed to appeal to women.

However successfully wedded with GM's market strategy, the contradiction of the Fisher craftsman's world within a modern world came to a head in the guild's contest itself. The image of a Napoleonic coach might have served marketing, public relations, and corporate organization strategies very well indeed, but it failed to fulfill the needs of the participants in the guild, who labored relentlessly at a task far beyond a world available to them. For a few years between 1930 and 1937, the world of the old crafts reigned supreme in the contest. Then, for another ten years, the old world of craft and the modern world of design were brought together in a delicate balance that worked as a compromise for a short time, but after World War II the modernist design ideal triumphed completely.[52]

The changes in the contest punctuated the shifts in the company and in the fate of the Fisher family firm. The announcement of the free model design in 1937 symbolized the imminent erasure of the Fisher family's past as coach builders and its direct claim to European lineage. While the Fisher Napoleonic Coach trademark continued to figure prominently in successive decades, the decision of the organizers to permit the design of free models announced both the integration of the Fisher family firm into GM's management structure and the firm's growing loss of autonomy. For years the Fisher brothers clung to their belief in the superiority of wood frames that were sheathed in steel and tried to hold onto their tradition of craft in the production of automotive bodies, but they lost out to GM's increased overall control in 1937.[53] In the same year that the guild adopted the free design competition based on plaster and synthetics, GM eliminated all wooden parts from their cars. That change in policy also marked the growing confidence of General Motors in a new marketing strategy, where women and style occupied center stage, pushing craft knowledge and technical innovations to the background and marketing strategies to the fore.[54]

Many other analogies existed between the requirements in the contest and the manufacturing of automotive bodies. When Harley Earl joined the guild as an official in 1937, it was also the first year the guild allowed the boys to enter a car model after their own design. As the head of GM's Art and Color Section, Earl stood at the center of the new marketing strategy emphasizing style. Funded by the Fisher Body Division, managers expected Earl "to direct general production body design and to conduct research and development programs in special car designs," in his newly established department.[55] He pioneered many new techniques in automobile design that made styling an institutional-ized and closely coordinated activity and crucial strategy to GM.

The contest's postwar requirements squarely reflected the policy shift from the craft tradition of coach building to streamlined design, personified by Earl. While in both versions of the contest (the Napoleonic coach and the free model), the emphasis fell on building from scratch and using raw materials with no prefabricated parts, the free model mirrored GM's focus on "style," one that came to dominate the automotive industry as a whole.[56] The decision to eliminate Fisher's Napoleonic coach from the contest altogether in 1947 effec-tively consolidated and completed the erasure of the Fisher family's coach-building past; it emphasized style rather than structure. If the lush and majestic interiors and the proper mechanical functioning of parts rendered the points essential for a boy to win the contest in the Napoleonic Coach competition, in the free-model contest, mechani-cally accurate movement had no bearing whatsoever on the outcome. After World War II, smooth exterior finishing and an eye-pleasing style formed the sole criteria for winning a scholarship or money award. "I was impressed," Tristan Walker Metcalfe recalls of a conversation he had with one of the top designers as a young boy at the guild's banquet in the 1950s, "[at] how unimportant the efficiency and performance were relative to appearance and style, in their attitude then."[57] Typical of the ideology of streamlined design, the guild's instruction books and newsletters reflected the change and defined bad design as those mod-els that appeared "slow, boxy, heavy, or square," and good design as "graceful, light, fast, flowing," cultural values that projected the new design curve of femininity.[58]

The parallels between the boy's world of model making and the internal workings of the corporation did not end here. During the 1950s and 1960s, the contest instruction manuals closely followed the first twelve months of the planning stages of GM's celebrated annual model change: sketching, drawing to scale, making a clay model, cast-ing a plaster model, and finishing. The manuals recommended that contest entrants use clay modeling as an essential part of the design process, just as GM designers employed the clay modeling technique pioneered by Earl to create fluid car lines.[59]

It is hard to say how far GM planned the nexus between the guild and the corporation, but the linkages forged were powerful indeed. Providing an easy source of design ideas might not have been the orig-inal intent of the guild's advocates when the contest was introduced in the 1930s, if only because the Napoleonic coach did not lend itself eas-ily to that purpose, but sometime in the 1950s the guild's promotional literature cast it as explicit contest policy in no uncertain terms: "it is possible that a submitted model may include a design or idea which General Motors Corporation may use at some time, and it is under-stood that the Corporation and its licensees are entitled freely to use any such design or ideas." Furthermore, officials warned those who participated in the competition that GM retained the right to "freely use, for advertising or publicity, reproductions of likenesses, statements, names and addresses of Guild members and the models or reproductions of models submitted by them."[60] The most successful model cars generated enough interest for GM's design department to go to the trouble of buying them, and in some cases displaying them at GM's headquarters.[61] James Garner recalls, for example, that "my 1955 model sports car entry was purchased by G.M., design rights included. It was on display at their headquarters. . . . It was in a traveling show throughout the U.S."[62] And James Sampson remembers seeing, "in the Fisher Body Office Building in Warren, Mich., storerooms on the lower level [containing] a number of models that they had purchased from Guildsmen," which were then loaned to Sampson when he went on a promotional tour for the guild in 1956.[63] Whatever the guild's initiators had in mind at first, these statements suggest at the very least that the nexus between the contest organization and GM's design had become unambiguous by the 1950s.

If the guild's instructions and practices copied or extended the adult world of automotive design, they also revealed major differences with GM and Earl's Art and Color Section. Styling at GM had become a coordinated, controlled, and institutionalized strategy. Fifty designers were employed in this department alone and worked at the introduction of a new model that took two years of planning. While the guild's manuals instructed teenagers to make models by themselves—a process including toolmaking, designing, modeling, and execution—in Earl's hands this was no longer left to the "haphazard activity of engineers or salesmen as the need for a new model arose," but involved teams of specialists working for over a year.[64] In contrast to the adult world—where the actual shaping and manufacturing of automotive bodies shifted from the hands of Fisher Body's engineers, foremen, and skilled workers to the creativity appropriated by GM designers in the styling department—the boys were instructed to accomplish the same results in seclusion in attics, cellars, and bedrooms at home.[65] No wonder many teenagers who entered the contest never completed it.

Other organizations tried to emulate the Fisher Body Craftsman's Guild, but never attained quite the same success. Ford's Industrial Arts Awards Program, for instance, sought to establish a similar program through high school industrial arts and vocational education classes in the 1960s, but organizers soon discontinued it due to lack of enthusiasm.[66] In 1962, the Bank of Dearborn and the Ford Motor Company Design Center established the Greater Dearborn Automotive Design Competition, known as the Thunderbird Design Contest in the period between 1962 and 1971. The distribution of literature, dependent on school cooperation, proved to be a major obstacle because attempts to lure teachers into the program failed. Ford decided to abandon the competition because the "number of participants, public relations and advertising value did not warrant the necessary investment in time, manpower and money."[67] These failures show by contrast just how successful the Fisher Body Craftsman's Guild had been in allying the school system with the corporation and how complicated the organization, maintenance, and reproduction of male technical knowledge and skills—all neatly lined up with a particular corporate ideal—actually was.

The success of the partnership between educators and GM during the thirties, forties, and fifties is perhaps best illustrated by the dramatic way in which the guild unceremoniously unraveled in 1968 when the company was forced to terminate the project. Standard promotional procedure had GM officials visit the high schools of the winners, but after John Jacobus won the contest at the state level during the 1960s, he recalled that "when GM came to my high school principal and requested permission to make a presentation to an assembly of 2,000 in my honor, the corporation was turned down."[68] Going against well-established expectations, such official neglect would be startling enough for a teenage boy who had spent many spare hours on his model. For another, it announced that the coalition between GM and the educational institutions could no longer be taken for granted. More dramatic signs flagged the ending of the once successful alliances among corporations, educational institutions, the teenager, and his family. By the sixties male teenagers no longer projected their future careers into the corporations, as canvassing corporate representatives were shocked to find out. Someone close to the organization remembered that "in the late sixties, [GM's] presentations at inner-city high schools were not that well-received." He thought that "often the disillusioned, turned-off young of that era felt little motivation to exercise the kind of self-discipline required for the creativity and craftsmanship it took to win even a college scholarship" and concluded, "I hate to say it, but I think a few of our Field Representatives felt fortunate to escape from some of those school assemblies in one piece—it got that bad."[69]

By the stark contrast they provide, these examples illustrate the sheer organizational resources, capital, and goodwill that had sustained the guild for over three decades. Even though it had grown to appear quite natural, the values of this corporate, male coalition could no longer be taken for granted by the late 1960s. Other and earlier signs signaled that all was not well in the corporations. Since World War II, for example, the immense popularity of a marginalized subculture of hot rods and drag racing, where young men with ties to the automobile and aircraft industries souped up and stripped down mass-produced cars and raced them illegally, announced the emergence of an exuberant, youthful male rebellion at a grassroots level. As historian Robert Post characterizes these early racing aficionados, they were "unmarried males, many of them ex-GIs, with plenty of spare dollars,

enhanced mechanical skills, an assertive bent, and a love of speed."
One could read their tinkering as a rebellion of sorts against gender
roles mapped out by the corporations. Their illegal activities implied a
rebellion against the modern corporate male identity of the "Organization Man" promoted by Sloan and by GM and against what they considered the frivolous effeminate designs coming from Detroit.[70]

In the postwar era, the guild's introduction of a free design model
sought to simultaneously convey and plan consumers' freedom of
expression. In contrast with the young men, who cherished the buoy-
ant grassroots and autodidactic culture of hot rods and drag racing, the
guild promoted a sense of individual expression that was essentially
corporate and adult-sponsored; it was carefully managed, supervised,
and circumscribed from above. Moreover, if hot rods and drag racing
emphasized high performance, mechanical ingenuity, exposed interiors, and adventure, GM and the guild merchandised smooth surfaces,
lush interiors, convenience and comfort associated with women and
family values. Hot-rodders relished stripped-down bodies; GM's automotive style relied on enhanced car bodies as a marketing strategy. As
the advocates of the Fisher free design contest instructed, the car's
body, not its interior, constituted the pièce de résistance in this new
design configuration. The miniaturized world of the guild's free design
contest replicated GM's famed annual model changeover that cosmet-
ically altered the car's exterior irrespective of interior technical specifications. GM's emphasis on enhanced bodies, smooth surfaces, and
female models had not been a matter of casual choice, but was part
and parcel of an elaborate effort to beat Ford's successful formula of
spartan utilitarianism associated with male virtues of thrift.[71] The
Fisher firm and its parent company, General Motors, confronted and
produced the female-gendered consumer through several institutional
means such as their establishment of the Art and Color Department,
their engagement of the advertising agency Batten, Barton, Durstine,
and Osborn, and their recruitment of famed illustrator McClelland
Barclay for the Fisher girl campaign. The strategy was so successful
that, when Barclay's Fisher girls appeared for the Fisher Body Company in *Life* magazine, *Motor* magazine editor Ray W. Sherman
described the change from Fordism to Sloanism as follows: "the automotive business has almost overnight become a feminine business
with a feminine market."[72] The strategy of smooth surfaces, convenience, and comfort consciously projected female values, however. As
a Fisher advertisement told retailers and other interested readers, "for
years Fisher Bodies have been built with feminine tastes in mind."[73] In
the new design curve of the automotive bodies that Fisher produced,
women and the female body played a prominent if not essential role,
as the hot-rodders sensed. The 1927 *Life* magazine "Body by Fisher"
advertisement (fig. 6.2) encapsulated GM's and Fisher's deliberate
marketing creation of women as consumers.

However successful, the automotive style as a consumable female-coded product proved to be a precarious enterprise, indeed.[74] If women were all surface and cosmetics, the automotive industry's content and operations, the company insisted, were to be left to men.[75] Establishing all-male organizations such as the Fisher Body Craftsman's Guild was one of many ways to reestablish firm, strict, exaggerated safeguards against possible female incursions. They helped maintain clear boundaries between designers and users, men and women, and between producers and consumers. While the corporation sought to tease out women as consumers, it recruited boys through the conduit of the YMCA, the Boy Scouts, and other all-male organizations.

The 1931 *National Geographic* advertisement (fig. 6.1) suggests, as has this article, that the playful world of model cars was not merely lighthearted, diverting, and amusing, nor was it inconsequential: it was a very serious business indeed. While Fisher boys found themselves making model cars with a view to an engineering scholarship, the future proposed to girls cast them as receivers—*consumers*—of what the boys produced. The world of Fisher Body provides us insights into the institutionalized ways in which boys, male teenagers, and adult men were channeled into the domain designated as technical; and conversely, the ways in which girls, female teenagers, and adult women were positioned as consumers, as the seemingly natural antitheses of the productive, masculine domain. If the gentle path to the showroom was open to all, the hard road to the design department demanded manly virtues acquired through boys' rites of passage, carefully constructed by just such coalitions as the Fisher Body Craftsman's Guild.

The smooth change from the Napoleonic coach to the free model showed how the craft ideal could be playfully adapted to the new requirements of mass production in a new phase of the automotive industry and consumerism associated with women's new roles: style was supposed to recapture notions of freedom and individuality in mass-produced and standardized consumer goods. But attempts to remake the past into the future by employing medieval rituals obscured pertinent facts about the present—including the changing representations of masculinity and femininity. The contest recruited boys to make models, casting them as knowledgeable producers, while Fisher girls were groomed to be models for the new consumer goods. These seemingly clear-cut roles nevertheless obscured a new truth about gender in the new phase of the consumer society. Boys, and for that matter men, were potential consumers as well, as even the supporters of the guild seemed to have acknowledged. The guild recruited not only at schools but also through automobile showrooms and department stores such as Macy's and Hudson's, while the organizers made sure to reserve ample time for contestants to shop in downtown Detroit. As we have seen, an industry trade journal considered the influence of boys in automobile purchasing significant enough to argue that, by way of the guild, General Motors meant to extend goodwill through the recruitment of boys for the model-making contest. By the same token, women and girls entered the buyer's market not merely as passive actors but as the essential builders of an expanding consumers' society. Yet in the tales of modern gender mythology told by organizations like the guild, boys' technophilia, whether as consumer or producer, was born of this role as potential designer.

## Notes

1. So far, the Fisher Body Craftsman's Guild has not been the subject of any scholarly treatment. John Jacobus generously shared his sustained childhood passion for the guild with this author and has generated most of the primary source material. Unless otherwise noted, all citations of primary source materials pertaining to the guild are to Fisher Body Craftsman's Guild Papers (FBCGP) donated by Jacobus to the Smithsonian, Division of Engineering and Industry, Division of Transportation, National Museum of American History. Jacobus also gave access to his personal collection on the guild.

2. W. A. Fisher to Walter S. Carpenter, W. S. Carpenter Papers, series 11, part 2, box 821, Hagley Museum and Library manuscripts, Wilmington, Del.

3. On the creation of the consumer as female by corporations and professional groups, see Roland Marchand, *Advertising the American Dream: Making Way for Modernity, 1920–1940* (Berkeley and Los Angeles: University of California Press, 1985); Virginia Scharff, *Taking the Wheel: Women and the Coming of the Motor Age* (Albuquerque: University of New Mexico Press, 1991); by women professionals, see Carolyn Goldstein, "Mediating Consumption: Home Economics and American Consumers, 1900–1940" (Ph.D. diss., University of Delaware, 1994); Jackie Dirks, "Righteous Goods: Women's Production, Reform Publicity, and the National Consumers' League, 1891–1919" (Ph.D. diss., Yale University, 1996).

4. On GM's advertising and marketing strategy, see Roland Marchand, "The Corporation Nobody Knew: Bruce Barton, Alfred Sloan, and the Founding of the General Motors 'Family,' " *Business History Review* 65 (1991): 825–75.

5. For examples of the "Body by Fisher" campaign, see the many advertisements from 1926 through the 1960s in such magazines as *Vogue, Life, Saturday Evening Post, National Geographic,* and *Woman's Home Companion.* Created by McClelland Barclay, the Fisher girl ran for nine years and established the genre for Fisher Body Company and GM. On Barclay, see the *National Cyclopedia of American Biography,* 34 (New York: J. T. White, [1898–1930]), 351; W. Blackman, *Facts and Faces by and about 26 Contemporary Artists* (n.p., 1937); *Art Digest* May 1939, 28; and *Current Biography,* 1940, 50–51. GM aligned itself also with the quintessential movie "flapper," Colleen Moore, who appeared in *Perfect Flapper* and *Flaming Youth;* see *International Dictionary of Films and Filmmakers* 3, *Actors and Actresses* (Detroit: St. James Press, 1992), 698, and Colleen Moore, *Silent Star* (Garden City, N.J.: Doubleday, 1968), 231–45. For a general history, see Marchand, *Advertising the American Dream.*

6. The classic statements are in Joan W. Scott, "Gender: A Useful Category of Historical Analysis," *Journal of American History* 91 (1986), 1053–75, and Sandra Harding, *The Science Question in Feminism* (Ithaca, N.Y.: Cornell University Press, 1986). On gender and technical knowledge, see Ruth Schwartz Cowan, foreword to Cynthia Cockburn, *Machinery of Dominance: Women, Men, and Technical Know-How* (Boston: Northeastern University Press, 1985).

7. Margaret W. Rossiter, *Women Scientists in America: Struggles and Strategies to 1940* (Baltimore: Johns Hopkins University Press, 1982) and *Women Scientists in America: Before Affirmative Actions 1940–1972* (Baltimore: Johns Hopkins University Press, 1995) are the best analyses of barriers to women's entering the fields of science and engineering. On engineering, see Martha Moore Trescott, "Lillian Moller Gilbreth and the Founding of Modern Industrial Engineering," in Joan Rothschild, ed., *Machina Ex Dea: Feminist Perspectives on Technology* (New York: Pergamon Press, 1983), 23–37, and "Women Engineers in History: Profiles in Holism and Persistence," in Violet B. Haas and Carolyn C. Perrucci, eds., *Women in Scientific and Engineering Professions* (Ann Arbor: University of Michigan Press, 1984), 181–205. See also Ruth Oldenziel, "Gender and the Meanings of Technology: Engineering in the U.S., 1880–1945" (Ph.D. diss., Yale University, 1992), chap. 6., and *Making Technology Masculine: Men, Women and Modern Machines in America, 1870–1945* (Ann Arbor: University of Michigan Press, 1999).

8. On the history of toys and consumer culture, see: Lawrence Frederic Greenfield, "Toys, Children, and the Toy Industry in a Culture of Consumption, 1890–1991" (Ph.D. diss., Ohio State University, 1991). More specialized information is provided by Erin Cho, "Lincoln Logs: Toying with the Frontier Myth," *History Today* 43 (1993): 31–34; Richard Saunders, "Pedal Power: The Kiddie Car," *Timeline* 6, no. 6 (1989): 16–25; "A Glimpse into the Magical World of Old-Time Toys," *American History Illustrated* 19, no. 8 (1984), 22–29; Robert K. Weis, "To Please and Instruct the Children," *Essex Institute Historical Collections* 123, no. 2 (1987): 117–49; Janet Holmes, "Economic Choices and Popular Toys in the Nineteenth Century," *Material History Bulletin* 21 (1985): 51–56; Mark Irwin, "Nineteenth-Century Toys and Their Role in the Socialization of Imagination," *Journal of Popular Culture* 17, no. 4 (1984): 107–15.

9. Carroll W. Pursell, "Toys, Technology and Sex Roles in America, 1920-1940," in Martha Moore Trescott, ed., *Dynamos and Virgins Revisited: Women and Technological Change* (Methuen, N.J.: Scarecrow Press, 1979), 252–67.

10. Donald W. Ball, "Toward a Sociology of Toys: Inanimate Objects, Socialization, and the Demography of the Doll World," *Sociological Quarterly* 8 (1957): 447, quoted in Pursell, "Toys," 254.

11. Wick Humble, "The Fisher Body Craftsman's Guild: GM's 34-Year Talent Search," *Special Interest Autos,* February 1981, 28; John L. Jacobus, "Once and Future Craftsmen: A Fisher Guild Scrapbook, 1930 to 1968," *Automobile Quarterly* 15, no. 2 (1987): 206.

12. These figures do not reflect the costs incurred by other organizations, such as the Boy Scouts' recruitment efforts on behalf of General Motors. Jacobus, "Craftsmen," 206; Arthur Pound, *The Turning Wheel: The Story of General Motors through Twenty-Five Years, 1908–1933* (Garden City, N.Y.: Doubleday, Doran, 1934), 300.

13. "This Is the Story of Fisher Body" (Detroit, 1952), General Motors Research laboratories Library Collection, Warren, Michigan, 10; all figures come from GM. Pound, *The Turning Wheel*, 300; "Fisher Guild Will Submit Car Designs," *Automobile Topics,* March 1, 1937, 157; Embury A. Hitchcock, *My Fifty Years in Engineering* (Caldwell, Idaho: Caxton Printers, 1939), 262; *Fisher in the News* (1966 pamphlet) and clippings, FBCGP; Jacobus, "Craftsmen," 206; Skip Geear, "The Fisher Body Napoleonic Coach," parts 1–3, *Generator and Distributor,* June 1988, 15–19; July 1988, 24–30; August 1988, 15–19.

14. Hitchcock, *My Fifty Years,* 262.

15. Raymond Doerr Scrapbook Collection (1931), Archives Center, National Museum of American History, Smithsonian Institution (hereafter, Doerr Scrapbook ); Humble, "Talent Search," 33.

16. Jacobus, "Craftsmen," 207.

17. Ken J. Dowd to Jacobus, February 21, 1985.

18. Ray Peeler to Jacobus, May 6, 1985. For similar reactions and assessments of the guild's influence on their career paths, see letters to Jacobus from Raymond Doerr, April 4, 1985; Leo C. Peiffer, April 9, 1985; Bert E. Ray, July 17, 1985; L. W. Jacobs, April 2, 1985; James Garner, February 23, 1985; David Rom, March 6, 1985; Gilbert McArdle, March 20, 1985; Art Russell, n.d.; Randall Wrington, March 8, 1985; M. B. Antonick,

March 4, 1985; James Barnett, n.d.; David P. Onopa, n.d.; Albert W. Brown Jr., February 1, 1985; Anthony Simone, n.d.; Lane Prom, February 8, 1985; Dale Gnage, January 22, 1985. The Soap Box Derby was established in 1934 by GM.

19. The sense of male fellowship can be gleaned from the extensive correspondence between Jacobus and other ex-guildsmen. Leo C. Peiffer to Jacobus, April 9, 1985; Jacobus, telephone interview with author, September 28, 1991; Jacobus, conversation with author, August 6, 1996.

20. The records primarily concern winners. Future research will concentrate on the differences and similarities between the winners and the rank-and-file members of the guild. The guild's organizers were self-conscious about the difference: "Guildsmen are cautioned not to compare their own model cars with the cars in the exhibit. They must keep in mind that the models in the exhibit are some of the best from among the top winners in past Guild competitions and are the products of four, five, even six different attempts at the project." *The Guildsman* 4, no. 4 (1951): 3.

21. Carroll M. Gantz to Jacobus, November 13, 1984.

22. Throughout the Doerr Scrapbook we find evidence of family cooperation in the families of other participants; Michael Pienmka to Jacobus, November 26, 1984. See also "Craftsman Remembered," *The Arkansas City Traveller,* August 16, 1983; Myron Webb to Jacobus, June 18, 1985; David Rom to Jacobus, March 6, 1985; Jacobus interview. In a still broader context, sisters also contributed to this household economy as they went to work to contribute to the family income, allowing their brothers to go to college. Upholstery was also a woman's job at Fisher; see "General Motors II: Chevrolet," *Fortune,* January 1939, 36–46, 103–4, 107–10; Sidney Fine, *Sit-Down: The General Motors Strike of 1936–1937* (Ann Arbor: University of Michigan Press, 1969), 156.

23. Humble, "Talent Search," 29.

24. "Building Tomorrow's Customers: How Fisher Body Is Securing the Good-Will of Boys through Its Craftsman's Guild," *Printer's Ink,* November 20, 1930, 11–12; "Guild Wins Goodwill," *System and Business Management,* March 1934, 135–36.

25. Pound, *The Turning Wheel,* 300.

26. Alfred P. Sloan, *My Years with General Motors* (1963; reprint, New York: Doubleday, 1986); Arthur J. Kuhn, *GM Passes Ford, 1918–1938: Designing the General Motors Performance-Control System* (University Park: University of Pennsylvania Press, 1986).

27. James J. Flink, *The Automobile Age* (Cambridge, Mass.: MIT Press, 1988), 232.

28. Presidents of engineering schools: Thomas Baker, Carnegie-Mellon; M. L. Brittain, Georgia Tech; S. W. Stratton, Massachusetts Institute of Technology; P. P. Kolbe, Brooklyn Polytech; R. A. Millikan, Cal Tech. Deans of engineering colleges: M. E. Cooley, University of Michigan; George J. Davis Jr., University of Georgia; W. F. Durand, Stanford University; E. A. Hitchcock, Ohio State University; D. S. Kimball, Cornell University; R. L. Sackett, Pennsylvania State College; T. A. Steiner, University of Notre Dame. See Hitchcock, *My Fifty Years,* 264; see also Mortimer E. Cooley with Vivien B. Keatley, *Scientific Blacksmith* (Ann Arbor: University of Michigan Press, 1947), 137; Dexter S. Kimball, *I Remember* (New York: McGraw-Hill, 1953); Pound, *The Turning Wheel,* 300, and various issues of *The Guildsman.*

29. In the 1960s the teenagers needed an average of 275 hours to finish a model of their own design.

30. This composite is based on biographical information supplied by two hundred participants collated from a variety of sources, including Jacobus's correspondence with a great number of former participants, several issues of *The Guildsman,* various guild pamphlets describing winners throughout the period between 1930 and 1968, and the rich descriptions contained in local newspaper clippings. In some cases a nearly complete biography emerges; in others only the mere outlines are generated in this manner.

31. Doerr Scrapbook; Humble, "Talent Search," 29. The exact class background of the guild participants and the role the guild played in their class aspirations remain in question, but some inferences may be drawn on GM's 1962 statistics on occupations of the fathers of guild entrants, the preponderance of immigrant names and places of res-

idence in the sample of two hundred members collated, and personal conversations with former participants Nil Disco, John Jacobus, Art Mollela, and Rudi Volti. The involvement of the Boy Scouts included more than active recruitment efforts since the organization also helped to formulate the guild's dress code and chaperoned winners of the state competitions from their home states to Detroit. Pound claimed that the guild was the only boys' organization sponsored by the Boy Scouts; see Pound, *The Turning Wheel*, 300.

32. Robert D. Smith to Jacobus, November 8, 1984; Humble, "Talent Search," 29; Jacobus, "Craftsmen," 206.

33. Doerr Scrapbook.

34. Geear, "Napoleonic Coach," 15; Humble, "Talent Search," 27, 29.

35. John Rempel Jr., to Jacobus, August 20, 1986.

36. David O. Burnett to Jacobus, March 10, 1988; *Fisher in the News,* and clippings (see n. 13 above).

37. James Barnett to Jacobus, n.d.

38. Doerr Scrapbook; Humble, "Talent Search"; Skip Geear to Jacobus, April 7, 1992; Herbert Lozier to Jacobus, August 10, 1984.

39. Despite his aversion to colorful personalities, Sloan himself did not fit the character of the "organization man," as Peter Drucker emphasizes in his introduction to Sloan, *My Years with General Motors*; see also Alfred P. Sloan and Boyden Sparkes, *Adventures of a White-Collar Man* (New York: Doubleday, Doran, 1941) and Flink, *The Automobile Age*, 232. For contrast, see Warren Susman, "Culture Heroes: Ford, Barton, Ruth," in *Culture As History: The Transformation of American Society in the Twentieth Century* (New York: Pantheon Books, 1984), 122–49.

40. Susman, *Culture As History;* Marchand, *Advertising the American Dream*.

41. Fisher Body Craftsman's Guild pamphlet, n.d., Henry Ford Museum and Greenfield Village Library and Archives, Dearborn, Michigan; see also *The Guildsman* for the year 1951 and thereafter.

42. Roland Marchand, "The Inward Thrust of Institutional Advertising: General Electric and General Motors in the 1920s," *Business and Economic History* 18 (1989): 188–96, and "The Corporation Nobody Knew."

43. Reynold M. Wik, "The Early Automobile and the American Farmer," 37–47, and Michael L. Berger, "The Great White Hope on Wheels," 59–70; both in David L. Lewis and Laurence Goldstein, eds., *The Automobile and American Culture* (Ann Arbor: University of Michigan Press, 1983).

44. Scharff, *Taking the Wheel*, chaps. 3–4. For a more general account, see David A. Hounshell, *From the American System to Mass Production, 1800–1932: The Development of Manufacturing Technology in the United States* (Baltimore, Md.: Johns Hopkins University Press, 1984), chap. 5; Flink, *The Automobile Age*; Kenneth T. Jackson, *Crabgrass Frontier: The Suburbanization of the United States* (New York: Oxford University Press, 1985), chap. 6. Electric cars had been catering to upper-class women at an earlier date, but had failed. Rudi Volti, "Why Internal Combustion?" *American Heritage of Invention and Technology*, Fall 1990, 42–47; Mark Schiffer, *Changing the Wheel: Women and the Electric Car* (Washington, D.C.: Smithsonian Institution Press, 1995).

45. Roger B. White, "Body by Fisher: The Closed Car Revolution," *Automobile Quarterly* 29 (1991): 46–63, and "Fisher Body Corporation," in George S. May, ed., *The Automobile Industry, 1896–1920* (New York: Facts on File, 1990), 187–92. Surprisingly, White's articles are the only scholarly treatment of the subject. I am grateful to him for sharing his research on the subject. See also Michael Lamm, "Body by Fisher," *Special-Interest Autos,* May–June 1978, 18–25, and Donald Finlay Davis, *Conspicuous Consumption: Automobiles and Elites in Detroit, 1899–1933* (Philadelphia: Temple University Press, 1988).

46. Pound, *The Turning Wheel*, 289.

47. "The Origin of the Emblem 'Body by Fisher'" (July–August, 1928), Fisher Body Papers, National Museum of American History, Division of Transportation, Division of Engineering and Industry, Smithsonian Institution.

48. White, "Body by Fisher" and "Fisher Body Corporation."

49. "Fisher Bodies," *Saturday Evening Post,* June 24, 1922, 37.

50. From 1926 until 1984, Fisher was a division of the GM company.

51. On the uses of history by major companies see Susman, *Culture As History.*

52. The annual competition ceased for several years because of the war.

53. White, "Body by Fisher," 63.

54. Richard Tedlow, *New and Improved: The Story of Mass Marketing in America* (New York: Basic Books, 1990), chap. 3; Marchand, "The Corporation That Nobody Knew" and "The Inward Thrust of Institutional Advertising."

55. Flink, *The Automobile Age,* 235.

56. *The Guildsman* explicitly stated that interiors were no longer important but that style was; *The Guildsman* 5, no. 1 (1957). In the 1960s, controversy arose over GM's emphasis on design and styling and would soon become the focus of consumer advocate Ralph Nader's indictment, *Unsafe at Any Speed: The Designed-In Dangers of the American Automobile* (New York: Grossman, 1965). In it, Nader accused GM of callous negligence in the design and manufacture of the rear-engine Corvair. For further criticism, see Jeffrey O'Connell, *Safety Last* (New York: Random House, 1966).

57. Tristan Walker Metcalfe to Jacobus, November 25, 1984.

58. For an example, see Fisher Body Craftsman's Guild, "How to Build a Model Car" (1957), General Motors Research Laboratories Library Collection, 2–3.

59. Flink, *The Automobile Age,* 201.

60. Fisher Body Craftsman's Guild, "Designing and Building a Model Car" (1958), General Motors Research Laboratories Library Collection, 26.

61. Harold C. Krysak to Jacobus, n.d.; James Garner to Jacobus, February 23, 1985; Art Russell to Jacobus, n.d. Norman Law sold his model to GM; see Fred C. Schollmeyer to Jacobus, February 21, 1985.

62. James Garner to Jacobus, February 23, 1985.

63. James T. Sampson to Jacobus, January 1, 1985.

64. Flink, *The Automobile Age,* 236; Jeffrey L. Meikle, *Twentieth Century Limited: Industrial Design in America, 1925-1939* (Philadelphia: Temple University Press, 1979), 12.

65. For some insights into the role of foremen and skilled workers in the styling of cars on the shop floor at Fisher, see White, "Body by Fisher"; on the rise of designers over engineers in Earl's styling department, see "General Motors II: Chevrolet," 47.

66. David L. Lewis to Jacobus, January 10, 1986.

67. H. Benson to Jacobus, March 13, 1974.

68. Jacobus interview.

69. Humble, "Talent Search," 34.

70. For a rich description of this subculture, see Robert C. Post, *High Performance: The Culture and Technology of Drag Racing, 1950–1990* (Baltimore, Md.: Johns Hopkins University Press, 1994). See also Gerald Silk, et al., *Automobile and Culture* (New York: Harry N. Abrams, 1984), 177–250. For an unsurpassed journalistic account, see Tom Wolfe, *The Kandy-Kolored Tangerine-Flake Streamline Baby* (New York: Farrar, Straus and Giroux 1965).

71. Meikle, *Twentieth Century Limited,* 12.

72. Scharff, *Taking the Wheel,* 115. On Batten, Barton, Durstine, and Osborn, see Sloan, *My Years with General Motors;* and Marchand, "The Corporation Nobody Knew" and "The Inward Thrust of Institutional Advertising." On the Art and Color Section see Meikle, *Twentieth Century Limited.* On the subject of Gibson Girls, flappers, and fashion, see Jennifer Craik, *The Face of Fashion: Cultural Studies of Fashion* (London: Routledge, 1994).

73. "A Coach for Cinderella," *Literary Digest,* February 27, 1932, 25.

74. For a general discussion on the precarious nature of the female market for the advertising profession, see Marchand, *Advertising the American Dream,* chaps. 1 and 2, and Scharff, *Taking the Wheel.*

75. "A Coach for Cinderella."

# Masculine Guidance

*Boys, Men, and Newspapers, 1930–1939*

---

TODD ALEXANDER POSTOL

"Well do I remember the newsboy of thirty years ago," Edward D. Hood of the *Savannah (Georgia) News and Press* recalled at a gathering of fellow circulation managers in mid-1933. "His face was seldom washed, his hair never combed, or his teeth brushed." The contrast with modern circulation conditions was extraordinary. In only a few short years, the industry had transformed the dirty, undersized "newsie" of 1900 into the "clean, upright, edu-cated 'newspaper merchant' of today." There was, Hood said, "no greater metamorphosis" in the history of the American newspaper business than the move from unregulated street trading to supervised home delivery work. At the heart of this change was the professional circulation manager. Unlike earlier managers who were little more than "slave bosses," the up-to-date circulation chief of the 1930s served as "a teacher, an instructor and guide" to the nation's half million work-ers in newspaper distribution. With so much attention being focused on New Deal programs, Hood thought it was time circulation man-agers tell people about their own "new deal for the newspaper boy."[1]

Though individual managers had experimented with carrier train-ing schemes as early as World War I, it took the jolt of economic col-lapse to spur the industry to collective action. The middle-class American newspaper boy was a product of the Great Depression, born of the need to boost sagging advertising revenues and improve carrier profitability. Print advertising revenues in the United States swiftly declined in the wake of Black Tuesday. Newspapers responded to dete-riorating market conditions with one of the few resources at their com-mand: inexpensive juvenile labor. In contrast to existing research, in this essay I follow Hood's lead in placing circulation managers directly at the center of this process. Circulation managers—not reformers, novelists, or philanthropists—conceived and implemented the person-nel policies that revitalized newspaper distribution in the United States in the 1930s. Operating in relative obscurity, managers forged an enduring alliance between daily delivery work and middle-class boyhood that shaped the occupational outlook of generations of American men.[2]

Scholars such as Susan Porter Benson, Stephen H. Norwood, and Patricia Cooper have probed the historical relationships among labor, consumption, and gender in American society through the single-industry case study. I believe this format, which has not been applied to juvenile workers, is ideal for investigating the internal evolution of newspaper distribution. Why did the newspaper industry expand the use of juvenile labor at a time when minors were disappearing from all other major industries in the United States? And why did middle-class parents approve of paper route work for their sons? The cultural implications of masculinity in the entry labor market have only begun to be investigated. One reason for this is a lack of detailed historical material on how boys were trained to assume the economic responsibilities of manhood. Written accounts of carrier training procedures, produced by the men who conceived and implemented those procedures, provide rare glimpses into how boys and men worked together in the maturing service economy. Only by looking at how boys were trained to assume their duties as workers can we begin to understand the broader significance of child work in modern America.[3]

Until fairly recently the historiographical literature on workers in the 1930s was devoted to the effects of mass unemployment on skilled workers and labor's epic struggles to organize key sectors of the American economy. Institutional labor history has paid much less attention to the experiences of nonunionized workers, the expansion of the consumption ethic, and the changing status of working children. The American newspaper circulation industry did not witness protracted sit-down strikes or bloody battles between striking wage earners and company goons. But it did undergo a quiet transformation that profoundly altered the relationship between middle-class boyhood and paid work in the United States.[4]

Drawing on connections linking men and boys in the marketplace, circulation heads created a gendered managerial philosophy that was distinctive to their industry. This philosophy, which I term *masculine guidance*, allowed managers to position themselves as guardians of the nation's newspaper boys in ways that would have been impossible with adult employees. The growth of masculine guidance raises important questions about gender and labor during the Depression. How, in the short term, did the economic scarcity of the 1930s shape managerial training policies? In what ways did managers prepare boys for route service, and how did managers structure incentives and rewards for working children? And, in the long term, how did these strategies influence the industry's new, commercialized vision of American boyhood?[5]

Historians who have written on the newspaper circulation business have largely ignored middle-class carriers, concentrating instead on

Todd Alexander Postol

the small, highly visible minority of working-class children in the street trades. Studies by Jon Bekken, David Nasaw, and others have focused on *newsboys*, who sold papers to pedestrians, to the virtual exclusion of *newspaper boys*, who delivered papers each day to the homes of subscribers. The history of working street children is of course valuable. But it is essential to recognize that by the time of the New Deal the overwhelming majority of juvenile workers in newspaper circulation were route carriers; many of these boys came from financially stable backgrounds. Their story has not been told. Authors intent on chronicling the economic exploitation of working-class newsboys have overlooked the earliest work experiences of millions of middle-class American boys.[6]

## Carriers, Managers, and the Depression

Writing about the industry in which these boys worked poses unique challenges. Most of the workers were below the age of sixteen. Carriers kept their routes for a short time, and when they departed they seldom left written records behind.[7] The industry lacked a geographic center, and managers were far too busy to record and preserve accounts of their experiences. Despite this, there is a wealth of material documenting the creation of the middle-class American paper boy. Any discussion of supervised delivery service must begin with the untapped archives of the International Circulation Managers' Association (ICMA). Originally founded in 1898 as the National Association, Managers of Newspaper Circulation, the ICMA was the sole professional organization for circulation managers for most of this century. By 1930 the ICMA was the largest body of its kind in the world, with seven hundred members in the United States and Canada. One of the Association's primary functions was to serve as a clearinghouse for local and regional materials produced by its members. The ICMA's monthly bulletins and the proceedings of its annual conventions contain thousands of reports, articles, and discussions dealing with every aspect of carrier supervision. They also include reprinted studies from the meetings of subsidiary regional circulation associations and even promotional items from individual newspapers that otherwise would not have survived.[8]

In addition to materials produced, collected, and preserved by ICMA members, trade journals such as *Editor and Publisher*, *The Bulletin of the American Newspaper Publishers Association*, *The American Newspaper Boy*, and *Circulation Management* contain useful information on circulation practices. Finally, managers produced an assortment of training manuals, guides, and circulation texts. Quite apart from industry records, government agencies during the Depression issued studies of working children in both the street trades and route work. All of these historical sources, it should be noted, reflect the attitudes and prejudices of the adults who produced them. The expectations of the boys who distributed newspapers, their motivation in acquiring a route, and the various tactics they may have used in circumventing managerial control are largely absent. But this limitation, characteristic of nonunionized industries with high employee turnover, does not invalidate the importance of either trade or government records. Investigations undertaken by the U.S. Children's Bureau, for example, are one of the few sources for determining the ages, hours, and earnings of working boys. And trade sources, which were never intended to be read by anyone beyond the narrow borders of the industry, unintentionally reveal how larger cultural constructions of gender, work, and boyhood redefined middle-class route work during a time of uncertain economic change.[9]

By the start of the Depression, newspaper circulation was the leading source of paid employment for school-aged children in the United States. During the 1930s, between 350,000 and 500,000 minors worked annually distributing the news. Since tabulations of working children were static, measuring only the number of boys at work at a given moment in time, the number of individuals who passed through the industry during these years may have been much higher. As the decade progressed, the share of juvenile workers in home delivery service steadily rose. Although figures are not available for the start of the decade, roughly two-thirds of the boys in the industry were engaged in delivery work in 1932. By 1939, fully 90 percent were daily route carriers.[10]

The masculine world of work defined newspaper circulation. Prior to the rise of supervised home delivery service girls had played a limited, but real, role in street selling. Following the progressive reform of the city, however, girls were driven from both the street and the route. By 1930, nearly everyone involved with newspaper circulation in the United States was male. In those rare instances where girls in the Depression were actually given the opportunity to have a daily route, they proved capable of offering dependable service. Manager George Williams, of the *Iola (Kansas) Daily Register*, was highly unusual: he utilized only girl carriers. "The boys I tried were no good," Williams noted in 1930, "and if I didn't want boys, girls were about the only other choice I had!" But Williams was a courageous exception; all other circulation managers on record during the Depression equated route work with the competitive masculine marketplace. A study of minors in newspaper distribution undertaken by the National Recovery Administration in 1933 indicated that nearly 99 percent of route carriers in the United States were male.[11]

Boys involved in route work differed in several key respects from boys in the street trade. In 1934 the Children's Bureau conducted an investigation of children in newspaper distribution in seventeen American cities. The study found that, on average, carriers were

FIGURE 7.1   *As managers looked to increase readership, they began training boys to market newspaper subscriptions to the general public, and promoted the value of the work for the news carriers.*

*From* American Newspaper Boys *(May 1937), p. 7.*

slightly older than street sellers. The median age for newsboys was 13.7 years; the median age for home delivery workers was 14.3 years. Significantly, there were fewer very young carriers. Most managers believed that children under 12 did not make suitable candidates for route training. As a result, just 6 percent of the carriers in the survey were under the age of 12. The corresponding percentage for street selling was nearly three times higher. Boys in home delivery also tended to do better in school and were arrested less frequently than street workers. These differences stemmed from the settings where the children worked. Newsboys who sold on the street often ventured far from their own neighborhoods. Route carriers delivered papers closer to home and were generally shielded from dangerous or illegal influences. Whereas delivery workers were trained by managers to sell subscriptions, street sellers won customers by "hollering and fighting" their way to supremacy on the corner. Boys who worked on the street, the Children's Bureau concluded, "are a radically different type from boys who deliver papers regularly."[12]

The hours of work associated with route service also distinguished delivery work from street selling. Unlike street boys, who sometimes sold papers late into the evening, carriers adhered to strict morning and afternoon schedules that dovetailed with the beginning and end of the school day. According to the Children's Bureau, most carriers delivered papers for just over an hour a day. Older boys often had longer routes, and hence spent more time at work; they also earned more from their routes. Very young carriers, under twelve, earned less than a dollar a week, but older boys between the ages of fourteen and fifteen took home more than twice this amount. Industry sources agreed with the findings of the Children's Bureau with respect to hours, but reported significantly higher earnings. In 1933 an ICMA survey reported that carriers earned, on average, $2.91 a week.[13]

No explicit data appear to exist for the industry as a whole on the class and ethnicity of route workers during the interwar years, but as early as 1928 one government study noted that the fathers of carriers earned slightly more than average for wage earners and junior salaried employees. Relative to street sellers, fewer carriers also had foreign-born parents. Managers rarely spoke of the race of newspaper boys. In regional markets where white workers were scarce, circulation chiefs recruited black boys, and appear to have trained them no differently from white youngsters. Thus, Jasper Rison of the *Louisville Courier Journal and Times* reported in 1936 that "our experience is that [race] makes little difference so long as the carrier meets the qualifications of a good carrier." Elsewhere, Mexican-American carriers distributed papers in El Paso, and Asian-American boys participated in sales demonstrations in California.[14]

Circulation men often professed a kinship with the boys they supervised on the basis of shared experience. Managers entered the industry as boys, and supervising juvenile workers remained, for most, the focus of their life's ambition. Within the industry, the presumption that managers began their craft as children was so widely accepted that no one bothered to comment on it. Only outsiders found the phenomenon remarkable. At an annual gathering of circulation managers in 1926, a guest speaker noticed that all the men in attendance seemed to have followed identical paths to becoming circulation managers. His spontaneous observation led to one of the most dramatic moments in the industry's history. The official running the meeting asked all those who had distributed papers as youths to please rise. To no one's surprise, "at least ninety-five per cent" of the audience stood up.[15]

Following hard on the profitable years of the 1920s, the Depression was an unexpected blow for these men. With print advertising declining after 1930, publishers looked to managers to boost readership. Market contraction, however, forced newspapers to slash circulation spending and this deprived managers of the ability to mount the kinds of subscription campaigns they had relied on in the past. It took investment capital to maintain circulation. Without adequate budgets for publicity, transportation, and supplies managers could not hope to give publishers the numbers that they wanted. "All of us know that there must be a steady stream of new orders coming in," Don R. Davis, of the *Birmingham (Alabama) News* said in 1932. But if newspapers eliminated the means for bringing in orders "a circulation loss must be expected, and in most instances, reductions in expenses which cause serious circulation losses are impractical economy."[16]

Beyond cutting expenses, how were circulation men to produce healthy results? Managers endorsed three broad plans for boosting

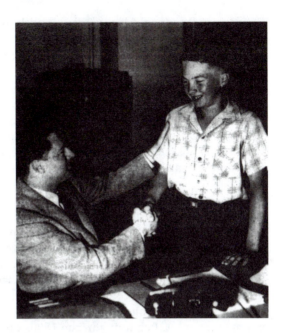

**FIGURE 7.2** *Masculine guidance: a circulation manager welcomes a new boy into the department.*

*From Texas Circulation Managers Association,* Newspaper Circulation: Principles and Development of Modern Newspaper Circulation Methods *(1948), p. 47.*

industry revenues: first, they argued that retail prices for their product were artificially low in relation to other goods; second, managers pushed for higher wholesale rates to distributors and news outlets; third, managers could bring in more advertising dollars by increasing readership. For most circulation managers, the power to stimulate demand depended on how wisely they deployed departmental personnel. In many cases this personnel consisted of a reduced staff of district managers and a large crew of carrier boys recruited from local sales areas. The possibilities for profit that these youngsters represented was too great for any intelligent manager to ignore. "During this present business depression," J. C. VanBenthem of the *San Francisco News* observed in 1931, "it is to the advantage of all of us to operate as economically as possible. One sure way of accomplishing this is with more intensified work among our carrier boys."[17]

The trend toward using middle-class boys to market newspaper subscriptions that began after World War I rapidly gained momentum during the 1930s. Managers who had employed adult solicitors in the past now abandoned the "professional door bell ringer" in ever greater numbers. Cost, reliability, and better subscriber retention gave the edge to juvenile labor. "I have conferred with many circulators in the past year," I. Isenberg of the *Jersey City Journal* announced before the Interstate Circulation Managers' Association in the fall of 1933, "and find that they are all turning to the carrier boy for new business. They are fully convinced that the carrier boy is the one who produces the best business at the least possible cost."[18]

## Taylorism, Personnel Management, and Impressionistic Management

In an age of system and uniformity, conditions in most circulation departments remained stubbornly resistant to rationalization. Topography, climate, patterns of urban growth and residential development, and approved custom and local preferences all conspired to preclude standardization between and within newspaper operations. Because distribution began at the printing plant and then spread outward, managers were rarely able to directly supervise the activities of working children. For the most part managers assumed a route was well run if there were few customer complaints and cancellations remained low. Supervision like this was at best reactive: managers had to wait for problems to come to them. By the start of the Depression circulation men were beginning to rebel against the limitations of such passive policies.

Historians examining patterns of managerial control in the United States have typically focused on attempts to improve employee productivity and policies designed to rationalize the work process. Two distinct managerial movements emerged during the early years of the twentieth century: scientific management, or Taylorism, and personnel management. Beginning in the 1890s engineer Frederick Winslow Taylor pioneered a form of management theory aimed at centralizing technical expertise and increasing worker efficiency. By cutting the number of steps involved in production and subdividing tasks performed by individual workers, Taylor and his followers hoped to introduce rational work principles onto the factory floor.[19]

In charting the application of these efficiency standards, observers have emphasized the destructive effects of scientific management on craft consciousness. David Montgomery has documented how managerial intrusions in the metal trades set off bitterly contested battles over job assignments, work pace, and wage levels. In a classic analysis of Taylorism, Harry Braverman discussed how workers in entire industries were "deskilled" of the knowledge critical to proper job execution. Social scientists, including Katherine Stone, Richard Edwards, and Dan Clawson have shown how scientific management separated physical from mental labor, and transferred oversight from the workshop to executive offices. This, in turn, bred resentment against impersonal white collar administrators.[20]

Some critics have questioned the extent to which workers were robbed of their occupational identity. Daniel Nelson has suggested that Taylorism was ideally suited to manufacturing plants where routinized machine operations could be performed by semiskilled workers. Less mechanized enterprises had little need for rationalization, and many firms could not afford to hire and train staffs of efficiency experts. According to Nelson, "In these establishments there was no separation of mental and physical labor, no transfer of skill to the plant office—or at least no more than would have occurred if Taylorism had never appeared."[21] Benson has noted that the ability of scientific management to regularize worker performance was even more circumscribed in service industries. "The core of scientific management in the factory—dividing and regularizing the work process—simply was not applicable to selling" in the retail sector, where the only product workers 'made' was a commercial transaction. Saleswomen proved remarkably adept at thwarting managerial intentions, resisting all attempts to regiment social behavior.[22]

Following World War I, personnel management evolved partly as a corrective to Taylorism. It sought to improve manager-worker relations without sacrificing gains in efficiency. Unlike Taylorism, personnel management forestalled union activism by training company experts to quickly defuse explosive work grievances. Personnel specialists who understood the source of problems encountered by employees could reduce the number of serious labor disputes, prevent labor turnover, and improve employee morale. The application of personnel management was suited to bureaucratic industries where employees were concentrated together for long periods of the work day. While Taylorism was a male domain, personnel management, with its emphasis on such "feminine" values as understanding and communication, attracted professional women. As corporate organizations integrated elements of personnel management into their operations the movement grew into an identifiable intellectual discipline, complete with journals and associations.[23]

The early response of circulation managers to Taylorism and personnel management influenced the subsequent development of welfare capitalism in the industry. Certainly the process of deskilling workers associated with scientific management did not happen in newspaper circulation. During the 1930s boys were taught for the first time about the products that they distributed, and were shown how to sell to a wide variety of customers. The human scale of labor did not fall away in daily home news delivery. Rather, it increased as circulation departments implemented sales training programs. Nor did managers endorse personnel management. Funding for personnel training was scarce, labor forces were scattered, and preventing carrier turnover was, given the young age of the workforce, hopeless. Characteristically, circulation managers formulated their own solutions, oriented around masculine symbols of achievement.

Since no one has examined managerial theory in relation to working children, there is no conventional model in the literature of industrial relations to describe this supervisory style. However, research on the history of the American insurance industry offers a useful basis for interpreting changes within newspaper circulation. Angel Kwolek-Folland has written that during the late nineteenth century managers developed a highly adaptable behavioristic approach to insurance sales training known as "impressionistic management." Stressing cooperation over coercion, impressionistic management recognized the inherent difficulty of measuring and controlling selling skill. Kwolek-Folland notes, "In contrast to scientific and personnel management, which were based in concern over workers, impressionistic management was aimed at motivating, controlling, and shaping the behavior of managers." The key to impressionistic management was understanding human nature. Successful managers knew how to "size up" both customers and salesmen, and had a knowledge of social psychology which allowed them to respond to an individual's changing interests.[24]

Circulation managers initially gravitated toward Taylorism, but soon rejected it in favor of a modified form of impressionistic management. The industry's first circulation text, published in 1915, reflected both tendencies: William R. Scott's *Scientific Circulation Management* presented circulation managers with "examples of efficient management and standard promotion methods." In a section titled "Controlling the Carriers" Scott cited the personnel policies of the *Indianapolis News*. The paper attempted to control nearly every aspect of carrier behavior. All route boys had to join the Indianapolis News Association of Carriers, and abide by the association's rules regarding delivery, collections, and complaints. Yet Scott did not suggest that carriers should be coerced into providing good performance. Modern managers knew that "one of the best assets any newspaper can have is a reputation for good treatment of its news and carrier boys." This meant "a square deal to the boy" with due "consideration of his interests and ambitions."[25]

In the years following, managers emphasized building esprit de corps among their carriers. In 1920 Phil M. Knox of the *St. Paul Daily News* told circulation heads that traditional managerial methods were inefficient. "I have seen many cases of bull-dozing and even dishonesty in the handling of the boys by circulation men," he stated. Knox thought the only way to "successfully meet the boy problem" in newspaper circulation was to study carrier policies "from a psychological standpoint." Knox shied away from lecturing boys, preferring to instruct them "in story form" by providing illustrations of how others had succeeded in similar situations.[26]

Over the next decade, more managers endorsed the norms of impressionistic management. In 1926 H. J. Smith of the *Waterbury (Connecticut) Republican* commented that "we believe in direct personal touch with our boys, keeping as far away from the boss idea as possible." When managers did have to enforce unpleasant rules, they softened the painful impact. In 1928 Neil C. Snyder of the *South Bend (Indiana) Tribune* related that he did not dismiss boys who failed to measure up—he let the boys fire themselves. Every *Tribune* substation had a large board listing the names of all the carriers. As boys received complaints, alphabet letters were hung beside names. By the time the phrase "I QUIT" was spelled out, everyone understood that the carrier had not met his responsibilities. Boys who realized their errors could redeem letters by acquiring new accounts.[27]

The rise of impressionistic management within newspaper circulation paralleled the development of a national child guidance movement. Margo Horn, in her study of the child guidance movement, has spoken of the discovery of the "problem child" in American society. Circulation managers similarly referred to the "boy problem" within their industry. Child guidance was a useful diagnostic approach for managers seeking to form profitable connections with their carriers. Though managers were hardly mental health experts, circulation men did speak in the parlance of popular psychology, utilizing metaphor and example to reinforce the idea that masculine guidance in the form of proper supervision required a thorough comprehension of boys' psychological as well as occupational needs. And just as the child guidance movement augmented "the status of mental health professionals" by endorsing "middle-class standards of behavior," masculine guidance improved the position of circulation managers by hastening the acceptance of carefully selected, thoroughly trained middle-class carriers.[28]

The success of carrier training programs encouraged managers to pursue psychology as a training aid. In 1931 manager A. Cohen of the *Santa Barbara Press* implored circulation men to "strike at the subconscious mind of the carrier" in order to develop the "habit part of the carrier brain." Two years later Lloyd Smith, of the *Kansas City Kansan*, emphasized the importance of psychology in establishing business relations with prospective carriers. Like Cohen, he believed that the mind of the working boy could be compartmentalized for maximum productivity. "Each newspaper boy is a peculiar mixture of part boy and part man," he wrote in the training text *Newspaper District Management*. "It is the man part of the boy that you put in charge of paper routes. Do not criticize the boy part. It is necessary and fine. It has its place, but not on the paper route."[29]

## Masculine Guidance in Action: Boy Welfare Programs

Their interest in psychology led circulation men to incorporate elements of both child guidance and impressionistic management into a coherent movement known as "boy welfare." At the very least, boy welfare included the offering of prizes for subscription sales contest winners and the production of morale-building carrier publications to keep boys and parents informed of the latest happenings on the route and in the department. A slightly expanded definition might also include dinners, outings and trips, recreational clubs and athletic facilities, savings plans, graded schemes to evaluate boys' selling skills, and academic programs designed to ensure that carriers remained in school. As circulation manager Jesse Birks noted in 1933, "Boy Welfare is so large, so complicated, that it cannot be covered in one paper. It is more the title for a thesis." All of these various welfare measures honored energetic carriers and downplayed the necessity of punishing poor performers.[30]

Kwolek-Folland has shown how managers in the insurance industry fostered images of family and corporate domesticity in dealing with employees. The absence of women and girls prevented this in newspaper work. Instead, circulation managers experimented with gendered notions of social convention between older men and younger boys. Overtly or by implication, managers portrayed themselves as teachers, as coaches, and as caring older friends. As teachers they prepared sales talks, administered written carrier exams, and maintained contact with school authorities. As coaches, managers gave pep talks and organized competitions to see who could obtain the greatest number of new customers. And as "faithful circulators," they took boys out to ball games, gave them presents during the holidays, and wrote letters of recommendation.[31]

The most powerful metaphor for depicting managerial interactions with working children was the most problematic. As men supervising boys, it was to be expected that managers might pattern occupational interactions on the father-son relationship. Yet this connection was rarely made explicit in the trade literature for fear of provoking public resentment. A central goal of juvenile sales training was to win parental approval for supervised route work. Managers did not want to upset family ties by suggesting that they might arrogate the place of biological fathers. Circulation managers recommended "friendly, paternal guidance" but usually refrained from assuming overtly parental positions of power. In early 1934 the *ICMA Bulletin* featured a didactic poem that placed a heavy burden of responsibility on the shoulders of circulators without once mentioning either fathers or sons. Entitled "The Boy," it began, "He is the person who is to carry on what you have started/He is to sit right where you are sitting/And when you are gone, attend to things you think are so important." Everything a manager did would one day be judged by the boy who carried the manager's papers. "Your reputation and your future are in his hands . . . SO—IT MIGHT BE AS WELL TO PAY 'THE BOY' SOME ATTENTION."[32]

Through the use of highly publicized welfare schemes, managers extended control over youngsters who operated beyond their immediate supervision. Of course, circulation chiefs were unable to implement the kinds of extensive programs that other industries introduced. Newspapers did not establish pensions or offer medical and housing programs for their route boys. But the impetus to give workers a "square deal" was every bit as strong in newspaper circulation as it was in adult enterprises. Operating according to the principles of masculine guidance, managers crafted a flexible, resilient system of entice-

Todd Alexander Postol

ments and rewards designed to satisfy the special needs of juvenile workers.[33]

"Boys always are enthusiastic about something," manager Oliver King of the *Arizona Republican* noted in 1929, "but as a rule not about their work." Creating a spirit of participation began at the top, with the circulation manager. "Take an interest in the boy," King suggested, "if he is doing good work, tell him so. He will break his neck to do even better." King recommended that all papers establish a publicity department to highlight the accomplishments of its boys. The methods that publicity departments used varied, but one rule was inviolate: carriers had to enjoy their work. Managers who made route service appear as desirable as a slot on a ball team were guaranteed "good delivery [and] more circulation than you can take care of."[34]

Staging subscription sales contests and offering prizes were essential elements in this strategy of transforming drudgery into fun. Manager A. R. Poyntz was a near genius at appealing to a boy's imagination and curiosity. In 1932 he told fellow managers about a "mystery drive" contest his department had recently completed. The promotion began when staff members draped delivery truck tarpaulins over the balconies of the carrier's meeting hall, enveloping the room in blackness. As unsuspecting carriers entered the hall they were propelled down a playground slide into a horror pit. Flickering red lights danced across the walls as ghosts in luminous paint pursued the boys. At one point in the chase an electric fan blew confetti directly into the faces of the startled youngsters. At length the boys reached the "room of rooms," where a red-robed attendant brandishing an immense sword guarded a glittering gold colored chest. After the boys escaped to freedom their district managers informed them that they could win the treasures inside the chest by securing five new starts. The promotion was a great success, bringing "gratifying increases" in readership.[35]

Managers strove to create contests that would motivate boys to sell more subscriptions. A central tenet of these contests was that involvement should never be compulsory; boys worked best when they felt good about what they did. "An organization of boys can be made to produce results daily," Davis of the *Birmingham News* noted in 1934, "only if sales effort does not become work. It must be play." On one level, this was obvious: nearly everyone would rather play than work. But what was key to supervisory policies in newspaper circulation was the nearly universal agreement that it was acceptable to proceed from this assumption. This, if nothing else, set the industry apart from all adult trades. It is difficult to imagine a shop floor steward or retail manager during the Depression encouraging his workers to play at their jobs. And the very definition of play was a juvenile, rather than adult, interpretation. Play, in home delivery work, involved a clearly articulated challenge associated with a highly desirable reward. As described in the literature of circulation management,

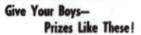

FIGURE 7.3 *Trade houses offered a variety of carrier prizes at discounted rates to circulation departments. This and the next three illustrations illustrate the rewards and arguments that would appeal to circulation managers planning the contests.*

From Circulation Management *(June 1936), p. 6.*

play was the expression of healthy competition through the controlled, supervised sales contest.[36]

The variety of playful contest formats was limited only by the imagination of the managers who staged them. Athletic themes were among the most common; promotions patterned after foot, auto, and airplane races were especially popular. Closely allied with these were

FIGURE 7.4   *"Do you want subscriptions?"*

*From* Circulation Management *(March 1936), p. 31.*

sports contests modeled along the lines of baseball, basketball, and golf. Within each type of promotion there was room for creativity. A baseball-inspired contest, for example, might simply draw on the metaphors of the game, or it could structure the entire process of selling according to the rules of big league ball, with route carriers receiving earned "runs" for each new customer that they acquired. One enterprising paper launched a fall football contest by bringing a man into a sales meeting dressed in a football uniform. To the boys' delight, the surprise guest "called" a fictional game play-by-play through a microphone. Managers also held seasonal contests at the holidays. As marketing specialist M. Zenn Kaufman observed in 1934, the only rules governing these contests was that they had to be fun, they had to be fair, and they had to offer prizes that boys wanted.[37]

Managers in search of prize ideas might turn to local retail establishments eager to sell bulk orders to newspapers, or they could thumb

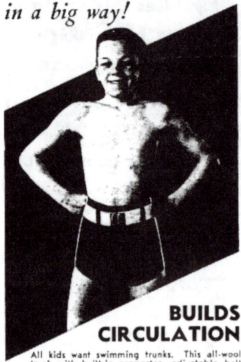

**KIDS "GO" FOR THIS**

*in a big way!*

**BUILDS
CIRCULATION**

All kids want swimming trunks. This all-wool trunk with built-in supporter, adjustable belt comes in all sizes and colors at $1.00 each. Send for a sample now—get the season's handiest, most desired premium.
We are also featuring Sport shirts ranging in price from $4.50 to $9.00 per dozen. Samples sent upon request.

**Milwaukee Knit Products
Corporation**

**342 N. Water St.** **Milwaukee, Wisconsin**
223-M

FIGURE 7.5   *"Kids 'Go'
For This in a big way!"*

From Circulation Management
*(May 1936), p. 30.*

through the glossy monthly publication *Circulation Management*. The magazine provided something that the *ICMA Bulletin* did not: photo advertisements from supply houses offering an assortment of attractions geared to the juvenile market. The Shelby Cycle Company assured managers that "every youngster" wanted one of its sleek, streamlined bicycles. A Shelby was "the ideal answer to the question of how to sustain interest for the long, strong pull in any campaign." The Goodyear Waterproof Company sold leatherette raingear "specially made" for newspaper boys, "the 'swellest' prize you can offer your carriers." Raincoat and hat together "cost you only $2.45. You'd pay at least double that at retail." An ad for the Chicago supplier N. Shure instructed managers

**FIGURE 7.6**   *"You bet - they'll <u>work</u> for a Shelby Bicycle."*

*From* Circulation Management *(June 1936), p. 3.*

to "Give Your Boys Prizes Like These!" Below the heading were photos of a softball, glove, and roller skates. Items shown in *Circulation Management* were usually purchased by circulation departments on the eve of a big subscription push or sales contest.[38]

Between promotions and sales contests, circulation men kept carriers motivated through the pages of publications printed especially for route boys. Most of these "junior papers" were a mix of gossip, jokes, humor, and cautionary tales to provide reliable service. Because it took time and skill to produce a quality publication, some managers subscribed to the generic national carrier paper, the *American Newspaper Boy (ANB)*. This instrument of boy welfare was published, improbably, by manager Bradley Welfare of the *Winston Salem Journal and Sentinel*. The paper featured carrier adventure stories, cartoons, advice on obtaining new accounts, recommendations for dealing with specific situations (such as dogs and deadbeat subscribers) and admonitions to "get rid of that old sales talk" and "try something NEW." In November 1936 the tabloid ran an editorial that neatly encapsulated the philosophy of masculine guidance. Delivering papers, the paper stated, was "not a sissy's job." Sometimes bad weather, plant delays, or the complaints of a rude customer made the task of delivering papers disagreeable, but the money a boy earned through honest labor was ample compensation for these hardships. "In the long run," the *ANB* reassured carriers, "the reward for taking the 'bitter' in your stride, is 'sweet'!"[39]

Boy welfare was, in effect, manager welfare. The same programs that transformed school children into subscription salesmen also turned circulation men into aspiring sales managers, joined now by common ambitions and responsibilities. Overcoming physical isolation and years of bitter competition, they came together to seek recognition from consumers and greater respect from their immediate superiors in the world of newspaper publishing. Managers of every persuasion discovered that they could not extend supervision over working children without acquiring the authority to determine personnel practices in their departments. Craving profits and prestige, circulation men saw juvenile sales training as a way to reinvent the American paper boy while improving the status of their own nascent profession.

## Eliminating the "Objectionable Term"

Managers' association with boys paradoxically hurt and helped them in the drive for full-fledged professional status. Barbara Melosh, in her study of twentieth-century nursing, has documented how nurses were stymied in their quest to attain professional standing by the sex-segregated nature of the industry. Most nurses were women, functioning within a medical establishment dominated by male doctors. If Melosh is correct that professional recognition is always "reserved for the most privileged" members of our society, then "nursing by definition cannot be a profession because most nurses are women." A similar exclusionary dynamic operated within newspaper circulation, but here the lines of professionalization were drawn according to age. The reason managers were destined never to receive credit for their efforts, to perpetually be treated as children by publishers and editors, was their association with untrained juvenile labor. Working in a world of children, circulation men would forever be denied entrance to the upper echelons of daily newspaper publishing. Yet only by improving the position of newspaper boys through instructional programs and supervision did managers have any realistic chance of bettering their own situation.[40]

No one understood this better than Howard Stodghill, circulation and business manager of the *Louisville Courier-Journal*. As president of the ICMA and head of its Newspaper Boy Welfare Committee, Stodghill worked tirelessly to promote a new kind of juvenile worker "comparable to the new type of circulation manager." At the association's 1930 convention, he spoke out on the need to implement higher professional standards for both managers and boys. The basis for Stodghill's remarks was a report issued by the U.S. Children's Bureau that had criticized the use of children in street trades. "Many boys sell papers only a few weeks or months," the government study found, "but the impression made by a few weeks may undo the work of years on the part of schools in training for citizenship." Speaking for all his fellow managers, Stodghill asked, "Is it possible that the circulation managers of today are so stupid that their organizations are but a haven to the thoroughly bad boy? Isn't our business an honorable one? Isn't the commodity we sell the most acceptable offered any public? Aren't we men of common sense and common decency?" It was small comfort that the moral abuses described in the Children's Bureau report applied to a minority of the youngsters in newspaper distribution who sold on the street.[41]

To improve the public image of the industry, Stodghill backed a resolution at the meeting endorsing a loosely written code of professional ethics. Pledging cooperation with parents and educational authorities, the code proposed "to maintain such standards as parents can be assured that their sons' connection with the circulation department will not be detrimental either by association or precept." No youngster would be allowed to continue where investigation disclosed "such boy's participation detrimental to the boy's own interests." Aside from this the resolution accomplished very little, for it lacked enforcement provisions. Its real significance was symbolic. For the first time managers had a common professional credo.[42]

Managers embraced the resolution with undisguised enthusiasm. In 1931 Stodghill printed the text of the resolution on poster stock beneath the legend "Lest Ye Forget." Circular letters announcing the offer were mailed to all association members; 265 managers availed themselves of the opportunity, promising to display the poster prominently. "I am going to have it framed and hung in my office," one delighted manager wrote. "In fact, I am going to do more than that. I am going to have copies of it made and put up in every one of our branch offices, of which we have seventy-three." Another circulation chief already had a copy of the poster under glass and intended to present a second to his publisher with the expectation that he, too, would hang it in his office. The pride that managers felt in finally having a physical confirmation of their professionalism could not be contained: "This is a splendid piece of work; one that shows there has been a great deal of thought put into it." The poster deserved "a place in the circulation department of every newspaper which is privileged to get one."[43]

In addition to printing "Lest Ye Forget" for managers to put in their offices, the ICMA attempted to alter what it considered to be the archaic, self-destructive terminology of the trade. In an ideal world youngsters who delivered papers to subscribers were carriers, while those who sold on the street were newsboys. But since neither class of worker received much formal training before 1930, many Americans conveniently referred to all minors in newspaper circulation as newsboys. If managers were ever to receive recognition this would need to change. New terms would be needed to reflect new conditions.

FIGURE 7.7    *During the Great Depression, circulation stressed virtues like neatness and politeness as part of their campaign to distance home delivery service from unregulated street selling.*

*From* Newspaper Circulation Manual: For Carrier Salesmen, Coaches, and District Supervisors *(1937)*.

The language of self-improvement, tied to the projection of socially acceptable behavior, played an important part in the "selling" of service industries between the wars. Kathy Peiss, in her landmark study of the American beauty business, has noted that large cosmetics firms in the 1920s successfully revised the vocabulary of their industry to meet changing expectations of beauty and femininity. Whereas many American women at the start of the century associated "painted" faces with prostitution and working-class street life, by the start of the Depression most middle-class women eagerly participated in the emerging "beauty culture." Contemporary women understood the value of their appearance. "The woman in the home, the woman in business, in society, must make up for the part she is to play in life," beauty writer Virginia Lee claimed in 1929. By purchasing the appropriate products, women could change not only their appearances but also their prospects for happiness and success.[44]

Circulation men displayed a similar concern with image and language in their industry. Managers objected to the term *newsboy* because it evoked memories of unsupervised, untrained labor. Conventional fiction, stage, and song depicted the newsboy as "poverty stricken, friendless, a truant from school." Middle-class route carriers, managers argued, did not fit this profile. They received careful instruction and guidance, worked reasonable hours, and their attendance in school was regularly monitored. Unlike turn-of-the-century street sellers, route workers were (in theory, if not practice) clean, well-dressed, and polite. Managers were fond of side-by-side visual comparisons, much in the manner of the "before and after" makeover advertisements of the cosmetics industry. Circulation texts inevitably contrasted scruffy, old-fashioned street boys with neatly groomed modern carriers. As early as the 1920s some newspapers were instructing boys on the proper way to dress for route work. During the Depression the construction of the socially respectable carrier was completed, and it was this image that managers now wished to sell to the American consumer.[45]

Before 1930, virtually no one in the United States spoke of newspaper boys. Within the industry, managers used "newsboy welfare" to mean programs devoted to both street sellers and route boys. When they wished to differentiate, circulation chiefs spoke of newsboys and, quite separately, carriers. For all practical purposes, the label *newspaper boy* was invented by Howard Stodghill to brighten the public's perception of working children and bring recognition to circulation management: "We, who are proud of the accomplishments of newspapers in advancing the interests of their newspaper boys want the public to become better acquainted with these juveniles." Stodghill cautioned managers to "make no mention of him in any way except as newspaper boy." Ordinary Americans conditionally approved the name change, abbreviating the somewhat bulky term to *paper boy*.[45]

Circulation men repudiated traditional stereotypes because the reputation of working boys was intertwined with their own professional status. This was clearly evident in the ICMA's relationship with the Audit Bureau of Circulations (ABC). From the time that the ABC was established in 1914 to provide advertisers with verifiable circulation figures, managers complained that it underestimated actual readership. In 1931 the feud between circulation men and auditors broke wide open, spurred on by the ICMA's labeling campaign. On July 4, 1931, the ABC unwisely ran an advertisement in *Editor and Publisher* featuring a "snub-nosed URCHIN crying the late edition." Four days later ICMA President Clarence Hixson wrote to ABC President P. L. Thomson, telling him that the ad "absolutely countered" the ideals of the association. After citing the "Lest Ye Forget" resolution in its entirety, Hixson asked for Thomson's assistance in stopping "further like advertisements." A war of letters ensued between the two organizations. By mid-July, the ABC pledged not to run any more ads endorsing or extolling street work, and submitted its next print advertisement to the ICMA for perusal.[47]

The ABC controversy may have contributed to the ICMA's decision to produce its own advertising to counteract negative portrayals of newspaper boys. In late 1932 the association prepared a series of boiler plate advertisements for its members. The following summer *Editor and Publisher* ran the ads. Each spot had its own theme, emphasizing training, thrift, and service. "The newspaper boy of today is receiving an education *plus,*" one piece declared. Beneath a photo of a well-groomed carrier was a note explaining that the ad was "designed to further public consciousness of the important work the newspapers are doing for the welfare and development of their boys."[48]

The promotional series was moderately successful, but many editors continued to lapse into the language of unregulated street trading. Managers would continue the labeling campaign, with varying degrees of success, for much of the decade. In 1934 the association ceased subscribing to a clipping service because it had prematurely concluded that "substantial progress in popularizing the favored term" had already been made. Association records in late 1935 showed that many editors still referred to minors in the industry as "newsboys." In 1936 the ICMA prepared sample letters to remind editors to use the correct terminology. As late as 1940, the ICMA's Newspaper boy Welfare Committee was still sending out approximately five hundred letters to editors "requesting the use of the term 'Newspaperboy' instead of the old undesirable terms 'Newsboy' or 'Newsie.'"[49]

By this time the labeling campaign had itself become redundant: managers had already transformed newspaper distribution in the United States. Nine out of ten boys were involved in supervised home delivery service. Whether editors recognized it or not, street selling was no longer a part of everyday life in most American communities.[50]

## Conclusion: Beyond the Depression

During the years of the Great Depression, newspaper circulation managers rejected established managerial approaches to working children, fashioning a new interpretation of commercialized boyhood in America. The training principles that circulation men devised in response to changing market conditions survived the 1930s and helped ensure the ongoing economic health of juvenile route service. During and after World War II the familiar profile of the paper boy endured with little modification, even as the country experienced military threats, demographic changes, McCarthyism, and social upheaval. Middle-class boys continued to pass through the industry as if carrying papers were an assumed, natural cycle of life. Though the physical landscape of home delivery became more suburban and dependent on automobiles, a study of daily route work in 1950, 1960, or 1970 would not look or feel very different from this study of the industry during the Depression years.

Despite inventing a new form of supervised route work that met with widespread approval, managers never obtained full professional status. Circulation men were always just on the verge of getting the recognition they felt they deserved. This state of delayed, perpetual professionalization remained a dependable fixture of the industry. In 1920 the *ICMA Bulletin* editorialized "the I.C.M.A. is fast becoming a power in the newspaper publishing world." In 1937 Floyd L. Hocken-hull of *Circulation Management* recalled "the time, not so many years ago, when the work of the Circulation Manager was grossly misunder-stood—when the circulation department in many a publishing plant was looked upon by other departments as being just slightly beyond the pale of responsibility." A decade later, the Texas Circulation Man-agers' Association claimed "until comparatively recent years, the cir-culation manager and the circulation department were regarded 'as that bunch that delivers the papers.' Now, however, this attitude has changed. . . . " In the 1970s a popular text stated that newspaper circu-lation "is a profession offering unlimited opportunities in a field of work now rapidly becoming a specialized occupation."[51]

As the 1970s progressed, the managerial philosophy of masculine guidance began to dissolve. For the first time girls entered home deliv-ery work in significant numbers. But even as the gendered composi-tion of route service changed, the basic structure of the industry remained intact. Then, in the 1980s, the system of supervised home delivery created during the Depression began to unravel. Women, who had traditionally looked forward each afternoon to the delivery of the evening paper, were leaving home for outside work in record num-bers. Children who had once turned to the daily paper for short stories and the funnies now had other options, including television, elec-tronic games, home computers, and videos. As this was happening, the advent of cable news channels made print reports of current events instantly out of date. The central importance of newspapers in Ameri-can life was being called into question as never before.[52]

The recession of the early 1990s hit newspaper advertising espe-cially hard. In an economizing move the ICMA was consolidated out of existence when it, and half a dozen other trade groups, combined to form the Newspaper Association of America in 1992. Given the insti-tutional stability of the ICMA, the decision to merge may have been premature. In spite of the declining economic fortunes of newspapers, ICMA membership reached a peak of 1,752 in 1989–90. Advertising in ICMA publications and the number of exhibit booths at the annual conferences also grew during the 1980s. Veteran members reacted to news of the association's dissolution with stunned sadness. Ray F. Mack, a forty-nine-year member of the ICMA, wrote that the associa-tion had been "the glue that held the nation's newspaper circulation operations together." Ron Anderson, a member for thirty-two years, said he was "Sorry to see ICMA go. Real sorry! I feel the industry is los-ing something very important." Most managers agreed with Dan Sid-bury of the *Sacramento Union*, who felt that the ICMA had been "gobbled up" by a "mega organization" that did not rate circulation issues very highly.[53]

Whether the consolidation was justified or not is debatable. One point, however, is beyond dispute: the merger robbed circulation men of the only collective voice they had ever known, irrevocably fracturing the long association between managers and boys in the American newspaper industry.

## Notes

My thanks to James R. Grossman, George Chauncey, and Patricia Cooper. This article grew out of a talk given in the Hagley Research Seminar series. Deepest appreciation goes to Roger Horowitz, associate director of the Center for the History of Business, Technology, and Society at the Hagley Museum and Library in Wilmington, Delaware. I am indebted to David B. Sicilia, associate editor of *Enterprise and Society*, and two anonymous reviewers for their encouragement and careful criticism. Joseph B. Forsee, past general manager of the International Circulation Managers' Association, and Yvonne Egertson, former librarian for the American Newspaper Publishers Association, provided essential help in locating industry source material.

1. "Ed. D. Hood Pleads Cause of Carriers," address given before the Southern Circulation Managers' Association, Pensacola, Florida. Reprinted in *Official Bulletin of the International Circulation Managers' Association,* September 1933, 8; hereafter referred to as *ICMA Bulletin.* Boys had distributed the news since the dawn of printing in America, but papers did not begin to systematically train carriers to deliver and market subscriptions until the Depression. This training distinguishes middle-class route work from all earlier forms of newspaper work. On the origins of vocational training for boys see Jan Cohn, "The Business Ethic for Boys: The Saturday Evening Post and the Post Boys," *Business History Review* 61 (1987): 185–215. For a firsthand account of nineteenth-century delivery service see Chase S. Osborn, *The Iron Hunter* (New York: Macmillan, 1919), 42–43. The appeal of twentieth-century supervised route work is briefly considered in Viviana A. Zelizer, *Pricing the Priceless Child: The Changing Social Value of Children* (New York: Basic Books, 1985), 82.

2. Newspapers lost advertising revenues during the Depression while broadcast advertising grew. See Frank Luther Mott, *American Journalism: A History of Newspapers in the United States through 260 Years: 1690 to 1950* (New York: Macmillan, 1956), 675 and 679. On circulation managers and radio see Todd Alexander Postol, "America's Press-Radio Rivalry: Circulation Managers and Newspaper Boys during the Depression," in Michael Harris, ed., *Studies in Newspaper and Periodical History: 1995 Annual* (Westport, Conn.: Greenwood Press, 1997), 155–66. In keeping with industry practices during the Depression, I use the terms *paper boy, newspaper boy,* and *newspaper carrier* interchangeably to refer to boys who delivered along regular routes; *newsboy* is restricted to street sellers.

3. Susan Porter Benson, *Counter Cultures: Saleswomen, Managers, and Customers in American Department Stores, 1890–1940* (Urbana: University of Illinois Press, 1986); Stephen H. Norwood, *Labor's Flaming Youth: Telephone Operators and Worker Militancy, 1878–1923* (Urbana: University of Illinois Press, 1990); Patricia A. Cooper, *Once A Cigar Maker: Men, Women, and Work Culture in American Cigar Factories, 1900–1919* (Urbana: University of Illinois Press, 1987). See also Margaret Creighton and Lisa Norling, eds., *Iron Men, Wooden Women: Gender and Seafaring, 1700–1920* (Baltimore, Md.: Johns Hopkins University Press, 1995); Mary H. Blewett, *Men, Women, and Work: Class, Gender, and Protest in the New England Shoe Industry, 1780–1910* (Urbana: University of Illinois Press, 1988); and Angel Kwolek-Folland, *Engendering Business: Men and Women in the Corporate Office, 1870–1930* (Baltimore, Md.: Johns Hopkins University Press, 1994). For a discussion of how children were traditionally socialized into the world of work see Daniel T. Rodgers, "Socializing Middle-Class Children: Institutions, Fables, and Work Values in Nineteenth-Century America," in N. Ray Hiner and Joseph M. Hawes, eds, *Growing Up in America: Children in Historical Perspective* (Urbana: University of Illinois Press, 1985), 119–32. On entry into the

job market see Walter Licht, *Getting Work: Philadelphia, 1840–1950* (Cambridge, Mass.: Harvard University Press, 1992); on masculine preparation for adulthood see David I. Macleod, *Building Character in the American Boy: The Boy Scouts, YMCA, and Their Forerunners, 1870–1920* (Madison: University of Wisconsin Press, 1983). For longitudinal treatments of childhood and adolescence during the 1930s see Glen H. Elder Jr., *Children of the Great Depression: Social Change in Life Experience* (Chicago: University of Chicago Press, 1974); and John A. Clausen, *American Lives: Looking Back at the Children of the Great Depression* (Berkeley and Los Angeles: University of California Press, 1993).

4. On organized labor in the Depression see, for example, Irving Bernstein, *Turbulent Years: A History of the American Worker, 1933–1941* (Boston: Houghton-Mifflin, 1970); Sidney Fine, *Sit-down: The General Motors Strike of 1936–1937* (Ann Arbor: University of Michigan Press, 1969); Robert H. Zieger, *John L. Lewis: Labor Leader* (Boston, Mass.: Twayne, 1988); and Nelson Lichtenstein, *The Most Dangerous Man in Detroit: Walter Reuther and the Fate of American Labor* (New York: Basic Books, 1995).

5. On changing definitions of boyhood see E. Anthony Rotundo, *American Manhood: Transformations in Masculinity from the Revolution to the Modern Era* (New York: Basic Books, 1993), 31–91; Leonard Harry Ellis, "Men among Men: An Exploration of All-Male Relationships in Victorian America" (Ph.D. diss., Columbia University, 1982), 1–60; and Kenneth Byron Kidd, "Bad Boys and Little Men: The Evolution of Boyhood in America" (Ph.D. diss., University of Texas, 1994).

6. On the history of juvenile street trading see Vincent DiGirolamo, "Crying the News: Children, Street Work, and the American Press, 1830s–1920s" (Ph.D. diss., Princeton University, 1997); Jon Bekken, "Newsboys: The Exploitation of 'Little Merchants' by the Newspaper Industry," in Hanno Hardt and Bonnie Brennen, eds., *Newsworkers: Toward a History of the Rank and File* (Minneapolis: University of Minnesota Press, 1995), 190–225; David Nasaw, *Children of the City: At Work and at Play* (New York: Oxford University Press, 1985), 62–87, 149–94; David E. Whisnant, "Selling the Gospel News, or: The Strange Career of Jimmy Brown the Newsboy," *Journal of Social History* 5 (1972): 269–309; Walter I. Trattner, *Crusade for the Children: A History of the National Child Labor Committee and Child Labor Reform in America* (Chicago: Quadrangle Books, 1970), 109–12, 193–95; Jeremy P. Felt, *Hostages of Fortune: Child Labor Reform in New York State* (Syracuse, N.Y.: Syracuse University Press, 1965), 57–61, 158–68; LeRoy Ashby, *Saving the Waifs: Reformers and Dependent Children, 1890–1917* (Philadelphia, Penn.: Temple University Press, 1984), 104–32; William J. Thorn and Mary Pat Pfeil, *Newspaper Circulation: Marketing the News* (New York: Longman, 1987), 35–54; and Alfred McClung Lee, *The Daily Newspaper in America: The Evolution of a Social Instrument* (New York: Macmillan, 1937), 287–300. One of the few studies of carriers is Marc Linder, "From Street Urchins to Little Merchants: The Juridical Transvaluation of Child Newspaper Carriers," *Temple Law Review* 63 (1990): 829–64.

7. A notable exception are the letters written by boys to the federal government during the New Deal period. See Todd Alexander Postol, "Hearing the Voices of Working Children: The NRA Newspaper Boy Letters," *Labor's Heritage* 1 (July 1989): 4–19.

8. A review of the ICMA's history is provided in *ICMA Update*, June 1992. All ICMA publications are available for viewing by appointment at the Information Resource Center, Newspaper Association of America, Vienna, Virginia. A second set of microfilmed ICMA records is housed in the Division of Special Collections and Archives, Merrill Library, Utah State University, Logan, Utah.

9. *Editor and Publisher* is available at the Columbia School of Journalism, Columbia University, New York. The Newspaper Association of America also has a complete set of *Editor and Publisher*, as well as the ANPA's *Bulletin*. Copies of the *American Newspaper Boy* from 1936 to 1939 are housed at the Library of Congress, Washington, D.C. *Circulation Management* is stored at the Science, Industry, and Business Library, New York Public Library.

10. On the number of workers in newspaper circulation, see *Editor and Publisher*, June 24, 1933, 10, and Henry Bonner McDaniel, *The American Newspaperboy: A Comparative Study of His Work and School Activities* (Los Angeles: Wetzel Publishing, 1941), 17. On the

proportion of boys in home news service see *American Newspaper Publishers Association Bulletin,* September 23, 1933, 554, where an industry survey found that 70 percent of juvenile workers were carriers. See also the unpublished government study "Summary of Report on Newspaper and Periodical Carriers and Street Sellers," which reported that 77 percent of minors in the industry delivered to subscribers. The summary is contained in Entry 44: Transcripts to Hearings, 507-1-05, Graphic Arts—Newspaper Publishing Business, 6/22/34, Records of the National Recovery Administration, RG 9 (National Archives). Percentage of carriers appears on page 13 of the transcript; hereafter referred to as NRA Hearing. Figure for 1939 appears in McDaniel, *The American Newspaperboy,* 43.

11. George Williams's all-girl carrier force is described in *American Magazine,* July 1930, 80. The percentage of boys in the industry appears in NRA Hearing, 93.

12. U.S. Children's Bureau, *Children Engaged in Newspaper and Magazine Selling and Delivering* (Washington, D.C.: U.S. Children's Bureau, 1935). Median ages of carriers and sellers appears on 4; percentage of boys under twelve selling and carrying appears on 5–6; the social aspects of selling are discussed on 20–22; quote appears on 9.

13. Ibid., 25–28. Industry earnings figure appears in *Editor and Publisher,* June 24, 1933, 10.

14. Family backgrounds of carriers discussed in U.S. Children's Bureau, *Children in Street Work* (Washington, D.C.: U.S. Children's Bureau, 1928), 39. Jasper E. Rison, "Supervision and Collections in Negro Communities," *ICMA Bulletin,* July 1936, 8; Mexican-American carriers described in *ICMA Proceedings* 24 (1922): 53; Asian-American carrier demonstration discussed in "Here's One Carrier That Wouldn't Take 'No' for an Answer," *ICMA Bulletin,* July 1932, 5.

15. Women circulation managers were rare. At the 1933 ICMA convention (attended by approximately three hundred managers), President John T. Toler announced, "I want to call your attention to the fact that we have two lady circulation managers here: Miss Hilda Larsen, *Valley Daily News,* Tarentum, Penn., and Miss Leonore Walker, *Palladium Item,* Richmond, Indiana. (Applause)." See *ICMA Proceedings* 35 (1933): 40. Former carriers quote appears in *ICMA Proceedings* 28 (1926): 111–12.

16. Don R. Davis, "Practical Economy," *ICMA Proceedings* 34 (1932): 99.

17. On raising retail prices see Russell Stokley, "Effect of Price Raise on Circulation," in *ICMA Proceedings* 36 (1934): 35–42. Frank Newell of the *Toledo Blade* argued that declining revenue left papers with no choice but to hike wholesale rates. See *Editor and Publisher,* June 24, 1933, 9–10. VanBenthem quoted in "Promotion through Carrier Organization," paper read at the California Circulation Managers' Association, Santa Barbara, autumn 1931. Reproduced in *ICMA Bulletin,* November 1931, 12.

18. The term "professional door bell ringer" was used by manager Alton H. Adams in a talk before the New York State Circulation Managers' Association in late 1930. See "Building Carrier Morale," reprinted in *ICMA Bulletin,* November 1930, 26. I. Isenberg, "Best Hour Plan," reprinted in *ICMA Bulletin,* January 1934, 16.

19. For overviews of scientific management see Daniel Nelson, *Managers and Workers: Origins of the New Factory System in the United States 1880–1920* (Madison: University of Wisconsin Press, 1975), 55–78, and *Frederick W. Taylor and the Rise of Scientific Management* (Madison: University of Wisconsin Press, 1980). On personnel management see Bruce E. Kaufman, *The Origins and Evolution of the Field of Industrial Relations in the United States* (Ithaca, N.Y.: ILR Press, 1993), 21–29.

20. David Montgomery, *Workers' Control in America* (New York: Cambridge University Press, 1979), 113–38, and *The Fall of the House of Labor: The Workplace, the State, and American Labor Activism, 1865–1925* (New York: Cambridge University Press, 1987), 214–56; Harry Braverman, *Labor and Monopoly Capital: The Degradation of Work in the Twentieth Century* (New York: Monthly Review Press, 1974); Katherine Stone, "The Origins of Job Structures in the Steel Industry," *Review of Radical Political Economics* 6 (1974), 113–73; Richard Edwards, *Contested Terrain: The Transformation of the Workplace in the Twentieth Century* (New York: Basic Books, 1979), 97–104, and Dan Clawson,

*Bureaucracy and the Labor Process: The Transformation of U.S. Industry, 1860–1920* (New York: Monthly Review Press, 1980), 202–53.

21. Daniel Nelson, "Scientific Management and the Workplace, 1920-1935," in Sanford M. Jacoby, ed., *Masters to Managers: Historical and Comparative Perspectives on American Employers* (New York: Columbia University Press, 1991), 79.

22. Benson, *Counter Cultures*, 127.

23. Sharon Hartman Strom, *Beyond the Typewriter: Gender, Class, and the Origins of Modern American Office Work, 1900–1930* (Urbana: University of Illinois Press, 1992), 109–71.

24. Kwolek-Folland, *Engendering Business*, 75–76. In the late 1930s the field of human relations echoed the behavioristic management theories first articulated by impressionistic management. This later movement, however, did not focus on the needs of managers in service and sales industries. For a discussion of the human relations movement see Kaufman, *Origins and Evolution*, 76–83.

25. William R. Scott, *Scientific Circulation Management for Newspapers* (New York: Ronald Press, 1915). "Efficient management" mentioned on vii; "controlling the carriers" appears on 98–99; the rules of the News' carrier association are reproduced on 261–67; proper treatment of carriers discussed on 137. Compare the title of Scott's work with a contemporary primer for adult salesmen also grounded in Taylorism; see Charles W. Hoyt, *Scientific Sales Management* (1912), cited in Timothy B. Spears, *100 Years on the Road: The Traveling Salesman in American Culture* (New Haven, Conn.: Yale University Press, 1995), 207.

26. "Newsboy Welfare Work in St. Paul," *ICMA Bulletin*, July 1920, 8.

27. "What Some Circulators Think about Carrier Welfare," *Editor and Publisher*, June 12, 1926, 9; "Methods Used to Minimize Complaints from Carrier Delivery," *ICMA Bulletin*, September 1928, 31.

28. Margo Horn, *Before It's Too Late: The Child Guidance Movement in the United States, 1922–1945* (Philadelphia, Penn.: Temple University Press, 1989), 186.

29. A. Cohen, "Building Carrier Morale," paper read before the California Circulation Managers' Association, San Francisco. Reprinted in *ICMA Bulletin*, September 1931, 29; Lloyd Smith, *Newspaper District Management: Including the Hour-a-Day Plan of Training Newspaper Boys to Sell* (Kansas City, Kans.: Lloyd Smith, 1933), 17.

30. Birks is quoted in *ICMA Proceedings* 35 (1933): 104.

31. On kinship imagery see Kwolek-Folland, *Engendering Business*, 129–64. On managers as coaches and carriers as team players see *The N.B.A. Handbook for Newspaper Boys* (Indianapolis: Newspaper Boys of America, 1932). The phrase "faithful circulator" appears in *ICMA Bulletin*, January 1930, 29.

32. "Friendly, paternal guidance" are the words of East St. Louis manager Rex Fisher. See *ICMA Proceedings* 37 (1935): 59. The poem appeared on the inside cover of *ICMA Bulletin*, January 1934. For a rare instance of overt father imagery see E. D. Hood, "Be a Father to the Newspaper Boy," *ICMA Proceedings* 36 (1934): 35.

33. Cradle-to-grave welfare capitalism is covered in Stuart D. Brandes, *American Welfare Capitalism 1880–1940* (Chicago: University of Chicago Press, 1976); "square deal" appears in Gerald Zahavi, *Workers, Managers, and Welfare Capitalism: The Shoeworkers and Tanners of Endicott Johnson, 1890–1950* (Urbana: University of Illinois Press, 1988), chap. 2. In keeping with the contrarian nature of newspaper distribution, newspaper boy welfare gained strength just as welfare capitalism lost potency in other major industries. See the discussions on the decline of welfare capitalism in Lizabeth Cohen, *Making A New Deal: Industrial Workers in Chicago, 1919–1939* (New York: Cambridge University Press, 1990), 238–46, and Sanford M. Jacoby, *Employing Bureaucracy: Managers, Unions, and the Transformation of Work in American Industry, 1900–1945* (New York: Columbia University Press, 1985), 219–21.

34. Oliver King, "How to Maintain Perpetual Enthusiasm among Carrier Boys," *ICMA Proceedings* 31 (1929): 90-91.

35. *ICMA Proceedings* 34 (1932): 169.

36. Davis quoted in *Editor and Publisher*, June 2, 1934, 26.

37. M. Zenn Kaufman, "How to Run Better Sales Contests," published weekly in *Editor and Publisher* between June 2 and August 4, 1934. Athletic and sports contests, June 23, 33; football announcer, June 9, 20; fairness, June 30, 36.

38. *Circulation Management* issues. Ad for Shelby Cycle appears in June 1936, 3; Goodyear raincoat appears in November 1935, 2; N. Shure Co. appears in September 1936, 6. Other firms specialized in premiums for new subscribers. The Moore Enameling and Manufacturing Co. offered a "Windsor Pot" with the promise "They Click Every Time." See September 1936, above.

39. The *American Newspaper Boy* was sold to circulation departments for free distribution to their carrier organizations. Welfare's affiliation with the *Journal and Sentinel* is recorded in *ICMA Proceedings* 32 (1930): 64. "Try something new," *American Newspaper Boy*, April 1937, 7; "bitter and sweet," *American Newspaper Boy*, November 1936, 8.

40. Barbara Melosh, *"The Physician's Hand": Work Culture and Conflict in American Nursing* (Philadelphia, Penn.: Temple University Press, 1982), 20.

41. Howard W. Stodghill, "The Newspaper Boy," *ICMA Proceedings* 32 (1930): 125–27. The study cited by Stodghill is U.S. Department of Labor, *Children in Street Work* (Washington, D.C.: U.S. Children's Bureau, 1928).

42. Although submitted to the membership by John Eisenlord of the *Chicago Daily News*, the resolution bore a strong resemblance to Stodghill's writings during this period on the need for professional standards. *ICMA Proceedings* 32 (1930): 141.

43. "Framing 'Lest Ye Forget' Posters," and "Comments on the Poster," *ICMA Proceedings* 33 (1931): 37.

44. Kathy Peiss, *Hope in a Jar: The Making of America's Beauty Culture* (New York: Metropolitan Books, 1998). The vocabulary of beauty is discussed on 121; Lee quote appears on 143–44.

45. Quote appears in "Asks Public's Respect for the Newspaper Boy—His Work Merits Dignity," *ICMA Bulletin*, January 1930, 5. As early as 1922 the *Chattanooga News* advised carriers to "dress neat and tidy," and to "take your hat off when a lady appears at the door." See "Makes Salesmen Carriers," *ICMA Bulletin*, September 1922, 20.

46. On separate terms for sellers and route workers see *ICMA Proceedings* 29 (1927): 32, where a questionnaire asked managers to "Give Age of Newsboys and Carriers." Stodghill quote appears in *ICMA Bulletin*, March 1930, 16.

47. "Writing It Out to a Better Understanding," *ICMA Bulletin*, July 1931, 8–10. Compare the ABC's ad with that of the *Detroit News* two weeks earlier, depicting a respectable middle-class boy in a suburban neighborhood. See *Editor and Publisher*, June 20, 1931, 25.

48. The genesis of the ad campaign is discussed in *ICMA Proceedings* 34 (1932): 60–61. Ads appear in *Editor and Publisher*, July 29, 1933, 31; August 5, 1933, 27; August 12, 1933, 33; and August 19, 1933, 37.

49. Decision to cease subscribing to clippings described in *ICMA Proceedings* 37 (1935), 34. Sample letters discussed in *ICMA Proceedings* 38 (1936): 37–38; quote appears in "Report of the Newspaperboy Welfare Committee," *ICMA Proceedings* 42 (1940), 172.

50. McDaniel, *The American Newspaperboy*, 43.

51. "The Membership Committee," *ICMA Bulletin*, March 1920, 10; *ICMA Proceedings* 39 (1937): 45; Texas Circulation Managers Association, *Newspaper Circulation: Principles and Development of Modern Newspaper Circulation Methods* (Austin, Tex.: Steck, 1948), 57; Robert A. Macklin, *Newspaper Circulation Management Training* (Washington, D.C.: ICMA, 1979), 6.

52. Decline in market penetration discussed in "Rethinking the Newspaper Business," *New York Times*, January 6, 1991. On the decrease in home delivery service see "Pages and Pages of Pain," *Newsweek*, May 27, 1991, 39. On the decline of juvenile carriers see "Deliver the Paper? No way! I'm Going to the Mall," *Forbes*, November 18, 1996, 40.

53. *ICMA Update*, June 1992, 60, 38, 55, 57.

# PART 3

# Manhood at Play

# Everyday Peter Pans

*Work, Manhood, and Consumption in*
*Urban America, 1900–1930*

WOODY REGISTER

> MRS. DARLING: Peter, where are you? Let me adopt you too.
> PETER: Would you send me to school?
> MRS. DARLING (*obligingly*): Yes.
> PETER: And then to an office?
> MRS. DARLING: I suppose so.
> PETER: Should I soon be a man?
> MRS. DARLING: Very soon.
> PETER (*passionately*): I don't want to go to school and learn solemn things. No one is going to catch me, lady, and make me a man. I want always to be a little boy and to have fun.
>
> —J. M. Barrie, *Peter Pan, or The Boy Who Would Not Grow Up*

In 1926, *The American Magazine* published an article on the enterprising puppeteer Tony Sarg, marveling that he wrote children's books, designed mechanical window displays and children's barbershops for department stores, sketched magazine illustrations, directed three marionette troupes, decorated public buildings, produced animated cartoons, collected toys, and managed workshops, laboratories, a studio, booking office, and staff of fifty. Yet, the article's headline declared, "Tony Sarg Has Never Done A Stroke Of Work In His Life!"[1] According to Sarg, work was not work; it was play. As one writer put it, "Playing with dolls, and making dolls play" was his "vocation."[2]

By any standard of the 1920s, Sarg was a hardworking, endlessly productive businessman, sleeping a few hours nightly, supervising workers, accumulating capital, and turning virtually every idea that came to mind into a moneymaking venture. What is striking here is not the question of whether he actually worked, but the way in which he and others characterized his exertions as a boy at play. Although he inhabited the "powerfully built" frame of a robust man in his mid-forties, by most accounts Sarg possessed ingredients for success that were more useful than his physical vigor: in particular, the "fun-loving" and "imp-ish" outlook and "tremendous energy and happy enthusiasm" of a boy.[3] Moreover, Sarg's achievements and wealth apparently resulted not from disciplined self-denial, but from unrestrained indulgence. As he explained, using a hedonistic vocabulary suitable to describing a day at the amusement park, "My pleasure, my thrills all come from the things I am doing. . . . To me the great secret is being able to do the thing you most like to do in life."[4]

These representations of work as play and man as boy were not lim-ited to enterprising puppeteers like Sarg. Rather, they conventionally were invoked to describe the actions and identities of a broad array of middle-class men who, between 1900 and 1930, helped lay the institu-tional foundation of twentieth-century consumer capitalism: the impresario Oscar Hammerstein I, the cartoonist Winsor McCay, the composer Victor Herbert, the architect Frank Lloyd Wright, the writer L. Frank Baum, and many others. The energy, reckless disregard of convention, and business success of these men were often attributed not to their self-possession and discipline, but to the fact that they had never "grown up." As a journalist observed in 1907 in an article on Hammerstein, "He has the shrewdness, the persistence, the humorous wisdom of the man, but he has the curiosity, the inscrutableness of the boy; and who shall say that is not a greater wisdom?" Hammerstein, the article's subtitle explained, was "A Boy Who Never Grew Up."[5]

Boys, toys, games, play, thrills, pleasure, personal satisfaction, never-ending childhood, and fun composed the strategic vocabulary of the commercial culture of Peter Pan, to borrow the title of the well-known play. Peter Pan, of course, is the boy who never grows up, who reminds us that we will kill the fairies if we do not believe in them, and who lives a life of play and adventure with the other "lost boys" in Never Land. Although British in origin, J. M. Barrie's drama has been among the most enduringly popular in the United States since its New York premiere in 1905. The commercial culture of Peter Pan draws particular attention to the business enterprises and businessmen who enlisted the figure of the eternal child—or, more accurately, the eter-nal boy—to explain themselves and to dramatize and legitimate con-sumer culture's powerful invitation to be like Peter Pan, a boy who plays, has fun, and never has to grow up. The central narrative of Peter Pan culture, promoted endlessly by many of the new consumer insti-tutions of the early twentieth century, promised beleaguered middle-class men that there were profits as well as pleasures awaiting them in the marketplace of goods. All they had to do was overcome their fool-ish aversion to fun and spending money, embrace the good life of play, and see the world through the eyes of children.

The men examined in this essay—the impresario Fred Thompson, the ethnologist Stewart Culin, and the stage comedian Fred Stone—all

**FIGURE 8.1** *Maude Adams as "Peter Pan, or The Boy Who Would Not Grow Up," in the original U.S. production of the J. M. Barrie play, ca. 1905–6.*

*Theater Collection, Museum of the City of New York.*

claimed to be boys who had never grown up and who craved, in Culin's words, "the joy of living and the world of delight."[6] They constructed their public identities with—or in the case of Stone, as—toys and sought to translate what they regarded as the magic and play of childhood into commodities for adults. As Peter Pans, these men who would be boys embodied a new consuming manhood that relieved even as it reflected anxieties arising not only from the association of consumption with women and femininity but also from older notions of responsible and controlled manliness that still cast a shadow over their commercial playgrounds. In the process, "everyday Peter Pans" helped relocate the traditional coordinates of middle-class manhood from the religious and civic obligations of the nineteenth century to what Jean-Christophe Agnew has called the "shifting ensemble of cultural and material commodities" that were distributed and promoted by the consumer marketplace in the twentieth century.[7] As Fred Thompson explained in 1915, "That's what's the trouble with this present age—too much work and too little play. We need to be educated up again to the child spirit."[8] This education involved demonstrating that what had once seemed the very negation of respectable middle-class manhood—the refusal to grow up and the insistence that work yield individual gratification and pleasure—were now the essential ingredients of manly success in a modern consumer economy. The lines of a popular tune from one of Thompson's Broadway productions defined the outlook of the commercial culture of Peter Pan and of the new boy-man who would represent and exploit its possibilities. "Cheer up and smile . . . ," insisted the song,

> If life isn't all that you'd like it to be,
> Remember this motto and take it from me:
> "Life is only a merry go round . . .
> when a man is dead and he's stuck in the ground,
> The merry-go-round'll go round and round."[9]

In the nineteenth century, a man who regarded life as a merry-go-round or his work as play would have been violating most normative expectations about the acceptable route to personal salvation, property ownership, and social respectability. The world of white middle-class men, according to Anthony Rotundo, "was based on work, not play, and their survival in it depended on patient planning, not spontaneous impulse."[10] "Play" described the untamed actions of children and "savages," and "boy" was a racial slur that denied African-American men their capacity for independent manhood. Citizenship, political participation, and property ownership were the essential markers of manhood in the early republic, and enfranchised men were expected to exercise their rights in a manner that demonstrated the distinction between the reckless antics of savages and the informed, responsible acts of civilized men. In other words, white males had to give up play as they matured from boyhood to manhood. And they had to exterminate it in others. Native Americans, according to Michael Paul Rogin, often were described as "playful, violent, improvident, wild, and in harmony with nature." Their "childish" communal ways had to be converted to the manly values of private property and commercial farming or forcibly removed to make way for white American civilization.[11] In the nineteenth century, then, manliness was measured by the degree to which (white) men abandoned or exterminated the "playful, hedonistic, libidinal quality" of boys, Indians, or African Americans, and achieved its negation by donning the mantle of duty, responsibility, self-control, and self-ownership.[12] The same logic applied to the republic as a whole; the (white) man was the nation writ small, and vice versa. In the words of the mid-nineteenth-century historian Francis Parkman, "Barbarism is to civilization what childhood is to maturity."[13]

In casting work as play, the ideal of the "eternal boy" celebrated in Peter Pan culture was part of the more general remaking of middle-class gender codes at the end of the nineteenth century in response to the erosion of self-made manhood and the civilization that it underwrote. Historians usually point to the broad social and economic changes of the period—the industrialization of the workplace; new social and economic roles for women; the growing social and political influence of working-class ethnic communities; and the rise of consumer culture—which weakened the material foundation of Victorian gender ideals and left middle-class men fretful about their manhood. Especially troubling was the decline of self-employment. Historians estimate that as many as four out of five white men owned their own farms, artisan shops, or businesses in the early nineteenth century. These conditions, which were experienced in the everyday lives of ordinary white men, helped define American manhood in class, age, ethnic, and racial terms. Manliness was not the exclusive condition of males, but of independent, property-owning men; boys, African-American slaves, and wage-working immigrant men were excluded from the category. However, by the end of the century, independent business ownership was in rapid decline; some historians estimate that by 1900 two-thirds of white middle-class men were bringing home salaries or wages, not profits, a condition that compromised the essential distinction between the prized condition of manly independence and the despised condition of dependent wage slavery. White middle-class men still valued freedom and independence, but as older ideals of manhood based on property ownership and control of one's labor seemed increasingly irrelevant (if not counterproductive) in a corporate, consumer economy, they had to reinvent the terms of manhood to preserve their sense of themselves as men, which was the basis of their economic, political, and sexual priority. Middle-class men began shifting emphasis away from much of what they had once regarded as the starting point of manliness: self-control, self-reliance, and the faith that manhood was achieved through productive work and property ownership.[14]

Much of the recent scholarship on twentieth-century manhood has focused on how such men sought to cultivate a virile body and sense of self to counteract their fears of being unmanned by the modern world. Once regarded as the mere framework of the manly character within, the male body assumed new importance as the basis of manhood itself. In the process men appropriated qualities as well as social behaviors that once had been regarded as subversive of manliness: the rough physical energy and activity of working-class men, but also the exuberant and rebellious playfulness of savages and boys. In the new rival but ascendant gender culture of "passionate" manhood, men who cultivated their male bodies rather than their manly characters and who preserved the untamed impulses of boys and savages within them emerged as culture heroes of manliness.[15] Many such men, according to Michael Kimmel, looked to "consumption, leisure, and recreation" to find "the danger, adventure, and risk-taking that used to be their experience in their working lives."[16]

Yet what about Tony Sarg, who was not interested in commodifying risk and danger? He wanted, in a telling allusion to Peter Pan, to make "people believe in fairies" and capitalize on their wish to do so.[17]

"Forty-five years old, he is," noted one writer, "and yet he plays with dolls and is not afraid of being laughed at."[18] As this quotation suggests, rival paradigms of manhood that valued either mature seriousness or the physically powerful male body still claimed the highest cultural authority. The lengths to which boy-men like Sarg went to demonstrate their unflagging physical energy and the profitability of their enterprises betrayed a defensiveness about being identified with a boy who would not grow up and who, according to convention, always was played on stage by a woman. Nevertheless, as the widely celebrated examples of men like Sarg show, the typology of passionate manhood needs both amplifying and revising to account for men who pointed the way to alternative masculine identities for middle-class men in a corporate consumer society.

Both what entrepreneurs like Sarg appeared to be (grown-up boys) and what they claimed to be doing (selling the freedom of childhood to adults) embraced play and magic to construct a new model of manhood in tune with what William Leach calls the "dream life" of consumer capitalism.[19] In the nineteenth century, the display and appeal of magic, fantasy, theatricality, and desire had been kept at a safe distance by a Victorian culture that both celebrated and feared the dynamism of American society.[20] These qualities were associated with deception and "out-of-control femininity," and their advocates—peddlers, urban confidence men, card sharps, vendors of patent medicines—scuttled in the margins of American society.[21] But after 1890, people who used illusion and fantasy to advance their interests gradually worked their way to the commercial center of American cities and towns.[22] Employed in new organizations that specialized in selling and advertising, these modern tricksters enlisted "magic" to sell goods. The older, Victorian manhood belonged to a culture of "solidity" and "needs" and warned of the "treacherous inconstancy and change" of the marketplace of goods.[23] By the end of the nineteenth century, the agents of the new consumer economy urged Americans to subject their longings and dissatisfactions to the alchemical wonders of the marketplace where people could be, as one of Fred Thompson's amusement attractions promised, "Anything They Wish."[24]

Accustomed to thinking of wealth, power, and manliness in terms of business ownership, land, and civic and religious duty, many middle-class white men were beset by corresponding concerns that a world built principally on catering to desires and selling dreams of ease and abundance was culturally subversive, inherently insubstantial, and personally compromising. Many of the American men who were inventing the forms and narratives of the urban consumer marketplace often felt like Barrie's orphans, the "lost boys" of Never Land, in a metaphorically feminized world of unrestrained desires and wishes, visions of abundance, and liquidity of identity that made any wish possible. At the same time, an economy shifting rapidly toward the manufacturing and marketing of consumer goods and services offered thrilling and unprecedented opportunities for profit. For "everyday Peter Pans" such contending emotions and concerns did not pose a "crisis of manhood" so much as opportunities, which they seized with enthusiasm, to explore and exploit what Jackson Lears calls the "pattern of tensions in commercial culture: between control and release, stability and sorcery."[25] The men who are examined in this article did not flee the artificiality and theatricality of consumer culture, but operated within its "pattern of tensions." Their struggles to secure their identity as men indicate that the form of masculinity they invented and performed was as unstable and ambiguous as Peter Pan himself: frozen by the playwright in a condition of arrested development and represented on stage by a woman. Everyday Peter Pans were not children at heart but new kinds of consuming men who used the concepts of play and eternal childhood to remap the coordinates of manliness to defuse the emergent associations of consumerism with women and femininity and to reconcile their expectations—social, political, and cultural priority—with the destabilizing, carnivalesque tendencies of the new economic world. Collectively, they suggest a demographic profile of the early-twentieth-century's commercial Never Land and the Peter Pans who helped engineer the transition from a nineteenth-century market culture that condemned play as the negation of productive manhood to a twentieth-century commercial culture that markets itself as the playground of boys who never grow up.

Fred Thompson, for instance, never doubted that the marketplace was his playground or that his mission to convert his dour male contemporaries to the "cheer up and smile" outlook represented anything less than fundamental human progress. During the first fifteen years of the twentieth century, Thompson was among the most visible and widely cited agents and symbols of the commercial culture of Peter Pan. The writer Samuel Merwin called him "a sort of everyday Peter Pan who has lived to carry out absolutely his boyish dreams."[26] He constructed his major commercial dreams—from Coney Island's Luna Park in 1903 and the New York Hippodrome in 1905 to the amusement park, Toyland Grown Up, at the 1915 San Francisco World's Fair—as "toys" for adults, not children. Celebrated as both the "toymaker of New York" and as a grown-up boy at play, Thompson reveals an important link between the more general remaking of middle-class gender codes of masculinity at the turn of the twentieth century and the emergence of the urban consumer playground.[27]

Born in Ohio in 1873, Thompson rose to sudden fame and wealth in the summer of 1903, when Luna Park, the amusement park that he himself designed and then operated with his partner, Elmer "Skip" Dundy, opened at Coney Island. Mobbed during its first season, Luna ignited entrepreneurial energies in cities throughout the United States, where speculators threw up larger and smaller versions of its "oriental" architecture and fantastic amusements. Luna's popularity established Coney Island as a synonym for middle-class joy and pleasure. Today Luna Parks exist throughout the world as amusement parks and night-clubs; the name is part of an international vocabulary of desire and pleasure and one of the earlier examples of the colonizing power of twentieth-century American popular culture.[28]

Thompson took his prescription of play to every variety of turn-of-the-century commercial amusement, whether it involved world's fair midways, amusement parks, electrical lighting spectacles, vaudeville, circus, "legitimate" and musical theater, or toy designing and selling. All were designed according to his conviction that women and men are simultaneously adults and children, and the self is not a fixed integer but a plastic, mutable substance. Adults, he contended in 1910, are not rational, utility-maximizing choice-makers, but "grown-up children [who] want new toys all the time. . . ." Thompson felt that "[e]ach season the grown children become more insatiable. They are thrill-hungry. They ask a new thought; they demand a new laugh; they clamor for a new sensation."[29] In other words, men and women were defined not by what they are, but by what they wished to be, and pity the businessman who thought otherwise. Thompson's description of consumer psychology and behavior amounted to more than a showman's schemes for dealing with a fickle public. By 1910, this vision of the "dynamic and malleable" consumer unencumbered by either custom or supply and demand also defined the market in general. At both the theoretical and practical levels, as Susan Strasser has shown, manufacturers were coming to see that they not only could but must energetically seek to make and develop products and markets even where the desire for them did not exist.[30] Thompson's statement about consumer desire indicates that his amusements were more than an aspect of a "leisure economy" growing up alongside an industrial-consumer society. Luna and his other ventures were part of a broader effort to reconceptualize human personality and to redefine manliness in a way that would liberate businessmen from being the passive respondents to consumers' needs and make them the agents of consumers' desires.

Although Thompson claimed to speak for all adults when he made his public pronouncements, he designed his major commercial ventures to manufacture sensations specifically for middle-class men who, as he described them, were overworked and needed cheering out of the straitjacket of "custom and habit" that alienated them from the pleasures of modern life.[31] Thompson still thought of manhood in terms of independence, but his amusements shifted the temporal location of "masterlessness" from adult manhood to the "golden days" of childhood. What men really wanted was to flee from duty and responsibility, the very concerns that defined manly rectitude in the minds of passionate men like the cowboy-reformer Teddy Roosevelt.[32] Men, according to Thompson, longed instead to return to the days "when play was everything; when responsibility had never been dreamed of . . . when we decided from personal experience what games we liked best."[33] Men, in other words, did not want to grow up; they wanted to live in Never Land.

In the nineteenth century, women and femininity conventionally were identified "with treacherous inconstancy and change," especially as these qualities were associated with consumption and the chicanery of the urban marketplace. Thompson's inclusion of middle-class men in the category of the irresponsible and impermanent, his characterization of their work as play, and his identification of their inmost desire, as Peter Pan put it, "always to be a little boy and to have fun" asserted a new masculinity. Thompson's "consuming" manhood blurred the boundaries between work and play, production and consumption, masculine civilization and feminine disorder, needs and desires. It further violated traditional as well as emerging gender codes and hierarchies that relied on the image of the imperturbable and mature male body as the cultural standard of masculinity. Yet, Thompson argued, such a model of boy-manhood did not constitute infantilization and loss of cultural authority; rather, it opened whole new frontiers of freedom, pleasure, and profit for middle-class men. In the dream world of consumption, boyish dreams of wealth and pleasure could come true.

Thompson's designs on the inviolable boundaries between work and play took the form of vastly oversized playthings for adults; in his words, they were "Fairy Picture-Books" into which patrons could enter and pretend to be children. For the showman, reclaiming the essential child liberated men to indulge not simply in pleasure, but in the pleasures of spending. As with all his amusements, Thompson explained, the idea behind Luna Park "was that of every showman—to erect a park where people would laugh, enjoy themselves, and would spend money while being amused."[34] Luna, then, was not just a pleasure resort, but "The Biggest Playground On Earth."[35] The Hippodrome, the largest theater in the world when Thompson completed it in 1906, was called "New York's gigantic toy."[36] Most of his many Broadway productions, from *Brewster's Millions* in 1906 to *Girlies* in 1910, were sensational fairy tales for adults that dramatized the pleasures of play and plenty. The clearest expression of Thompson's designs was his last major amusement enterprise, Toyland Grown Up, a fourteen-acre "playground for the human race" that he planned but never fully executed for the Joy Zone, the commercial midway of the 1915 Panama-Pacific International Exposition in San Francisco. He designed the amusement, which one writer called a "Barrie-like fantasy," according to his "principle that no one changes."[37] Work, Thompson contended, was play, and the man most likely to reap both fun and profit was the one who remained, like him, a boy at heart.

The genteel patrons of the larger fair were not willing to concede this point. As a number of scholars have argued, the Panama-Pacific

FIGURE 8.2 *An artist's rendering of Fred Thompson's Toyland Grown-Up, ca. 1913.*

*Reproduced by permission of the Larson Collection, Special Collections Library, California State University, Fresno.*

was the "last" of the great Victorian fairs.[38] Such fairs were supposed to be "colossal" universities, as boosters of the 1901 Buffalo fair expressed it, "instruct[ing] the people by means of the best object lessons the Western Hemisphere can produce."[39] The San Francisco fair was little different in this regard. By design, the fair was supposed to celebrate the world-transforming power of masculine industry and innovation. Its official representation showed the muscled form of Hercules splitting the isthmus for the Panama Canal, the "thirteenth labor of Hercules."[40] Here was man's conscious triumph over nature, a fitting

FIGURE 8.3    *Fred Thompson and San Francisco children planting the "seeds" for Toyland Grown-Up at the site of the Panama-Pacific International Exposition in October 1913*

San Francisco History Center, San Francisco Public Library.

symbol for a nation that had joined the two oceans and for a city that had rebuilt itself from the 1906 earthquake. As with other "Victorian fairs," the amusement midway was a negative analogue that demonstrated, by example, the cultural might and industrial progress of Western civilization. The designers positioned the fair's other, the Joy Zone, away from the Exposition City, behind the screen of the vast Machinery Hall and across the great metaphorical divide of the Avenue of Progress. The Joy Zone's "riotous *melée* of flimsiness and sham," as the art critic Eugen Neuhaus described it, showed the "fatal results of the utter disregard of all fundamental laws of balance, harmony, and unity so uniformly and persistently applied through the seriously designed main body of the Exposition." The "final and lasting effect" of the Exposition, asserted Neuhaus, "will be found in the great enduring lesson of beauty" that the main body of the fair would teach.[41]

The 1915 fair did represent enduring continuities, but it also suggested important discontinuities. Within weeks of its opening, some writers were declaring that the exposition was not a "noble educational institution" at all but a "great play-place." "Educational bosh!" a writer for the *San Francisco Bulletin* exclaimed. "Education only as it lures, as it is had in the spirit of the child at play, not in a sense of strenuous stern duty." The fair should have been called "Titania's Playground," according to another writer: "Can't you shut your eyes and see the Fairy Queen and all her fays flitting along [its broad avenues]?"[42] The vision of the Panama-Pacific as a playground for the cast of *A Midsummer Night's Dream* suggests that, although the Herculean fair still spoke for, as one guidebook put it, "the Spirit and Romance of Man's Development, Energy, Adventure, Aspirations and Achievements," another less rational and more intuitive voice also laid claim to the fair's meanings.[43] This voice belittled industry as the "fumbling and groping of earth's creatures" and proclaimed that the truth of the fair was glimpsed through nonrational, intuitive eyes, like those of a child.[44] This exposition voice, as another writer put it, "just won't stand for seriousness. It laughs and wants the world to laugh with it."[45]

Thompson was the fair's principal architect of the assault on seriousness, and from his perspective, progress and history were on his side of the Avenue of Progress. His designs indicate that he aimed for Toyland to engineer a Gulliverian transformation of his customers, making them feel as if they were entering a Brobdingnagian child's playroom. From the entrance guarded by ninety-foot tall toy soldiers to the Toyland Grand Hotel, outfitted as a five-story-high Mother Hubbard's cupboard inside of which patrons danced on a "plate 100 feet across," the surreal cityscape of outsized toys, animated fairy tales, nursery rhymes was meant to destabilize the solidity of identity and needs. Thompson wanted the patron of Toyland never to be certain whether he was big or small, a man at work or child at play.[46] For Toyland's groundbreaking in 1913, Thompson travestied the exposition's inauguration as the "thirteenth labor of Hercules" by employing children wielding toy shovels and rakes, blowing noisemakers, and planting "toys" as magical seeds that would grow into Toyland's fantastic architecture.[47] He designed the Toyland roller coaster as a treacherous urban construction site; automatons raced wheelbarrows loaded with passengers along a winding, treacherous pathway of scaffolding.[48] Throughout the park, automatons appear to perform the actual labor, freeing men and women from the drudgery and discipline of work.[49] Thompson was no more willing to question the sanctity of industrial capitalism than either the fair's major patrons or the 1920s generation of social scientists who encouraged workers to "play" as compensation for the "monotonous, meaningless, fragmented, dreary, and irksome" character of industrial labor.[50] In Toyland, work settings were simply inverted as playgrounds, a rendering of delight that would appeal to white-collar men increasingly distanced by managerial structures from the actual point and act of production. This idea, that work in a modern industrial society can be like play, also made sense from the perspective of the new brokers of goods who had an emotional and financial stake in the dream life of consumer capitalism. "We're playing games," Thompson explained, "and the toys may be the theater, the mart of trade, the stock ticker, the factory or the laboratory, but they're toys just the same."[51]

Stewart Culin conjured up similar visions of iconoclastic childish freedom, work as play, and commodities as toys with his innovative ethnological work at the Brooklyn Museum, where he worked from 1903 until his death in 1929. Culin's quarter-century in Brooklyn coincided with the ascendence of New York City as the powerful center of retailing, fashion, and entertainment in the United States. During that period, he built the museum into one of the most influential cultural institutions in America by allying its rich storehouses of primitive artifacts with the emergent consumer industries of retailing, fashion, design, and toymaking. Culin believed, like Thompson, that modern methods of industrial production had robbed the world of the enchanting fantasy and stirring excitement of light, color, and play, which both men associated with childhood and found distressingly absent in the twentieth century. His work at the Brooklyn Museum, no less than Thompson's at Toyland, aimed to restore a primitivist belief in things as living beings to the material world of the modern consumer economy.

Culin was born in 1858 and grew up in Philadelphia, where his father was a merchant actively involved in the overseas trade. Wealthy Philadelphians had maintained an abiding interest in natural history since the late eighteenth century, when Charles Wilson Peale opened a museum displaying natural and scientific curiosities, attracting the avid support of Enlightenment naturalists like Thomas Jefferson and Benjamin Franklin.[52] Although the Federalists satirically derided the Republicans' interests in fossils and woolly mammoths as misguided and distasteful fantasies, natural history gained respectability in the nineteenth century through scholarly societies supported by Philadelphia's social elites: the American Philosophical Society, the Academy of Natural Sciences of Philadelphia, and the Numismatic and Antiquarian Society of Philadelphia.[53] By the time Culin graduated from secondary school and joined his father's business in overseas trade in the mid-1870s, the support of natural history and anthropology had begun the transition from the nonprofessional leadership of wealthy collectors to the control of professionals affiliated with the new disciplines of anthropology, ethnology, and archaeology at major universities like the University of Pennsylvania. Culin himself had become an obsessive collector of oriental artifacts through his business in the China trade and was active in the Numismatic and Antiquarian Society, which was presided over by Daniel Brinton, a professor of archaeology and linguistics at the university. Brinton was a leader in the professionalization of anthropology and in 1889 convinced Culin to leave commerce to serve as the first secretary of the oriental section of the new museum at the university. Culin stayed at the museum,

FIGURE 8.4 *The ethnologist Stewart Culin posing with gun on hip and rifle in hand during a collecting expedition to the Navajo reservation, ca. 1906–9.*

St. Michaels Collection,
St. Michaels Parish.

aggressively building its collections until his disagreements with its directors forced his removal in 1903 to the Brooklyn Academy of Arts and Sciences, otherwise known as the Brooklyn Museum.[54]

Instead of abandoning commerce for academia and science, Culin combined his passion for primitive artifacts and his merchandising sensibility in his work with the museums in Philadelphia and Brooklyn by breaking from the evaluative and display practices of nineteenth-century natural history. The traditional wisdom of the science of natural history, laconically summarized in 1831 by the European anthropologist E. F. Jomard, held that "there is no question of beauty [in primitive artifacts] . . . but only of objects considered in relation to practical and social utility."[55] Culin professed undiluted contempt for this rigidly wooden perspective and confessed that museums interested in fact and utility alone depressed and annoyed him. "Known Facts," he observed, are "among the most capricious and undependable of all the creatures that came out of [literature's] Ark."[56] One need only look, he asserted, whether at prehistoric relics or at the handicrafts of contemporary savage cultures, to "find evidences of an aesthetic sense, of an effort, not only at mere utility, but at decoration and ornament . . . "[57] His faith in the aesthetic value of primitive cultures reflected his upbringing in the commercial world of the Philadelphia merchant. Culin was acutely aware of the merchandising revolution occurring in the city under the leadership of John Wanamaker, in whom he found an enthusiastic sponsor during his years at the University Museum. The Wanamaker stores in Philadelphia and New York led in the development of the modern department store, pioneering merchandising and display methods, services for customers, advertising, and expanding the array of goods available to American consumers. Wanamaker envisioned his store as a people's art museum. He patronized archaeologists and paleontologists and in 1895 became a manager of the University Museum, a powerful position from which he helped, with Culin's aid, to enlarge the collection and to shape its public display. Wanamaker, according to his biographer, "hated the bizarre or incongruous in the display of anything beautiful," a broad category that embraced the artifacts collected by natural historians. "In museums," Wanamaker flatly stated, "'[al]most everything looks like junk even when it isn't, because there is no care or thought in the display. If women would wear their fine clothes like galleries wear their pictures, they'd be laughed at." Wanamaker determined that museums, no less than department stores, were involved in the display of the beautiful and needed "the merchant instinct to show it off to best advantage." He found such an instinct and ally in Stewart Culin. Wanamaker funded many of Culin's earliest and most important expeditions among western American Indians for the University Museum and, in turn, displayed many of the artifacts collected by the young ethnologist in his Philadelphia department store.[58]

Culin proclaimed a new epoch in museum display that closely followed the display practices of the new retail houses. Culin believed that department stores were the modern reservoirs of the magic, play, and color that were cherished and idolized by primitive and preindustrial cultures. He longed to capture in his museum displays the drama, color, and animation with which the stores staged their goods. "Enter one of our great department stores," he urged his audience in a lecture in 1900 at the Free Museum of Science and Art in Philadelphia, "and examine the fabrications of cotton and silk, of glass and metal, wood and lacquer; mere utility is quite insufficient to justify the profusion of form and color with which we are surrounded."[59] Utility alone was equally insufficient for displaying and studying primitive artifacts, although, he admitted with dismay, usefulness was the theme governing most ethnological exhibits. "Ten thousand people visit a department store to gratify their curiosity, to see new things, to one who resorts to a museum or similar educational institution."[60] The reason for the disparity in popular appeal, according to Culin, was that museums, unlike department stores, did not convey an understanding or reveal in their displays the excitement of things. To appreciate things, he said, "we must be stirred, not with a critical spirit of comparison and evaluation, but patiently, with a feeling and respect for beauty."[61] He proposed that the museum adopt the display practices of the department stores and provide not just walls on which to hang tagged objects but a stage on which artfully arranged exotica could be dramatized and made to come alive, stirring the imagination and enthusiasm of the audience as deeply as department store displays engaged the imaginations of window-shoppers. What Culin admired about modern retailing was the ability to work magic with goods, to present them not as they are but as "they are thought to be," an incantatory power that he identified with and passionately envied in children and "childlike" primitives.[62] Culin stated his display creed as a rejection of utility and objectivity as sufficient in themselves: "I have continued on with no other thought than of making things tell me their story, and then in trying to coax and arrange them to tell this story to the world."[63]

The study of premodern or ancient cultures transported Culin to a kind of primitivist Never Land where, in his words, the people seemed "younger and not older than the people of our own age." Among the Zuñi, for instance, he felt "old beside the oldest member of the tribe." From them, he "learned something of the secret of youth and its happiness" and felt "younger and more vital" from the experience.[64] No things rejuvenated and delighted Culin quite the way toys did. Although best known for his studies of games, Culin claimed little other than "academic" interest in the subject. "Far different," he said, was his passion for the "Friends of Children." He had discovered the "secret of toys" during his expeditions to Asia and the American Southwest. He recalled blindly stumbling into the invisible "little playhouses" that Zuñi children had constructed of sticks and pieces of basketry. At first he "pitied them and their poor toys," but gradually he began to see what the Zuñi children saw. In play, he discovered, "[e]very child is naturally and instinctively a magician, able to transform a stick or a stone into something infinitely precious." He especially loved the "toy-like country" of Japan, where work and play, utility and magic, adulthood and childhood seemed the least artificially divided. "Fondly I would linger there," he said. "I feel young always in Japan."[65]

Most of all, Culin longed to paint the modern world in the radiant colors he associated with his earliest and fondest memory of childhood play, a game in which he arranged variously hued cards according to the gradations of color. "Whatever keen[n]ess and appreciation I may have for color I date from that childhood pastime," he said. "Even now I can recall the many shades of yellow." Color, for Culin, was associated not only with child's play but also with playful "primitives" whose artifacts he collected for the museum. Culin translated his primitivist, childlike "eagerness," "desire," and "craving" for color into his efforts to inspire the museum's display techniques.[66] In 1925, he opened a new ethnological gallery, which was called "Rainbow House" after a Zuñi creation myth. Culin arranged the exhibits of the various cultures not according to an evolutionary scale of development, but by designating each with a single color that evoked the subjective spirit he had detected in a particular people. "I would assign anew the colors of the world," Culin explained: for the Zuñi, pink; a sea blue for the Caribbean islands; "tawny yellow" for South American aborigines; "the green of shallow waters the islands of the Pacific, and the deep green of the tropical jungle shot with sunlight, the great river valley of the African Congo."[67] Culin thus played with color in two ways: assigning new value to the supposed color-sense of childish nonwhite "primitives" and redeploying color as a magical language for bringing things to life.

The boundless identity and magic-working powers of children and the "magic-filled world" of the primitive formed the conceptual center of Culin's identity, his museum innovations, and his efforts to place his collection at the service of modern commerce. Like Thompson and other boy-men, Culin seemed unbound by the adult's body or straitjacket of custom and habit. He "has no principles. Nor has he any rules," observed his friend, the ethnologist George A. Dorsey. "To his friends he is . . . always perpetual youth."[68] Culin was fond of quoting Oskar Seyffert, a German classicist who had written the preface to a collection of illustrations of German-made toys. To understand or to design toys, according to Seyffert, adults must learn to regard objects with a child's eyes; that is, not with the sense organs alone but with an "inward eye" that sees beyond the material world.[69] Culin seemed to possess this "eye" and urged others, especially toy manufacturers, to follow Seyffert's advice. That is, they had to believe in fairies in order not to kill them. Culin believed and thus claimed a kind of freemasonry with children. "I know secrets about toys," he said, "which I may not tell if I would."[70] Like a child, he prized museums that were worlds of sensory delight, not facts, like the Museum of National Arts in Bucharest, which he called an "Aladdin's cave" of treasures. "Indeed I am an ethnologist," he wrote in 1925, "in so far as that science has to do with magic and wonderworking, with spells and incantations. . . . Fairyland . . . may be esteemed as the true kingdom of my science. . . ."[71] Dorsey called him a "museum magician," although Culin himself claimed only to be "a student of magic and a recorder of its mysteries."[72]

Whether recorder or practitioner, Culin sought to expand the usefulness of play and color in contemporary American culture. He maintained that the cultural distance between the work of his museum and that of American consumer industries was arbitrary and unnecessary. To lessen that distance, he enlisted his museum Never Land as an active, even aggressive producer of new markets and ideas for commodities. He allied his department with major retail stores and design schools, lectured on fashion and design, judged window display and interior decoration competitions, and contributed articles to popular as well as trade publications like *Women's Wear Daily*.[73] Although he urged these shapers of the modern consumer economy to enlist the magic of childhood and primitive or preindustrial life to sell or design goods, playing or conjuring in this context did not disqualify a man from economic success; it improved his chances. In 1925 Culin saluted color technicians at their annual meeting as fellow "magicians" and dispatched them to enrich "the color sense . . . of the American people." To play with color, according to Culin, was not to surrender power but to seize the supreme instrument of magic, "the concrete expression of nature's most vital forces, a quality that has decisive influence on man's happiness and a determinant of the value of most of the material things he prizes." Aversion to color signifies "weakness," but a "vigorous color sense is a no mean index of the quality of a people."[74]

Playthings also promised untold possibilities for riches, and Culin had no reservations about translating the secrets of toys into the trade secrets of toys. The toy industry publication *Playthings* reported in 1920 that in response to an invitation from the curator, toy manufacturers were mining the museum's collections for new ideas. Selchow and Righter's orientalist Parcheesi was one result of this cooperation. "I constantly think of the possibilities of the practical adoption of games which I encountered in remote places to the requirements of our own American industry," Culin explained in 1920 in *Playthings*.[75] Culin promised "a great prize" to the manufacturers "who will make toys that will strike a responsive chord in the minds of American children."[76] Businessmen could profit, in other words, from making friends with the "friends of children."

Culin's promise to translate magic and play into practical market forces confirms recent scholarship on early-twentieth-century advertising and merchandising, which has shown the "persistence of irrationalist and animistic countertendencies" within the rational structures of managerial, corporate capitalism.[77] As William Leach has observed, businessmen in the early twentieth century often spoke in two rival or contradictory voices. "For work and production, business (as much of the culture at large) emphasized repression, rationality, self-denial, and discipline; but for selling and consumption, it opened the door to waste, indulgence, impulse, irresponsibility, dreaming, or qualities thought of as non-Western."[78] Everyday Peter Pans usually spoke in the vocabulary of impulsive play and carefree childhood, and often struggled to affirm their masculinity against the competing claims of the "individualistic model of controlled, unified selfhood."[79] Culin and his fellow boy-men defended their contested masculinity by defining a new version of male identity that eased nineteenth-century producerist anxieties about the unmanliness of the irrational by asserting the productivity dividends and profit value of never growing up and insisting on having fun. Culin's wish to dwell in Aladdin's cave, his rejection of materialist science, and his determination to ally the magic and color of childhood and the childlike primitive with emerging consumer industries outlined a consuming ethos for middle-class men, which showed them how to live and prosper in, without being subsumed by, the effeminate world of consumption. An investment in childhood returned the "great prize" of renewed force, wealth, and fun to any man who preserved an "inward eye" for its profitable opportunities. Peter Pans, in other words, did not just play; they made play *pay*.

Force, vitality, youth, pleasure, and profit were precisely what the preservation of the child within and a life in Never Land seemed to have rewarded Fred Stone. By offering new ways of thinking about and enacting masculinity in and for a culture of consumption, Stone's stage career as the "human doll" fully exploited the "pattern of tensions" of the emerging commercial culture.[80] At the same time, however, his efforts to reconcile older expectations about manliness with the new economic world of consumption reveals the contested, tentative nature of the Peter Pan ideal and the gender trouble produced by a life enacted in Never Land.

Fred Stone, who claimed he never read a fairy tale until he was almost twenty-nine years old, became one of the most popular figures in American theater between 1900 and 1930 by acting in fairy tales retooled for adult consumption, the first and most famous of which was the original stage adaptation of L. Frank Baum's *The Wonderful Wizard of Oz* in 1902.[81] With his version of adult play, Stone created stage fairy tales for adults that merged the fantasy world of children's literature with stage illusion technologies and his own personal vitality and athletic self-culture. Stone invariably portrayed a human doll, a tirelessly agile marionette without strings whose identity was as plastic as the fantasy worlds he inhabited on stage. He could play a Mandarin doll in one scene, a clumsy circus equestrienne in the next; neither his form nor his sex was impervious to dramatic manipulation or limited by the narrative demands of the plot. Stone's protean identity and acrobatic and elastic comic style equipped him ideally for the theatrical representation of the unfixed, volatile commercial culture of play and playthings. He was a man, a boy, and a toy.

Stone was born in Colorado in 1873 and was, by his account, the son of a bumbling, romantic father who was constantly moving his family from one dust-ridden Western town to another. Stone remembered his "queer sort of childhood" as departing from bourgeois norms of fairy tales and playrooms, but it was also, by established Victorian ideals, strikingly unmanly. Stone's parents actually encouraged his early interest in performance, especially the circus and trapeze artistry. His mother made him a spangled suit of tights, and neither parent, if Stone can be believed, objected when a traveling circus hired him as a ten-year-old highwire artist. His first performance, in a ballet skirt, tights, and a curly blond wig as "Mlle. Amy d'Artago, the Human Doll," humiliated the boy: "My pride received a jolt and my manhood suffered an

**FIGURE 8.5** *Fred Stone as the "Scarecrow" and Dave Montgomery as the "Tin-man" in the original stage production of L. Frank Baum's* The Wizard of Oz, *ca. 1902–3.*

*The Billy Rose Theatre Collection, The New York Public Library at Lincoln Center, Astor, Lenox and Tilden Foundations.*

insult." The unschooled circus troupe mistakenly called him "Milly," which made his "flesh crawl." When an elderly woman sympathetically exclaimed "Poor little girl!" in the middle of a performance, Stone defiantly shouted back, "I ain't a little girl. I'm a boy." But the protest did little to change the essential ambiguity of his stage personality, which foreshadowed the gender confusion of the commodity identity that shaped his entire theatrical career.[82]

Stone's gender trouble and his identity as a boy who never grew up were founded, in part, by almost thirty years of acting in children's literature translated to the stage as spectacles for adults. Although he got his theatrical break as part of a minstrel act with his partner Dave Montgomery, the role of the Scarecrow in *The Wizard of Oz* in 1902 launched him on a career in fairy land. It was followed by *The Lady of the Slipper*, Victor Herbert's musical rendition of *Cinderella* in 1912; *Chin-Chin,* in 1914, based on the story of *Aladdin*; *Jack O'Lantern,* a musical comedy version of *The Babes in the Wood*; and *Tip Top* in 1920, with a libretto that the *New York Times* called "one of those nursery-flavored books."[83] *Stepping Stones,* in 1923, was an adaptation of the stories of *Red Riding Hood* and *Prince Charming*. Following lengthy runs in New York, each of these productions was put on a national road tour for a year or more, spreading the clown's fame and identity beyond the immediate boundaries of Broadway.

The Scarecrow was the formative role of Stone's career, and an important indicator of the new masculinity he embodied. In adopting the role and switching from a career in vaudeville minstrelsy to the "legitimate" stage, Stone, like Culin, was playing with racial "color" by staking out important new meanings for the word *boy*. This common racial slur for a black man not only named his inferiority and incapacity for the privileges of whiteness; it also rewarded the white name-caller with a gendered "sense of superiority and security [that] was gained by being white and *not* being black."[84] Minstrels, according to David Roediger, exploited the slur by depicting black men as playfully boyish and sexually potent. "Blacking up" affirmed the privileges of whiteness as it appropriated the "wildness" of being black.[85] Even as the color of his stage face changed, Stone did not abandon the racial appeal of minstrelsy. In the most obvious sense, he integrated some of his most popular blackface routines in *The Wizard of Oz* and other productions.[86] In a less literal sense, Stone's performances as the Scarecrow and other human dolls may have served as a form of "racial disguise" similar to that of minstrelsy. His routines indicated that white men could retain what they loved about the boyishness of African-American men—their supposed innate irresponsibility, love of play, and joyfulness—while suppressing, behind the whiteface of the eternal boy at play, the degradation and subordination associated not only with blackness but also with the diminished expectations and dependent conditions of white-collar work.[87] Stone's adult play also promised to contain the erotic potential conventionally portrayed in minstrel routines. As he explained, from *The Wizard of Oz* on, all of his musical comedies would be "based on a fairy tale and clean as a whistle."[88] His boyishness, as he represented it for the next thirty years, probably never fully suppressed the powerful derogatory associations of childish behavior with blackness; but at the same time, Stone made eternal boyhood more appealing to middle-class men by rendering it as the boundless energy, ungoverned freedom, and cheerful irresponsibility of white children at play.

In addition to subverting and reorienting the racial coding of boyishness, Stone's four years playing the Scarecrow in theaters throughout the United States linked his identity to the emerging urban marketplace and its playgrounds of consumption. *The Wonderful Wizard of Oz* was made to order for a boy who would never grow up. As William Leach has shown, Baum's various occupations as theatrical producer, dry goods merchant, display designer, fairy tale writer, and playwright revealed rather than a fragmented personality a brilliantly imaginative fascination and passion for the urban marketplace developing in major cities like Chicago and New York. Baum's *Wizard* was a cheerful, therapeutic text of and for the new industrial order of consumer capitalism. According to Leach, Baum rejected the religious and ethical culture of the nineteenth century, especially its valuation of work and its consciousness of human and material limitations, for a mind cure or "positive-thinking" philosophy in tune with consumer culture's promises of "a life of ever-increasing abundance, comfort, and bodily pleasure."[89] Baum found his greatest joy in the new urban playgrounds of consumption, especially department stores and theaters. In 1900, the same year as *The Wonderful Wizard of Oz*, he published *The Art of Decorating Show Windows and Dry Goods Interiors*, the first book on the subject and widely valued among urban retailers.[90] Baum permanently left merchandising to write children's fiction in 1900, but the integration of his imagination into the urban marketplace and the new art of displaying goods cannot be separated from his literary fairy tales. In effect, Baum urged window trimmers to excite with their commodity displays the same sensations of marvel and fascination that he linked to his own childlike obsession with animation, dreams, artificiality, fantasy, and joy. Five years before *Peter Pan*, the writer described his own eternal childhood: "I have no shame in acknowledging that I . . . am also a child, for since I can remember my eyes have always grown big at tales of the marvellous [*sic*], and my heart is still accustomed to go pit-a-pat when reading of impossible adventures." The "nature of children," according to Baum, is "to scorn realities" for joyful dreams, and this outlook was at the core of *The Wizard of Oz*, consumer culture in general, and the boy-man who played its Scarecrow, which, from its opening night in Chicago, was the chief sensation of the show.[91]

From the moment he was brought to life by Dorothy and slid from the pole in the cornfield, Stone's Scarecrow was a dancing, gymnastic rag doll. Other doll roles followed, permanently linking Stone to the new commodity world of children. Virtually nonexistent before 1905, American-made toys by 1925 amounted to a $58 million industry, the beneficiary of new mass-production techniques, the interruption of toy imports during the Great War, and, especially, the soaring consumer demand for toys after 1912.[92] Stone's fame as the "Human Doll" followed the path of the revolutionary expansion of American toy manufacturing. But Stone did not have to adopt the actual part of a doll to be understood as one. Descriptions of Stone's flying, tumbling, and bouncing about the American stage during the first two decades of the twentieth century tended to highlight the almost mechanical execution of his stunts. Critics portrayed Stone as a living doll or a marionette without strings. The *New York Times* observed, "Stone has defied those deeper laws of gravity that weigh upon us all. It is clowning, if you will, but clowning with so light a toe, so airy a body, and a spirit so elementally gay and free that it rises to the altitude of the fine arts."[93] Gilbert Seldes, writing in *Vanity Fair*, found Stone a magically half-human and half-mechanical toy, "humanized Jack-in-the-Box; you feel his astonishing virtuosity in being so mechanically perfect and so humanly attractive at the same time."[94]

Stone's athletic virtuosity was a defining aspect of his stage career. By all accounts he had been born with extraordinary physical agility, which he cultivated through a stridently active life, outside the theater, of singleminded conditioning and then integrated into his productions as impressive feats of bareback riding, ice skating, acrobatics, lassoing, and highwire walking.[95] "There seems to be no position he cannot assume, no leap or tumble or step he cannot take," Seldes noted.[96] Another critic credited Stone with discovering "physical culture as an infallible means of amusing the masses."[97]

Stone's virility and talent for calling "practically every muscle into play" in his performances resembled what Anthony Rotundo calls "passionate manhood."[98] Yet the translation of his physical endowments into theatrical comedy complicated the solidity and controlled selfhood that his athletic body implied. His signature comic style combined physical agility and athletic training with what was by all accounts an amazingly flexible, even liquid body. Among other talents, Stone was able to bend his ankles inward or outward at right angles to his legs and walk or dance on his joints in this manner.[99] The contorted maneuver seemed to dissolve his skeleton while making him appear simultaneously clumsy and nimble. As a Chicago critic observed, "Stone is as boneless as shredded cod and as graceful as a squirrel. . . ."[100]

Many of Stone's roles similarly compromised his virile self-mastery by making his comical clumsiness indistinguishable from his acrobatic gracefulness. Though only a few seconds long, a 1907 silent film clip that shows Montgomery and Stone sparring in boxing gloves concisely expresses this comic style. When Montgomery stings him on the chin, Stone retaliates with wildly uncontrolled roundhouse swings, which, striking nothing but air, lift him off his feet. In one seamless motion, Stone throws himself topsy-turvy, lands on his head, spins, twists, and nimbly springs to his feet.[101] His Broadway productions incorporated this agile clumsiness, usually as a trademark stunt invented by Stone himself to illustrate his physical self-culture and irrepressible boyish-ness. In a sensational scene from *The Lady of the Slipper*, which used a series of hidden trampolines, the actor stepped onto a stairway landing and began uncontrollably to bounce and somersault before stumbling down the stairs and falling onto a sofa, which catapulted him onto a table. Jumping back to the floor, he ricocheted off another hidden trampoline, which hurled him headfirst through an ancestral portrait hanging on the wall.[102] Such comical propulsions and blunders depicted Stone as the embodiment of disciplined recklessness, at once graceful and klutzy, managed and out of control. Stone's usual roles as an antic, boyish clown or mischief maker were extensions of his divided self. In *Stepping Stones* (1923–24), according to Seldes, Stone divided "himself into two characters, one stealing and eating tarts, the other watching and preventing him. It is beautifully timed, the slide across the stage to assume the guardian character just as the last crumb is swallowed, and back again."[103] In this scene Stone gave repressive self-denial and indulgent irresponsibility equal time, but the joke was on the guardian of moral order.

Stone's commitment to his forceful, managed body reveals his enduring unease about the subversive implications of living in the Never Land of unending childhood. At the same time, however, his ability to be both controlled and out of control—the tart-eating thief and the stalwart protector of moral order—enacted the alluring promise of consumer capitalism to preserve the antic adventure of boyish play within its rational managerial and marketing techniques for generating profits. Stone's stage roles captured the color, fluidity, mutability, animation, play, joy, and childish impulse that composed the visual and narrative forms of the commercial culture of Peter Pan. "Stone lives and breathes—and sings, and dances, and does stunts—in the air of the Brothers Grimm and Hans Christian Andersen," Seldes observed. "He creates a modern fairy tale with mechanical hobgoblins, and radiolite spirits, and good fairies blazing with electricity."[104] As the "Human Doll" he was an object of play and a stimulant to the pur-ported child spirit of his adult audience—a man, a boy, and a toy. This "grown-up boy acrobat," as *Leslie's Weekly* called him, seemed himself a child at heart who lived consumer capitalism's "dream life" of abun-dance and play.[105] Like Culin, he claimed to possess an inward eye that enabled him to dwell always in what he called the child-world of "Let's pretend." Moreover, his work eluded the pinch of sacrifice and duty. "I was a happy man and a fortunate one," Stone recalled reflecting late in his career. He had a family that was his "delight" and work that was "the kind I liked best." His cup running over with fun, yet troubled that he "had never been grateful enough for" the bounty of his life, Stone achieved "final peace" by joining a Protestant church, an act that left him feeling "better and happier" than ever before.[106] He truly was, at this point, as a newspaper ad had described him several years before, "First in the Land of Fun—The Peter Pan of Clowns."[107]

In any earlier period of American history, a respectable white man who valued work and religion for their fun quotient would have invited scorn from men of his own class and race. Work and play, by definition, were incommensurable. For Stone, however, the fusion of these antinomies in his stage representations rewarded dividends of pleasure and profit. "The world has been good to me," he concluded his autobiography. "I have been a happy man."[108] By 1940, when the puppeteer Tony Sarg died, a rival was able to eulogize him as "a good business man, a hard worker, and one who also knew how to play."[109] By this time the unending childhood of men like Fred Thompson, Stewart Culin, Fred Stone, and many other everyday Peter Pans was beginning to make sense. Such men radiated vitality; their energies were boundless, their incomes of the first order. And they always had fun.

Although challenged from many angles, everyday Peter Pans endorsed an insurgent form of masculinity and man's work that defied and undermined, without fully subverting, the dominant culture's investment in the model of the controlled, masculine man. In doing so, they made a vital contribution to middle-class male identity by charting a new economic frontier for manly endeavor within the stigmatized world of consumption. With independence and selfhood redefined in the vocabulary of fun and play, manliness and work became matters of unfettered consumer choice; they meant, in Tony Sarg's words, "being able to do the thing you most like to do in life," or, as Fred Thompson put it, playing the "games we liked best." Under these terms the center of social value was liberated from the traditional matrix of economic, religious, and civic obligations, the ownership of property, and the actual making of goods that had defined manliness in the nineteenth century. By embracing consumption and the consumer marketplace as the workplace stage for achieving and performing one's manhood, these "boys and their toys" embodied a new manhood that announced new opportunities for pleasure and profit in a culture built upon the conception, representation, and consumption of commodities.

Peter Pan manhood began as a small revolt on the margins against the restrictive bourgeois economy of productive labor, repressed desires, and rational leisure in a new era of abundance and pleasure. Its celebration of play and flight from care and responsibility sketched the contours of a new bourgeois man for the twentieth century and suggests that the rebellion of the "playboy" and its hedonistic attack on what Barbara Ehrenreich calls the masculine "convention of hard-won maturity" began long before Hugh Hefner's glossy publications emerged in the 1950s.[110] Everyday Peter Pans did not directly challenge monogamy, but they did implicitly subvert the breadwinner ethic by identifying middle-class men's alienation from and longing for the "joy of living and the world of delight" that were consumer culture's principal enticements. Joy and pleasure, as Fred Thompson and other Peter Pans argued, were what a man really wanted out of life, and the way to find them was by playing, which meant doing "the opposite to the things he HAS to do. . . ." [111]

This consuming ethos and the form of masculinity it endorses remain today as an expression of the undercurrent of discontent felt by middle-class men. Critical voices still denounce the Peter Pan model of manhood; authors of books like *The Peter Pan Syndrome* lament what they call men's flight from responsibility and the "commitment to noncommitment." [112] Yet one need only look at contemporary child-men like Steven Spielberg and Robin Williams, who collaborated on *Hook* (1991), the most recent big-budget version of *Peter Pan*, to see the continuing appeal of eternal childhood. Or at Tom Hanks, whose films *Big* (1988) and *Forrest Gump* (1994) preserve the myth that arrested development or eternal childhood, while scorned by those without an "inward eye" for its potential, can revitalize moribund capitalist enterprises and generate huge financial as well as sexual rewards. In *Big* in particular, the grown-up child that Hanks portrays restores zest and prosperity to a toy company whose commodities have gone stale under the leadership of its excessively rational and grown-up managers. Hanks's character does not actually make any goods or own any capital, but he does come up with ideas for commodities that make people—stockholders as well as toy buyers— happy. He also is sexier than the manager with the M.B.A. If the popularity of these films is any indication, the commercial culture of Peter Pan still preserves the century-long middle-class hope that the diminished expectations and disenchantment of life can be reversed and the compromised sense of what it means to be a man in a corporate and now postindustrial capitalist society can be revitalized—if we will only believe in fairies. [113]

## Notes

I am most grateful to Bruce Dorsey, John Grammer, Roger Horowitz, Peter Laipson, and Gayle McKeen for their indispensable and generous advice, and to Dean Robert Keele of the University of the South, who provided vital funding for some of the research. The most important help came from my favorite historian, Julie Berebitsky.

1. John Monk Saunders, "Tony Sarg Has Never Done a Stroke of Work in His Life!" *American Magazine* 101 (1926): 26–28, 100–108.

2. Ruth Kedzie Wood, "Puppets and Puppeteering," *Mentor* 9 (1921): 35.

3. "Testimonial," n.d., 1, 3, Tony Sarg Collection, Detroit Institute of the Arts.

4. Saunders, "Tony Sarg Has Never Done a Stroke of Work," 28, 108.

5. Walter Prichard Eaton, "Oscar Hammerstein: A Boy Who Never Grew Up," *American Magazine*, May 1907, 34.

6. Stewart Culin, "The Road to Beauty" [unpublished typescript]. Research and Writings: Road to Beauty [5,2,006] chap. 1–4, 1925, 49–50, Stewart Culin Archival Collection, Brooklyn Museum of Art Archives (hereafter cited as BMA).

7. Jean-Christophe Agnew, "Coming Up for Air: Consumer Culture in Historical Perspective," *Intellectual History Newsletter* 12 (1990): 15.

8. Pauline Jacobson, "Forty Winks at the Exposition," *San Francisco Bulletin*, February 13, 1915, 13.

9. "Life Is a Merry Go Round," words by John L. Golden, music by Benjamin Hapgood Burt, from Fred Thompson's *Girlies* (New York and Detroit: Jerome H. Remick, 1910). *Girlies* was produced by Thompson at the New Amsterdam Theatre Roof Garden, beginning in June 1910, for eighty-eight performances.

10. E. Anthony Rotundo, *American Manhood: Transformations in Masculinity from the Revolution to the Modern Era* (New York: Basic Books, 1993), 55, 56–74.

11. Michael Paul Rogin, *Ronald Reagan, the Movie and Other Episodes in Political Demonology* (Berkeley and Los Angeles: University of California Press, 1987), 135.

12. Rotundo, *American Manhood*, 71.

13. Francis Parkman, *The Conspiracy of Pontiac*, 10th ed. (New York: Collier, 1962), 182–83, quoted in Rogin, *Ronald Reagan*, 137.

14. Rotundo, *American Manhood*, 167–283; Michael Kimmel, *Manhood in America, A Cultural History* (New York: The Free Press, 1996), 13–116; Gail Bederman, *Manliness and Civilization: A Cultural History of Gender and Race in the United States, 1880–1917* (Chicago: University of Chicago Press, 1995), 10–15.

15. Rotundo, *American Manhood*, 5–6, 222–46.

16. Michael Kimmel, "Consuming Manhood: The Feminization of American Culture and the Recreation of the Male Body, 1832–1920," in Laurence Goldstein, ed., *The Male Body: Features, Destinies, Exposures* (Ann Arbor: University of Michigan Press, 1994), 21.

17. Anne Stoddard, "The Story of Tony Sarg and His Varied Art Activities," *Mentor* 16 (1928): 25.

18. "A Man Who Plays with Dolls, and Admits It," *Literary Digest* 94 (1927): 58–60.

19. William Leach, *Land of Desire: Merchants, Power, and the Rise of a New American Culture* (New York: Pantheon, 1993).

20. Karen Halttunen, *Confidence Men and Painted Women: A Study of Middle-Class Culture in America, 1830–1870* (New Haven, Conn.: Yale University Press, 1982); Jackson Lears, *Fables of Abundance: A Cultural History of Advertising in America* (New York: Basic Books, 1994).

21. Victoria de Grazia, *The Sex of Things: Gender and Consumption in Historical Perspective* (Berkeley and Los Angeles: University of California Press, 1996), 15.

22. Ann Fabian, *Card Sharps, Dream Books, and Bucket Shops: Gambling in Nineteenth-Century America* (Ithaca, N.Y.: Cornell University Press, 1990); Leach, *Land of Desire*.

23. Joyce Appleby, *Capitalism and a New Social Order* (New York: New York University Press, 1984), 42, 93; de Grazia, *The Sex of Things*, 13–15.

24. See Thompson's rendering of "The Wishing Well," in the Illustrations of Toyland Grown Up Amusements, 1913, Larson Collection, Special Collections Library, California State University-Fresno (hereafter cited as CSUF).

25. Lears, *Fables of Abundance*, 42–43.

26. Samuel Merwin, "Thompson and his Hippodrome," *Success* 9 (1906): 528.

27. "Frederic Thompson's Tribute to Toys," *Playthings* 7 (1909): 115.

28. For examples of Luna Parks on other continents, see the following: for Melbourne, Australia (1912), see the web site http://www.lunapark.com.au/history.html, which reports that seven Luna Parks were opened in Australia on the Coney Island example, but only those in Melbourne and Sydney still exist; for Buenos Aires, Argentina (1912), see "Un poco de historia" on the web site http://www.lunapark.com.ar/main. htm; for a photograph of Luna in Berlin, see Volker S. Berghahn, "Germany America; How Germans Perceived America As a Society and a Culture," *American Heritage* 46, no. 3 (1995) 62ff.; for the former Soviet Union, see the film *Luna Park* (1991), directed and written by Pavel Lungin; 105 minutes, IMA Films/New Yorker Video 1994, videocassette.

29. Frederic Thompson, "Amusing People," *Metropolitan* 32 (1910): 604–5, 610.

30. Susan Strasser, *Satisfaction Guaranteed: The Making of the American Mass Market* (New York: Pantheon, 1989), 159, 161, and the chapter "Designing Markets," 124–61.

31. Thompson, "Amusing People," 610.

32. On Roosevelt, see Bederman, *Manliness and Civilization*, 170–215.

33. "Frederic Thompson's Tribute," 115.

34. Fred Thompson, "Amusement Architecture," *Architectural Review* 16 (1909): 87–88.

35. Advertisement, *Brooklyn Daily Eagle*, May 27, 1911, Coney Island Section, 1.

36. William Wood Register, "New York's Gigantic Toy," in William R. Taylor, ed., *Inventing Times Square: Commerce and Culture at the Crossroads of the World* (Baltimore, Md.: Johns Hopkins University Press, 1996), 243.

37. "Toyland Grown Up," *New York World*, September 28, 1913, magazine, 12; "First Fair Concession Is Dedicated; Children Loath to Bury Pretty Toys," *San Francisco Examiner*, October 14, 1913, 3.

38. Robert W. Rydell, *All the World's a Fair: Visions of Empire at American International Expositions, 1876–1916* (Chicago: University of Chicago Press, 1984), 208–33; James Gilbert, "World's Fairs As Historical Events," in Robert W. Rydell and Nancy Gwinn, eds., *Fair Representations: World's Fairs and the Modern World* (Amsterdam: VU University Press, 1994), 13–27.

39. "Some Information Regarding the Pan-American Exposition," *Pan-American Exposition Literature*, Bound Pamphlets, n.p., 1901, New York Public Library.

40. See the cover of *Panama-Pacific International Exposition, San Francisco, 1915*, Booklet No. 1, 2d ed. (San Francisco, Calif.: Panama-Pacific International Exposition Company[?], 1914[?]). The illustration of "The Thirteenth Labor of Hercules" was the work of the artist Perham Nahl.

41. Eugen Neuhaus, "The Architecture of the Exposition," *University of California Chronicle* 17 (1915): 292–95.

42. Jacobson, "Forty Winks," 13; Katherine Dunlap Cather, "Titania's Playground: A Glimpse of the Panama Exposition," *St. Nicholas* 42 (1915): 516–24.

43. Stella Perry, *The Sculpture and Murals of the Panama-Pacific International Exposition* (San Francisco: Wahlgreen, 1915), 1.

44. Cora Lenore Williams, *The Fourth-Dimensional Reaches of the Exposition* (San Francisco: Paul Elder, 1915), 7–16.

45. "A City of Lovely Light," *San Francisco Examiner*, February 21, 1915, n.p.

46. " 'Toyland' at the Panama Fair," *Playthings* 12 (1914): 76–78; Gus R. Kinsley, "Playthings at the Panama Fair," *Playthings* 12 (1914): 96–98; Illustrations of Toyland Grown Up, 1913, CSUF; Frances A. Groff, "Exposition Moths," *Sunset* 35 (1915): 133–48.

47. Frank Morton Todd, *The Story of the Exposition: Being the Official History of the International Celebration Held at San Francisco in 1915 to Commemorate the Discovery of the Pacific Ocean and the Construction of the Panama Canal*, 5 vols. (New York: G. P. Putnam, 1921), vol. 1, 184–87; "Seeds of Toyland Planted; 'Kids' Revel in Rare Treat," *San Francisco Chronicle*, October 14, 1913, 4; "First Fair Concession Is Dedicated," *San Francisco Examiner*, 3.

48. Illustrations of Toyland Grown Up, 1913, San Francisco History Center, San Francisco Public Library.

49. See "Toyland G.U. Hand Car Ride" and "The Town Pump, Principality of Toyland G.U.," in illustrations of Toyland Grown Up, 1913, CSUF.

50. Quoted in Benjamin Kline Hunnicutt, *Work without End: Abandoning Shorter Hours for the Right to Work* (Philadelphia: Temple University Press, 1988), 141.

51. " 'Toyland' at the Panama Fair," 76.

52. Neil Harris, *Humbug: The Art of P. T. Barnum* (Chicago: University of Chicago Press, 1973), 34–36.

53. Linda Kerber, *Federalists in Dissent: Imagery and Ideology in Jeffersonian America* (Ithaca, N.Y.: Cornell University Press, 1980), 67–94.

54. Simon J. Bronner, "Object Lessons: The Work of Ethnological Museums and Collections," in Simon J. Bronner, ed., *Consuming Visions: Accumulation and Display of Goods*

*in America, 1880–1920* (New York: Norton, 1989), 217–54; William Leach, "Strategists of Display and the Production of Desire," in Bronner, ed., *Consuming Visions*, 128–30; Regna Darnell, "The Emergence of Academic Anthropology at the University of Pennsylvania," *Journal of the History of the Behavioral Sciences* 6 (1970): 80–83.

55. Elizabeth Williams, "Art and Artifact at the Trocadero: Ars Americana and the Primitivist Revolution," in George W. Stocking Jr., ed., *Objects and Others: Essays on Museums and Material Culture* (Madison: University of Wisconsin Press, 1985), 147.

56. Culin, "The Road to Beauty," (1925), 29.

57. Stewart Culin, "The Origin of Ornament," *Bulletin of the Free Museum of Science and Art* 2 (1900): 235.

58. Herbert Adams Gibbons, *John Wanamaker*, vol. 2 (Port Washington, N.Y.: Kennikat Press, 1971), 71–86; Bronner, "Object Lessons," 233–34; Leach, "Strategists of Display," 128.

59. Culin, "The Origin of Ornament," 235–42.

60. "Department Store a Great Influence for Culture," *Toys and Novelties* 24 (1927): 349.

61. Stewart Culin, "Creation in Art," *Brooklyn Museum Quarterly* 11 (1924): 97.

62. Stewart Culin, "The Friends of Children," October 31, 1925 (Games [7.3.006]: Japanese, 1925), n.p., BMA.

63. Stewart Culin, "The Road to Beauty," *Brooklyn Museum Quarterly* 14 (1927): 41.

64. Culin, "The Road to Beauty" (1927), 43.

65. Stewart Culin, "Stewart Culin Talks of Toys," *Playthings* 25 (1927): 161–63.

66. Stewart Culin, "The Magic of Color," *Brooklyn Museum Quarterly* 12 (April 1925): 103.

67. Culin, "The Road to Beauty" (1927), 41–44.

68. George A. Dorsey, "Stewart Culin," *American Magazine* 75 (1913): 37.

69. Oskar Seyffert, *Toys* (Berlin: Ernst Wasmuth A.G., 1921), 3–8.

70. Culin, "Stewart Culin Talks of Toys," 161–62.

71. Culin, "The Road to Beauty" (1925), 8, 47.

72. Dorsey, "Stewart Culin," 37; Culin, "The Magic of Color," 99.

73. Leach, *Land of Desire*, 166–73.

74. Culin, "The Magic of Color," 99, 103.

75. "World's Wonder Toys at Brooklyn Museum," *Playthings* 18 (1920): 105; "Modern Toys Share Stage with Ancient," *Toys and Novelties* 24 (1927): 126; Culin, "Stewart Culin Talks of Toys," 161–63; Stewart Culin, "Dolls," *Playthings* 25 (1927): 94–96; Stewart Culin, "Puzzles, European and American and Their Oriental Analogues," *Playthings* 25 (1927): 111–13; Paula Petrik, "The House That Parcheesi Built: Selchow and Righter Company," *Business History Review* 60 (1986): 410–37.

76. "A Big Message to U.S. Toy Makers," *Playthings* 18 (1920): 79.

77. Lears, *Fables of Abundance*, 2.

78. Leach, *Land of Desire*, 107.

79. Lears, *Fables of Abundance*, 2.

80. Fred Stone, *Rolling Stone* (New York: Whittlesey House, 1945), 23.

81. Ibid., 129–41.

82. Ibid., 1–31.

83. Alexander Woolcott, "Review of Tip Top," *New York Times*, October 6, 1920, Brown Collection, Billy Rose Theatre Collection, New York Public Library at Lincoln Center; hereafter, the Rose Collection will be cited as TCNYPL.

84. Robin D. G. Kelley, *Race Rebels: Culture, Politics, and the Black Working Class* (New York: The Free Press, 1996), 29–30.

85. David Roediger, *The Wages of Whiteness: Race and the Making of the White Working Class* (London: Verso, 1991), 116–22.

86. Stone, *Rolling Stone*, 99–106.

87. Eric Lott, *Love and Theft: Blackface Minstrelsy and the American Working Class* (New York: Oxford University Press, 1995).

88. Stone, *Rolling Stone*, 135.

89. Leach, *Land of Desire*, 259.

90. L. Frank Baum, *The Art of Decorating Show Windows and Dry Goods Interiors* (Chicago: Show Window, 1900).

91. L. Frank Baum, "To the Reader" (preface), *A New Wonderland: Being the First Account Ever Printed of the Beautiful Valley, and the Wonderful Adventures of Its Inhabitants* (New York: R. H. Russell, 1900), n.p.

92. "New and Old Merchandising Problems in the Toy Industry," *Toys and Novelties* 24 (December 1927), 177; "Keep and Use This Book," *Playthings* (1925): 361; William Leach, "Child World in the Promised Land," in James Gilbert, Amy Gilman, Donald M. Scott, Joan W. Scott, eds., *The Mythmaking Frame of Mind: Social Imagination and American Culture* (Belmont, Calif.: Wadsworth, 1993), 209–17. On the rapid growth of American toy manufacturing and retailing after 1900 in general, see Gary Cross, *Kids' Stuff: Toys and the Changing World of American Childhood* (Cambridge, Mass.: Harvard University Press, 1997), 1–81; Leach, *Land of Desire*, 85–90.

93. "Fred Stone Brings Jack O'Lantern," *New York Times*, October 17, 1917, *Jack O'Lantern* clipping file, TCNYPL.

94. Gilbert Seldes, "Fred Stone and W. C. Fields," *Vanity Fair*, April 1924, Brown Collection, TCNYPL.

95. Stone, *Rolling Stone*, 144–212.

96. Seldes, "Fred Stone."

97. "Jack O'Lantern review," n.d., *Jack O'Lantern* clipping envelope, TCNYPL.

98. "Jack O'Lantern review"; Rotundo, *American Manhood*, 222–46.

99. Stone, *Rolling Stone*, 59.

100. Amy Leslie, "Plays and Players," Clipping of Chicago review, June 16, 1902, Townsend Walsh Scrapbook No. 4543, TCNYPL.

101. *Dancing Boxing Match*, 1907, Winthrop Moving Picture Co., in *The American Variety Stage: Vaudeville and Popular Entertainment, 1870-1920*, American Memory Historical Collections for the National Digital Library, Library of Congress, Washington, D.C. Available from http://lcweb2.loc.gov/cgi-bin/query/r?ammem/varstg:@field(NUMBER(0763)).

102. Stone, *Rolling Stone*, 183–84; *The Lady of the Slipper*, reviews, n.d., *The Lady of the Slipper* clipping envelope, Brown Collection, TCNYPL.

103. Seldes, "Fred Stone."

104. Ibid.

105. Clipping of "How Two Western Comedians Won Their Way into Public Favor," *Leslie's Weekly*, October 8, 1903, in Locke Scrapbook, series 2, volume 280, TCNYPL.

106. Stone, *Rolling Stone*, 221–23.

107. Advertisement, *Columbus Dispatch*, February 1 (?), 1918, Brown Collection, TCNYPL.

108. Stone, *Rolling Stone*, 246.

109. "Testimonial," 2, Sarg Collection.

110. Barbara Ehrenreich, *The Hearts of Men: American Dreams and the Flight from Commitment* (Garden City, N.Y.: Anchor Books, 1983), 11–12, 42–51.

111. "Toy-Maker for Grown-ups," *New York Journal*, May 5, 1916, Thompson and Dundy clipping envelope, Brown Collection, TCNYPL.

112. Dan Kiley, *The Peter Pan Syndrome: Men Who Have Never Grown Up* (New York: Dodd, Mead, 1983); William O'Malley, "The Peter Pan Syndrome," *Spirituality for Today* 1, no. 2 (1995), available at http://www.spirituality.org/issue02/page06.html.

113. *Big*, directed by Penny Marshall, produced by Robert Greenhut and James L. Brooks, 104 minutes, Twentieth Century Fox, 1988, videocassette; *Hook*, directed by Steven Spielberg, produced by Kathleen Kennedy, Frank Marshall, Gerald R. Molen, 144 minutes. Amblin Entertainment/Steven Spielberg Film/TriStar Pictures, 1991, videocassette; *Forrest Gump*, directed by Robert Zemeckis, produced by Wendy Finerman, Steve Tisch, Steve Starkey, 142 minutes, Paramount Pictures, 1994, videocassette.

# Masculinity, the Auto Racing Fraternity, and the Technological Sublime

## The Pit Stop As a Celebration of Social Roles

BEN A. SHACKLEFORD

F orty bright blurs dashing around an oval track inches apart, speed punctuated by brief and frenzied pit stop action, and concluding victory lane celebrations filled with happy racers, race queens, and adoring fans present powerful images of masculine daring combined with skill and speedy machines in a dangerous setting. These symbols and rituals, as components of the growing stock car entertainment spectacle managed by NASCAR (National Association for Stock Car Automobile Racing) are both cause and consequence of powerful notions of masculine work environments. As a cause, auto racing brings these traditional views of masculinity, machinery, production, and danger to millions as mass spectacle. As consequence, racing bears the imprint of traditional attitudes about dangerous machinery and masculine productivity. As negotiated by racers, NASCAR officials, fans and sponsors, the rules that create race events celebrate and encourage an exclusively masculine, distinctly stratified, labor-intensive relationship between man and machine. Furthermore, the rituals in which stock car racers engage feed on and are nourished by a regional flair for competitive masculine behavior in potentially violent circumstances. This essay is an attempt to untangle the relationships among the ritual, technology, and governance of events at stock car racing's highest level. It is an attempt to understand how the vehicles, drivers, rule makers, mechanics, officials, and pit crews of NASCAR combine weekly to create a popular masculine allegory.

The idea that stock car racing celebrates mechanized danger is not new. Among historians of Southern culture, stock car racing is regarded as a modern extension of traditionally violent and competitive themes in Southern life. Pete Daniels asserts that "Stock car racing combines Southerners' love of automobiles, daring, violence, heroes, and hell-raising."[1] In *Honor and Violence in the Old South*, Bertram

Wyatt-Brown describes how "Southerners . . . loved sports, hunting, games of chance and skill—in fact, any event that promised the excitement of deciding the inequalities of prowess among men, or among men and beasts."[2] The twentieth-century substitution of race cars for swift horses continues the dangerous contests whereby Southern men assert their masculinity.

The perception that Southern culture spreads with the popularity of stock car racing is also not new. In *The World's Number One, Flat-Out, All-Time Great Stock Car Racing Book*, Jerry Bledsoe cites NASCAR as partly responsible for the growing national influence of Southern culture. In reference to the "Southernization of America" he writes, "I suppose you could even point to stock car racing, the only big-time sport to come out of the South, as part of the evidence. You could see a Saturday night stock car race in almost any state in the country now, [1975] and those old lead-footed country boys from North Carolina and Tennessee and other points south who had made the big time were going to Michigan and California and Texas to race on new "super-speedways" that had been built for them, and all the big races could be seen now live on network TV."[3] In the past two decades, the influence of stock car racing has continued to grow. During the nineties, all thirty-five races in the biggest stock car series, as well as most of the preliminary events, became live televised events. In 1996, as estimated by Nielson Media Research, each race drew an average television audience of just under 4.8 million viewers.[4] As a consequence of such popularity, corporate advertisers fueled the phenomenon by spending whatever necessary to finish well in races. Subsequently, stock car racing invaded nearly every sphere of consumer culture. Today, advertising for teams competing in NASCAR's premier championship series, The Winston Cup, seems to be everywhere; magazines, ice cream cartons, facial tissues, soap, tools, bedroom slippers, watches, towels, and snack food packaging all bear the mark of Winston Cup. In 1997 alone, thirty million cereal boxes featuring Winston Cup drivers, teams, and cars served as testament to stock car racing's growing popularity.[5]

The full consequence of all the growing attention lavished upon stock car racing remains unclear. However, one conclusion seems evident. Regional culture, and the technologies that convey such culture, do matter.[6] They help set the stage for the conduct of NASCAR events that now transmit embedded features of regional culture whenever a race is run. Indeed, the grassroots origins of NASCAR events, and the traditions that govern the technological and operational details of such events guarantees that the regional affinity for dangerous confrontation and violent competition remain central to the sport even as it is embraced nationally.[7] Because it is beyond the scope of this inquiry to fashion a clear picture of the influential models created by all dimensions of stock car racing, it seems most effective to concentrate on the pit stop, that portion of a stock car race that brings the maximum number of professional racers and their technology into the competitive spotlight. During these periodic breaks in competition on the track, the attention of the crowd is cast upon competing teams of men using technology in rituals of productive speed.

## The Pit Stop

A pit stop is the period during a race when a car is allowed to enter a detour off the main race course and receive fuel, tires, and quick repairs from the pit crew. The crew members, some mechanics, some pit stop specialists, along with managers constitute the race team. The pit road, the area designated for pit stops, is a strip of pavement inside the racing oval and it is divided into pit stalls. Each pit stall corresponds to a race team. The "hot pits," an area designated for team members and their management, are separated from the action on the pit road by the pit wall.

In a typical pit stop, the driver brings the car to a screeching halt into the pit stall and parallel to pit wall, its grill centered on a distinctive team sign attached to a pole held over the wall by his pit crew. As the car stops, the crew leaps the wall and into the arena of masculine action. A "jack man," two tire changers, and two tire carriers charge to the far side of the car. The jack man lifts the right side of the car as the lug nuts and the old tires are removed. Tire carriers position the new wheels and tires, fresh rubber, on the car's hubs for eager air wrenches to attach them. Two more team members scramble over the wall with a gasoline "dump can" to refuel the car. The "gas man" hefts the spout of a huge funneled can into a special spill-proof "dry break" socket as the "vent man" holds the second can of fuel and a vent can to a tube belching air and bubbling gasoline from the fuel cell. With one can empty, the "gas man" tosses the empty "dump can" over the wall to a teammate, and receives the second can from the "vent man." As two eleven-gallon cans of fuel are poured in, the tire changers, tire carriers, and the jack man sprint around the car to complete tire changes on the near side, the side of the car closest to the pit wall (see fig. 9.1). As the tire changers and carriers work on the near side, the tire carriers move to perform chassis adjustments and clean the windshield and radiator grill. With the last of the fuel flowing in, the jack man, a sort of job foreman, lowers the near side of the car, thus signaling the end of the pit stop. When all four wheels contact the ground, the car roars off to rejoin the race. In less than sixteen seconds, the car returns to the fray with four new tires, a full tank of gas, a clean windshield, and a debris-free grill.

FIGURE 9.1    *In this photo a NASCAR pit crew is half way through an intense pit stop. Seemingly intent on rapid service, the jack man and front tire changer race to the near side of the car to complete the pit stop. Note the fuel "dump can" in use at the rear of the car.*

*Photo courtesy Sidell Tilghman.*

## The Stock Car Racing Fraternity

To understand how the masculine ritual of the pit stop persists as a vital component of racing's spectacle, and how the resulting images and masculine notions are propagated, we need to first look at the structure and objectives of the governing organization. By designating the scope of the technology and the rules of events, as well as the specifics of pit stop practice, rules produced and enforced by NASCAR do much to perpetuate the thrill and spectacle of the pit stop. Within the racing community as well as the sanctioning body, relationships that foster masculine exhibitions of skill and rigor in the face of danger display continuity with the often violent, rural, and working-class, dirt-road moonshining roots of NASCAR's past.[8] During the brief interlude on the pit road, elements of danger, brotherhood, potential violence, hierarchy, and intense labor in competitive sport are combined in an outward display of the masculine hubris upon which the NASCAR fraternity is built. As a productive ritual, both symbolically and strategically, the pit stop provides an opportunity for each racing team to publicly express itself as a productive subset of the larger racing fraternity.

The stock car racing fraternity constitutes a close-knit community. The rigors of a schedule built around the championship circuit, a yearly journey that takes teams to venues around the country, helps build a sense of fraternity that builds cohesion among team members and extends beyond race teams to the larger community of stock car racers. For around forty weeks a year, these teams work alongside each other to create competitive spectacle. A daily schedule that includes long hours of work at the track and exhausted nights sequestered in hotels keep racers separate from the rest of society, building a strong community through shared experience.

Racers share powerful sensory experiences that help to strengthen the fraternal bond. Competing with complex technological systems pushed to the limit of their performance provides circumstances where factors as unpredictable as another racer's error, lax component quality control, or even the weather can bring about utter failure. As a part of weekly competition, intense and unpredictable struggles with human and technological performance occur in close proximity to other racers in the garages, paddocks, and pit roads of the race circuit. The capricious fortunes inherent in auto racing provide ample opportunity for celebration or commiseration of shared experiences.

Other factors contribute to the strong sense of fraternal brotherhood among racers. Given strong familial connections within the sport and the tight clustering of race shops around Charlotte, North Carolina, racers are also largely racially, culturally, and geographically homogenous.[9] For example, three well-known racing dynasties, the Pettys, the Earnhardts, and the Jarretts are but one example of the literal kinships that often bind teams together and limit diversity.[10] These factors and the tacit fraternity that exists ensure that stock car racing remains the domain of white Southern men. Competitive struggles in a complex sport and the existing traditions of masculine culture in the South form the common experiences through which the proprietary bonds of the stock car racing fraternity are built.

Though the label *fraternity* conjures up images of houses filled with beer-guzzling undergraduates or service-minded middle lodges replete with middle-aged burghers, unusual hats, and bingo tournaments, the fraternal structure offers a viable and informal organizational logic utilized by racers. Indeed, the axiom *racing fraternity* describes an organizational matrix that closely resembles more formally defined fraternities. That NASCAR is not formally regarded as a fraternity does not mean that its rules and practices do not produce the equivalent fraternity of more traditional masculine organizations. By defining the practice and boundaries of the racing fraternity, we can compare it to the traditional fraternal structure while developing an understanding of the negotiations and regulations that both created and preserve gender as an organizing bias within the sport.

Though not formally defined as a brotherhood, racers act in many ways to promulgate and enjoy the advantages of fraternal membership. Besides occasional reference to themselves as a fraternity, NASCAR racers exhibit other features of more traditional fraternities such as the Masons, Moose, or Knights of Pythias. In her careful discussion of fraternal construction during the nineteenth century, Mary Ann Clawson describes four distinguishing features.[11] First among these features is masculine constituency: racers are almost exclusively male. Traditionally it was though to be bad luck to have women at trackside. This masculine exclusivity was even institutionalized within some sanctioning organizations such as NASCAR that officially excluded women from the pit stalls until 1973.[12] Second, fraternities are bounded by proprietary knowledge. Such secrets for racers generally include technical knowledge used to groom technology for competition as well as practical knowledge such as what hotel parking lots can accommodate race trailers and where the good places to eat are while traveling.[13] Third, fraternities practice rituals that build solidarity. Like most sporting contests, racing is highly ritualized. For our purposes, the public ceremony of the pit stop presents racing as a team sport. Like ritual in more typical fraternities, the pit stop builds solidarity by presenting the members in cooperative action apart from society. Fourth, fraternity members operate within a corporate idiom, a world divided into groups. Like the local chapters of a typical national fraternity, race teams operate as the basic subsets within the larger racing fraternity. Indeed, like the hats or jerseys of more traditional fraternities, the outward appearance of automobile racers conveys expressions of the corporate idiom. Unlike those of Shriners or campus "Greeks," racers' uniforms convey both the literal and metaphorical meanings of corporatism. Racers are adorned with similar uniforms that distinguish teams with distinct corporate advertising symbols. In a sense, the corporate and cooperative action during races reinforces the relationship of racers to one another and to society at large.

The fraternal logic of race organization does not end with the behavior and disposition of racers themselves. Like more conventional fraternities, the racing fraternity could not exist without centralized direction. The sanctioning bodies that regulate racing mimic the role of centralized governing entities within traditional fraternities. By writing and enforcing rules that organize and sustain exclusive knowledge systems, masculine rituals and the corporate idiom, NASCAR keeps stock car racing a male sport. NASCAR as the largest sanctioning body concerned with stock car racing performs functions analogous to the highest officers of traditional fraternities.[14] They preside over the constitution of fraternal life by instituting systems of rules and organizing the location and creation of events. Such rules determine the location and duration of competition, criteria for victory, and most important, the configuration of the race technology. The rules and

Ben A. Shackleford

subsequent race vehicles also embody features that facilitate and perpetuate the action of the pit stop. These rules determine both the
human action and the technological component of the ritual. As structured by the rules, the technology of the race vehicle provides a tangible
prop for the gendered relationships expressed during the pit stop.

NASCAR creates rules that not only help make stock car racing an
extremely successful business but also help perpetuate the relations and
violence of Southern masculine culture. As Robert J. Thomas writes,
"The technical system of an organization can be at one and the same
time objective—that is, reflexive of a logic, a set of rules and conditions
independent of the social system—and infused with objectives—that is,
reflective of the interests or goals of particular groups within the social
system. Technology can appear as determinant when its objective features become indistinguishable from those who occupy a position of
dominance."[15] The technical format dictated by NASCAR and rendered
by stock car racers is a circumstance where technology carries the
agenda of a smaller group into the public sphere, simultaneously sat-
isfying the needs of NASCAR sponsors and the racing fraternity.
Reflecting the interests and needs of the white, Southern men who
participated in the creation of NASCAR stock car racing, the rules were
created as ad hoc responses to technical and promotional dilemmas as
they influenced the sport. Their current manifestation reflects the
nature and location of this process.

## NASCAR Technology and Governance

By indirectly fashioning the technology of competition, the rules
administered by NASCAR help set the tone of action on the track. The
durability and resilience of the stock car format have influenced the
degree of violence possible within NASCAR events. For example, when
racing the open wheeled cars used at the Indianapolis 500, it is impossible to "put a fender on someone" to force them out of your way.
Because the wheels of an Indy car are exposed at the end of elongated
chassis components, any attempt to muscle around a competitor most
often results in wheel contact, thereby somersaulting both cars and
ending that day's efforts if not the careers of the drivers. In stock car
racing, additional bodywork and heavy cars with extensive roll cages
prevent such catastrophic encounters and allows drivers to bang into
each other with relative impunity. Rather than ending the race for the
competitors, "trading paint" only enhances the entertainment value of
struggles for track position. Such close racing within an oval track,
where traction loss centrifuges competitors into the surrounding wall,
results in frequent violent crashes. The low cost of a NASCAR race
vehicle also means that more frequent damage to the equipment can
be easily afforded. Simple components minimize replacement cost.

While other forms of motor sports also include elements of violent danger, they remain less emphasized than in NASCAR. Rules intended to keep the sport inexpensive provide durable equipment at once suited to rough racing and advertising.

Though the business of NASCAR racing today discourages overt demolition-derby tactics, it has not changed the rules governing vehicle construction or competition to prevent contact between vehicles. It is important to note that violence in the pursuit of a larger goal, in this case victory, is tolerated if not condoned. In the same way, men dueling for their honor in the antebellum South used violence as a means to an end rather than an end unto itself.[16] Violence for the sake of violence was and still is considered bad form, but violence in the pursuit of some higher end, even if the end offers rewards as ethereal as racing in circles or adherence to a code of honor, is absolutely acceptable. Comfortable acceptance of the violent texture of NASCAR racing resounds in the common parlance of description. Epithets such as "the intimidator"[17] describe particularly successful drivers, and heat races are called "shootouts." Though races today do not wholly resemble events of earlier years described to me (as when every "Saturday night at the local dirt track there was a fight and sometimes a race"), they still carry the stamp of regional masculine violence.[18]

In addition to allowing for dramatic wrecks, the race vehicle's size and simplicity reflect the financial and technical capacities of early racers. It permits fierce racing action and maximum commercial exposure for low investment in equipment. Unlike other race vehicles, the relatively large stock car body can carry large advertisements and withstand rigorous, violent action on the track and in the pits. Begun when sponsorships were lean and all that rural Southern racers could afford were modified stock vehicles (literally, what the autodealers "stocked" for the consumer), the stock car format is maintained in an effort to attract factory sponsorships and permit fan association with the vehicles. Continuous development of the race chassis has created contemporary vehicles that are a combination of stock components under a body built to maintain stock appearance. As developed by generations of racers, the current stock car configuration, though not at all "stock," serves as technically similar terrain for the tuning and innovative efforts of fraternity members. It is the common factor that informs the proprietary knowledge of the fraternity.

The stock car format combines a highly modified chassis and drivetrain technology with a physical exterior that bears direct resemblance to contemporary road vehicles. Other forms of racing such as the Indy Racing League use "purpose-built" cars that resemble short-winged airplanes with oversized landing gear. Although in no way a stock production vehicle, the "stock car" format offers spectators direct association with the race vehicle and offers sponsors ample space for advertising. The fraternal corporate idiom is enhanced by distinctive commercial logos and colors that define each team in relation to their vehicle(s) while describing them as members of the larger community of racers.

The mechanical details ruled legal by NASCAR also serve as a means of common association for fraternity members. Indeed, the tacit knowledge necessary to compete successfully builds a boundary of proprietary knowledge that binds the NASCAR fraternity together. Beneath the recognizable bodywork, contemporary stock cars are in fact purpose-built machines utilizing an unusual agglomeration of regionally evolved technology. For example, the peculiar combination of chassis geometry borrowed from 1960s stock passenger vehicles and sophisticated shock-absorber technology produces a wholly unusual vehicle, the mastery of which is accessible only through experience as a fraternity member. In other racing series such as the Sports Car Club of America (SCCA), competitors use a variety of vehicles. Thus, while SCCA racers do demonstrate strong fraternal tendencies, they lack a standardized technical reference with which to build proprietary technical knowledge and violent spectacle. In NASCAR racing, the rule-configured, empirically developed vehicles demand experientially based judgment accessible only to fraternity members.

But the proprietary knowledge, and the exclusivity that it promotes, is also institutionalized within unpublished rules. Fraternal neophytes must master the craft of race car preparation and adjustment with respect to rules that must be interpreted through trial and error as well as advice from other competitors. Fielding a competitive car requires experience as a member of the racing fraternity rather than simply capital and intent. As racing consultant and ex-NASCAR racer Amos Johnson put it, "The first NASCAR car I built they sent me the rule book, I built the car by the rule book and when I took it to the race track they laughed at it. . . . If you're around the track you know what everybody is doing and how it's interpreted in the rules."[19] This system of unpublished rules forms a threshold, a rite of passage guarding the fraternal ranks and fraternal resources. Just as members of conventional fraternities share secrets that bind them together, racers share the accretion and application of proprietary knowledge. This information separates initiates from the larger society while cementing individual loyalty to participation within the sport.

Apart from supporting proprietary knowledge, NASCAR rules, perhaps most importantly, also ensure the practice of ritual. The speeds allowed, the tires provided, the minimum weight of the car, the length of race events, and the size of fuel cells as specified in the NASCAR rule book in effect mandate the ritual of the pit stop. The race vehicles are heavy, have small tires, and run long races, necessitating regular pit stops during the course of an event. Informally, the pit road and the hot pits continue to be predominantly masculine space reserved for the manipulation of powerful technologies; it is a publicly visible stage dedicated to the struggle of men and machines in contest. Fuel cans, loud exhaust, hot tires, and powerful air wrenches are sanctioned in the rules and combine to produce an area of possible danger and intense sensory stimulation. The central location of pit road, a detour cut across the infield of the oval tracks, places the ritual at the geographic center of racing action. Indeed the terms *hot pits* and *going over the wall*, which describe the location and action of ritual, resonate with masculine martial themes and focus attention by conjuring dramatic images of danger and contest (see fig. 9.2). Race events are therefore, through the demands of the car and the construction of the arena, structured by NASCAR's rules to include the public spectacle of service in the pits, setting the stage for manly confrontation with technology within the context of potential violence.

NASCAR stock car rules are also notoriously vague, a measure that allows tremendous breadth for interpretation. This flexibility permits officials the latitude to groom technology in order to ensure close competition, thereby drawing attention to the spectacle while meeting the marketing needs of sponsors. A wide "gray area" permits NASCAR to limit technological developments made by specific teams and ignore developments made by others in an effort to maintain the excitement of close competition.[20] Mark Donohue, professional race engineer and NASCAR Grand American series champion wrote of entering the NASCAR Winston Cup series, "In Sports Car Club of America racing we knew the game, and we knew what we could get away with. But NASCAR rules are so vague, it's hard to know what to do."[21] NASCAR champion, car builder, and team owner Junior Johnson comments, "I never read the rule book because they [NASCAR officials] never go by it."[22] The judicious, often selective, enforcement of rules prevents technological advantages from causing a boring one-sided race.

Such supple guidelines also mandate the continual participation of racers trying to remain competitive. Understanding how to build a car to remain competitive but not too far outside the rules requires knowledge of the prevailing interpretation of the rules that govern the racing fraternity. For example, for the 1968 Daytona 500, innovative car builder Smokey Yunik showed up with a car sporting an offset frame which, while it maintained the engine on center between frame rails as stipulated in the rules, moved weight advantageously to the left side of the car. This weight bias would advantage Yunik's driver by defeating much of the weight transfer inherent on an oval race track with only left turns. By achieving more neutral balance through the corners, the car would handle much more easily and the right front tires (which normally are the first to wear out) would last much longer. Though this car was built within the published rules, it was disqualified because of the tremendous advantage wrought by its unconventional construction.[23] Subsequent rulings designed to limit such creativity dictated that the front suspension components on Winston

Ben A. Shackleford

FIGURE 9.2  *When the circumstances of a race demand, teams service their vehicles along pit road, the road through the center of the racing arena designated as the stage for masculine confrontation with the machine. This photo reveals the fraternal subgrouping of each team and both literal and figurative expressions of the corporate idiom.*

*Photo courtesy Sidell Tilghman.*

Cup cars must all share antiquated steering geometry in common with a 1965 Ford Galaxy or a 1969 Chevrolet Camaro.[24] Likewise, the rear suspension setup common to all NASCAR race cars shares geometry with an early 1960s Chevrolet pickup.[25] These standards are maintained today despite significant advances in the design and construction of racing suspension components. The seemingly contradictory aims of promoting competition with a single winner while regulating vehicles into equality are reconciled in the interest of maintaining fraternal structure and presenting exciting race spectacle. NASCAR manages race car technology so that it possesses impressive qualities of power and speed without allowing technological advantage or advances to defuse the excitement of competition.

## The Rationalization of Labor in the Pit Stop

By ensuring competition on the track rather than on the drawing board, rule enforcement effectively develops all of the race cars in unison. The resulting uniformity of vehicles and close competition set the stage for competition in the pit stop. As little advantage can be gained through technological innovation, and subsequently competition on the track remains close, the onus of improved performance is cast elsewhere. The pit stop, an instance in which many members of each team are called on to contribute, offers an excellent opportunity for the team to earn track position through rationalized and intensified production. Action to this end within the dangerous competitive arena enhances the spectacle of competition while providing an opportunity for masculine confrontation with the competitive task. In producing exciting, often violent race spectacle, the NASCAR fraternity continues traditions of violent masculine competition that find widespread expression in the region where it began. Thus by becoming a competitively critical break from action on the track, the pit stop has come to constitute a vital part of the main shared resource of the racing fraternity, the spectacle of masculine work within a dangerous, potentially violent context.

Beginning in 1962 the Wood Brothers Racing Team transformed the pit stop ritual into part of competitive spectacle. By improving the tools and organization of the pit stop, organizing in detail each crew member's responsibility, and enlarging the pump cylinder of their hydraulic jacks to lift a car in three handle strokes, they shaved precious time off hitherto haphazard pit stops.[26] Up until that time, pit stops were relatively disorganized and relaxed affairs using unmodified mechanics' tools and no particular organization. Other teams continued to use slower conventional hydraulic floor jacks, requiring up to fourteen strokes, until they caught on to the Wood Brothers' clever time-saver. Soon they, too, followed the closely planned division of labor, implementation of specialized tools, and management hierarchy. Through the specialized modification of standard mechanics tools and the time-efficient organization of previously hurried but haphazard actions, the Wood Brothers introduced the deliberate, mechanized rationalization of the pit stop ritual.

Competition then spread into the pits as the efforts of the pit crews became ever more important to the outcome of the race. Rationalization of the pit stop continues at an unrelenting pace which drives improvements in organization and hardware. The equipment of the pit stop—race cars, helmets, and pneumatic tools, common objects used in protective/productive combination—introduce the elements of danger, power, speed, and routine efficient action to which participants and fans respond with vigor. Exercising proprietary knowledge and arrayed hierarchically, the racers service their cars in a thoroughly rehearsed ritual of masculine mechanical virtue and productive organization. Colorful flame-retardant uniforms, gloves, and knee pads adorn and protect the crew members. Fuel dump cans matching specialized receptacles on the cars permit rapid tank refill. Specially built hydraulic jacks resembling those of the typical automotive garage but with the machine finish of a Swiss watch and weighing only a dozen pounds can lift a 3,400-pound car in two handle strokes. Modified impact wrenches, again similar to equipment used by the average mechanic, equipped with purpose-built auto-ejecting six-tooth sockets turn lug nuts over "space-shuttle" alloy, long-pilot wheel studs at 10,000 revolutions per minute. Special weight jacking screws permit suspension changes during brief pit stop service. The implementation of specialized equipment and rehearsed actions allow seven crew members to drop the time needed to service a race car from a few minutes (in 1962) to under sixteen seconds.[27]

Besides masculine confrontation with technology, the fraternal format ensures adherence to and acceptance of hierarchy. The propriety of hierarchical relationships in traditional fraternities was organized around a system of degrees of brotherhood directly associated with levels of ritual achievement and experience.[28] Within stock-car racing these degrees are defined in relation to skill accumulated and the responsibility of command during competition. Crew chiefs, the commanders of the pit area, must have experience as crew members, mechanics, and often as a driver before they are given charge of managing a race. Position within the racing fraternity's hierarchy depends largely upon investments in time and subsequent mastery of race technology. By keeping technological mastery contingent upon participation, and by revising the competitive terrain to ensure that any established base of technical information must be accompanied by experiential knowledge, the rules mandate hierarchy in the pits. Again we find the central governing institution, NASCAR, indirectly implementing a fraternal structure through the medium of the race vehicle.

Because participation in the pit stop spectacle involves competitive manipulation of the race vehicle, only a limited number of team members can be involved. The specific responsibilities given through the implementation of hyperrationalized work fosters strict hierarchy. The crew chief determines strategy with advice and data from team engineers, the driver, spotters in radio communication from positions around the track, and occasionally, the team owner. Subsequent decisions about the timing and extent of the pit stop and vehicle adjustments are then relayed to the crew via radio headset. Having been told the extent of the pit stop by the crew chief—just gas, gas and two tires, a mere suspension change, or a normal pit stop with four tires and a tank of gas—the necessary crew members diligently prepare to leap the wall. During the actual stop, the jack man assumes the role of foreman, determining the pace of work. After the tire changers and the fuel men have signaled the completion of their work, the jack man signals the end of the pit stop by lowering the car. The crew, driver, spotters, engineers, crew chief, and jack man occupy different levels of command and public acclaim as they fulfill specific roles during a stop. These roles are built by the specialized nature of the vehicle. Under the aegis of managed competition, the rationalization begun by the Wood Brothers has prompted the development of a hierarchically based model of efficiency.

The fraternal relationship to hierarchy also builds a sense of obligation into the stratified crew. Intense, hyperrationalized action is viewed in relation to the technology in competition rather than in relation to stratified power relationships. The concept of team and fraternal obligation thoroughly obscures the reality of work intensification. During the race season, for at least one day a week, the pit crew rehearses the action of the pit stop,[29] celebrating the sort of brotherly spirit of intensification described by historian Wayne Lewchuck in other contexts. He writes that employers "consciously excluded women from the workplace and created a fraternal system, a men's club, to help male workers adjust to a world of monotonous repetitive work."[30] Fraternity provides coercion to intensify work and incentive to acquiesce to hierarchy by conflating mechanical work and masculinity. Fraternal status, especially within the subset of the race team, becomes equated to competitiveness, in this instance linking masculinity with productive speed. Thus, the practice of traditional masculine technical virtue is transformed into an expression of brute productive speed.[31] The model of the pit stop projects the powerful message that rationalization and radically intensified work conducted under hierarchical control is both masculine and good.

In *Shop Floor Culture: Masculinity and the Wage Form* Paul Willis writes, "One of the marks of the lived and contemporary culture of the shop floor is a development of this half-mythical primitive confrontation with the task. It is a familiarity and experiential sense of control

Ben A. Shackleford

of technology, or at least of sharing its power."[32] This relation to technology, though describing factory production, is also consistent with the rural tradition described by Ronald Kline and Trevor Pinch where "competence in the repair and operation of machinery formed a defining element of masculinity."[33] As a publicly visible shop floor built through the patronage of largely rural fans, the pit arena reinforces conventions suggesting that technically difficult and physically demanding work is best left to male hands.[34] Within racing, especially within the pits, we find a re-creation of the masculine circumstance of production. Willis describes this gendered arena, a place such as the hot pits, where "[d]ifficult, uncomfortable or dangerous conditions are seen . . . for their appropriateness to a masculine readiness and hardness."[35] The absence of women from the scene of competitive action infers that they are somehow unsuited to the intense, technically demanding productive efforts of the racing world.

The main resource of the racing fraternity is the awesome spectacle of race action, a marketable form of what David Nye terms the "American technological sublime." Such spectacle involves both the sensory and visceral impact of technology on human perception. Recognition of the technological sublime can be divided into three stages. First, perception registers nothing out of the ordinary. For example, on a sunny spring day in the grandstands of a track, cars resembling many of the vehicles in the parking lot rumble past on a pace lap with loud but tolerable unmuffled exhaust and at a moderate speed. In the second phase of the sublime, reality becomes distorted by the magnitude of events wrought by technology. In unison, the procession of forty stock cars roars loudly to life as the pace car ducks off the oval track. In a synchronous streak of colors and a crescendo of exhaust noise and high-octane smell, they launch forward, approaching two hundred miles per hour at the close of the first lap. Third, perception recovers from the shock of tremendous scale and power to register the subsequent events with a perspective forever changed by a new relationship to spectacle. The racers continue to roar around the oval course, bumper to bumper, door to door, at speeds that stretch the limits of imagination and physics. Within the sublime created by the vehicles at this speed, the ritual of the pit stop assumes mythical significance. As necessary during the course of events, drivers drop from the intense action on the banked oval track into the pit area inside the oval to receive more fuel and tires in this hyperintensified productive ritual. The exertion of the pit stop seems commonplace amid the din of competitors still roaring about on the track.[36]

Like the example of Apollo space rockets described by Nye, race events involve intellectual and sensory confrontation with impressive, active manifestations of human technical ability. The fascination lies within the violent potential coupled with the power vested in a mass of expertly driven machines in a carefully orchestrated contest of speed. Within the ritual of the pit stop, the pit workers demonstrate a similar coupling of violent confrontation and controlled intensity. The frenzied, powerful exertion of masculine effort combined with the controlled intensity of hyperrationalized rigor resonates with the duality of masculine workplace culture described by Stephen Meyer in this volume.[37] However, unlike the male workers on mass-production shop floors, the actions of the pit crew achieve a relatively placid combination of respectable and rough working-class culture by finding expression not in a social context but through a publicly scrutinized celebration of productive competition. Furthermore, the brotherhood among fraternal members smooths any potentially rough edges of masculine productive ritual by focusing upon the event as a component of spectacular sport.

## Racing and the Commercialization of the Technological Sublime

Enthusiasm for the sublime also finds expression in the participation of avid fans, and, not surprisingly, the sublime sells well. Advertisers eager to associate themselves with the racing spectacle fund and promote racers. NASCAR presents race series as fair contests to guarantee the spectacle of the technological sublime. By keeping competition close and under strict control, the fraternal organization ensures the financial well-being of the series, providing for initiates and devotees alike a weekly renewal of the forceful attraction of a massive, powerful, technologically based spectacle. When combined with the potential of the mass media, the influence of the masculine celebrations within stock car racing comes into focus outside the race venue.

Bob Post writes that for drag racing, "[o]f all the technological transformations. . . none was ultimately as significant as television."[38] With all events televised live, and over two hundred million television viewers in 1995,[39] this statement is no less true for the Winston Cup series. Since the first live race coverage of the Daytona 500 in 1979,[40] electronic media have brought more racing, and sponsors, to the fans each season. Television is the catalyst enhancing the influence of the fraternal mode of organization, the forum wherein dangerous masculine confrontation with the machine and seemingly appropriate hierarchical organization enjoys public celebration. The American affinity for stock car racing can in some ways be explained by the action of cars on a race track. However, it is unlikely that 390 million annual viewers could be brought in front of their televisions without the additional lure of the spectacle in the pits.[41] The pit stop offers opportunities for fans to equate stock car racing with more traditional sports. It offers evidence that racing is a team sport dependent upon the cooperation of skilled team members while providing an occasion where humans can fully be distinguished from machines.

Evidence that television connects the demands of eager race fans with the racing fraternity can be found in the ways television has changed the sport. Just as electronic technologies have helped to amplify, project, and celebrate models presented by the racing fraternity, they have helped to intensify the action of fraternities themselves. Pit stops are frequently timed and critiqued by television broadcast crews. As Winston Cup champion turned television announcer and author Benny Parsons writes, "Pit stops are more and more competitive, thanks in part to television which zooms in on the action, and runs digital elapsed time on the screen. The pit crews compete with one another as hard as the drivers do. They video tape every stop and study the tape, looking for ways to be faster."[42] In this instance of self-exploitation, we find video technology used to represent the demands of the competitive spectacle.

In response to the benefits of public recognition, the relationship between television technology and race teams has changed. Whereas during the early 1980s racers demanded payment to carry in-car cameras, thirty pounds of weight situated inefficiently high in the chassis along with a protruding camera fin atop the car, they now actively seek camera installation.[43] Heightened use of the vehicle as a "200-mile-an-hour-billboard" has changed the names of parts of the race car;[44] the back of the vehicle, once known as a rear valence, has become known as the "TV panel," the most highly prized advertising space on a stock car.[45] It derives its name and value from the extended periods of television time given by the front bumper cameras of following cars.

Electronic media not only bring the technological sublime to the masses, they help familiarize the public with the technology and techniques of the fraternal ritual. Radio and television announcers instruct novice fans on subtle nuances of strategy and scoring as well as the procedure of the pit stops. Scanners allow spectators to eavesdrop on the radio conversation between driver and crew, affording a vicarious connection with racers within the sublime. The potential of bringing spectacle into the consciousness of fans is not lost on advertisers. Such immediate involvement with the spectacle of the sublime helps the NASCAR Winston Cup Series claim a brand loyalty for participating sponsors of 71 percent as fans actively seek out the products of NASCAR sponsors. Compared to brand loyalty among fans of major league baseball—the so-called national pastime—of 38 percent, the messages of racing seem to leave a deeper impression.[46]

Advertisements using the race vehicles as exemplars frequently ignore the difference between racing technology and real-world technology. Rules that perpetuate the use of stock bodies facilitate frequent though incongruous comparisons of reality to the technological sublime. In this way salable advertising space is created within spectacle. For example, while NASCAR maintains the stock car moniker through the race, cars are roll-cage filled, custom built, pure race vehicles whose silhouette only *resembles* showroom "stock." Although race vehicles are wholly unsuited for operation outside the arena of competition, advertisements consistently refer to the rigors of racing and how utilitarian refinement results from motor sports. Technical qualities that ensure racing performance become associated with credible automobiles off the track. Televised advertisements that make claims such as, "Ford: we race, you win," and "The Chevrolet Monte Carlo, whose winning performance and winning design can go straight from the race world to your world" fail to mention that the only part your car will have in common with a race car is the roof panel.

The suitability of exclusively masculine relationships to racing technology finds frequent expression within advertisements. For example, a Ford Quality Care advertisement reads, "Dale Jarrett's got NASCAR in his blood from his father. . . . And on race day, he's got a pit crew led by Todd Parrott. It's a lot like the expertise you get with Quality Care at Ford and Lincoln-Mercury Dealers."[47] Fraternal relations are celebrated for the larger public when advertisements regularly draw comparisons between car care offered by pit crews and car care outside racing. Such intentional associations between the masculine world of racing and the consumer automotive world extend the racing fraternity to least as far as the selling floor of dealerships nationwide. Other clues reveal that fraternal relations are celebrated as the productive norm. By inferring that race teams have the best mechanics, behaving as a race mechanic is presented as the proper way to work on a car. Association between typical automotive maintenance environments and the pit road are made easier by the similarity between the equipment used in each arena. In such advertisements, images of masculine technical skill and the propriety of hierarchically controlled work intensification are projected through association with race performance.

## Conclusion

Popular fascination with the action and potential violence contained within stock car racing helps explain the fraternal relationships stemming from NASCAR's careful control of technology. The repeatability of NASCAR's carefully managed technological sublime stands in contrast to Nye's more irregular examples. Whereas the goals of the Apollo program or the atomic bomb were the manipulation or conquest of nature, the true end of Winston Cup racing is the creation, demonstration, and conclusion of competition.[48] Rather than a consequence incidental to pursuit of some larger goal, the use of technology to create spectacle is the intention of a sanctioning body.

However, the fraternal traditions and the technological enthusiasm that nourishes the sublime do not ramble on unfettered by context in an endless, mutually reproductive dialectic. Just as organizations promote the continuation of events in a certain way, so too does the public shape the parameters within which the spectacle works. Thus, NASCAR is both a product of the rural South and the needs of contemporary culture. With each passing year, and every session of personal presentation coaching provided to a driver by a hopeful sponsor, many features of the Southern roots of NASCAR fade. And yet the violence that served as a cornerstone of Southern masculine relations persists along with masculine rituals of technological prowess and fraternal models of hierarchy. To understand the persistence, indeed the expanding popularity of such rituals, the spectacle of NASCAR must once again be viewed in relation to the technological sublime.

To begin with, NASCAR presents a safe allegory; the sublime in NASCAR is carefully managed. Humans are allowed to indulge their Promethean fascination with technology and to express or enact this technological enthusiasm. While technology is enjoyed, fans and participants can indulge in the suspense wrought by technological power that remains barely under the control of a mortal master. With the proliferation of television within NASCAR events, spectators can vicariously become—like the racers—empowered by being involved. If only electronically, fans can feel within the action of the sublime from within. Even if the threat of violence is fulfilled, it is seldom punctuated with the remorse of truly injurious consequence. Stout roll cages, fire extinguishers, and safety harnesses developed through years of violent experiment assure the cathartic rebirth of the unharmed driver from the wreckage of a dead car. In a sense, stock car racing offers control of or association with powerful technology in a world where the unmanaged sublime—a nuclear holocaust, unbridled genetic manipulation, or biological warfare—is unimaginable.

Thus, the cathartic potential of NASCAR events, the demonstration of humankind's tenuous control over powerful technology, brings the message of the racing fraternity into seductive focus. On a level more purely masculine in its effect, NASCAR racing, in particular the action of the pit stop, also offers a chance for men to publicly demonstrate the potency of rough confrontation with the task in combination with the responsibility of the rationalized, cerebral method.[49] Races offer men a chance to publicly associate with the power of masculine aggression in combination with the socially acceptable potency of mental rigor.

Gone are the days when someone who was able to drive a race car, who was handy with tools and had a few mechanic buddies, could go racing for a living. The rationalization of professional racing has dictated a hierarchy of experienced, well-equipped specialists such as spotters, engineers, crew chiefs, and crew. Under the demands of competition, the refinement of the pit stop provides an exaggerated model of work intensification. Within the pit stop ritual, conceptions of masculine technical virtue have become represented within a context of rationalized intensity and hierarchical specialization, the fraternity of racers shaped as much by instrumental concerns as social networks. Through the spectacular interplay of subset teams, the maintenance of male membership, the practice ritual, and the preservation of propri- etary knowledge, the Winston Cup fraternity trundles into the twenty- first century. The rural Southern values long ago embedded in the practice of racing spectacle—albeit in an intensified and celebrated mutation the men of the Saturday night dirt track era could hardly imagine—carry their message into the living rooms of America each week. The overlap of technological systems, the combination of empir- ically refined racing knowledge and modified mechanic's tools (the "stuff" of fraternal proprietorship) with the communicative and organi- zational catalyst of radio and video, amplifies the messages coded into the ritual of the pit stop. Fascination with the technological sublime and subsequent popularity of NASCAR Winston Cup racing has also brought these models of masculine mechanical ability, intense work, and hierarchical organization to the fore, casting the ideologies of the racing fraternity's historical tradition and regional roots center stage.

## Notes

1. Pete Daniels, *Standing at the Crossroads* (Baltimore, Md.: Johns Hopkins University Press, 1986), 199.

2. Bertram Wyatt-Brown, *Southern Honor* (New York: Oxford University Press, 1986), 131. See also Frank E. Vandiver, "The Southerner As Extremist," in Frank Vandiver, ed., *The Idea of the South: Pursuit of a Central Theme* (Chicago: University of Chicago Press, 1964), 43–55; Edward L. Ayers, *Vengeance and Justice, Crime and Punishment in the Nineteenth- century American South* (New York: Oxford University Press, 1984), 3.

3. Superspeedways are oval tracks over a mile and a half in length, built with high banked turns (usually paved at an angle above 20 degrees) to facilitate continuous dri- ving at maximum speed.

Jerry Bledsoe, *The World's Number One, Flat-Out, All-Time Great Stock Car Racing Book* (Asheboro, N.C.: Down Home Press, 1975), 34.

4. Richard Huff, *Behind the Wall* (Chicago: Bonus Books, 1997), 115.

5. Rob Sneddon, "A Third Generation of France Family Asserts Its Influence on Stock Car Racing." *Stock Car Racing* 32, no. 7 (1997): 32–48.

6. As the most visible active elements within stock car spectacle and the vehicles for sponsor branding, race cars are placed at the center of fan consciousness. The cars are such important nodes of association that most teams have dozens of proselyte "show cars" traveling the nation, soliciting attention at strip malls and grand openings year round.

7. It should be noted that as a more egalitarian motor sport, stock car racing initially offered the thrills of racing for fewer dollars. Consequently, racing equipment was often more prone to failure than purpose-built race cars. To its credit, NASCAR learned from each accident and sought cheap, simple technological solutions that permitted contin- ued competition—and real danger. Technological innovations such as vehicles that can withstand severe contact and continue to compete carry the imprint of the culture from

which they came, promoting the reproduction of the sort of racing behavior that attends their origin.

8. More than a few of NASCAR's early stars gained experience building and driving hot-rod cars running illegal liquor out of the hills of Alabama, Georgia, South Carolina, and North Carolina. For an informed discussion of moonshining and NASCAR see the chapter "The Last American Hero" in Tom Wolfe, *The Kandy Kolored Tangerine Flake Streamline Baby* (New York: Farrar, Straus and Giroux, 1965).

9. The geographic clustering around Charlotte is largely a consequence of the dominant teams of the Pettys and the Ford-sponsored Holmans and Moodys during the fifties and sixties as well as the industrial resources of the textile trade in the "Queen City."

10. Lee Petty began racing NASCAR stock cars in 1949 and raced until 1960. Son Richard Petty, also known as "King Richard," won more races and more championships than any driver before or since. Even after the death of his son Adam, grandson Kyle Petty continues to race in the NASCAR Winston Cup series. In addition, engine builder Maurice Petty continues to build motors for competition. Dale Earnhardt's father, Ralph, raced NASCAR until his death in 1973. Dale's son has recently joined the ranks of NASCAR's Winston Cup Series racers. Announcer Ned Jarrett, NASCAR champion in 1960 and 1963, has two sons actively involved in NASCAR. In addition to announcing, Glen Jarrett runs a racing marketing company while Dale was 1999 Winston Cup champion. Other families—the Wood brothers, the Flock brothers and sister, and the Allisons—have also contributed to stock car racing.

11. Mary Ann Clawson, *Constructing Brotherhood: Class, Gender and Fraternalism* (Princeton, N.J.: Princeton University Press, 1989), 38. Clawson describes a theoretically robust framework of boundaries and behavior that define fraternal relations both internally and externally. Four key elements define a fraternity in relation to society. These features are the corporate idiom, publicly experienced ritual, proprietorship, and masculinity.

12. Bledsoe, *Racing Book*, 89. Bledsoe writes, "To be a race queen is about the only way a woman can be involved in big-time stock car racing. Oh, wives and girlfriends of drivers are allowed to keep lap scores [repetitive clerical records maintained by each team and NASCAR simultaneously], but there are no women drivers, no women mechanics, or crew members. No women but race queens. . . . Indeed, until 1973, when a female photographer threatened to bring suit, women were not allowed in the pits of most of the big stock car tracks."

13. Race teams are also separated from the public geographically. Because stock car racing (like most American automobile racing) occurs on oval tracks, the infield location of competitor's garages, the pits, and the equipment trailers is at the center of attention but symbolically and literally separated by the moat of speedway action. For the public, race teams are both central and separate.

14. Clawson, *Brotherhood*, 211.

15. Robert J. Thomas, *What Machines Can't Do: Politics and Technology in the Industrial Enterprise* (Berkeley and Los Angeles: University of California Press, 1994), 19.

16. Wyatt-Brown, *Southern Honor*, 350.

17. "The Intimidator" is a nickname commonly attached to Dale Earnhardt, a successful driver from the eighties and nineties.

18. Jack Lewis, professional race driver, interview with the author.

19. Amos Johnson, interview with the author.

20. Mark D. Howell, *From Moonshine to Madison Avenue: A Cultural History of the NASCAR Winston Cup Series* (Bowling Green, Ohio: Bowling Green State University Press, 1997), 24.

21. Mark Donohue, *The Unfair Advantage* (New York: Dodd, Mead, 1975), 226.

22. Howell, *Moonshine*, 25.

23. John Craft, *The Anatomy and Development of the Stock Car* (Osceola, Wisc.: Motorbooks International, 1993), 29.

24. Ibid., 32.

25. J. D. Gibbs, interview with the author.

26. Peter Golenbock, *American Zoom: Stock Car Racing from the Dirt Tracks to Daytona* (New York: Macmillan General Reference, 1993), 143.

27. Gibbs interview.

28. Mark Carnes, "Middle Class Men and the Solace of Fraternal Ritual" in Mark Carnes and Clyde Griffen, eds., *Meanings for Manhood: Constructions of Masculinity in Victorian America* (Chicago: University of Chicago Press, 1990), 48; and Clawson, *Brotherhood*, 25.

29. Gibbs interview.

30. Wayne A. Lewchuck, "Men and Mass Production: The Role of Gender in Managerial Strategies in the British and American Automotive Industries," in Haruhito Shiomi and Kazuo Wada, eds., *Fordism Transformed* (Oxford: Oxford University Press, 1995), 223.

31. On masculine technical virtue, see Clay McShane, *Down the Asphalt Path* (New York: Columbia University Press, 1994), 139; and Lesley Hazelton, *Everything Women Always Wanted to Know about Cars but Didn't Know Who to Ask* (New York: Doubleday, 1995), 201, 260. See also Willis, "Shop Floor Culture, Masculinity and Wage Form" in J. Clark and R. Johnson, eds., *Working Class Culture: Studies in History and Theory* (New York: St. Martin's Press, 1979), 197.

32. Willis, "Shop Floor Culture," 185–98.

33. Ronald Kline and Trevor Pinch, "The Social Construction of the Automobile," *Technology and Culture* 37 no. 4 (1996): 763–95.

34. Virginia Scharff, *Taking the Wheel: Women and the Coming of the Motor Age* (New York: The Free Press, 1991).

35. Willis, "Shop Floor Culture," 190.

36. David Nye, *American Technological Sublime* (Cambridge, Mass.: MIT Press, 1994), 12.

37. Stephen Meyer, "Work, Play and Power: Masculine Culture on the Automotive Shop Floor, 1930–1960" see esp. 15–19 in this volume.

38. Robert Post, *High Performance: The Culture and Technology of Drag Racing 1950–1990* (Baltimore, Md.: Johns Hopkins University Press, 1994), 237.

39. Joe Gibbs Racing, promotional literature (Concord, N.C., 1997), 2.

40. Golenbock, *Zoom*, 168.

41. Attendance/Television in Motorsports Marketing (www.motorsports2000.net/attendan. htm).

42. The pit stop presents people running around, working on the race car. Other reference to individuals in competition generally describes a driver buried in the roll cage of a race car, all but inseparable from the machine. I would like to suggest that fans can associate more easily with the pit crew than the driver because they appear as humans rather than part of a machine.

43. Benny Parsons and George Bennett, *Inside Track: A Photo Documentary of NASCAR Stock Car Racing* (New York: Artisan Workman, 1996), 114.

44. Ned Jarrett, interview with the author.

45. Golenbock, *Zoom*, 382.

46. Gibbs interview.

47. Joe Gibbs Racing, 2.

48. Ford Motor Company, "What's Behind the Guy Out Front" in Matt DeLorenzo, ed., *Autoweeks Official Fan Guide* (Detroit: Autoweek, 1997), 137.

49. Nye, *Technological Sublime*, 9, 225.

50. Michael Kimmel, *Manhood in America* (New York: The Free Press, 1996), 320.

# Rights of Men, Rites of Passage

*Hunting and Masculinity at Reo Motors of Lansing, Michigan, 1945–1975*

LISA FINE

Toward the end of Ben Hamper's *Rivethead: Tales from the Assembly Line*, there is an important episode that provides a clue into the sources of gender identity among male autoworkers. Hamper had started to receive attention for his columns in Michael Moore's *Michigan Voice*, and "[i]t all ran smoothly until the fateful day that I allowed my editor to talk me into writing a piece about deer hunting, the most sanctified of blue-collar blood rituals." Hamper did not partake or even approve of the sport and his article "celebrated the fact that these yahoos often ended up shootin' each other's brains out in their orgasmic frenzy to go boingin' some Bambi. . . . To hell with 'em. I liked deer just fine. The whole idea of slingin' a deer carcass over the hood of your Buick seemed rather unhinged." Hamper featured a coworker named Polson, a white, 6' 2", 245-pound former Marine and member of the National Rifle Association in his article. When Hamper caught wind of the fact that someone had brought the journal with his article on hunting into the shop, he decided to make a preemptive strike and present Polson with a copy. After twenty minutes of reading, Polson confronted Hamper, "I should kick your worthless faggot ass!. . . I bet all your candy-ass writin' pals think you're clever. Let me tell you what I think. You're nothin' more than a dumb cunt with diarrhea mouth. The only way you can get your garbage printed is by suckin' up to commie assholes who've got nothin' better to do but sit around, all doped up, tearin' this country down." Round two came after lunch, as Polson continued, "Where the hell do you get off writin' that I rented my wedding tux from *Outdoor Life*? . . . And what about this part where you state that the NRA stands for Nuts Run Amuck? Where do you come up with this crap?" Hamper replied that it was just a joke, to which Polson informed Hamper that hunters keep the deer population down and healthy. Hamper suggested, foolishly, "I think you just enjoy killing things," and Polson exploded, "And faggots are at the top of my list!"[1]

Hamper's antipathy notwithstanding, the activity of hunting does need to be explored as an important nonwork activity of male autoworkers (and certainly a large group of white men of all classes in Michigan and elsewhere), and as a source of this group's evolving identity as white, male, worker citizens. Even though workers hunted both before and after World War II, the war represented a watershed for the popularity and extent of this outdoor activity for auto men. Through the United Auto Workers union and as individual, private citizens, autoworkers pushed for and enacted their own rights to the public lands and the game those lands contained. Polson represents an important constituency in auto factories in Michigan that needs to be addressed and understood. That a man like Polson had so much invested in his identity as a hunter and gun owner and the gendered language he used to disparage those not like him ("faggot," "dumb cunt") speaks to the importance of these activities to the masculine identity of many of these workers.

Even though I intended my project on the history of the workers, community, and management of the Reo Motor Car Company to be sensitive to gender, I was caught off guard by the constant refrain on hunting in the materials in the archives, company journals, personnel records, grievance reports, and union materials. These materials concerned the opening and closing of various hunting seasons; information about places, gear, and weather conditions; the arrangement of time off for these various seasons; the accounts of humorous or dangerous hunting trips; controversies over unauthorized vacations always around hunting time; and reports about behaviors related to hunting (drinking, card playing). The frequency of these accounts increased after World War II and through the 1950s and 1960s. Individually, these were prosaic scraps of daily life; together, they began to take on meaning. Two informants of the Reo Oral History Project, Otto and Layton Aves, came from Reo families (their grandfather, father, and various other relatives all worked at Reo) and worked for Reo between the 1940s and 1970s; both talked about their yearly excursions to their hunting camp "up north" with male coworkers and relatives. As they both insisted, farming was better than working in the factory, and hunting was better than farming. Their eyes sparkled and their voices became animated when they talked about hunting pheasant or deer.[2]

The three areas of scholarship that might address the issue of auto work and hunting (or even the general issue of masculinity and hunting in the twentieth century)—masculinity studies, auto work/labor history, and work culture/leisure studies—are virtually devoid of any discussion on this relationship. In the new area of "men's studies" or masculinity studies, working-class men are relatively understudied; yet, when hunting is considered, it is presented as a throwback, a carryover of a primitive male behavior—the discussion is ahistorical. Peter Stearns, in his important *Be a Man! Males in Modern Society,* asserts the fundamental relationship between early man, hunting, and war and suggests that a great deal of the history of modern masculinity is some version of re-creating the challenges, skills, bonding, and values associated with this activity. Ancient hunting societies "provided models for personal identification that long survived their economic basis and remain valid simply because models are needed." Because we live in a "post-hunting" society, other forms such as war, sports teams, and secret societies took the place of hunting as a site for the enacting and transmission of these characteristics and values. Perhaps because Stearns focuses primarily on European working-class men, the actual activity of hunting itself is not explored as an enduring, if changing, source of masculine identity;[3] however, recent works on manhood in U.S. history are similarly silent on hunting and the working class in the twentieth century.[4]

Even though there is a growing body of excellent historical, anthropological and sociological work that considers working-class leisure and culture, there is virtually nothing about hunting.[5] Pathbreaking works by Roy Rosenzweig and Kathy Peiss propose that an exploration of leisure or nonworking activities of the working class can reveal spaces where alternative (although not necessarily oppositional) working-class culture can be forged and worked out.[6] Historians like Ron Edsforth, Lizabeth Cohen, and Robert Lipsitz, interested in the rise of mass consumer culture in the twentieth century and its affect on the working class, have explored consumption patterns, radio, television, the roller derby, car customizing, country music, rock and roll, and film. Often these types of nonwork activities are understood as a safety valve, a source of alternative (or diversionary) identity to class consciousness, a site for resistance or opposition in a safe, managed way, and/or a means by which a worker becomes a participant in (or is co-opted by) a national consumer culture.[7]

Hunting in the twentieth century does not lend itself to this kind of analysis. Even though hunting is an ancient activity freighted with meaning, bound up with notions of masculinity, it changed and evolved throughout the century. Scholars in many fields have revealed that it was and continues to be a sort of craft passed on from father to son, often in ritualized fashion.[8] Even though hunting involves the consumption of gear (and ultimately and hopefully game), it is not consumption in the same way one consumes soap or soap operas. It is a sport, but it is not organized or attended like a baseball game. And even though there are a multitude of local variations, all hunting regulation throughout the twentieth century came under the purview of the state.

Even though I do not think that it is accurate to understand hunting by twentieth-century Michigan autoworkers as a form of resistance, the literature on workers' resistance to state hegemony does prove helpful. E. P. Thompson, in *Whigs and Hunters,* describes how state law and policies regarding game and the land it inhabits can reveal political tensions brought about by changing conditions of capitalism; James Scott, in *Domination and the Arts of Resistance,* understands poaching in Europe as a way that powerless, subordinate groups could exercise their own understanding of traditional rights to the forest and its game. Poaching was not a safety valve, weakening "real resistance"; rather, it was a performance of rights denied.[9] This way of conceptualizing hunting is presented in the most recent (and I think most helpful) book on hunting, Louis Warren's *The Hunter's Game: Poachers and Conservationists in Twentieth Century America.* Warren's book provides two insights that helped me understand the material I had heretofore encountered. First, the twentieth century witnessed the construction of the idea of public lands and game as a common or a public good that the state controlled, and to which it sold access. Even though this certainly did not prevent the political manipulation of these public holdings, it allowed conservationists in service to the public to "deflect local charges that poor people were being shunted from the hunting grounds to make them a playground where the rich could recreate." The second important issue Warren raises is that "disputes over what constituted proper hunting were clashes over rival masculine ideals." For example, "killing female deer or songbirds might have been considered unmanly, even cowardly, in [upper class] sporting circles, but for many locals it was a part of life."[10] Perhaps then, through the twentieth century, members of the working class came to understand their own access to the land and its game as both a right of American citizenship and an emblem of a particular type of working-class masculinity. This isn't just "boinging Bambi" anymore.

Finally, the conclusions drawn from exploring this association between autoworkers and hunting need qualification. Not all members of the working class are hunters, and not all hunters are members of the working class. The fit is certainly not perfect and the link between hunting and the working class may be stronger in Michigan than elsewhere, but the association is strong, and what is most important from the perspective of a historian is that the changes over time reveal links between the growth of an automotive working class and hunting, specifically, and outdoor activity as leisure, generally. Two of the most distinctive features of the state are the automotive industries and hunting, and it seems fruitful to explore how work and leisure are linked to illuminate gender identity in Michigan automotive industries.

## Hunting Has a History

Even though the activity of hunting has a transhistorical, transcultural dimension to it (men and women everywhere have hunted since the beginning of recorded history, and undoubtedly before), the activity, regulation, and ideas about—and those who could, couldn't, and did engage in—hunting have a history. In the United States, the two most important figures regarding hunting nationally are probably Theodore Roosevelt and Aldo Leopold.[11] The crises or questions of the late nineteenth century—urbanization, immigration, industrialization, race and gender equity—all challenged elites to redefine the experiment of United States republicanism (or to revert and reassert older ideas.) As Gail Bederman has skillfully and provocatively described, all of this suggests a challenge to ideas of manhood at the turn of the century, addressed and resolved in a number of ways.[12] Christian values, vocational training, organized sports in the inner-city playground and at universities, military service, the Boy Scouts, and getting close to nature, whether you explore a remote and dangerous wilderness or pursue a large animal, could be acceptable outlets for masculine urges as well as ways to mold good men.

The turn of the century saw the state's first meaningful efforts at regulating the taking of game. In response to the depletion of deer by market hunters supplying out-of-state suppliers and loggers with venison and fur, Michigan passed its first law limiting seasons, regions, and the amount of deer taken in 1895. It has been a popular refrain from the 1920s to today for hunters to reminisce about the good old days when herds of hundreds of deer roamed in full view, but one would probably have to go back to Michigan before 1850 to see anything closely resembling that golden age. Three constituencies were interested in making some effort to preserve a variety of game animals and the habitat they were found on: professional conservationists, sportsmen who tended to be from more elite classes, and workers. Sportsmen, "in high boots and whipcords, armed with fine gunnery, who kill for sheer joy of the hunt and seeing things die," formed their own private sportsman's clubs to assure their access to land and game in light of the poor enforcement of the early regulations.[13] The growing urban labor force's—particularly the autoworkers'—desires for outdoor recreation placed a greater strain on an already stressed resource. Researchers for the Works Progress Administration doing research for a book on the history of Michigan fish and game identified the growth of the auto industry, the availability of inexpensive cars, and the improvement of roads as the key factors bringing more people to the woods throughout the state to hunt.[14] Urban workers invaded farming regions contiguous to cities during various game seasons, and the "city amateurs respected the rights of neither the farmer nor the sportsman, but raided the farm and reserve alike, sometimes killing pets and livestock. This stirred hot rural resentment and eventually brought the farmer into the sportsman's camp." The result was the creation of the Department of Conservation in 1921, which began to innovate to accommodate these various constituencies. In his 1931 report on game management in the Northern Midwest states, Aldo Leopold identified

Michigan, with its "able leadership in the conservation and an extraordinary pressure of hunters by reason of the heavy industrial populations of the automobile manufacturing towns," as having not only distinguished in its efforts at providing public lands for hunting, but also for establishing creative ways to ease hunter-farmer conflicts.[15] As the Department of Conservation became entrenched in the state bureaucracy, hunters from many constituencies became concerned that appointments and policies would reflect political patronage rather than hunters' admittedly diverse interests. To respond to this, sportsmen in 1937 formed the Michigan United Conservation Clubs (MUCC), an amalgamation of the scores of sportsman's clubs throughout the state. Functioning as a clearinghouse and a lobbying group, MUCC (which is presently one of the largest sportsman's clubs in the nation) disseminated information about hunting throughout the state and monitored the Department of Conservation (which later became the Department of Natural Resources) to make sure they kept hunters' interests foremost in their minds.[16]

Even though the number of hunters reflected changes in the law, economic and ecological conditions, and historical circumstances such as war, the long trend was relentlessly upward. Surveys done by the Michigan Department of Resources Research and Development Division during the 1960s and 1970s documented that:

(1) Since 1920, the number of resident firearm deer hunters has generally increased much faster than the Michigan population.

(2) The proportion of the Michigan population that hunted deer in 1968 was about seven times the proportion in 1920.

(3) In 1968, about 20 percent of all Michigan males 15 years old and older hunted deer with a gun. Between the ages of 25 to 44, over 26 percent did. Nearly 30 percent of all males 25 to 44 years hunted deer or small game or both.

(4) All but 6 percent of deer hunters in 1968 were male.

(5) In 1961/2, when 10.2 percent of the population of Southern Michigan was listed as Negro [sic], only 2.8 percent of hunters surveyed self-identified as such.[17]

(6) A study of the 1961/2 hunting season reported that, "almost three-fourths of the hunters were employed in some form of skilled, semi- or unskilled labor. . . .The professions, sales, and managers were less represented than they existed in the population." A 1966 survey reported that 49.5 percent of firearm deer hunters listed their occupations as craftsman, foreman, operatives or kindred workers.[18]

Firearm deer hunters were/are not the only type of sportsman in Michigan, just the largest group. By the 1960s, a sportsman could organize his whole year around the openings and closings of various fish, fowl, small and large game seasons, using rod and reel, bow and arrow, or firearms. Tourism, including hunting and fishing, is the second largest industry in Michigan behind auto work (farming is third), and hunting is the most popular form of recreation in the state of Michigan. Hunters were overwhelmingly white, male, and workers and these associations became stronger as the state took on the regulation of hunting and the land on which it was done throughout the twentieth century.

## The Rites of Masculinity

The activity of hunting, as it came to be understood in the twentieth century, tapped into a number of enduring sources of masculine identity that changed slowly over time. Because hunting was traditionally a sport of rural people, hunting's initial popularity either continued or evoked the rural roots and ways of many factory workers.[19] Throughout Reo's history, ties to the land, like evidence of hunting, was another quiet yet constant refrain. During August of 1919, for example, the company gave 111 employees the "privilege of volunteering to assisting the farmers of Ingham and surrounding counties," holding these employees' jobs until they returned. An analysis of the names of the employees and the names of the farmers they were helping reveals that at least forty-one were related, suggesting that these were workers released to help their families.[20] The annual labor reports of the Reo Motor Car Company reveal that between 1918 and 1938 the number of workers leaving to "go to farms" was consistent, yet peaked during years of economic crisis.[21] Many worked on farms *and* in the factory. As Glen Green, who worked at Reo between 1937 and 1975 and was a member of a Reo family, told us, "Reo started in working winters because they could hire farmers that couldn't work on the fields, . . . and then in the spring when it came time for planting they'd shut down and maybe build up a supply of parts to work the next winters." Green's father Howard had a farm north of Potterville in the 1920s and 1930s; he would "come home from work, jump on the tractor and go out after work and run until dark, come back up and milk cows, go back out and run until close to midnight, get up at 3:00 in the morning to go down, he had 26 cows to milk by hand and milk those cows, go down to Reo, work all day and come back out."[22] During its heyday in the 1920s the company sponsored a popular annual "fun fair," which took place in late summer or early fall and resembled, in many ways, rural country fairs. (To commemorate the fiftieth anniversary of Reo, one more fair was organized in 1954, and it is probably no accident that the annual Reo retirees luncheon takes place in August.) This rural identification persisted into the post–World War II period. At least one-third of the individuals interviewed for the Reo Oral History Project had come from farming backgrounds. Two of our interviews were actually conducted in the farm homes of former Reo workers and these were farms they had lived in since the 1940s and 1950s.[23] Through the 1950s, farmer-workers at Reo were still being identified as a distinctive group in the plant in the *Lansing Labor News*.[24]

Even more important as a source of masculine identity, however, was the association of hunting with war. Throughout the century, but particularly during the periods around the world wars, the links between the activity of hunting and military preparedness were common. Theodore Roosevelt stated in 1905 that "the qualities that made a good soldier are . . . the qualities that made a good hunter."[25] The *Michigan Sportsman* echoed this sentiment in 1919 in an article entitled "Sport and National Security" arguing that "free shooting and fishing must not be allowed to disappear, for directly thereon rest not only the health and happiness of thousands of our citizens, but in a large measure our national security." The editors called upon the federal government, the states, associations, or philanthropic individuals to "set aside at once as many public hunting preserves as possible to ensure that our nation is "composed of strong, healthy men, not only . . . prepared for future military service, but . . . better able to withstand the duties of a successful civil life."[26]

The workers at the Reo Motor Car Company in Lansing were already reading about the association between hunting and military preparedness in their company journal, the *Reo Spirit*. In 1918, an editorial first humorously declared, "Hunting is a disease that attacks human beings, but comes in the most virulent form during the fall and winter months . . . making men do strange things," then turned serious claiming that "just now there seems to be much good in it, for several gentlemen so infected are in Europe, hunting the Kaiser. That gentlemen thinks Huntergetis a bad disease, wishes that all who have it had been quarantined [*sic*]."[27] This language undoubtedly resonated with the scores of Reo employees who joined the Reo National Rifle Club during the first two decades of the twentieth century.[28]

By World War II, hunting was even more popular among autoworkers. As the rationing of various foods became a tedious reminder of a long war, autoworkers in Lansing took to the woods to supplement the diets of their families. On November 14, 1944, the *Lansing State Journal* reported that the "hunter army" was "crippling war factories. Excessive absenteeism due to deer hunting season" brought on an unprecedented number of cases of "grip, severe headache, rheumatism, and other ailments" affecting production at Reo, Motor Wheel, and Fisher Body, with whole shifts canceled at Oldsmobile. It was reported that Carl Swanson, regional director of the United Automobile Workers-Congress of Industrial Organizations (UAW-CIO) region for Flint and Lansing had suggested to local civil defense committees that, "we in the state of Michigan should get to-gether all the DeerHunters and put them in squadrons to help with the home defense . . . they have high powered rifles and if put together they could help in case of invasion as a temporary relief." Swanson, who was himself a deer hunter, said that there were "over 100,000 deer hunters in the state of Michigan. . . ."[29] The offices of the Michigan State Police and Military District who became aware of this information while infiltrating the CIO during World War II were not anxious to empower these deer hunters in the national defense, but veterans clearly took to hunting after the war. One of the largest single increases in hunting was right after World War II, when veterans returning to the factories sought an outlet for their new skills, cash, and leisure. During the late 1960s, in an era of protests against militarism and the unpopular Vietnam War, the number of worker/hunters increased even as workers became more defensive about their right to bear arms and pursue game. The "Reo Local Sportsman," a column in the *Lansing Labor News,* reported in 1969 that "the anti-gun forces have been quietly awaiting an opportunity to force their 'hang-ups' on you the sportsman. . . . Don't let Clubwomen and sentimental popgun crusaders disarm you and arm the criminal."[30]

If the association of war and hunting was only reinforced episodically, certainly the association of masculine qualities with hunting presented an enduring source of appeal. Nevertheless, characteristics of masculinity in general, and working-class masculinity specifically, were not fixed or unitary throughout the first three quarters of the twentieth century. From Theodore Roosevelt's initial endorsements of hunting as a character-building activity for men, workers and their various representatives have identified hunting as an activity that produced and reproduced characteristics of multiple (although not necessarily dichotomous) masculine identities. Before World War II, it was recognized by conservation officials that hunting both instilled and reflected democratic values. In 1932, the Michigan Conservation Department described providing "everyone, regardless of financial status, a chance to fish and hunt," as a form of "social welfare."[31] Gerald Fitzgerald, who wrote the "Outdoor Corner" column for the *Michigan CIO News* through the 1950s, used the Christmas holiday to remind worker-hunters of more spiritual lessons: "If only everyone knew the God of the sportsman. . . . We are all neighbors who share the fields and streams . . . we share our knowledge and the products of the rod and gun . . . this is truly the season of the true sportsman."[32] The mutualism and fairmindedness of the sportsman and union man went hand in hand.[33]

In the late 1940s and 1950s hunting was endorsed as an antidote to two basic concerns of the era: domesticity and the new factory system. As veterans and female war workers were "homeward bound," hunting represented a form of family leisure although this usually meant that it provided an opportunity for fathers and sons to play together. As one poem that appeared in a Grand Rapids journal, the *Sportsmen's Voice* (1948) began, "If you have a son mister, give him a gun, plus a dog and a reel and a rod. / For the lad who knows both water and wood has a keener knowledge of God."[34] Hunting was also described as an antidote to the stresses of modern life, a way to have an adventure and to refresh and renew. After reporting on those who had returned victorious from the "battle of the North," the writer of the "Reo Items" column in the *Lansing Labor News* described the condition of those who returned emptyhanded as: "long and lean from the need of a well-cooked meal; bleary eyed from lack of sleep and glassy eyed, not always from driving straight through; perhaps disappointed but not dismayed; full of stories and an experience never to be forgotten. They'll invade the woods again en mass[e] next season. Even if only a brief respite, you're not thinking of all your everyday problems while peering in the quiet woods for the sign of a spike."[35]

These values associated with hunting continued through the 1960s, when they were joined by less lofty appeals. As the above quote hints, the less "respectable" aspects of postwar masculinity could also emerge during the yearly hunting excursion. Hunting was an opportunity to escape women (wives, really, as one hunter I know suggests that the season should also be called "dear" hunting), abandon daily rituals of hygiene, play cards, and drink a lot. As one joke put it, "Six men on a deer hunting trip ran out of provisions and sent one of their men to a nearby town to shop. He returned with six bottles of wine, a case of beer, a bottle of whiskey, and loaf of bread. One of the group was heard to exclaim, 'Good boy! You've even brought something for the birds.'"[36] The values associated with hunting ranged from the sacred to the profane, all masculine and having enormous appeal for all men.

## The Rights of Men

Hunting was not just a masculine *rite*, an activity associated with the land and war and manly characteristics and values; it was also a *right* that needed to be negotiated. It is in this process of negotiation that we can see how workers at Reo and perhaps automotive workers in Michigan generally came to see this as a condition of employment and an emblem of identity.

In 1957, Michigan's CIO unions proclaimed that they were proud that Michigan was the best year-round vacation state in America and that they intended to keep it that way "by actively pushing for better and better recreational facilities and more and more time for people to enjoy them." In this way, workers, through their unions, made claim to more space (i.e., land for recreation) and more time (freedom to pursue these activities). Even though these contests over space and time were not as dramatically featured in dailies, periodicals, and histories as workplace conflicts, they were passionately argued by workers. They demonstrate that important sources of identity for and ideas about rights of white, male worker-citizens existed outside as well as inside the workplace. And the local labor periodicals recognized this even if the national leadership did not.[37]

By the post–World War II era, a great deal of land had already been set aside for recreational use, including hunting. Because of the state's retrieval of marginal and abandoned farmlands, particularly around urban areas, there was a well-established network of nature areas after the war.[38] Workers applauded any increase in available land or better accessibility to that land, and they protested any restrictions. Workers and their unions understood this issue of land accessibility as a class issue. In 1958, for example, there was universal praise for the building of the Mackinac Bridge, which connects the lower part of the state and the Upper Peninsula (UP). "Thanks to the new bridge at the Straits," workers could make it back from the UP, "in about six hours. In the past years they "waited longer than that just to cross the ferry."[39] Sunday hunting bans persisted through the 1950s, although they were determined by individual localities, creating a patchwork of regulations throughout the state. Farmers in localities that allowed Sunday hunting, particularly around large cities, felt invaded during open seasons. Workers pushed for uniform laws that allowed them to engage in hunting on their day of rest.[40] Workers and their union representatives responded most vociferously to any efforts to limit access to existing public lands. When fishermen became aware that a state-owned fish hatchery had become a private fishing club supplied with fish from the state, the letters in the *Lansing Labor News* went on about it for months.[41]

In the postwar period, Michigan autoworkers had developed a collective consciousness about their rights to the land. In 1957, when the Republican legislature was preparing to get Governor C. Mennen Williams to sign a bill allowing for the creation of private game preserves with longer hunting seasons and virtually no restrictions, the Michigan CIO Council asked him to veto. The president of the council, August Scholle, wrote, "This is the worst kind of class legislation. It permits wealthy people who are able to spend large sums of money to hunt on these preserves to buy themselves a license to hunt 120 days of the year, while the rest of the population of Michigan would be restricted to the very limited season for bird hunting. . . . " Many of these preserves would be created, "gobbling up every potential bird hunting area in the state. It would ultimately evolve into the same situation as prevailed in most European countries where hunting was reserved for the aristocracy, and the only sport in which a working man could indulge would be bush-beating for the aristocrats."[42] Space for hunting had become an inalienable right of the Michigan autoworker.

It was not enough to have the space to hunt if you had no time to do it, and to get that you needed to bargain with your employer. Workers in Michigan understood that the timing of the opening of hunting seasons was also a class issue. An editorial in the *Saginaw Valley Sportsman* in 1949 proclaimed, "They ought to open the season on Saturday so we'll all get an even start without missing work. . . . Saturday openings for bird and deer hunting seasons would give working men a chance to participate without time from work."[43] Contests over time to hunt between Reo management and its employees surfaced in three ways: discussions about absenteeism, grievances regarding workers who simply took off to hunt without authorization, and finally, the special provisions in vacation stipulations oriented to hunters.

Whether the company liked it or not, it had to contend with absenteeism, some authorized and some not, during the openings of various game seasons. During negotiations over piecework rates on October 12, 1948, a remarkable exchange took place between management and labor. From the mid-1940s through the early 1950s, Reo was plagued by dozens of unauthorized work stoppages, most of which were the result of piece-rate changes or heavyhanded foremen (and the two often went hand in hand.) The union/management bargaining committee met at least weekly during these contentious times and then on October 12, 1948, Ernst Miller, a union representative, asked if the plant would be open on Friday to which management answered yes.

Miller responded that "some of the supervision . . . do not seem clear on the agreement that we arrived at as far as deer hunters are concerned." The union representative, Ralph Barnes, continued, "People that waived a portion of their vacation in the summer time, it was agreed when we set up the vacation period, they would take it during deer season." Management responded that if the supervisor had been informed and had given the O.K. then the worker could go hunting. Barnes then added, "From what I hear and the people have told their supervisors, about 50% will not be here Friday." Russell Smith, the company attorney asked Barnes, "All day, Ralph?" "Yes" said Barnes. And when management pointed out that the deer season didn't open until noon, Barnes responded, "By the time they get oiled up and their guns ready it would be noon."

President of the union Raymond Reed added, "Last year they did shut down for the day if I recall."

To which Gerald Byrne, director of personnel replied, "We were forced to shut down. We attempted to start the line."

Smith added, "The year before last, wasn't that?"

Barnes: "It was the year before and we sent them home at 10."

Smith, "Last year, we found in advance we were going to have the same situation so they did not run at all, as I recall."

Al Foust (management): "There is just as good hunting on Saturday as on Friday."

Reed: "It is only normal they want to go out the first day."

Byrne: "You are telling us now that we can expect about 50% absenteeism on Friday."

Barnes: "I would not say it would be full 50% but there will be a
  lot of them off."
Reed: "This is every year."[44]

This candid interchange occurred in the middle of a negotiating session devoted to resolving important issues, but both sides had to resign
themselves to the fact that this absenteeism around the opening of
hunting season was not open for negotiation. Certainly there was a
give and take here, but both parties understood that given the history
of hunting and their workers, altering these practices would be futile.
Even union officials suffered the same fate whenever their meetings
were scheduled in October and November.[45]

Official and legitimate leave for hunting was dispensed by the foreman, which allowed for a great deal of favoritism and inequality.
Grievances and sometimes dismissals resulted when certain employees were held to the letter of the law as others around them experienced privileged treatment.[46] In many ways, the dispensation of
hunting leave might be one of the last vestiges of the prerogative of the
foreman in the twentieth century.

From the middle of the 1940s through the 1950s, the company and
the union sought to codify in print the relationship between vacation
leave and hunting leave undoubtedly to avoid excessive absenteeism
and grievances. The company made it clear through its stated vacation
leave policy statements, as well as through its representatives on the
management bargaining committees, that "[t]ime off during fishing or
hunting season should be discouraged excepting to employees eligible
for regular vacations," and objected to the practice of some supervisors
who granted so-called deer hunting leaves to employees without seniority or who had previously used up their vacation time.[47] Reo's management not only had their hands full with errant workers, anxious to
exercise their rights to make their annual exodus to the forests, but also
had to keep their foremen and supervisors in line with regular
reminders regarding the language of the contract.[48] None of this seemed
to make any difference: In 1957 the workers reported an "epidemic of
Asian Flu" on Monday, October 21—the start of pheasant season.[49]

During the 1960s and early 1970s, the history of hunting in Michigan and the history of Reo intersected in profound ways. As hunting
reached new heights of popularity during the 1960s and early 1970s,
Reo (then called Diamond Reo because of the many buyouts it had
experienced) was in decline. With remote and changing ownership
and uncertain government contracts, in part because of the Vietnam
War, the company declined as hunting became more important to the
workers who remained. In the increasingly depressing Reo columns in
the *Lansing Labor News,* the juxtaposition of items describing the company's decline to items joyfully recounting hunting activities is striking. In October of 1963, along with news that the company that had

taken over Reo had engaged in yet another merger, the men formed a "buck club," and every year thereafter had Buck contests.[50] In 1968, the year the Reo local formed its own sportsman's club and signed 150 members in its first month, the company changed its production manager, personnel director, supervisory staff, and foremen.[51] In 1969, amid continuing concerns over the viability of the company in Lansing and the threat of the plant moving, the men of the Reo Sportsman's club affiliated with the MUCC and began publishing their own column, "Local 650 Sportsman's Club Column," in the *Lansing Labor News*, the only Lansing CIO local to do so.[52] Filled with information, the first column alone announced classified ads relating to hunting and the opening of a club library at the union hall, wholesale buying at a sportsman store if one showed his union card, a fishing contest, information about shooting carp, news about the smelt run, a special turkey season in May, state congressional hearings about financing of state recreational facilities, meetings of the MUCC, and information about a local shooting range. These sorts of activities continued until the Lansing plant's demise.

## The Bonds of White Working-Class Manhood

> Class is defined by men as they live their own history, and, in the end, this is the only definition.
> —E. P. Thompson, *The Making of the English Working Class*

It's not that hunting provided a subterfuge for class consciousness, diverting the energies and attention of workers from useful protests against their alienated work, their place in the increasingly global capitalist system, the increasing bureaucratization (or ineffectiveness) of their union, or the threat to their jobs and pensions. Perhaps some of the workers at Reo recognized these developments and used the retreat to the woods as a way to respond; perhaps some were even motivated enough to engage in a range of political activities (on the left and right) to address these issues. As scholars, we might decide that it was the deskilling of the workplace, the bureaucratization of the unions, the co-optation of the workers by good wages and fringe benefits, the politically repressive atmosphere of the Cold War, or the challenges to traditional masculinity made by the civil rights and women's movements that contributed to the growing popularity of hunting as a form of leisure for Michigan autoworkers. Perhaps hunting can be understood as a particular response of the working class to their "blue collar blues" during the 1950s and 1960s, similar to the middle-class men's flight from job and family that Barbara Ehrenreich describes in *The Hearts of Men*.[53] Perhaps the increasing popularity and importance of hunting among the automotive working class is evidence of the "remasculization" occurring during the 1960s and 1970s that Susan Jeffords describes in her *Remasculinization of America: Gender and the Vietnam War.*[54] Hunting might also be seen as a Midwest automotive version of the hypermasculine "hard hat" phenomenon of the late 1960s and early 1970s so well described by Joshua Freedman.[55]

The reason for the increasing popularity of hunting among autoworkers in the twentieth century and its importance as a source of white, working-class masculine identity needs to be understood as proactive rather than reactive. There is no question that many men who took (and take) to hunting did so because it was considered one of the few remaining authentically masculine and white, male-only activities left in an increasingly feminized and integrated world. Yet there is a danger in using the hunter-worker presented at the start of this paper, Polson, as representative of all hunter-workers. The act of hunting, the yearly ritual of taking to the woods with workmates, friends, and male kin cannot be simplified to an act of resistance or the reaction of men under assault. Because of hunting's long history in the state of Michigan (and elsewhere) its regulation by the state, century-long secular increase in and seeming importance for those who partake of it, and the consistent and varied ways working men sought to ensure and extend their rights to land and game, it needs to be understood as a right won. As surely as Reo's workers came to expect to earn enough to support their families, to rely on the state to ensure minimum wages, hours, working conditions, and fringe benefits, to be treated equally and fairly in their workplace and communities, they also expected to have the time and space to hunt. For Reo workers, the right to hunt was all they were left with after 1975, when their plant closed down.

Just as they had probably been doing for the forty years since the building of the Reo Clubhouse, a group of men were sitting around the lunch table in the cafeteria. It's September 1957, and "fishing is nearly done at the lunch table and the boys have started killing deer. Biggest deer killed Tuesday at lunch was by Gene Lewis, weight 566 pounds with 42 points. Longest deer carried was by Eddie Phile, who said he chased the deer eight miles thru a swamp then carried him eleven miles back; deer weighed 220 pounds. Ed said he didn't mind the weight of the deer as much, but horns kept probing his back."[56] After World War II, for many white male workers in automotive industries, and certainly for the men who worked at Reo, hunting and other outdoor activities became a key dimension of their identities. For Eddie, Gene, and many of the men at Reo, it was the activity of hunting that tied them to their fellow workers, filled their days and minds with excitement and joy, and provided an important and enduring source of their masculine, white, working-class culture and identity.[57]

# Postscript

Even though Reo's story ended in 1975, the story of this association between hunting and the automotive working class was far from over.[58] Deer hunting and all outdoor activities are still enormously popular. During the 1998–99 hunting season in Michigan, over 500,000 hunters (mostly men) bought firearm deer licenses.[59] Throughout the twentieth century, hunting was one of the fastest growing leisure activities in the state that brought the automobile to the United States and the world. The region that saw the birth of the second industrial revolution, with mass production, mass consumption, Fordism, and Americanism also provided for its worker-citizens to have historically unprecedented access to public land and game. What does it mean to twentieth-century labor history when we include working-class white men's access to land and game as a key feature of their masculine identities? What does it mean to studies of twentieth-century masculinity when we include an understanding of hunting, not as a reaction to a crisis of twentieth-century masculinity, but as the creation of a new masculine norm and right within the working class? Clearly the millions of men (and some women, but that's another essay) who engaged in this activity throughout the twentieth century need to be included in our studies of white male workers.

## Notes

I would like to thank Peter Berg, Leslie Moch, Lewis Siegelbaum, Mark Kornbluh, Peter Beattie, Daniel Ernst, and the members of the panel and the audience of the session on "Motor Men" at the North American Labor History Conference (October 1998), especially Kevin Boyle and Eric Guthey for comments and support. Thanks also to the two anonymous reads for *Journal of Social History* as well as my first-year graduate student Tom Adams, who although new to history is a longtime autoworker and hunter. All faults in the piece are, of course, my own.

1. Ben Hamper, *Rivethead: Tales from the Assembly Line* (New York: Warner Books, 1986), 135–39.

2. Oral interviews conducted with Otto Aves, January 4, 1993, and Layton Aves, August 8, 1995.

3. Peter Stearns, *Be a Man! Males in Modern Society* (New York: Holmes and Meier, 1979), 18.

4. See for example, Michael Kimmel, *Manhood in America: A Cultural History* (New York: The Free Press, 1996.)

5. E. Anthony Rotundo, *American Manhood: Transformations in Masculinity from the Revolution to the Modern Era* (New York: Basic Books, 1993) has a few pages on hunting. Eli Chinoy, *Automobile Workers and the American Dream*, 2d ed. (Urbana: University of Illinois Press, 1992); David Halle, *America's Working Man: Work, Home and Politics among Blue-Collar Property Owners* (Chicago: University of Chicago Press, 1994); and Kathryn Grover, *Hard at Play: Leisure in America, 1840-1940* (Amherst: University of Massachu-

setts Press, 1992) have little on hunting. Both David D. Gilmore, *Manhood in the Making: Cultural Concepts of Masculinity* (New Haven, Conn.: Yale University Press, 1990), 113–17, and E. E. Masters, *Blue-Collar Aristocrats: Life-Styles at a Working-Class Tavern* (Madison: University of Wisconsin Press, 1975), 132–36 have short but good sections on hunting.

6. Roy Rosenzweig, *Eight Hours for What We Will: Workers and Leisure in an Industrial City, 1870–1920* (Cambridge: Cambridge University Press, 1983); Kathy Peiss, *Cheap Amusements: Working Women and Leisure in Turn-of-the-Century New York* (Philadelphia: Temple University Press, 1986.)

7. See Lizabeth Cohen, *Making a New Deal: Industrial Workers in Chicago, 1919–1939* (Cambridge: Cambridge University Press, 1990); Ronald Edsforth, *Class Conflict and Cultural Consensus: The Making of a Mass Consumer Society in Flint, Michigan* (New Brunswick, N.J.: Rutgers University Press, 1987); George Lipsitz, *Rainbow at Midnight: Labor and Culture in the 1940s* (Urbana: University of Illinois Press, 1994.) Lipsitz has the best example of this: "On the job, at home, and in popular culture, workers and others paid a terrible price for their inability to convert grass-roots militancy into a social movement capable of fighting to reform society along democratic and egalitarian lines. But the traces of working-class consciousness within popular culture in the postwar period also show the limits of corporate-liberal hegemony. They testify to profound popular dissatisfaction with the hierarchies and exploitations of the cold war era. They also demonstrate the emergent possibilities of the affinity between electronic mass media and working-class culture, an affinity most powerfully demonstrated by the class dimensions of popular film and popular music during the postwar years" (276).

8. See Stuart Marks, *Southern Hunting in Black and White: Nature, History, and Ritual in a Carolina Community* (Princeton, N.J.: Princeton University Press, 1991). I would also like to thank Peter Rachleff and Kevin Boyle for their insights on this point.

9. E. P. Thompson, *Whigs and Hunters: The Origin of the Black Acts* (New York: Pantheon, 1957); and James C. Scott, *Domination and the Arts of Resistance: Hidden Transcripts* ( New Haven, Conn.: Yale University Press, 1990), 188–92.

10. Louis Warren, *The Hunter's Game: Poachers and Conservationists in Twentieth Century America* (New Haven, Conn.: Yale University Press, 1997), 12, 14.

11. Aldo Leopold, the famous author of *The Sand County Alamanac and Sketches Here and There* (1949) was a well-known writer and scholar on the relationship between humans and the environment. According to the editors of a recent anthology of his works, "Leopold was a leader and innovator in the young profession of forestry, especially in recreation planning, game management, and soil erosion control. He is considered the father of the national forest wilderness system and the father of the profession of wildlife management in America. . . . Leopold occupied the nation's first chair of game management, which was created for him at the University of Wisconsin. . . . He offered his remarkable leadership talents to more than a hundred conservation organizations, agencies, and committees." Susan L. Flader and J. Baird Callicott, *The River of the Mother of God and Other Essays by Aldo Leopold* (Madison: University of Wisconsin Press, 1991), ix.

12. Gail Bederman, *Manliness and Civilization: A Cultural History of Gender and Race in the United States, 1880–1917* (Chicago: University of Chicago Press, 1995).

13. Ed Langenau, "100 Years of Deer Management in Michigan," Michigan Department of Natural Resources, Wildlife Division Report Number 3213 (1994); I would like to thank Dr. R. Ben Peyton of the Michigan State University Department of Fisheries and Wildlife for sharing this pamphlet with me. "Outline of Fur and Game History" manuscript by Richard Briley, dated 1940, 6, Department of Natural Resources—Game Division: Michigan Writers' Project, 1941–1943.

14. See Briley, "Outlaw," and, S. E. Sangster, "Tentative Outline for Proposed History of Michigan Fish and Game," dated 1940, 2. Department of Natural Resources—Game Division: Michigan Writers' Project, 1941–1943.

15. Aldo Leopold, *Report on a Game Survey of North Central State for the Sporting Arms and Ammunition Manufacturing Institute* (Madison, Wisconsin: n.p., 1931), 198, notes,

"Michigan is the only State in the north central group which is so far embarked on a systematic program of acquiring refuges and public shooting grounds on forest lands and putting them under management." On these issues see also 244–46. On the amelioration of the hunter-farmer conflicts see the discussion of the Williamston Pool, 131–33.

16. See Harry R. Gaines, "History of MUCC," *Michigan Out-of-Doors,* January 1947, 12.

17. Walter L. Palmer, "An Analysis of the Public Use of Southern Michigan Game and Recreation Areas," *Michigan Department of Conservation Research and Development Report* 102, March 14, 1967, 41.

18. L. A. Ryel, G. C. Jamesen, and L. J. Hawn, "Some Facts about Michigan Hunters," *Michigan Department of Natural Resources: Research and Development Report* 197, April 9, 1970.

19. The Lansing autoworkers featured in Ely Chinoy's *Autoworkers and the American Dream* expressed powerful nostalgia for the land, and many either owned or desired to own farms. Chinoy, *Autoworkers and the American Dream,* 86–96.

20. In other words, they had the same last name. Therefore, many more may have been related by marriage. "In the Harvest Field," *Reo Spirit,* August 1919, 22–23. The average monthly total of all employees for the year 1919 was 4,475, so this was hardly an exodus—only about 2 percent of the workforce. *Annual Report of the Labor Department—From February 1, 1919–February 1, 1920,* February 10, 1920, Reo Motor Car Collection Box 66, Folder 4.

21. See Appendix 1.

22. Interview with Glen Green, December 22, 1992.

23. Interview with Herbert Heinz, Dansville, Michigan, March 16, 1993; interview with Raymond Fuller, Mulliken, Michigan, March 19, 1992.

24. See, from the *Lansing Labor News,* "Reo News," (August 7, 1952, 3), where it was reported that "many of the farmer members of the Reo family are quite worried lately about the harvest of wheat and oats. Rain in excessive quantity has damaged grain very seriously"; see also "Reo Items" (April 18, 1958, 4): "What's with these farmers, Harvey? They plow all night and come in and drag all day." On April 25, 1958, my interviewee, Ray Fuller was referred to as the "Mullican Sodbuster," [*sic*], page 6.

25. Theodore Roosevelt, *Outdoor Pastimes of an American Hunter* (New York: Charles Scribner's Sons, 1905), 228, and his essay "The American Boy," in *The Strenuous Life* (New York: The Century Co., 1904): "In the Civil War, the soldiers who came from the prairie and the backwoods and the rugged farms where stumps still dotted the clearings and who had learned to ride in their infancy, to shoot as soon as they could handle a rifle, and to camp out whenever they got the chance, were better fitted for military work than any set of mere school or college athletes could possible be" (156–57).

26. "Sport and National Security," *Michigan Sportsman,* August 1919, From papers of the Department of Natural Resources Game Division, Michigan Writers' Project, 1941–1943, folder 9, excerpts from publications, State of Michigan Library, Lansing, Michigan.

27. "Hunting," *Reo Spirit,* December 1918, 4.

28. "The Reo National Rifle Club," *Reo Spirit,* April 1916, 13. News of the club appears in almost every issue through the 1920s.

29. Memorandum from Arlo A. Emery, Lt. Col. J.A.G.D. Officer in Charge, Detroit District, Michigan Military Area, To: Assistant Chief of Staff, G-2 Sixth Corps Area, Chicago, Illinois, Subject: CIO Dated April 3, 1942. Includes report. Copy sent to Captain Olander. Records of the Michigan State Police: Intelligence and Security Bureau, 1942–1947. Even though it is impossible to verify the spy report, I have confirmed that the number of hunters was roughly correct, and according to the oral history of Carl Swanson on deposit at the Reuther Library, Walter Reuther Library at Wayne State University, Detroit, Michigan, Swanson was a hunter and did do civil defense work. See Jack W. Skeels, Oral History Interview with Carl Swanson, University of Michigan/ Wayne State University, Institute of Labor and Industrial Relations, August 8, 1960, 30, 46.

30. "Local Sportsman," *Lansing Labor News,* November 6, 1969, 12. See also: "Reo News," *Lansing Labor News,* July 11, 1968, 8, and Fred Parks, "Local 650 Sportsman's Club Column," *Lansing Labor News,* May 1, 1969, 5.

31. "Hunting and Fishing for Everyone," *Michigan Conservation*, December 1932, 2. Later they described it as a basic freedom; see "Relax—You're Not So Darned Important," August 1946, 2: "Citizens of a democracy need to relax together as well as work together in order to understand one another."

32. See, in *Michigan CIO News,* December 24, 1953, 7, and December 22, 1955, 6.

33. See, for example, "Unionism Benefits the Fisherman," *Michigan CIO News*, July 29, 1954, 7.

34. Gomer Reeves, "If You Have a Son," *Sportsmen's Voice*, June 1948, 6.

35. "Reo Item," *Lansing Labor News,* December 13, 1957, 6.

36. " The joke came from the newsletter of the Reo sales staff. "Newsletter from J. M. Struble, Advertising Department to Sales Personnel," November 30, 1953, and August 4, 1954. Reo Motor Car Company Collection, Box 156, Folders 16 and 30.

37. "Michigan Is a Vacation Paradise All Year Round," *Lansing Labor News*, August 2, 1957, 6. I do not mean to imply that the national leadership of the UAW did not pay attention to issues of leisure and recreation. The UAW recreation and sports programs did sponsor a number of activities including Sportsman's Nights, but they did not concentrate on hunting. See, in *Michigan CIO News*, "UAW Spring Sport Program in Full Swing," April 21, 1955, 8; "Sportsnight Scheduled for Wednesday," October 6, 1955, 7; and "Union Recreation," March 10, 1955, 7.

38. See, for example, "Play Space for Millions," *Lansing Industrial News*, October 4, 1946, 3. This article describes the ring of a dozen parks and wildlife areas around Detroit. See also "Welcome Sign for Hunters," *Lansing Labor News*, October 20, 1966, 9, which describes the opening of 100,000 acres of land for hunters in southern Michigan.

39. "This Bear Made Him Late for Picket Duty," *Lansing Labor News*, October 17, 1958, 4; and "Deer Hunters Looking Forward to Mackinac Bridge," *Lansing Labor News,* November 7, 1958, 1.

40. See, for example, "Deer Herd Controversy Grows," *Michigan CIO News*, December 2, 1954, 7; and Mort Neff, "Inequity in Hunting Laws," *Michigan CIO News,* September 7, 1955, 6.

41. See, for example, "More Readers Comment on Favored Fish Club," *Lansing Labor News,* July 12, 1951, 1.

42. "Hit Hunting Bill for Wealthy," *Lansing Labor News*, May 31, 1957, 5; and "Special Hunting Privileges for the Rich Hit by Scholle," *Michigan CIO News*, May 16, 1957, 3.

43. Editorial, *Saginaw Valley Sportsman*, February 1949, 12.

44. Piecework negotiations, October 12, 1948, in Reo Motor Car Company Collection, Box 68, Folder 59.

45. "Hunters Wreck Council Meet; Date Is Moved," *Lansing Labor News*, November 5, 1953, 1.

46. I have not done a systematic search of grievances on this matter but intend to in the future. See for example, "Grievance, William Earl Bailey," November 24, 1944, Reo Motor Car Company Collection, Box 54, Folder 1; "Grievance # 10386—Otto J. Bell," Minutes of the Management-Union Bargaining Committee Meeting (December 11, 1946), UAW Local #650, Material Box 7, Reuther Library; and "Office Memo dated November 16, 1943," from Charles Parr, Plant Protection, To E. D. Stinebower, re: G. C. Sigourney, Reo Motor Car Company Collection, Box 51, Folder 64.

47. "1953 Vacation Procedure for Hourly Rated Employees, April 7, 1953," Reo Motor Car Company Collection; See also, "1954 Vacation Procedure for Hourly Rated Employees, May 7, 1954," Reo Motor Car Company Collection; "Meetings of the Management-Union Bargaining Committee Meeting, November 6, 1945," UAW Local # 650, Material Box 7, Reuther Library; "Minutes of the Management-Union Bargaining Committee Meeting, October 21, 1947," UAW Local # 650, Material Box 8; and "Minutes of the Executive Board Meetings, November 12, 1952," UAW Local # 650, Material Box 6.

48. See, for example, "Memorandum to all Reo Deer Hunting Employees" from Byron F. Field, Personnel Manager, dated November 9, 1942, Reo Motor Car Company Collection Box 51, Folder 26; "Memorandum to All Superintendents and Foremen" from Gerald

Byrne, Director of Personnel, dated October 31, 1951, Reo Motor Car Company Collection, Box 27, Folder 28; and "Memorandum to All Superintendents, Department Heads and Foremen" from Gerald Byrne, Director of Personnel, dated October 16, 1953, Reo Motor Car Company Collection, Box 27, Folder 29.

49. "Reo Items," *Lansing Labor News*, October 25, 1957, 6.

50. "White Division," *Lansing Labor News*, October 10, 1963, 16.

51. "Diamond Reo News," *Lansing Labor News*, April 18, 1968, 11, and May 16, 1968, 14.

52. "Diamond Reo News," *Lansing Labor News*, January 23, 1969, 6; and Fred Parks, "Local 650 Sportsman's Club," *Lansing Labor News*, May 1, 1969, 5.

53. Barbara Ehrenreich, *Hearts of Men: American Dreams and the Flight from Commitment* (New York: Anchor, 1983).

54. Susan Jeffords, *The Remasculinization of America: Gender and the Vietnam War* (Bloomington: Indiana University Press, 1989).

55. Joshua B. Freeman, "Hardhats: Construction Workers, Manliness, and the 1970 Pro-war Demonstrations," *Journal of Social History* 26 (1993): 725–44.

56. "Reo Items," *Lansing Labor News*, September 13, 1957, 2.

57. As Eliot Gorn puts it, "most workers did not spend their free time reading the *Rights of Man,* toasting Tom Paine, and struggling to resist oppression. Probably more hours were consumed at cockfights than at union meetings in the nineteenth century. Radicals there were of course, and they have been studied brilliantly. But if historians are to understand working-class people, they must look closely at their folklore and recreations, their pastimes and sports, for it has been in leisure more than in politics or in labor that many men and women have found the deepest sense of meaning and wholeness." Eliot Gorn, *The Manly Art: Bare-Knuckle Prize Fighting in America* (Ithaca, N.Y.: Cornell University Press, 1986), 14.

58. During the post–Vietnam War era, the association between hunting and war would be used to promote an antiwar message. Michael Cimino's popular film *The Deer Hunter* (1978) ended with the battle-worn, disillusioned, and probably unemployed steel worker (played by Robert DeNiro) coming face to face with a big buck in a surreal mountainous terrain. He doesn't shoot; he lets the deer go. See Tom Zaniello, *Working Stiffs, Union Mains, Reds, and Riffraff: An Organized Guide to Film about Labor* (Ithaca, N.Y.: Cornell University Press, 1996), 68–69; Zaniello says, "When Michael chooses at the end of the film to let a deer escape although it is in his sight, we know that he is on his way to healing." Jeffords, *The Remasculinization of America,* 94–102, also provides a rich and provocative analysis of the importance of masculine identity represented in *The Deer Hunter.*

59. The exact number is 502,395. As well, 202,953 archery deer licenses and 97,664 antlerless deer licenses were sold. Last year's figures were roughly the same. I would like to thank the public relations division of the Michigan Department of Natural Resources for sharing these figures with me.

## Appendix 1  *"Going to Farms"*

| Year[1] | Number of Voluntary Quits[2] | Number "Going to Farm" | Percentage "Going To Farm"[3] |
|---|---|---|---|
| 1918 | 4045 | 272 | 6.7 |
| 1919 | 5059 | 259 | 5.1 |
| 1920 | 5435 | 527 | 9.7 |
| 1921 | 984 | 129 | 13.1 |
| 1922 | 1212 | 67 | 5.5 |
| 1923 | 1996 | 94 | 4.7 |
| 1924 | 885 | 68 | 7.7 |
| 1925 | 994 | 51 | 5.1 |
| 1926 | 947 | 61 | 6.4 |
| 1927 | 1343 | 63 | 4.7 |
| 1928 | 2276 | 75 | 3.3 |
| 1929 | 1959 | 87 | 4.4 |
| 1930 | 871 | 66 | 7.6 |
| 1931 | 432 | 26 | 6.0 |
| 1932 | 106 | 12 | 11.3 |
| 1933 | 147 | 6 | 4.1 |
| 1934 | 363 | 14 | 3.9 |
| 1935 | 606 | 10 | 1.7 |
| 1936 | 467 | 14 | 3.0 |
| 1937 | 513 | 9 | 1.8 |
| 1938 | 105 | 3 | 2.9 |
| 1939 | 90 | 0 | 0 |

1.   All materials from "Annual Reports of Labor Department," 1918–1938, *Reo Motor Car Company Collection*, box 66, folders 2–54.
2.   Voluntary Quits include these categories provided: "better job in city"; "better job out of city"; "leaving the city"; "dissatisfied with wages"; "dissatisfied in other ways"; "sickness and poor health"; "can't make good on job"; and "other." Some early labor reports provided more reasons. Voluntary quits does not include "no work, out of stock."
3.   Rounded to nearest tenth.

# Contributors

**Janet F. Davidson** is a historian with the "America on the Move" exhibition team at the Smithsonian Institution's National Museum of American History. A recent recipient of a National Historical Publications and Records Commission fellowship with the Samuel Gompers Papers Project at the University of Maryland, her article is part of her dissertation, "Women and the Railway: The Gendering of Work during the War Era, 1917–1920" (University of Delaware, 2000).

**Lisa Fine** is an associate professor of history at Michigan State University. She received her Ph.D. from the University of Wisconsin-Madison. Fine has published *The Souls of the Skyscraper: Female Clerical Workers in Chicago, 1870–1930* (1990) and is presently working on a book on the Reo Motor Car Company of Lansing, Michigan. Earlier parts of her work in progress on Reo have appeared in *Labor History* (1993) and the *Journal of Social History* (2000).

**Roger Horowitz** is associate director of the Center for the Study of Business, Technology, and Society at the Hagley Museum and Library, Wilmington, Delaware. He is author of *"Negro and White, Unite and Fight!" A Social History of Industrial Unionism in Meatpacking, 1930–1990* (1997) and coeditor, with Arwen Mohun, of *His and Hers: Gender, Consumption, and Technology* (1998). Currently he is writing a book on meat consumption and production in America.

**Stephen Meyer** is a labor historian and professor of history at the University of Wisconsin-Parkside. He is author of *The Five Dollar Day: Labor Management and Social Control in the Ford Motor Company, 1908–1921* (1981) and *"Stalin Over Wisconsin": the Making and Unmaking of Militant Unionism, 1900–1950* (1992), and a coeditor with Nelson Lichtenstein, of *On the Line: Essays in the History of Auto Work* (1989). He is currently researching and writing a book, tentatively titled *Bearing*

*Manliness: The Gendered Cultures of American Automobile Workers, 1900–1970.*

**Ruth Oldenziel** is an associate professor at the University of Amsterdam. She coedited the special issue of *Technology and Culture,* "Gender Analysis and the History of Technology" (1997), and is the author of *Schoon Genoeg* (1998), *Making Technology Masculine: Men, Women and Modern Machines in America* (1999), and *Crossing Boundaries, Building Bridges: Comparing the History of Women Engineers* (2000).

**Todd Alexander Postol** received his Ph.D. from the University of Chicago and is an assistant professor at St. Joseph's College in Patchogue, New York. His work has appeared in *Enterprise and Society,* the *Journal of Social History,* and *Labor's Heritage.*

**Nancy Quam-Wickham** is an associate professor of history at California State University-Long Beach. Previously, a full-time maritime worker, she is completing a book manuscript on the history of the oil industry in California and the American West.

**Woody Register** teaches U.S. history and American studies at the University of the South in Sewanee, Tennessee. His cultural history of the Coney Island showman Fred Thompson, *The Kid of Coney Island,* will be published in 2001.

**Ben A. Shackleford** is a historian of technology working toward a Ph.D. at the Georgia Institute of Technology. His dissertation continues his study of NASCAR, focusing on technology as a medium between communities of users in Southern stock car racing. Before entering academia he worked as a race car fabricator, mechanic, and crew chief.

**Jeffrey Ryan Suzik** is a Ph.D. candidate in history at Carnegie Mellon University. He is currently the chairperson of the history department at Shady Side Academy, where he also teaches. The article in this collection is drawn from his dissertation in progress, " 'Work As Paradise': The Civilian Conservation Corps and the Social Gendering of Male Youth, 1933–1942."

**Paul Michel Taillon** is a lecturer in U.S. history at the University of Auckland, New Zealand. He received his Ph.D. from the University of Wisconsin-Madison. Taillon is completing a book on the railroad brotherhoods and conservative unionism in the U.S. railroad industry, 1877–1916.

# Permissions Acknowledgments

Lisa Fine, "Rights of Men, Rites of Passage: Hunting and Masculinity at Reo Motors of Lansing, Michigan, 1945–1975" from the *Journal of Social History* (Summer 2000), 805–23.

Stephen Meyer, "Work, Play, and Power: Masculine Culture on the Automotive Shop Floor, 1930–1960" from *Men and Masculinities* vol. 2, no. 2 (October 1999), 115–34.

Ruth Oldenziel, "Boys and Their Toys: The Fischer Body Craftman's Guild, 1930–1968, and the Making of a Male Technical Domain" from *Technology and Culture* vol. 38, no. 1 (January 1997), 60–96.

Todd Alexander Postol, "Masculine Guidance: Boys, Men, and Newspapers, 1930–1939" from *Enterprise and Society* vol. 1, no. 2 (June 2000), 355–90.

Nancy Quam-Wickham, "Rereading Man's Conquest of Nature: Skill, Myths, and the Historical Construction of Masculinity in Western Extractive Industries" from *Men and Masculinities* vol. 2, no. 2 (October 1999), 135–51.

Woody Register, "Everyday Peter Pans: Work, Manhood, and Consumption in Urban America, 1900–1930" from *Men and Masculinities* vol. 2, no. 2 (October 1999), 197–227.

Ben A. Shackleford, "Masculinity, Hierarchy, and the Auto Racing Fraternity: The Pit Stop As a Celebration of Social Roles" from *Men and Masculinities* vol. 2, no. 2 (October 1999), 180–96.

Jeffrey Ryan Suzik, "'Building Better Men': The CCC Boy and the Changing Social Ideal of Manliness" from *Men and Masculinities* vol. 2, no. 2 (October 1999), 152–79.

# Index